THE SECRET OF RUNNING

Gerard Nijboer, Olympic Silver Medalist and European Champion Marathon

"Most interesting! Reading this book brought back memories of my first running book *The Complete Book of Running*. Just like James Fix's book it is a real page-turner, each and every page fascinates the committed runner with an eye for details!"

Hunter Allen, Legendary Coach and Co-developer of TrainingPeaks' WKO+ software

"When Dr. Coggan and I wrote, *Training and Racing with a Power Meter*, there were some very elite coaches that took this information and became experts around the world. The authors of this book are such experts. They used the laws of nature to describe and calculate the performance in running as well as in cycling. This book will help to take your running to the next level and the concepts written inside are foundations to creating success."

Asker Jeukendrup, Sports Nutrition Scientist, Professor of Exercise Science

"One of the best books about endurance performance I have ever seen, with an evidence based analytical approach to performance in running. The many practical examples make it easy for the reader to understand and apply this to improve their own performance. The breakthrough of power meters is analyzed critically, including the possibilities to increase running economy and running performance."

Maria Hopman, Professor of Integrative Physiology, Radboud University, Nijmegen

"I like the quantitative approach to the physics and physiology of running in this book. I feel this is important to understand and improve the performance in sports. I believe this book will help coaches and runners as theory and practice are combined in a highly understandable way."

HANS VAN DIJK I RON VAN MEGEN

THE SECRET OF

RUNNING

MAXIMUM PERFORMANCE GAINS THROUGH EFFECTIVE POWER METERING AND TRAINING ANALYSIS

Meyer & Meyer Sport

The Secret of Running
Maidenhead: Meyer & Meyer Sport (UK) Ltd., 2017
ISBN 978-1-78255-109-6

Auckland, Beirut, Dubai, Hägendorf, Hong Kong, Indianapolis, Cairo, Cape Town,
Manila, Maidenhead, New Delhi, Singapore, Sydney, Teheran, Vienna

 Member of the World Sports Publishers' Association (WSPA)

Manufacturing: Print Consult GmbH, Munich, Germany
ISBN 978-1-78255-109-6
E-mail: info@m-m-sports.com
www.m-m-sports.com

Contents

WHY DID WE WRITE THIS BOOK?

In theory, there is no difference between theory and practice. In practice, there is!

The Success of Our Books on the Dutch Market

Our previous Dutch books[1,2,3] were an instant success in the running and cycling communities in the Netherlands and Belgium. Apparently many thousands of runners and cyclists share our passion to understand, quantify and optimize the power of our human engine and to calculate and predict our attainable performance in sports. More than 10,000 copies of our books have already been sold in the (relatively small) Dutch market. We get tons of enthusiastic reactions from fans, who call our quantitative approach "a revelation in sports books." The calculators at our websites www.thesecretofrunning.com and www.thesecretofcycling.com are visited by many thousands of runners and cyclists, who enjoy calculating how they can optimize their performance.

How to Get Fitter and Faster

We share a lifelong passion for running and science. The remarkable story of our books starts in 2011 when Hans retired (at the age of 57) from his position as full professor at Delft University of Technology. Hans decided to devote his time to running and studying the science of running to see if he could get fitter and faster. Hans has been a committed runner since 1980, but over the years his race times had declined slowly as shown in the figure below. Obviously, the decline in performance with age will not surprise our readers, but the fact that he got significantly faster after 2011 should! From 2013 onwards he even managed to become a multiple Dutch Masters Champion (M60)! The reasons for this amazing improvement are the topic of our books. You will gain insights into the factors that determine your performance and how you can get fitter and faster.

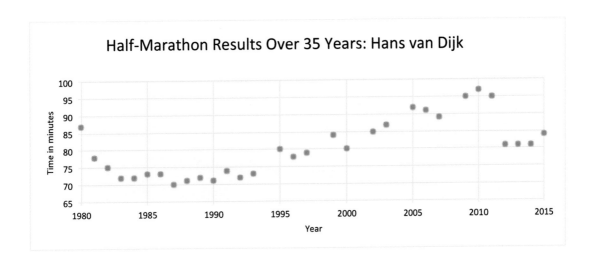

The Quantitative Approach to Running

As scientists and engineers, we were not satisfied with the traditional handbooks on running which are based mostly on the experiences of runners and coaches. They do describe the factors which influence the performance, but only in a qualitatively way. We were interested in hard numbers and formulas that would enable us to calculate the performance exactly. We also wanted to differentiate between scientific proof and the opinions of runners and coaches, so we have set out to develop science-based models for all factors influencing the running performance and to test these models with hard data from measurements.

One simple, but important, example is the impact of your body weight on your VO_2 max and your running performance. In 2012, Hans rationed his diet, which resulted in a decrease of his body weight in six months by 15% (from 67.5 kg to 57.5 kg). As shown in the figure below, his VO_2 max increased consistently and proportionally to his weight loss (finally by the same 15%). This confirms the theoretical relationship between body weight and running performance, as explained in a later chapter. So, if you want to get fitter and faster, our first tip would be to shed some body fat!

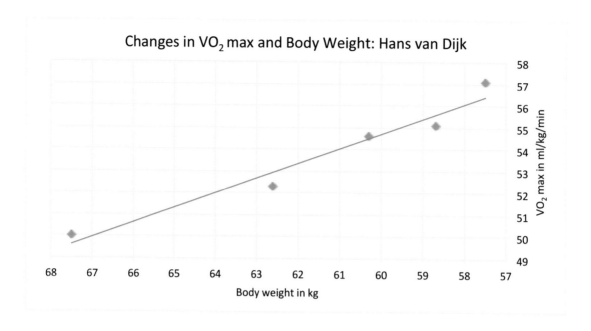

Changes in VO$_2$ max and Body Weight: Hans van Dijk

Running Science:
The Laws of Physics and Physiology

We have developed a new and complete running model based on the laws of physics and physiology. The figure below illustrates the model, which enables us to calculate the race time exactly.

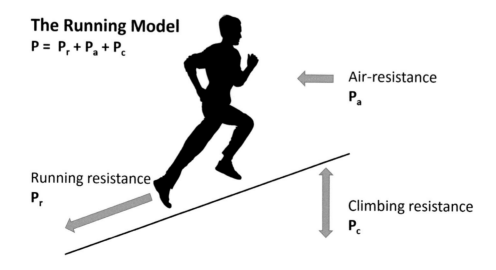

The Running Model
$$P = P_r + P_a + P_c$$

Air-resistance P_a

Running resistance P_r

Climbing resistance P_c

The model is based on the fact that your muscles and cardiovascular system form your human engine. Your human engine has a certain capacity, which can be described in terms of the traditional notion of oxygen uptake capacity (VO_2 max) or, more accurately, in terms of the amount of power (P, in watts). Obviously, the power (P) depends on factors such as talent, training, time or distance, altitude, tapering and so on.

In the equilibrium condition, the power of your human engine (P) is used to surmount the running resistance (P_r) the air-resistance (P_a) and the climbing resistance (P_c). Consequently, we can calculate your running speed and race time when the conditions of the race (such as footing, distance, wind, temperature, hills and altitude) are known.

We believe that our running model is a major step forward as compared to the existing running models such as the well-known VDOT model of Jack Daniels[8]. These models were not based on the laws of physics and physiology, and as a result they are less accurate and do not allow exact calculations based on the impact of many variables.

Another major step forward is our model of the human physiology. Based on the biochemistry of the four energy systems of the human muscles, we managed to calculate the ultimate limits of human power as a function of time, as illustrated in the figure below.

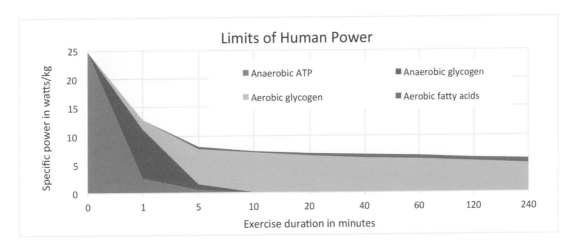

Our calculations show that these ultimate limits of human power match perfectly well with the current world-class performances in running, cycling and other sports.

The Theory of Nearly Everything: How to Calculate and Optimize Your Race Time

We have never met a runner that did not want to get faster. Moreover, most runners are keen to learn the impact of all factors that may affect their performance. Consequently, in this book we have systematically analyzed the impact of nearly everything on your running performance. In 79 chapters, you will find the answers to questions like:

» How big is the power of your human engine?

» How fast can you race with your human engine?

» How much slower do you get with age?

» How much faster can you get by shedding body fat?

» How much faster can you get from training?

» How fast should you train?

» What is the ultimate limit of the human power and the world records?

» Is it possible to run a marathon in under two hours?

» What is the energy cost of running a flat course?

» What is the impact of the air resistance on your race time?

» How much time do you lose on account of wind?

» How big is the impact of pacemakers and running in a pack?

» How much faster could Usain Bolt run the 100-meter race in Mexico?

» How much slower do you run uphill and how much faster downhill?

» What is the impact of your running economy (RE)?

» What is the impact of your running dynamics (i.e., cadence and stride length)?

» How much faster are racing shoes?

» How big is the impact of nutrition and carbo-loading?

» How good and reliable are running power meters?

» Can you improve your RE using power meters?

Power Meters: A Revolution in Running

Recently, the first running power meters have been developed[4]. This means you are among the first generation of runners who can actually measure the power of your human engine in real time, each and every day. We tested the Stryd power meter and were quite impressed. The figure below shows that the Stryd data were as good as those of the VO_2 measurements in the lab, the gold standard of physiological research!

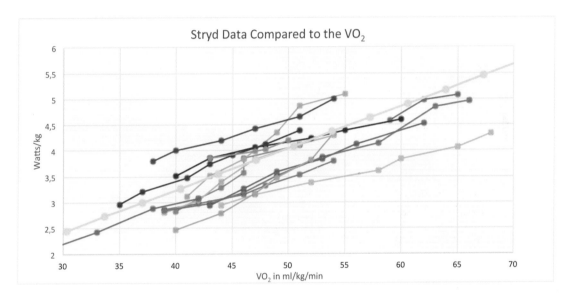

Based on our research we believe that power meters may have an equally revolutionary impact on running as they have had in cycling. Using the data from their power meter, runners can now optimize their daily training and races. Also, it is now possible to quantitatively determine your running economy (RE). This means you can now optimize your RE and running form, based on hard data on the specific energy cost of running.

Who Are the Authors?

Hans van Dijk is a lifelong runner and scientist. Since retiring from a full professorship at Delft University of Technology, he has devoted his time to studying the laws of sports, developing new concepts and models and writing books and columns on running, cycling and other endurance sports. Hans has also developed the running and cycling calculators, enabling the readers to analyze and calculate their own performances. As an added bonus, his research has led to a spectacular improvement in his race times at the age of 60!

Ron van Megen is a lifelong runner, engineer and managing director. He has been a friend and running mate of Hans for over 30 years. He enjoys quantifying his running results and using new running technologies, including power meters. Just like Hans, he is also keen on improving his race times, and was happy to see them go down by 20% at the age of 55! He has organized the production of the book and provided many of the photographs.

Hans van Dijk (right) and Ron van Megen (left), authors of this book.

Website and Calculators

The website www.thesecretofrunning.com contains many papers, columns, media reports, Q&As and our calculators, which the readers can use to calculate and predict their race times, depending on many variables. We welcome reactions from readers and runners around the world, and hope that the readers will enjoy the calculators and share their feedback!

Hans van Dijk and Ron van Megen

Leusden, the Netherlands, September 2016

PART I

THE BASICS OF RUNNING

1. RUNNING IS GOOD FOR YOU!

I have two doctors, my left leg and my right.
—George M. Treveyan

A Dutch magazine once summarized the advantages of running with the headline "Miracle cure within reach!" A daily routine of exercise and running indeed provides a miracle cure. The best thing you can do if you want to improve your fitness and health is to become a runner.

A daily run has an amazing positive impact on your physical and mental health, while a lack of exercise is the single largest health risk in Western society—even larger than the risk of smoking! A paper in The Lancet of July 20125 concluded that presently 1 out of 10 people die from insufficient exercise. This adds up to 5.3 million premature deaths worldwide as opposed to 5.1 million from smoking.

Anima Sana In Corpore Sano

The importance of physical fitness has been known through the ages, as evidenced by the above Roman proverb which translates to "A healthy mind in a fit body." Running improves your fitness and health in many ways:

1. The daily training has a direct and large positive impact on your physical fitness. Your body will slowly be transformed into that of an athlete.
2. Your habits will automatically become healthier. You will start to eat and drink less and more healthily, you will stop smoking and you will drink only the occasional glass of alcohol.
3. Your blood values and other health indicators will change for the better.
4. Your disease risk will decrease and your resistance to diseases will increase.

Running also has a big positive impact on your mental health, as millions of runners experience every day. This will be discussed in the next chapter.

Positive Impact of Training on Physical Fitness

1. The oxygen transport capacity of your heart–lung system increases substantially.
2. Your heart rate drops (both at rest and during exercise).
3. Your heart gets stronger and more efficient.
4. Your blood pressure lowers and your blood vessels become more flexible.
5. Your lungs get stronger and more efficient.
6. Your muscles become stronger (particularly the muscles of the legs, heart and lungs).
7. Your bones become stronger.
8. Your joints stay agile and flexible.
9. The energy production in your muscles becomes more efficient.
10. You lose weight and become leaner.
11. Your metabolism and bowel movement improve.

Medical professionals and sport coaches know that the human body has a tremendous capacity to adapt to training. By training on a daily basis, you can gradually transform your body. On a long-term basis, your body gets fitter. Your body is then able to achieve better results with less effort. Many aspects of fitness respond to training, such as endurance, speed, strength, agility and coordination. The box summarizes this miracle of training.

We have not found any scientific papers detailing why runners automatically change their lifestyle, but this is by no means less certain. We have never met a serious runner who smokes, and canteens of athletic clubs have been nonsmoking zones long before legislation made this mandatory. Also almost all runners change their eating and drinking habits after some time. They realize that their fitness and performance will improve when they eat and drink less and healthier. Runners are aware of their body and the need to take care of it. You are what you eat!

If You Could Stuff the Impact of Running in a Pill, You Could Make a Fortune!

Positive Impact of Training on Health Parameters

1. Your cholesterol levels change for the better (LDL lower, HDL higher).
2. Your insulin values get better (lower).
3. Your blood glucose values get better (lower).
4. Your bone density increases.
5. Your body fat percentage (BFP) decreases markedly.
6. Your blood volume increases.
7. The level of hemoglobin and myoglobin in your blood increases.
8. The buffer capacity of your blood increases.
9. Your immune system becomes more effective.
10. The hormone levels in your brain change for the better (adrenalin lower, serotonin higher).
11. The enzymes in your muscles become more efficient.

The positive impact of running is really amazing. Obviously, you get fitter and your body looks much better. Additionally, many processes in your body change with the result that many blood values and other health parameters improve. The box summarizes the positive impact of training on health parameters.

Prevention Is Better Than Cure

Proverbs like "Good health is above wealth" and the above "Prevention is better than cure" sum up the importance of the positive impact of running on the risk of disease, as indicated in the box below. No wonder that some health insurance companies offer runners a rebate on their premium! Running is also used as a therapy in the treatment of mental health issues. In general, running is considered to be an excellent therapy for many physical and mental complaints.

Physical and Mental Complaints Positively Affected by Training

1. Heart and coronary diseases
2. Diabetes
3. Osteoporosis
4. Stroke
5. Certain types of cancer (colon, uterus, breast)
6. Certain lung diseases (bronchitis, emphysema and asthma)
7. Depression, fears and stress
8. Rheumatoid arthritis
9. Cystic fibrosis
10. Aging problems
11. Gout

Of course, running should not be seen as a panacea to all problems for all people. However, we feel that running has strongly improved the quality of our own lives and many others. We hope that you will have the opportunity to try it and experience the advantages for yourself, just like we have.

The best thing you can do if you want to improve your fitness and health is to become a runner. Enjoy a workout in the great outdoors, take a shower and feel fit and strong!

2. RUNNING IS FUN!

Every day is a good day when you run!

Runners are positively addicted; they enjoy their sport and rejoice in life and running outdoors, preferably in nature. The authors of this book have run almost every Sunday morning for over 30 years in the beautiful scenery surrounding their home town of Leusden in the Netherlands. During these long runs, they enjoy the splendor of the landscape, which includes stunning heath fields, mysterious forests and historical landmarks. They spot deer, squirrels, woodpeckers and buzzards, while talking about work and life. When they return home after 25-30 kilometers, they are tired, but happy and full of beans!

At their Sunday morning runs Hans and Ron enjoy the splendor of the landscape, which includes stunning heath fields, mysterious forests and historical landmarks.

Positive Impact of Training on Mental Health and Well-Being

1. You feel better.
2. You sleep soundly and wake up smiling.
3. You become more calm and relaxed.
4. You enjoy your body and your performance.
5. You feel younger and fitter.
6. Your concentration improves.
7. You get good ideas and see things more clearly.
8. You enjoy life and feel more energetic.
9. You feel free and in control of your life.
10. Your willpower increases.
11. You become more resistant to stress.
12. The quality of your life increases.

These are the moments when life is lived most intensely. You experience strong feelings of freedom, happiness and power. Most probably, this is related to some subconscious memories of prehistoric man, who roamed the landscape in search of his prey. The positive impact of running on our mental health and well-being is very broad and diverse. They are summed up by the ancient Roman proverb Anima sana in corpore sano, meaning "A healthy mind in a fit body." The box gives an overview of these positive effects and experiences.

Somebody who does not run may find it hard to believe all these advantages. But they are experienced by almost everybody who starts running! You leave your home, meet the elements and enjoy running in the great outdoors. Soon, your body becomes your friend, and you feel fitter and happier. Even beginners soon become ambassadors of the sport and advocate the many advantages.

Scientific research has established that the natural hormones endorphin and serotonin are produced during running. These are the hormones that stimulate a euphoric sense of happiness, often called a runner's high. Unfortunately, not everybody produces the same amount of these hormones and it may take some time before you feel more happy than tired. But research has shown that the level of endorphin in our brain is statistically increased by running. Our ancestors may have needed this in order to escape

predators and survive in the prehistoric landscape. We can enjoy the feelings of happiness without the use of drugs. As a matter of fact, most runners are pleasantly addicted to their sport.

Running can be done at any available time slot and you can do it by yourself, relaxing or meditating, and listening to the birds or to the music on your iPod. It is also great fun to run with some friends and chat and exchange ideas. The most serious runners join an athletic club. Together with their comrades they travel to the great races, telling tall tales en route and celebrating their performances and successes. One of the nicest things about running is that everybody is a winner. You mainly compete with yourself, trying to improve your performance and running times. Once you have made your first progress, your sense of pride and self-esteem will only grow.

There is also a belief that runners enjoy happier marriages and do not divorce. Although this has not been studied scientifically, it is true in our own circle of running friends!

Finally, running is a tested cure for aging problems and guaranteed to improve the quality of the life of the elderly. In many places, running therapy is used to improve the mental well-being of senior citizens.

Youngsters and seniors enjoy their sport and rejoice in life and running outdoors, preferably in nature.

The authors of this book enjoy running in the beautiful scenery surrounding their home town of Leusden in the Netherlands.

3. SPORTS PHYSIOLOGY

The heart of a runner is a superior and more efficient organ. —Cardiologist Dr. J. Wolffe, MD

In this chapter we will give some background information on the human engine. In short, the human engine is made up of the leg muscles and the cardiovascular (or heart–lung) system, which ensures the supply of oxygen to and the disposal of metabolites from the muscles.

Which factors determine the capacity of the human engine? Which fuels are used by the muscles and how much power can be produced? And what is the impact of training? Training leads to huge adaptations in our body as a result of which we become fitter. In many handbooks[6,7,8,9] and papers, this miracle of training has been described. Below, we present a summary of the most important aspects of the human engine.

Training Effects

Consistent and balanced training leads to the following adaptations of the muscles and the cardiovascular system:

1. **Muscles**

   The leg muscles become stronger. There is an increase of:

   - the number of mitochondria (the energy producers of the cells);
   - the number and size of the muscle fibers;
   - the number of capillaries and the blood flow through the capillaries;
   - the stockpile of ATP (adenosine triphosphate) and glycogen;
   - the number and activity of enzymes (improving the breakdown of glycogen and fatty acids).

   Recent research has shown that training can even lead to a modification of the ratio of fast-twitch (FT) muscles to slow-twitch (ST) muscles. As a consequence, both speed and endurance can be improved by training. Such training should be continuous and focused. As a result of the training stress, initially some muscles will be damaged. You can feel this, as your muscles may ache the first days after the training. However, in time your body will react by strengthening the muscles. Consequently, they can better cope with the training load. Training your leg muscles is a protracted process and you have to put many miles in the tank to get the best results. The majority of the training can be done at an easy pace, but in order to develop the FT muscles it is necessary to do some speed work as well.

2. **Heart**

The adaptation of the heart to the training is most remarkable. The number of heart muscle fibers increases and so do the number of the capillaries and the blood flow through the capillaries, in particular those of the left heart chamber. As a result of this, the sports heart is much more efficient than the heart of untrained, sedentary people. We can illustrate this by considering the heart as a pump. The discharge of this pump (called cardiac output or heart minute volume) is the number of liters of blood pumped per minute. This equals the stroke volume (in liters) times the heart rate (HR, in beats per minute). The stroke volume of a trained runner can be twice as large as that of an untrained person. Consequently, at rest the heart of a trained runner has a large spare capacity and the HR can be quite low. It is quite common for well-trained runners to have a resting heart rate (RHR) of 40 or even lower! During exercise, the sports heart is capable of pumping much more blood, leading to an increased oxygen transport to the leg muscles. As the muscles need oxygen to produce energy, this oxygen transport capacity is the single most important factor to determine the performance in sports in general and in running in particular. The increase in stroke volume and the corresponding decrease of the RHR are important physiological adaptations of the heart. These adaptations increase the capacity of the heart. The sports heart is able to increase the blood flow during exercise from 5 l/min to 40 l/min, thus by a factor of eight. This is achieved by a combination of the increase in the stroke volume and the HR. The adaptation of the sports heart depends mainly on the intensity of the training (a high HR and thus a high intensity of the training is required) and can occur relatively quickly. It is possible to achieve a significant reduction in the RHR in as little as six weeks.

3. **Blood**

The blood volume of a well-trained runner is some 10% larger than that of an untrained person. This is mainly caused by an increase of the plasma volume. Of course this increase has a positive impact on the oxygen transport capacity. Another important adaptation is an increase in the flexibility of the blood vessels, leading to a decrease in blood pressure. The blood composition also changes: the cholesterol levels decrease, in particular those of the bad LDL and the total cholesterol. The good HDL increases. The level of hemoglobin may increase as a result of altitude training. Hemoglobin is vital for the oxygen transport by the blood. One gram of hemoglobin can transport 1.34 ml oxygen (O_2), so an average hemoglobin level of 15 g/100 ml blood leads to an oxygen transport capacity of 15*1.34 = 20 ml O_2/100ml blood or 20%. A low level of hemoglobin may indicate an iron deficiency in the nutrition or increased iron loss. A high level of hemoglobin may be the result of blood or EPO doping. Finally the blood vessels dilate during exercise, leading to a reduction of the peripheral resistance and an automatic increase of the blood flow to the leg muscles. Less blood is diverted to nonessential body parts, such as the digestive system.

4. **Lungs**

As a result of training, your breathing muscles become stronger and the tidal volume (functional lung volume) increases. We illustrate this in the same way as we did for the heart: by considering the lungs as a pump. The capacity of this pump (called respiratory minute volume) is the tidal volume (in liters) times the breathing frequency (in breaths per minute). At rest, we breathe around 10-15 times per minute and the tidal volume is around 0.5 liter, so the respiratory minute volume is 5-7.5 l/min. During exercise, the respiratory minute volume can increase dramatically to 180-200 l/min for well-trained athletes. This is the result of an increase of both the breathing frequency (to 60 breaths per minute) as well as the tidal volume (to 3-4 liters). The increase in the capacity of the lungs is even larger than that of the heart, so the lungs are usually not the limiting factor. Consequently, we can conclude that normally the oxygen transport capacity of the cardiovascular system is the main factor that determines the performance in endurance sports. However, we should remark that the breathing muscles themselves need a significant amount of oxygen. This can amount to some 10% of the maximum oxygen transport capacity or VO_2 max.

Energy Systems

In order to run we need energy. This energy is produced in our muscle cells, to be precise in the mitochondria. The cells can do this by using any (or a combination) of the four following energy systems:

1. **ATP**

Adenosine triphosphate (ATP) is the primary fuel for sprinters. ATP can be transferred to ADP very quickly, releasing a large amount of energy and thus providing the muscles with the largest amount of power. Moreover, the process does not require oxygen. However, the stockpile of ATP in the muscles is extremely small, lasting only for a short sprint of some 10 seconds. During recovery, the muscle cells are able to regenerate the ATP from the ADP. This process requires energy, which has to be supplied by the aerobic (using oxygen) breakdown of glycogen. The amount of oxygen needed to regenerate the ATP is called the oxygen debt. So, the energy debt is created during exercise and needs to be redeemed during recovery. As a result of training the efficiency of the stockpiling and the use and recovery of ATP can be increased. This requires many repetitions of short sprints at top speed.

Relief by the Dutch sprint queen Dafne Schippers on Naomi Sedney in the 4 x 100-meter relay at the World Championships Athletics 2015 in Beijing.

2. Anaerobic glycolysis

The anaerobic breakdown of glycogen or glycolysis is the most important energy system for the middle (400-800 meter) distances. Glycogen is composed of large chains of glucose (sugar) units. Glycogen is stored in the muscles and the liver. The blood also contains a small amount of glycose. Glycogen can be broken down anaerobically (without the use of oxygen) into lactic acid. This lactic acid may accumulate and cause exhaustion and pain in the muscles. During recovery, the lactic acid can be broken down using oxygen, thus redeeming another oxygen debt. With training the efficiency of the glycolysis can be improved. This requires training at a high intensity so that lactic acid is accumulating. This occurs only at a high HR, around 85-90% of the maximum HR (MHR). This is called the anaerobic limit or threshold limit. The anaerobic breakdown of glycogen produces less power than the ATP system, but it is somewhat more durable. The time to exhaustion is a few minutes, depending on the speed and fitness.

3. **Aerobic breakdown of glycogen**

The aerobic breakdown of glycogen is the main energy system for endurance athletes, including long-distance runners. Glycogen is broken down into carbon dioxide and water, using oxygen. The carbon dioxide is removed from the muscles by the blood and the lungs. The oxygen is supplied to the muscles by the lungs and the blood. This is a very durable process that can be maintained for a very long time when the oxygen transport capacity of the cardiovascular system is large enough. This oxygen transport capacity can be increased by training at an intensity just under the anaerobic or threshold limit. Training at a lower intensity (e.g., 70% of MHR) is also useful as it stimulates the muscles themselves. The aerobic breakdown of glycogen produces less power than the glycolysis, but the stockpile of glycogen lasts for at least 1.5 hours. With training and optimized nutrition (e.g., carbo-loading), this period can be increased to 2-3 hours.

4. **Aerobic breakdown of fatty acids**

The aerobic breakdown of fatty acids is the main energy system for ultra-runners and triathletes. Fatty acids are broken down into carbon dioxide and water, using oxygen. Consequently, this system is quite comparable to the previous one (the aerobic breakdown of glycogen). The main drawback is that it produces less power. This is the reason for the well-known phenomenon of hitting the wall in the marathon. This happens when the stockpile of glycogen in your muscles is exhausted, so the muscles have to transfer to the breakdown of fatty acids. From that moment onwards, your power output is greatly reduced and your speed drops dramatically. The main advantage of the breakdown of fatty acids is that the stockpile is extremely large and sufficient to run for many days. We use this system during rest and when exercising at low intensities. When the exercise intensity increases, our muscles switch to the other systems. This depends on the required amount of power: so first fatty acids, then glycogen, then glycolysis and finally ATP. The efficiency of the fatty acid system can also be improved by training. This should be done by long runs at low intensity (less than 70% of your MHR). Eating less carbohydrates may also help, as well as early morning trainings prior to breakfast. We should realize that the fatty acid system is used by all runners at low and moderate intensities. When we run slowly, the amount of fatty acids in the fuel mix of our muscles may be as high as 90%. At marathon pace this percentage may be only 30% and at 3,000-meter pace only 10%.

The box summarizes some important aspects of the four energy systems of the human engine.

1. ATP

ATP → ADP + energy

Small stockpile, 10 seconds, sprint, maximum power and speed

2. Glycolysis

Glycogen → Lactic acid + energy

Limited time to exhaustion, few minutes, middle distances, high power and speed

3. Aerobic breakdown of glycogen

Glycogen + $6O_2$ → $6CO_2$ + $6H_2O$ + energy

Large stockpile, 1.5 hours, long distance, endurance power and speed

4. Aerobic breakdown of fatty acids

Fatty acids + $23O_2$ → $16CO_2$ + $16H_2O$ + energy

Very large stockpile, many days, ultra-distance, low power and speed, higher oxygen use

The theory on the human engine applies to all endurance sports. The performances of elite cyclist Robert Gesink (left) and multiple world champion speed-skater Sven Kramer (right) can be compared with our unified model.

4. TRAINING PRINCIPLES

Listen to your body!

Many textbooks[6,7,8,9,10] describe the principles and practices of training. However, it is not easy to distinguish the scientific research and facts in these writings from the practical experiences, hearsay and personal opinions of runners and coaches. Moreover, we should realize that most scientific studies have a limited scope in terms of the number of athletes (usually no more than 20) and the timespan (usually no more than a few months). Obviously, it is hard if not impossible to draw statistically sound conclusions from these limited studies. In practice, we want to know how we can optimize our training with subtle variations (with relatively small effects of each variation) and on a long-term basis (over many years). This problem is further complicated by the variability of the impact on training: what is good for one person may not be good for someone else.

Nevertheless, some training principles have been well studied. They are based on the science of sports physiology and have a general validity. Coaches and runners should use these training principles to design a training program and—even more importantly—to modify the program based on the actual results. In this chapter we will give a review of these nine training principles, including some practical applications.

1. **Principle of stress and recovery**

   This is the most essential training principle. Our body has the unique capacity to strengthen itself when exposed to cycles of stress and recovery. This principle was first studied by the Hungarian physician and endocrinologist Hans Selye (1907-1982). He found that a training impulse will initially lead to fatigue, strain and some damage to muscles and cells. After sufficient recovery time, the fatigue disappears and the cells adapt and get stronger. As a result, they are better able to cope with the next training impulse. After a workout, the damaged cells are broken down by enzymes and replaced by new and stronger cells. This means that the pain that we sometimes feel after a hard workout is actually a good sign as it means this process is taking place ("No pain, no gain"). It is essential to time the cycle of work and recovery accurately. If we do not allow sufficient recovery time, the body will be overloaded and the runner may get overtrained (stress on top of stress equals breakdown). If we allow too much recovery time, the impact of the training will be small. The goal is to find a perfect match of training impulses and recovery time, so an optimal progress is achieved (super compensation).

Consequently, the training should be composed of the right combination of work and recovery to get the best training impact. Rest and recovery are an essential part of the training program (stress followed by recovery equals progress). In practice this means that hard days and easy days should always be sandwiched. Which training load should be considered hard and which easy depends of course on the quality of the runner and his training status.

2. **Principle of sufficient intensity and variation**

This is an important principle, which is too often neglected. In order to get the best training results, it is necessary not to limit the training to one aspect (e.g., long, slow runs). Instead you have to make sure to incorporate enough other training forms so that all relevant muscles are trained (when you do what you have always done, you will get what you have always gotten). Also you have to do part of your training at high intensity in order to develop all energy systems. Consequently, in practice you have to pay attention to both volume and intensity. Many miles are required to develop your leg muscles (building the muscles) and high speed is required to develop your VO_2 max and the four energy systems (the aerobic breakdown of fatty acids, the aerobic breakdown of glycogen, the anaerobic glycolysis and the anaerobic conversion of ATP). Many long distance runners neglect the speed work, but this is not wise as only the aerobic energy systems are developed with such training. In order to make progress, the high intensity speed work is by far the most effective! Finally, it is important to try to consistently incorporate new impulses in your workouts. Remember that effective training impulses are always out of your comfort zone, so it is necessary to dig deep in part of your training.

3. **Principle of moderation and consistency**

Don't increase your training too fast or too much or you will suffer injuries. In practice you should increase the work load by no more than 5-10% per month. Listen to your body! Pay attention to signs of overtraining and avoid injuries as these will set you back severely. In general it is wise to maintain a training impulse for six weeks. During this period, your body adapts and you will be ready for the next step, either in volume or in intensity. Try to incorporate sufficient variation in the training (e.g., repetitions of sprints can be useful to allow the body to get used to high speeds which may optimize your running economy).

4. **Principle of diminishing returns**

For novice runners, the training will have a large effect. Both endurance and speed will increase rapidly and to a large degree. Unfortunately, the training effect will become smaller and slower as we train more. Elite runners have to train extremely hard—both in terms of volume and intensity—to achieve a gain of a few seconds at the 5K or 10K. Normal runners will experience a rapid improvement until the moment that they train almost daily and achieve a volume of 50-80 kilometers per week, including

at least one high-intensity (interval) session. From then on, progress will be slow and small. The good news is that even after many years of consistent training you may still progress further; often the best results are achieved after 5-10 years of training.

5. **Principle of specificity**

This principle implies that you will see the effects of training specifically on the muscles and energy systems that have been stressed in the training. In long-distance running mainly the leg muscles and the muscles of the heart are developed, while the arm and other muscles are hardly affected. There is even a difference between the development of the leg muscles in runners and cyclists. In cycling the quadriceps are tested more, whereas the hamstrings are the main muscles of the runners. The practical consequence of this principle is that a runner should run during the vast majority of his training program. This is the best way to prepare his body for the race. Fitness and strength training in a gym are of limited value to a runner, and should only be used as a supplementary training (e.g., to maintain and improve the core stability). Another consequence of this principle is that it is wise to focus the training on the race distance as well. This applies mainly to the development of the energy systems. A sprinter will have to develop his ATP system and a long distance runner his aerobic systems. Of course, it is always good to vary the training somewhat, as long distance runners also face a sprint finish.

6. **Principle of periodization**

This principle was developed by Arthur Lydiard (1917-2004), the New Zealand runner and coach of Olympic champion Peter Snell. Based on his experiences, Lydiard concluded that many athletes could not maintain a continuous high-level training program. After some time, his athletes petered out and their performance dwindled. Consequently, he was the first to develop a cyclic training program. His training plans distinguish the following periods:

- **Base period:** building aerobic endurance by increasing mileage with limited intensity
- **Building period:** increasing speed while maintaining volume
- **Peak period:** reducing volume, focusing on high-intensity speed work
- **Race period:** mainly speed work with low volume
- **Transition period:** allowing the body to recover and to start a new cycle

Nowadays, almost all training programs of elite runners are based on this structure. Usually, within the annual or macro cycle they also incorporate smaller (meso- and micro-) cycles of work and recovery (e.g., a building block of three weeks followed by a recovery block of one week).

7. **Principle of reversibility**

The effects of training are highly reversible. The bad news is that you may lose the gains of years of training within a short period of illness or overtraining. One month without training may lead to some 10% loss in performance ("Use it or lose it"). The good news is that retraining also proceeds quickly. Within a month you may regain most of what was lost.

8. **Principles of individuality and flexibility**

This is a very important principle which underlines that people react very differently to training. Obviously the training program of a sprinter has to include much more speed work as compared to the program of a long-distance runner. But some long-distance runners gain a lot from speed work, whereas others benefit more from endurance runs. This is related to genetic differences and the trick is to find what works best for you. That is also why you need to be flexible in adapting the program to the results. Make sure you avoid overtraining and injuries! In general it is wise to use your natural abilities ("Go with your strengths").

9. **Principle of maintenance**

Once you have reached a high level of fitness, it is possible to maintain a good performance over a longer period with only limited training. During this period you should keep up the speed work, but you can reduce the volume to a minimum without much negative effects. Arthur Lydiard used this principle to strongly reduce the training of his runners in the race period, so they were always fresh and hungry for the speed sessions and the races.

The track provides opportunities for many training modes and intensities.

5. TRAINING PLANS

Keep varying the program. Your body will tell you what to do. —Joan Benoit-Samuelson

This chapter deals with the most popular topic in the literature on running. No wonder, as training (next to losing weight) is the most effective way to get better and faster. Many books and papers have been written on training plans, including such aspects as training goals, training modes, training paces and training mileage. Almost all writings are based on the experiences of coaches and runners in the daily practice of training and racing. Scientific reasoning and support is usually limited.

Fortunately, some high-quality scientific textbooks[6,7,8,9,10] and papers have also been published on the topic. They all conclude that intensity is the most important factor of training. Most progress can be made when at least part of the training is performed at a high intensity. This means that the training should be done at a high speed, high heart rate (HR) and a high percentage of the VO_2 max. Of course a runner must have a sufficient base before he can train at a high intensity. This means he will already have completed a proper base training with sufficient mileage at low intensity. It also goes without saying that a high-intensity training can only be maintained for a short period. This means the training will always be done in intervals: short blocks at high speed sandwiched between short blocks at low speed, during which the runner can recover. The reason for the effectiveness of high-intensity training is the fact that all energy systems are stressed and developed in this way. Next to the aerobic breakdown of fatty acids and glycogen, the anaerobic glycolysis and the direct conversion of ATP are stressed at high intensity. The aerobic energy systems are also trained during the recovery parts of the training. As these parts are run at low speeds, interval training also fulfills the requirement of sufficient variation.

Training Goals

The following training goals can be distinguished:

1. **Building the muscles and stamina**

    The body of the runner will slowly adapt to the daily work load. Both the leg muscles and the heart–lung system will get stronger. As a result of the training, part of the cells will be broken down by enzymes and replaced by stronger cells, which will form stronger fibers and stronger muscles. In order to fully achieve this adaptation, it is necessary to run many miles on a long-term basis (to put sufficient mileage in the bank). This training should be done at an easy pace, approximately 70% of the maximal heart rate (MHR) and the VO_2 max. A trained runner can maintain such a pace for 2-3 hours and the risk of injuries is small.

2. **Increasing functional threshold power (FTP)**

    The goal of this training is to adapt the body to running at the functional (lactate) threshold level (i.e., the level at which the anaerobic glycolysis starts to kick in and lactate starts to accumulate). We feel this accumulation of lactate as an acute fatigue in our legs, which limits our performance. The training is focused on the capability of the body to cope with some lactate. This means that the intensity should be high, around 85-90% of the MHR and VO_2 max. Well-trained runners can maintain this level for about an hour during a race, so the speed is around that of a one-hour race. In a later chapter, we will discuss more details of this level, which we will call the Functional Threshold Power (FTP). In training, a few intervals of 5-10 minutes are usually run at this level, sandwiched between low-speed blocks to allow recovery and to limit the training stress. At this intensity, mainly the aerobic systems are stressed.

3. **Increasing VO_2 max**

    This is a very important goal, as the VO_2 max is an essential factor in determining the performance in long-distance races. In order to increase the VO_2 max, it is necessary to train at an even higher intensity than the FTP level, around 90-100% of MHR and VO_2 max. In practice the speed will be around that of a 3,000-meter race. Training at such a high intensity, work can only be done at intervals of 2-4 minutes at high speed, sandwiched between low-speed recovery blocks of a few minutes. At this high intensity, both the aerobic and the anaerobic systems are stressed severely. Such training is hard and should only be done once or twice a week.

4. **Increasing speed**

   This is an essential training for track runners at the middle distances (400-1,500 meters). It requires training at such a high speed that the anaerobic systems are fully tested. The intensity should be above 100% of the VO_2 max and the HR will be around the MHR. In practice the speed will be similar to that of a 1,500-meter race. Training at such a high intensity can only be done at short intervals of around one minute, again sandwiched between low-speed recovery blocks of some minutes. At this very high intensity, the anaerobic systems need to supply the power required above the capacity of the aerobic systems. This training should also be limited to once or twice a week. A good combination would be to do one speed training and one VO_2 max training weekly.

5. **Increasing running economy (RE)**

   This training is focused on adapting the body to run economically at race speed. Running economy (RE) is a complicated phenomenon. It deals with the amount of energy required to run one kilometer. The RE depends on your body composition, the efficiency of your energy systems and your running form and technique. The running form includes many factors, such as stride length, cadence, vertical oscillation and many more. In later chapters we will discuss the running form and the RE in much more detail. In order to run economically at race speeds, you need to train many repetitions at race speeds. Consequently, the intensity of this training will depend on your race distance and goals.

Training Modes

1. **Aerobic endurance run**

   This is definitely the most popular training mode. Worldwide millions of runners jog at an easy pace in their neighborhood or nearby forest, enjoying their fitness and the great outdoors. Meanwhile, they develop their stamina and their muscles. The short endurance run of around one hour does not put great stress on your body and can be done daily. When preparing for a marathon, it is wise to include one long endurance run of around 2.5-3 hours in your weekly schedule. The pace of an aerobic endurance run should be slow, around one minute per km slower than your marathon pace. At this pace, your HR will be limited to 70% of your MHR. The volume will be around 10-15 kilometers daily or 50-100 kilometers per week for the average committed runner. It is wise to include some other training impulses during the run, like hills sprints, a few accelerations or a climax finish. This will provide some variation, which is desirable.

2. **Threshold run**

    This training is used to increase the functional (lactate) threshold power (FTP). It consists of fast runs of 2-5 kilometers at a speed around half of your marathon pace. At this pace, your HR will be around 85-90% of your MHR. The fast runs should be alternated with slow recovery parts, also of 2-5 kilometers, during which your HR will drop to below 70% of the MHR. The total volume will be around 10-20 kilometers. Such trainings are stressful and should not be done more than once a week.

3. **Climax run**

    This is a combination of the endurance run and the threshold run. Start easy at around 70% of MHR and increase the pace slowly during the run so that in the final kilometer your HR approaches MHR. The volume is around 10-15 kilometers. This training mode combines the advantages of the endurance run and the threshold run. It poses only limited stress on the body and mind while still stimulating both the aerobic systems and part of the anaerobic systems.

4. **Interval training**

    Interval training is considered the holy grail of competitive running. It is by far the best way to improve race performances at almost all distances. It became famous by the example of Olympic champion Emil Zatopek, who pushed the limits of interval training to 50 times 400 meters at blistering speed. His famous quote was "Why should I practice running slow? I already know how to run slow. I want to learn to run fast."

    We can distinguish two interval modes:

    - **VO_2 max intervals**

      These longer intervals should be done at an intensity of 90-100% of VO_2 max. The speed should be around 3,000-meter pace. At this pace, the HR will be 90-100 % of the MHR. They consist of a limited number of repetitions of 800, 1,000 or 1,200 meters. The total volume should be around six kilometers.

    - **Speed intervals**

      These are the shorter intervals of 200-400 meters. They should be done at an intensity of more than 100% of VO_2 max. The speed should be around 1,500-meter pace. At this pace the HR will approach the MHR. The total volume will be around 5-6 kilometers, so the number of repetitions will be larger.

    Interval sessions are hard, so they should only be done once or twice weekly. Recovery periods should be timed to allow the HR to drop to below 70% of MHR.

A popular alternative interval mode is high-intensity training (HIT), in which 20-second blocks of sprinting are sandwiched with 10 seconds of recovery. As a result of the high intensity, the HR will approach the MHR during the sprints. During the recovery HR will remain quite high, making this a very effective training mode which can be completed in 30 minutes.

5. **Fartlek**

    Fartlek training originates from the history of endurance running in Sweden. It is in fact a playful way to execute speed training (in Swedish *fart* means speed and *lek* means play). Traditionally it is done in nature, using hills, sand and other natural elements to sandwich speed work with recovery periods. The volume is usually one hour and the intensity varies significantly, between 50-100% of the MHR. Fartlek is a very pleasant training mode which offers a broad spectrum of training impulses.

6. **Hill training**

    This is a very effective training mode, as gravity assists the training load. Uphill, your HR will increase quite rapidly to the MHR. Another advantage is that this is running-specific strength training. Uphill, the forces acting on ankles and leg muscles are much higher than on a flat course. This provides an additional training impulse. Hill training is usually executed as 10-20 short (100 meter) or long (200-400 meter) sprints uphill with recovery downhill. It is possible and recommended to combine hill training with endurance runs or fartlek training.

In summary, we conclude that it is very important to train with sufficient variation. Make sure that all energy systems and muscles are stimulated and developed. In order to get faster, it is essential to do enough speed work ("Running slow will make you slow"). Provide sufficient recovery time between workouts so you are always fresh and ready to perform high-intensity work. The Dutch multiple champion Klaas Lok even advocates a training method based entirely on interval training. He recommends refraining from endurance runs altogether, as they will make you slow. Instead he insists on daily flexible intervals of 200, 400 or 1,000 meters at a relatively comfortable pace. He has used this method with great success for many years.

Hill training is a very effective training mode, as gravity assists the training load. Uphill, your HR will increase quite rapidly to the MHR.

6. SPORTS NUTRITION

Let food be thy medicine and medicine be thy food.
—Hippocrates

A great many books have been written on the topic of food and most of them sell well! Many books detail a specific diet with the promise to lose body fat and gain fitness and health, but a scientific base for the claims is usually lacking. Nevertheless, our food has a big impact on our health, as Hippocrates already stated in the above quote. What can science tell us about the effects of nutrition on health in general and on our performance in running in particular?

You Are What You Eat

Our body is made of and maintained by the elements in our food. If our diet lacks certain elements, we can get a deficiency disease like scurvy from lack of vitamin C and rickets from lack of vitamin D. Other examples are goiter from lack of iodine and anemia from lack of iron.

These deficiency diseases have all been documented scientifically. Based on the acquired knowledge, we have modified our diet with the result that these diseases do not occur anymore in most Western countries. A proper and varied diet nowadays contains sufficient trace elements, minerals and vitamins, so in general we don't have to fear deficiency diseases anymore.

Our modern problem is actually the opposite: our health suffers from too much food. On average we eat too much and too fat, as a result of which obesity, diabetes and coronary diseases abound. These problems are caused primarily by the fact that we simply eat more energy (calories) than we use for our base metabolism and our physical activities. The result is that the surplus is stored in our body in the form of body fat. So our body weight increases and in time we develop Western diseases. Many scientific studies have proven that eating too much is bad for your health. Obesity was found to decrease the life expectancy by 2.5 years. Presently 60% of the U.S. population is considered to be overweight or obese. Consequently, if we want to become healthier our first priority should be to eat less and be more active. The goal should be that our daily energy balance stops being positive. As a result our body weight will no longer increase.

In later chapters we will discuss in more detail the energy balance and the impact of your body weight on your performance in running. We will also detail how you can achieve an optimal racing weight.

Sources of Energy in Our Food

The main sources of energy in our food are carbohydrates, proteins and fats. The boxes below give some information on these compounds[11,12]. The ratio of these compounds in our food may vary to a large degree, depending on diet and tradition. An example are the Inuit, who eat mainly fish and seal, a diet consisting primarily of proteins and fats. The traditional foodstuff of the Kenyan athletes is ugali, which consists mostly of carbohydrates. Various theories exist on what is best for your health. The high life expectancy of the Japanese has been attributed to the fact that they eat a lot of fish. It has also been suggested that the Mediterranean kitchen has a positive health impact because of the widespread use of olive oil.

Proteins

» Small energy source for endurance runners (4 kcal/gram, 5% of total energy intake)
» Essential for the production of cells and muscles
» Present in meat, fish, chicken, dairy products, legumes, tofu
» Found in a varied diet so vegetarians can meet the daily requirement

In the animal world, classic examples exist of species that live either on a fat diet (the Inuit sled dog or husky) or on a protein diet (African wild dogs) or on a carbohydrate diet (thoroughbred horses).

Fats

» Second energy source for endurance runners (9 kcal/gram, 10-35% of total energy intake)
» Stored in the body as fatty acids and triglycerides (a few to many kilograms)
» Risk factor for increased cholesterol levels in the blood and for vascular diseases
» Present in meat, sausages, butter, oil, cookies, French fries, cheese, chocolate
» Also a source of vitamins
» The intake of saturated fatty acids should be limited (butter, sausage, cookies, French fries).
» Unsaturated fatty acids are less harmful (olive oil, sea fish, nuts).

One author[13] has hypothesized that bread and other grain products are less healthy because prehistoric man was a hunter-gatherer and did not yet eat grain. However, these theories have not been proven scientifically. Of course, many other factors have an impact on health such as smoking, physical activity, environmental pollution and professional diseases.

Carbohydrates

» Main energy source for endurance runners (4 kcal/gram, 60-90% of total energy intake)
» Stored in the body as glycogen. The muscles contain 300-600 grams, the liver 100-130 grams. The blood also contains a little glucose (5 grams).
» Present in vegetables, fruit, potatoes, whole-wheat pasta, whole-wheat bread, oatmeal
» Generally a healthy source of energy
» Single, refined sugars such as glucose, syrup, soda and white bread are less healthy. They contain less minerals and vitamins and are considered empty calories.

The one thing that all scientists agree on is that the average Western diet contains too much fat and proteins, as indicated in the table below.

Main Energy Sources in Diet			
	Carbohydrates (%)	Proteins (%)	Fats (%)
Average Western diet	45	20	35
Recommended for endurance athlete	70	15	15

The endurance athlete should limit the percentage of fats and proteins in his diet. This will also have a positive impact on the energy balance and thus on his weight. A reduction in the percentage of fats and proteins in the diet can easily be achieved with a heathy diet. Such a diet should have a base of:

1. Vegetables and fruit
   • Three portions of each daily are recommended.
   • They consist mainly of carbohydrates and contain fibers, vitamins, minerals and water (a limited amount of calories).

2. Whole-wheat bread, potatoes, pasta and oatmeal
   • Six portions daily are recommended.
   • They also consist mainly of carbohydrates and contain fibers, vitamins and minerals.

Additionally the athlete can use some (no more than three portions daily) low-fat dairy products such as cheese, milk and yoghurt. He should eat meat in moderation and try to replace it partially with fish, chicken or tofu (no more than two portions daily). Butter, soda, beer, French fries and cookies should be avoided and replaced by low-fat products. Water and tea (no sugar!) may be consumed as desired, coffee in moderation. No snacks! In later chapters we will discuss in much more detail the impact of nutrition, vitamins, minerals, antioxidants and supplements on the performance of the athlete.

Carbo-Loading

It has become good practice for marathon runners to eat a lot of carbohydrates during the final three days before the marathon. Many scientific studies have proven that this leads to an increased level of glycogen in the muscles and the liver. These levels are vitally important to prevent hitting the wall (caused by a low blood glucose level or hypoglycemia) in the later part of the marathon, as we will see in later chapters. During these final three days the athlete should strongly reduce his training (called tapering) and eat mainly carbohydrates, the so-called carbo-loading. The marathon diet can be characterized by the absence of meat and the presence of carbohydrates like pasta, bread, honey, raisins, bananas and oatmeal. The traditional pasta party on the eve of the marathon is a feast for all marathon runners. In a later chapter we will discuss carbo-loading in more detail. There we will also elucidate the use of a sports breakfast (necessary to compensate for the reduction of the liver glycogen level during the night) and the use of sports drinks during the marathon (necessary to compensate for the losses of water, minerals and glycogen during the race).

Nothing is tastier than a homemade marathon pasta party.

PART II

THE PHYSICS OF RUNNING

7. ENERGY

Look deep into nature and then you will understand everything better. —Albert Einstein.

In this book we will use the laws of physics to study running, so we can understand the fundamental factors that determine our performance. In running we use a certain amount of energy (E), which of course depends on the distance. Our muscles and our heart–lung system provide this energy; we will call this our human engine. Our human engine has a certain capacity or power (P), which is the amount of energy per unit of time. Elite athletes obviously have a human engine with a larger capacity than ordinary people, so they can run faster. The general relationship, which we will use frequently in this book, is such that you can calculate your race time (t) for a certain distance if you know the power (P) of your human engine and how much net energy (E) is required to run that distance:

$$t = E/P$$

Example for the marathon:

E = 2,961 kilojoule (net)

P = 235 watt

t = 2,961,000/235 = 12,600 seconds

   = 3 hours 30 minutes

Of course, the trick is to know the numerical values of E and P. Once you know these, you can calculate your race time easily. In later chapters we will outline how you can determine the numerical values of E and P and on which factors these values depend. With this new knowledge, you will be able to understand which factors determine your racing performance so you can make a more informed decision on what you can do to improve your performance. We will also prove that the numbers in the example are exactly right for our Marathon Man, a hypothetical 35-year-old man who runs the marathon in 3 hours and 30 minutes. In this book we will use Marathon Man frequently to illustrate the impact of various factors on his race times.

In this chapter, we will first discuss the concept of energy (E). We will give some examples from daily life and illustrate how you can use the concept of energy to make useful calculations.

Energy in Our Food

The concept of energy is best known in daily life from the amount of kilocalories (kcal) in our food. Most readers will be aware that we consume some 2,500 kcal daily (of course heavyweight champion Tyson Fury will consume much more than supermodel Naomi Campbell). As 1 kcal is equivalent to 4,184 kilojoule (kJ), we can calculate that 2,500 kcal equals 10,460 kJ.

Weight Loss Resulting From the Marathon

We should note that the efficiency of our human engine (metabolic efficiency) is around 25%. This means that the gross energy consumption of our body is four times the net energy use of running. Consequently, our Marathon Man uses a total of 4*2,961 = 11,844 kJ of metabolic energy to run the marathon. When we compare this to his daily food consumption of 10,460 kJ, we can calculate that the energy requirement of the marathon is only 11,884/10,460 = 113% of the daily energy (calorie) intake with his food. Obviously, running a marathon will not result in a large weight loss (apart from the weight lost through sweating which will be quickly replenished by drinking water).

How much weight do you actually lose from running a marathon? We can calculate this when we realize that our body fat has an energy density of 9 kcal/gram or 37.6 kJ/gram. Consequently, the Marathon Man will lose 11,844/37.6 = 316 grams of body fat. A modest amount which may not inspire heavyweights to run a marathon as a means to lose body fat! Of course, in the long run daily training will definitely lead to a sizable and stable weight loss, as many runners have experienced.

Energy in Our Daily Life

At home, the concept of energy is best known to many of us from the electricity consumption (in kWh) for lighting, the fridge and other household uses. When we realize that 1 kWh is equivalent to 3,600 kJ, we can calculate that the amount of energy in our daily food is equivalent to 10,460/3600 = 2.9 kWh. A very small number indeed, in particular when we consider that 1 kWh costs only some US$0.12. In theory, we would thus need only 2.9*0.12 = US$0.35 to provide the daily energy for our metabolism. It is a pity that we cannot eat electricity as this would be a lot cheaper than our groceries!

Another example from daily life is the gas consumption of our cars. The energy density of petrol is 28,800 kJ/l, so if we could eat petrol we would need only 10,460/28,800 = 0.4 liter per day! With a gas price of some 0.6 US$/l, our daily cost would be as low as 0.4*0.6 = US$0.24, so even cheaper than electricity! Of course the energy density of petrol is quite high, which we can see when we calculate that the energy content of a small tank of 40 liters is equivalent to 40*28,800 = 1,152,000 kJ. This is the same amount of energy that we consume with our food in 1,152,000/10,460 = 110 days! Apparently, the gas mileage of our body is far superior to that of our car!

How Much Energy Do We Use for Running?

When we neglect the air resistance, we can calculate the energy cost of running with the formula:

E = cmd

In a later chapter, we will show that the numerical value of the specific energy cost of running (c) can be set at 0.98 kJ/kg/km. The body weight (m) of our Marathon Man is 70 kg, so the energy cost of running a marathon (d = 42.195K) is 0.98*70*42.194 = 2,985 kJ. This number is slightly lower than the one in the box, because there we have included the air resistance. In later chapters we will discuss the air resistance in much more detail. The figure shows the energy cost of running as a function of the distance (for the Marathon Man, 70 kg, excluding the air resistance).

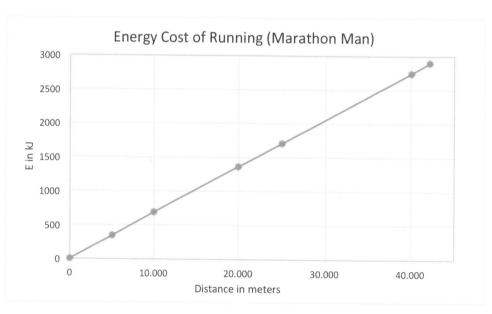

How long do you need to run in order to lose 1 kg of body fat? We can calculate that easily as 1 kg of body fat is equivalent to 37,600 kJ. Taking into account the metabolic efficiency of 25%, the Marathon Man needs to run d = E/cm = (37,600/(0.98*70*0.25) = 137 km to burn 1 kg of body fat! This seems impressive, but with regular training you will reach this easily, so you will definitely lose weight (provided you do not increase your food consumption of course).

8. POWER

Knowledge is power. —Sir Francis Bacon

In the previous chapter, we discussed the general relationship which you can use to calculate your race time (t) for any distance, once you know the power (P) of your human engine and the energy cost (E) of running that distance:

> $t = E/P$
>
> Example for the marathon:
>
> E = 2,961 kilojoule
>
> P = 235 watts
>
> t = 2,961,000/235 = 12,600 seconds
>
> = 3 hours 30 minutes

In this chapter, we will look more closely at the concept of power (P). Once again, we will give some examples from daily life and illustrate how you can use the concept of power to make useful calculations.

The Average Power of the Human Engine

One way to approach this is by simply dividing the daily energy intake from our food (E = 10,460 kJ) by the number of seconds in a day (t = 86,400 sec). The result is an average power (P) of 121 watts, about equivalent to an old-fashioned lightbulb. However, we should realize that this is just a theoretical calculation of the average thermal power. In practice, we need to take into account that the metabolic efficiency is only some 25%, so the average mechanical power of the human engine is just 121*0.25 = 30 watts.

Of course our human engine is quite capable of supplying more power during a short time. As an example we mention the fact that professional cyclist Chris Froome pushed 415 watts during 39 minutes while climbing to the summit of the Alpe d'Huez in the Tour de France of 2015.

We can appreciate the meaning of 30 watts by considering that we use it to produce electricity with a home trainer. If we cycled for an entire working day (8 hours), we would produce 8*30/1000 = 0.24 kWh of electricity, with a monetary value of just 0.24*0.12 = 0.03 US$!

Other Examples of Power

In 1777, James Watt defined the unit of horse power (HP) as the amount of power that a horse produces by hoisting a weight of 150 kg up a height of 30 meters in one minute. The energy cost of this can be calculated as:

E = mgh

With the gravity constant g = 9.81 m/s^2, E becomes 150*9.81*30 = 44,145 joule.

Consequently, the HP is equivalent to:

P = E/t = 44,145/60 = 736 watts

As we know that a horse can easily maintain this power, we may conclude that the endurance power of the horse engine is substantially larger than that of the human engine.

The power of modern cars is much higher still. Many a car is equipped with an engine of 100 HP or 73,600 watts. In the previous chapter, we saw already that the energy content of a small 40-liter tank of petrol is equivalent to 40*28,800 = 1,152,000 kJ. Consequently, we can conclude that the tank will be empty after a time t = E/P = 1,152,000/73,600/3,600 = 4.3 hour drive at full power.

How Can You Calculate Your Race Time?

In the previous chapter we already saw the formula to calculate the energy cost of running a flat course:

E = cmd

This means that for our Marathon Man the energy cost of running one kilometer is equal to 0.98*70*1 = 68.7 kJ (c = 0.98 kJ/kg/km, m = 70 kg). When we know his power (P), we can calculate his race time with the formula:

t = E/P

In this chapter we will simply assume that his power is constant and equal to 235 watts. With this assumption, we can calculate that his time per km will be 68,700/235 = 292 seconds or 4 minutes 52 seconds. The figure below gives the race time as a function of the distance.

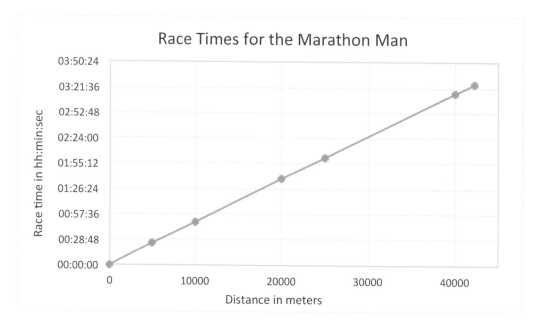

Race Times for the Marathon Man

We should note that the figure is the result of some simplifications:

1. We have not yet taken into account the effect of the air resistance. This has a small, but not negligible, impact.
2. In practice the power will not be constant, but decline with time. As a result of this, the race times at short distances will be somewhat better than calculated.

In later chapters, both aspects will be taken into account, so exact running times can be calculated.

Haile Gebreselassie at the 2007 FBK Games in Hengelo (the Netherlands).

9. POWER REQUIREMENTS FOR SPORTS I

Study the past to succeed in the future!

In this chapter and the next one, we will make some simple calculations to illustrate how the power of the human engine determines your performance in various sports. One of the nice things about our theory is that it can be applied to many endurance sports. Once you know the power of your human engine, you can calculate your approximate race times in different sports. In this chapter, we will use the examples of stair climbing and cycling. In the next chapter speed skating and running will be discussed.

We will show that in some sports (like speed skating and cycling on a flat course) your performance is determined by the total power (P, in watts) of your human engine. In other sports (like running and cycling uphill), the specific power (P/m, in watts/kg body weight) is the decisive factor.

Before we start the calculations, we should make one comment. Our calculations are based on the assumption that the power of your human engine is the same in different sports. This does not mean that a runner can automatically cycle or skate as well as he can run. Of course he will have to train for this and even then it may appear that he is less talented in the other sports. But we do believe that in general the power of your human engine gives a pretty good indication of what you could achieve in other sports as well, provided you have trained for it!

How Fast Could You Run Up the Stairs of the Empire State Building?

The annual Empire State Building Run-Up (ESBRU[14]) has become an elite bucket list item that the general public vies to participate in. Thousands of runners from around the world enter, all seeking one of a select few spaces. The ESBRU includes climbing 1,576 steps to a height of 320 meters. The record time of 9 minutes 33 seconds was set by Australian Paul Crake in 2003.

We can calculate the energy cost of the ESBRU with the formula:

E = mgh

The Empire State Building Run-Up includes climbing 1,576 steps to a height of 320 meters.

As we know that g = 9.81 m/s^2 and h = 320 meter, we can calculate the race time as:

t = E/P = mgh/P = m*9.81*320/P = 3139/(P/m)

The result is quite interesting; we see that the race time depends inversely on the specific power (P/m, in watts/kg) of the human engine. So far, we have neglected the running resistance. To compensate for this, we have added a 25% margin to the theoretical formula. The figure below shows the resulting relationship between the climbing time and the specific power.

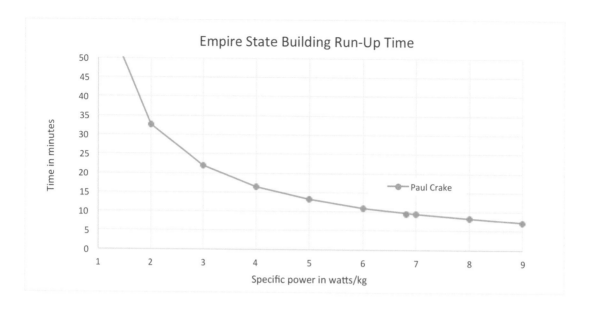

This relationship makes sense as a heavyweight has to carry much more weight upstairs, so he uses more energy for the climb. In comparison to a featherweight, the total power (P, in watts) of his human engine should be much higher in order to reach the top at the same time.

The record time of 9:33 means that the specific power (P/m) of Paul Crake must have been 6.8 watts/kg. We don't know his body weight, but at 60 kg he would have needed a total power (P) of 6.8*60 = 408 watts. If his body weight were 80 kg, he would have needed a total power (P) of 5.48*80 = 544 watts. This last number is even higher than the 415 watts that Chris Froome pushed on the climb to the Alpe d'Huez, as we saw in the previous chapter. Of course, we should remark that Chris weighs only 67 kg, so his specific power was also quite high at 415/67 = 6.2 watts/kg. Moreover, he did this in the third week of the Tour de France and at the end of a tough stage, so some fatigue will definitely have been there already. Also he did this in the thin mountain air (which has a negative impact on human performance) and he maintained this power for 39 minutes instead of 9.5 minutes. In later chapters, we will discuss the impact of all these factors in more detail. Finally, we can now calculate the race time that we may expect from our Marathon Man. His power output is 235 watts and his weight is 70 kg, so his specific power is 235/70 = 3.37 watts/kg. This means he will reach the top after 19 minutes. He might even be a little faster as his power output during these 19 minutes can be somewhat higher than the 235 watts which is his power output during the marathon. This will also be discussed in later chapters.

Bradley Wiggins during a time trial in the Tour de France of 2012.

How Fast Could You Bike on a Flat Course?

For now, we will assume that in this case the power of the human engine is used completely to overcome the air resistance. This means we have neglected all other losses in cycling (the rolling resistance of the wheels, the climbing resistance of hills and the mechanical resistance of chain and hubs). Without wind, we can then use the following formula:

$$P = 0.5\rho c_d A v^3$$

In this formula ρ is the air density (1.205 kg/m^3 at 20°C), $c_d A$ is the air-resistance coefficient (0.21 m^2 for a streamlined cyclist) and v is the velocity in m/s. Consequently, we can calculate the attainable velocity as a function of the total power (P) in watts. To compensate for the other losses, we have added a 10% margin to the theoretical formula. With this, we have determined the power–speed relationship as shown in the figure below.

In spite of the simplifications that we used, the graph appears to be pretty good. We have indicated the recent world hour record by Bradley Wiggins[15]. In 2015 he set the record at 54.526 km/h. His power output during this race has been calculated at 468 watts or 6.1 watts/kg as Bradley weighs 77 kg.

Our Marathon Man could attain a speed of 43.2 km/h with his total power of 235 watts, provided of course that he has trained sufficiently, is talented and is able to ride with the same perfect aerodynamics as Sir Bradley did.

In summary, we conclude that in cycling on a flat course your total power output (P, in watts) is the decisive factor and not the specific power (P/m, in watts/kg). Consequently time trial specialists are usually somewhat heavier and more powerful than the lightweight climbers.

How Fast Could You Bike to the Top of the Alpe d'Huez?

Here we can use the following formula to calculate the cycling time to the summit:

$t = E/P = mgh/P = 9.81 * 1,071 * (P/m)$

We know that the summit is at an altitude (h) of 1,071 meters[16]. Just like in the run up the Empire State Building, we find that the specific power (P/m, in watts/kg) is the decisive factor. In climbing every kilogram that you have to carry to the top weighs heavily! As a result, the top climbers are always featherweights with as little body fat as possible.

The figure below gives the attainable climbing times as a function of the specific power in watts/kg. In preparing this figure, we have added 40% to the theoretical formula to compensate for the weight of the bike and the other losses (rolling resistance, air resistance and mechanical resistance).

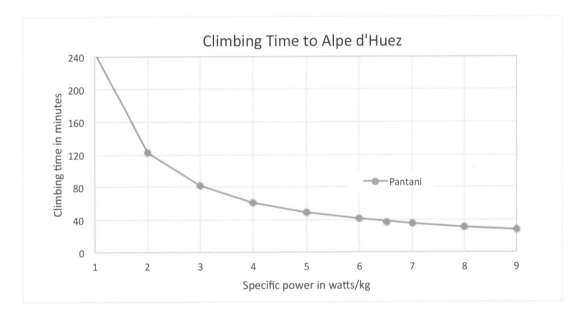

We can see that a specific power output of 6.5 watts/kg is required for the record of Marco Pantani (37:35). This is higher than the 6.2 watts/kg that Chris Froome pushed and it should be considered with suspicion, particularly as Pantani did it in the thin mountain air. In a later chapter, we will discuss these factors in more detail. Here, we remark that Pantani weighed considerably less than Froome (57 kg vs 67 kg), so his total power output was lower than that of Froome (370 watts vs 415 watts). With only 370 watts Pantani climbed almost three minutes faster than Froome did with 415 watts. This corroborates the fact that in climbing the total power output in watts is not the decisive factor; the specific power in watts/kg is!

Finally, we have calculated that our Marathon Man could reach the top after 73 minutes with his specific power output of 3.37 watts/kg, provided he has trained sufficiently.

10.POWER REQUIREMENTS FOR SPORTS II

Life is lived forwards, but understood backwards.

In this chapter, we will investigate how fast you can skate and run with the power of your human engine. We will show that in speed skating the total power (P, in watts) is the decisive factor, whereas in running the specific power (P/m, in watts/kg) determines how fast you are. Consequently, speed skaters are usually somewhat bigger and more powerful: the Dutch multiple Olympic and World Champion Sven Kramer weighs 84 kg! Runners on the other hand benefit from being skinny: Haile Gebrselassie weighs only 56 kg!

Before we start the calculations, we should make the same remark as in the previous chapter: you are not automatically as good in speed skating as in running. You should definitely train sufficiently in order to perform up to the potential of your human engine!

How Fast Could You Skate?

We can compare speed skating with cycling. In both sports the air resistance is the main factor that determines the attainable speed. Consequently, we can use the following formula, neglecting the sliding resistance of the skates with the ice:

$$P = 0.5\rho c_d A v^3$$

In this formula ρ is the air density (1.293 kg/m^3 at 0°C), $c_d A$ is the air-resistance coefficient (0.28 m^2 for a speed skater) and v is the velocity in m/s. Consequently, we can calculate the attainable velocity as a function of the total power (P, in watts). To compensate for the sliding resistance, we have added a 35% margin to the theoretical formula. With this, we have determined the attainable speed and the race time at the 10,000 meter, the domain of Sven Kramer. The result is shown in the figure below.

Sven Kramer wins the European Speed Skating Championships Allround 2016 in the Belarus city of Minsk.

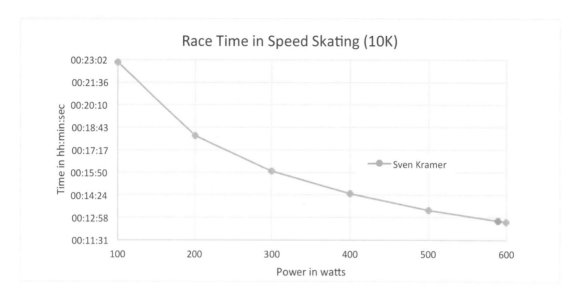

In spite of the simplifications that we used, the graph appears to be pretty good. We have indicated the track record of 12:45 that Sven Kramer set at the Thialf Centre in Heerenveen, the Netherlands[3]. According to our calculations, his power output during this race was 589 watts or 7.0 watts/kg. These numbers are quite high, but we should remember that he only had to maintain this effort for less than 13 minutes.

Our Marathon Man could skate a time of 17:17 with his power of 235 watts, provided of course that he has trained sufficiently and has the same perfect skating technique that Sven has.

In summary, we conclude that in speed skating the total power output (P, in watts) is the decisive factor and not the specific power (P/m, in watts/kg).

How Fast Could You Run?

When we neglect the air resistance and consider running on a flat course, we can use the formula:

P = E/t = cmd/t = cmv

As we mentioned in an earlier chapter, the numerical value for the specific energy cost of running (c) can be set at 0.98 kJ/kg/km. Consequently, we get an interesting result:

v = (P/m)/0.98

This means that your speed is directly proportional to your specific power (P/m, in watts/kg). Because we are used to expressing the speed in km/h and not in m/s, we need to multiply with a factor of 3.6. The result thus becomes:

$$v = 3.67*(P/m)$$

This is a simple and very powerful formula for the relationship between specific power and speed. In order to compensate for the air resistance, we have added a factor of 10%. With this assumption, we have calculated the attainable speed and converted it to the race time for the 10,000 meter. The result is shown in the figure below.

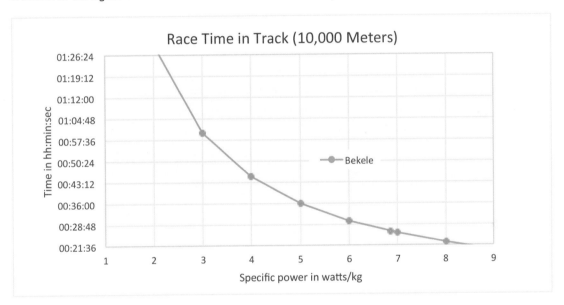

In spite of the simplifications that we used, the graph appears to be pretty good. We have indicated the world record of 26:17 of Kenenisa Bekele[3]. According to our calculations, his specific power output during this race was 6.8 watts/kg. Bekele weighs 56 kg, so his total power output was 383 watts. We see that his total power output (in watts) is much less than that of Sven Kramer and Bradley Wiggins. However, his specific power (in watts/kg) is quite high, considering the fact that he had to maintain this for more than 26 minutes. In later chapters we will give more details on the power–time relationship. There we will also show that the limit of human power can be set at a value of 6.4 watts/kg for an endurance time of one hour. In general the power that you can maintain for one hour is called the functional threshold power (FTP). With the abovementioned formula, we can calculate that the attainable speed for an FTP of 6.4 watts/kg equals (3.67/1.10)*6.4 = 21.35 km/h. Presently, the world hour record on the track is held by Haile Gebrselassie at 21.285 km, which is quite close.

Our Marathon Man could run a time of 53:31 with his specific power of 3.37 watts/kg, provided of course that he has trained sufficiently.

In summary, we conclude that it is possible to make simple and interesting calculations on the attainable performance in all kinds of endurance sports. The total power (in watts) is the decisive factor in sports where the air resistance is important, like speed skating and cycling on a flat course. The specific power (in watts/kg) is the decisive factor in sports where gravity is important, like stair climbing, cycling uphill and running (also on a flat course as your legs have to lift your weight each step).

So far, we have made simplified calculations in which several factors have been neglected or estimated, like:

1. The impact of the endurance time on the power output of the human engine
2. Various losses, like the air resistance, the climbing resistance, the rolling resistance, the gliding resistance and the mechanical resistance
3. The impact of the thin air in the mountains on the human engine
4. The impact of training and other factors (like age, sex and gear) on the power output of the human engine

In the next chapters, we will derive a complete model of the physics of running and of the human engine. In the remainder of this book, we will then use this model to calculate the impact of many factors on the attainable race time. We hope and expect that the reader will be able to use this knowledge to assess the power of his own human engine and to see what performances he could reach (e.g., at different distances or under different circumstances). Finally, the reader may then evaluate the options that are available to him to optimize his performance (e.g., training, losing weight and optimizing his pace and gear).

Multiple Olympic and World Champion Kenenisa Bekele (left) with Mukhlid Alotaibi, the first Saudi who participated in four successive Oympic Games.

11. THE RUNNING MODEL

Everything should be made as simple as possible, but not simpler. —Albert Einstein

So far we have used very simple models to calculate the race times based on the available power (P in watts) of the human engine. This has already given promising and interesting results. Now we want to make a complete model of the physics of running. In order to do this, we need to know how much power is needed to run in different conditions. Obviously, additional power is required to run against the wind. Consequently, we need to know the amount of power required to overcome the air resistance (P_a, in watts). Running against a hill also requires additional power, so we need to know the amount of power required to overcome the climbing resistance (P_c, in watts). Running on a flat course without any air resistance also requires power; by analogy we call this the amount of power required to overcome the running resistance (P_r, in watts). The figure below illustrates our running model.

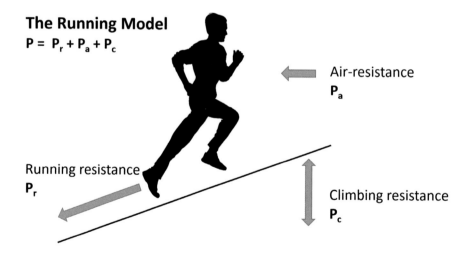

The Running Model
$$P = P_r + P_a + P_c$$

Air-resistance P_a

Running resistance P_r

Climbing resistance P_c

In the equilibrium situation, the available power of the human engine should be equal to the sum of the power required to overcome these three resistances: the running resistance, the air resistance and the climbing resistance:

$$P = P_r + P_a + P_c$$

We call this the running model. In this chapter we will analyze the three resistances that define the running model.

The Running Resistance

Theoretically, we can calculate the amount of power (P_r, in watts) required to overcome the running resistance from the specific energy cost of running (c, in kJ/kg/km), the body weight (m, in kg) and the speed (v, in m/s) of the runner, as given in the box.

> ## The Running Resistance
>
> $$P_r = cmv$$
>
> Example:
> c = 0.98 kJ/kg/km, m = 70 kg , v = 12.06 km/h
> P_r = 0.98*70*12.06/3.6 = 230 watts

The example is valid for our Marathon Man, who weighs 70 kg and runs the marathon in 3 hours and 30 minutes, a speed of 12.06 km/h. In the next chapter we will give more details on the specific energy cost of running (c in kJ/kg/km). There we will show that a sound value for c is 0.98 kJ/kg/km (for the average runner). We can also relate the specific energy cost (c) to the notion of the running economy (RE), which is used by many authors to describe the amount of energy used in running. The RE is usually given as the specific amount of oxygen used (in ml O_2/kg/km). In a later chapter we will show that 1 ml O_2 has an energy value of 19.5 joule, so with the muscle efficiency of 25%, we can calculate that a c value of 0.98 kJ/kg/km is equivalent to an RE of 0.98*1,000/19.5/0.25 = 201 ml O_2/kg/km. In later chapters we will discuss the specific energy cost (c) and the running economy (RE) in more detail. There we will also discuss how you can improve your RE and reduce your c value, so you will need less energy and run more economically.

The formula for the running resistance shows that the required power is directly proportional to the body weight and the speed, as seen in the figure below.

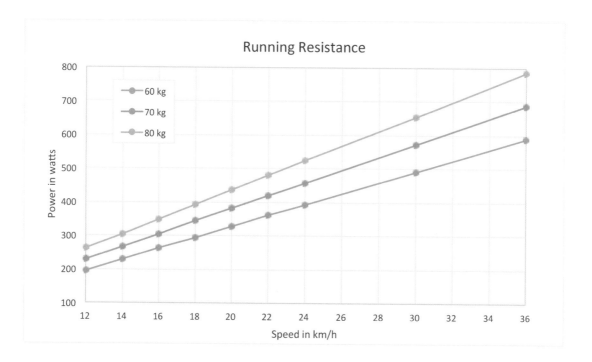

The figure shows that for sprinters the required power is quite high. When we look at the numbers of Usain Bolt (100 meters in 9.58 seconds, so a speed of 37.6 km/h and a body weight of 94 kg), we can calculate that his running resistance is 963 watts. And this figure does not even include the air resistance and the power required for his initial acceleration!

As the formula shows, the specific power (in watts/kg) determines the achievable speed, as shown in the figure below.

The figure shows that in order to achieve a speed of 20 km/h, a runner should be able to mobilize at least a specific power of 5.45 watts/kg. Also this number does not yet include the air resistance!

For completeness we have to remark that we should have included a factor cos(arctangent (i/100)) in the formula, with i being the gradient (in percent). In practice this factor is very close to one, also at steep hills (at an extreme gradient of 20%, the factor is still 0.98). Consequently, we did not include it in the box. However, we have included it in our model calculations in this book and in our computer program.

The Air Resistance

The power (P_a, in watts) required to overcome the air resistance depends on the air density (ρ, in kg/m³), the air resistance factor (c_dA, in m²), the speed (v, in m/s) and the wind speed (v_w, in m/s), as shown in the box.

The Air Resistance

$$P_a = 0.5\rho c_d A(v+v_w)^2 v$$

Example:
$\rho = 1.205$ kg/m³, $c_dA = 0.24$ m², $v = 12.06$ km/h, $v_w = 0$ km/h
$P_a = 0.5*1.205*0.24*(12.06/3,6)^3 = 5$ watts

The example is valid again for our Marathon Man, who runs at a temperature of 20°C (at this temperature the density of the air is 1.205 kg/m³) and in ideal, windless conditions. We see that the power (P_a, in watts) required to overcome the air resistance due to his own wind is rather small, 5 watts or 2% of his running resistance (P_r) of 230 watts. However, the formula also shows that P_a increases to the third power of the speed. Consequently, the impact of the air resistance is much higher for elite runners, as can be seen in the figure below.

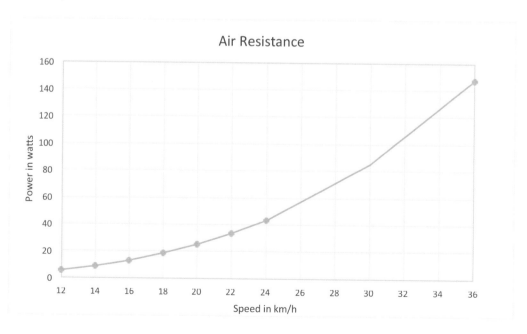

The figure shows that for sprinters P_a is quite high. When we look at the numbers of Usain Bolt (100 meters in 9.58 seconds, so a speed of 37.6 km/h and a body weight of 94 kg), we can calculate that his P_a has been 167 watts or 17% of his P_r of 963 watts. This also means that Usain could easily improve his world record if he ran at altitude. In a later chapter, we will calculate how much faster Usain could run in Mexico City, where the density of the air—and thus P_a—is 25% lower than at sea level. In other chapters we will also show the impact on the race times of the other factors that impact P_a, such as the wind conditions and the assistance of pacemakers.

The Climbing Resistance

The climbing resistance depends on the gradient (i, in %), the body weight (m, in kg) and the speed (v, in m/s), as shown in the box.

The Climbing Resistance

$P_c = (i/100)mgv$

Example:
i = 7.4%, m = 70 kg, v = 12.06 km/h, g = 9.81 m/s^2
$P_c = 7.4/100*70*9.81*12.06/3.6 = 170$ watts

The example is valid again for the Marathon Man, who attempts to run to the top of the Alpe d'Huez. The numbers show that uphill he cannot maintain a speed of 12.06 km/h, as this would require a climbing resistance of 170 watts on top of the 230 watts that he needs for the running resistance and the 5 watts for the air resistance. So he will have to reduce his speed until the sum of the three resistances equals the power of his human engine (235 watts for the Marathon Man). In a later chapter, we will show that in reality the muscle efficiency is slightly higher uphill than on a flat course, so P_c is somewhat less than follows from the theoretical formula.

The climbing resistance (P_c, in watts) increases proportionally with the speed (v) and the gradient (i), as can be seen from the formula. As the running resistance (P_r, in watts) also increases proportionally with the speed (v), the ratio of P_c/P_r depends only on the gradient (i). This ratio is given in the figure below.

In later chapters we will discuss all factors that impact the climbing resistance and the speed uphill and downhill. For completeness we have to remark that we should also have included a factor sin(arctangent (i/100)) in the formula. In practice this factor is very close to one, even at steep hills (at an extreme gradient of 20%, the factor is 0.98). Consequently, we did not include it in the box. However, we have included it in the model calculations in this book and in our computer program.

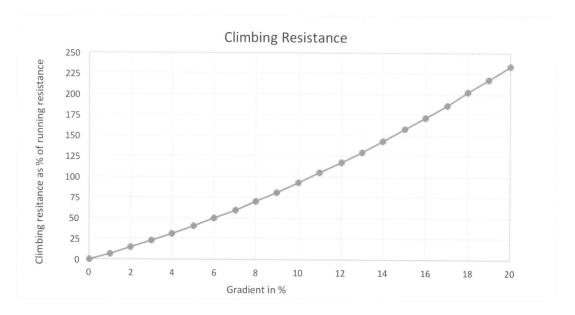

Conclusions

The physics of running comprises the formulas that describe the three resistances. In the equilibrium situation, the power output of the human engine will be equal to the sum of these three resistances: the running resistance, the air resistance and the climbing resistance:

$P = P_r + P_a + P_c$

The final result is the fairly complicated third-power formula given in the box below. In the next chapter we will explain how we have solved this equation. There we will also show how we can use the formula to calculate the attainable speed and race time depending on the power of the human engine and the race conditions.

The Physics of Running

Running resistance: $\qquad P_r = cmv$

Air resistance: $\qquad P_a = 0.5\rho c_d A(v+v_w)^2 v$

Climbing resistance: $\qquad P_c = (i/100)mgv$

Running formula: $\qquad P = cmv + 0.5\rho c_d A(v+v_w)^2 v + (i/100)mgv$

Running in a pack reduces the air resistance.

12. THE ENERGY COST OF RUNNING A FLAT COURSE

Anybody can be a runner. We were meant to run. It is the easiest sport. —Bill Rodgers

---

The Running Resistance

$P_r = cmv$

Example:

$c = 0.98$ kJ/kg/km, $m = 70$ kg, $v = 12.06$ km/h

$P_r = 0.98*70*12.06/3.6 = 230$ watts

In the previous chapter, we saw that we can calculate the power (P_r, in watts) required to overcome the running resistance from the specific energy cost (c, in kJ/kg/km), the body weight (m, in kg) and the speed (v, in m/s) of the runner, as given in the box.

The example is valid for our Marathon Man, who weighs 70 kg and runs the marathon in 3 hours and 30 minutes, so with a speed of 12.06 km/h.

The Specific Energy Cost of Running or the Running Economy

In this chapter we will discuss the specific energy cost (c, in kJ/kg/km) in more detail. How did we come to conclude that 0.98 kJ/kg/km is a sound value that we can use for our calculations?

In various textbooks the specific energy cost of running is set at a standard value of 1 kcal per kg of body weight per kilometer. As 1 kcal is 4.184 joule and the metabolic efficiency can be set at 25%, this is equivalent to 4.184*0.25 = 1.05 kJ/kg/km, so slightly more than our value of 0.98.

Many authors also use the notion of running economy (RE) to describe the specific energy cost of running. The RE is usually expressed as the specific oxygen cost of running (in ml O_2/kg/km). As 1 ml O_2 has an energy value of 19.5 joule and the metabolic efficiency can be set at 25%, we can calculate that a c of 0.98 kJ/kg/km is equivalent to an RE of 0.98*1000/19.5/0.25 = 201 ml O_2/kg/km.

We have made a review of the values for c and RE that are given in literature[1,17,18,19,20,21,22,23]. The table gives a summary of the results for running on a track course or treadmill (i.e., in ideal conditions).

Specific Cost of Running and Running Economy in Literature			
	c	c	RE
	(kcal/kg/km)	(kJ/kg/km)	(ml O_2/kg/km)
HGVH	**1.000**	1.046	214
ACSM	**0.934**	0.977	200
Sherman	**0.897**	0.938	192
Slawinski	0.897	0.938	192
Zamparo	1.056	**1.104**	226
Sassi	0.961	**1.005**	206
Vroemen	0.841	0.879	**180**
Léger	**0.980**	1.025	210
Léger	**0.927**	0.970	198
Model number	0.938	0.981	201

The bold numbers in the table are the ones originally stated by the authors; we have recalculated these to the equivalent other parameters and units. When we realize that the methods and circumstances of the investigations have been quite different, it seems surprising that all numbers are actually quite close to each other. Consequently, we conclude that it is realistic to use a model value for c of 0.98 kJ/kg/km (equivalent to a model number for RE of 201 ml O_2/kg/km). From the table we can also conclude that deviations of some 10% from this number may occur in practice.

Does Everyone Have the Same Running Economy?

Obviously, the specific cost of running (c) and the running economy (RE) will not be the same for everybody and in all conditions. In literature it is often stated that in particular the elite Kenyan and Ethiopian runners run very economically, so they use less oxygen and energy than the average runner.

The notion of running economy covers many aspects, but the impact of all of them is not fully known. Some relevant aspects are:

1. Body length (smaller is better)
2. Body stature (long legs, narrow calves, narrow and flexible hips are better)
3. Running form
   - Foot strike (bouncing, short ground contact, avoid rear foot striking)
   - Arm swing (synchronized, avoid excessive movement)
   - Stride pattern (high cadence, large stride length)
   - Vertical oscillation (impact not fully known)

We cannot influence our body length and body stature much (besides losing weight), but we can try to optimize our running form. However, many runners and coaches differ in their opinion on what constitutes the best running form. In later chapters we will discuss this in more detail, including what you can do in training to improve your running economy. We will also discuss the impact of running on a non-ideal footing, such as sand, grass, trails or clinkers.

Running Resistance as a Function of Speed

Based on the c value of 0.98 kJ/kg/km, we can now easily calculate the specific power (in watts/kg) which is required to run at a certain speed; see the table below.

Running resistance	
v	P/m
(km/h)	(watts/kg)
8	2.18
10	2.73
12	3.27
14	3.82
16	4.36
18	4.91
20	5.45
22	6.00
24	6.54
30	8.18
36	9.81

We see that in order to run his world record on the marathon (2:02:57, equivalent to a speed of 20.6 km/h), Dennis Kimetto apparently had to mobilize a power output of 5.6 watts/kg. Even more impressive are the numbers of David Rudisha at the 800 meter (1:40:91, equivalent to a speed of 28.5 km/h or 7.8 watts/kg) and Usain Bolt at the 100 meter (9.58 seconds, equivalent to 37.6 km/h or 10.2 watts/kg). Of course, all these numbers are still without the impact of the air resistance! The examples also show that the human engine can provide a much higher power output during a short time (short distance). This power–time (distance) relationship was first described in literature by Peter Riegel[24,25]. In later chapters we will discuss this relationship in more detail.

The World Championship Marathon 2013 was held at a flat course in Moscow. The runners completed four laps along the embankment of the Moskva river.

13. THE ENERGY COST OF THE AIR RESISTANCE

You never have the wind with you—either it is against you or you're having a good day. —Daniel Behrman

In the chapter on the running model, we saw that the power (P_a, in watts) required to overcome the air resistance depends on the air density (ρ, in kg/m^3), the air resistance factor (c_dA, in m^2), the speed (v, in m/s) and the wind speed (v_w, in m/s), as shown in the box.

The Air Resistance

$$P_a = 0.5\rho c_dA(v+v_w)^2v$$

Example:
$\rho = 1.205$ kg/m^3, $c_dA = 0.24$m^2, v = 12.06 km/h, $v_w = 0$ km/h
$P_a = 0.5*1.205*0.24*(12.06/3.6)^3 = 5$ watt

The example is valid again for our Marathon Man, who runs at a temperature of 20°C (at this temperature the density of the air is 1.205 kg/m^3) and in ideal, windless conditions. We see that the power (P_a in watts) required to overcome the air resistance is rather small, 5 watts or 2% of his running resistance (P_r) of 230 watts. However, the formula also shows that P_a increases to the third exponent of the speed. Consequently, the impact of the air resistance is much higher for elite runners, as can be seen in the figure below.

The Air Resistance Factor (c_dA)

In this chapter we will discuss the air resistance factor (c_dA) in more detail. How did we come to conclude that 0.24 m^2 is a sound value that we can use for our calculations?

Theory tells us that the factor (c_dA) consists of the product of the drag coefficient (c_d (dimensionless)) and the cross-sectional area (A in m^2) of the runner. The value of c_d depends on the air flow and turbulence and can be set at 0.9. The cross-sectional area (A) of the runner depends on the size of the runner and his posture.

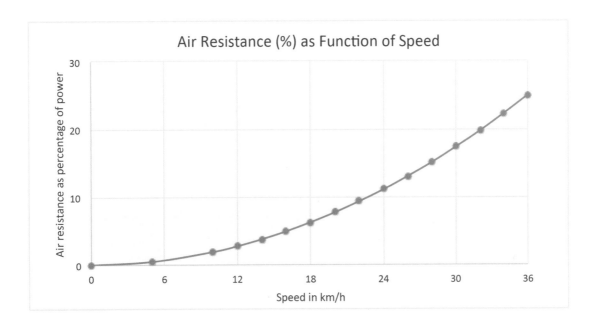

In the literature four studies[26,27,23,28] have been reported on the topic of the air resistance in running. In general, the authors measured the oxygen uptake of runners at a certain speed, both in situations without wind and with a head wind or tail wind (artificially created by means of a fan). The authors then correlated the measured oxygen uptake to the air resistance due to the speed of the runners. The following formulas were derived.

Formulas for Air Resistance in Literature			
Pugh 1	$\Delta VO_2 = 0.002v^3$	VO_2 in l/min	v in m/s
Pugh 2	$\Delta VO_2 = 0.0017v^3$	VO_2 in l/min	v in m/s
Léger	$\Delta VO_2 = 0.000525542v^3$	VO_2 in ml/kg/min	v in km/h
Davies	watts/kg $= 0.003335v^3$		

We have recalculated the oxygen uptake data of Pugh and Léger to the specific power (watts/kg) by using the fact that the energy value of one liter of oxygen is 19.5 kJ and the muscle efficiency is 25%. Finally we took the body weight of the runners into account and compared the resulting formulas with the theoretical formula from the box with a c_dA value of 0.24 m². The results are given in the tables below. We conclude that there is a very good match, so the c_dA value of 0.24 m² is a sound value to calculate the air resistance in practice.

Recalculated Formulas		
Pugh 1	$P/m = 0.002485v^3$	watts/kg
Pugh 2	$P/m = 0.002145v^3$	watts/kg
Léger	$P/m = 0.002135v^3$	watts/kg
Davies	$P/m = 0.002446v^3$	watts/kg
Theorie	$P/m = 0.002452v^3$	watts/kg

Required Power for Air Resistance					
v	Theory	Pugh 1	Pugh 2	Léger	Davies
(km/h)	(watts)	(watts)	(watts)	(watts)	(watts)
0	0	0	0	0	0
5	0	0	0	0	0
10	3	3	3	3	3
12	5	6	5	5	5
14	9	9	8	8	9
16	13	13	11	11	13
18	18	19	16	16	18
20	25	26	22	22	25
22	34	34	29	29	34
24	44	44	38	38	43
26	55	56	48	48	55
28	69	70	61	60	69
30	85	86	74	74	85
32	103	105	90	90	103
34	124	126	108	108	124
36	147	149	129	128	147

The Effect of Head Wind and Tail Wind

Davies and Pugh have also reported formulas for the additional oxygen uptake due to head wind and tail wind. For a head wind, their formulas are given in the table below.

Formulas for the Impact of Head Wind	
Davies	$\Delta VO_2 = -0.700 + 0.109 * v_w^2$
Pugh1	$\Delta VO_2 = 0.0089 * v_w^2$
Pugh2	$\Delta VO_2 = 0.00757 * v_w^2$

We have recalculated these formulas and compared them with the theoretical formula with a c_dA value of 0.24 m². The results are given in the figure below.

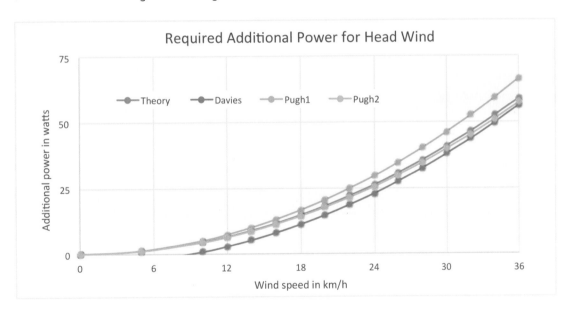

Again the results match very well, as can be seen from the figure.

Finally, Davies and Pugh have reported that the advantage of a tail wind was only 50% of the disadvantage of a head wind. They reasoned that this difference could be explained by a lower muscle efficiency during a tail wind due to the depressing effect of a tail wind. This can be compared to the lifting effect of a head wind as we know it from airplanes.

Based on this, we have concluded that for a tail wind we should use a c_dA value of only 0.12 instead of 0.24 m².

Impact of Air Resistance on Required Power and Achievable Speed

Now that we have established the air resistance coefficient, it is interesting to calculate the required power to overcome the air resistance exactly. We have done this in the table below. From the table, we can see that the impact of the air resistance is significant. As an example, we use the world record of Kenenisa Bekele at the 5,000 meter, 12:37.35. The average speed during this race was 23.8 km/h, which means that the air resistance was 43 watts or more than 10% of the running resistance!

By running behind pacemakers, it is possible to reduce the air resistance by some 30%, which offers a significant advantage at the elite level. In later chapters, we will show the effect of pacemakers on the race time. Also we will discuss the impact of wind, which can be quite big at strong winds. Later we will also show the impact of running on a treadmill, where there is no air resistance at all.

Air Resistance	
v	P_a
km/h	watts
10	3
12	5
14	9
16	13
18	18
20	25
22	34
24	44
30	85
36	147

In summary, the air resistance in running is small in comparison to the running resistance, but it can definitely not be neglected, even at ideal, windless conditions. The impact is bigger at higher speeds and consequently the biggest for the elite runners and sprinters. Obviously, strong winds will have a big negative impact on the race time.

What can runners do to limit the negative impact of the air resistance? Try to hide behind pacemakers or inside a pack of runners! Sprinters can have an advantage by running at altitude, where the air resistance is much lower. In a later chapter, we will calculate how much faster Usain Bolt could run the 100-meter race in Mexico City. Unfortunately, long-distance runners cannot improve their race time by running at altitude. This is due to the negative impact of the thin air on the oxygen uptake and thus the power output of the human engine. This will also be discussed later. Finally a slightly better race time can be expected during a depression. At a low air pressure, the air density, and consequently the air resistance, is somewhat lower.

Try to hide behind pacemakers or inside a pack of runners to limit the negative impact of the air resistance.

14. THE ENERGY COST OF HILLS

For every uphill, there is a downhill. —Mike Hodges

The power required to overcome the climbing resistance depends on the gradient (i, in %), the body weight (m, in kg) and the speed (v, in m/s), as shown in the box.

> ## The Climbing Resistance
>
> $P_c = (i/100)mgv$
>
> Example:
> i = 7.4%, m = 70 kg, v = 12.06 km/h, g = 9.81 m/s^2
> P_c = 7.4/100*70*9.81*12.06/3.6 = 170 watts

The example is valid again for the Marathon Man, who attempts to run to the top of the Alpe d'Huez. The numbers show that uphill he cannot maintain a speed of 12.06 km/h, as this would require a climbing resistance of 170 watts on top of the 230 watts that he needs for the running resistance and the 5 watts for the air resistance. He will have to reduce his speed until the sum of the three resistances equals the power of his human engine (235 watts). In practice, it was found that the climbing resistance (P_c) is somewhat less than follows from the theoretical formula. This will be discussed in this chapter.

The Hill Factor

In literature, various investigators[17, 26,27,28,29] have established that the climbing resistance is somewhat less than could be expected from theory. They explain the difference with the muscle efficiency. According to physiology, the muscle efficiency is higher when positive work is executed (as in running uphill) and lower when negative work is done (as in running downhill). The muscle efficiency can even be negative, at extreme downhill slopes when brake forces are dominant. In their research, the authors measured the oxygen demand for various gradients. We have recalculated the oxygen demand to the specific power in

The climb to Alpe d'Huez known from the Tour de France is a common thread in calculation examples in this book.

watts/kg, by using the fact that the energy value of one liter of O_2 is 19.5 kJ. Finally we have determined a hill factor (η in %) as the ratio of the measured power (P) and the theoretical required power (P_c):

$$\eta = P/P_c *100$$

The results are given below

Hill Factor in Literature	
	η in %
ACSM (running)	39.6
ACSM (walking)	79.3
Pugh (running)	51.5
Pugh (walking)	77.2
Davies (running)	59.9
Davies (downhill)	28.7

In spite of the different results, we see a consistent pattern. The hill factor and thus the required power is always less than 100%. Moreover, the hill factor is always less downhill than uphill. This means that the energy advantage of going downhill is always less than the disadvantage of going uphill. This is consistent with the explanation of a lower muscle efficiency downhill as a result of brake forces. Finally, the hill factor for running is always lower than it is for walking.

The Research of Minetti et al.

The most convincing investigation in this field has been carried out by Minetti et al[29]. They measured the energy cost of running up and down an extreme range of gradients, from -45% to +45%. We have calculated the hill factor equivalent to their results as seen in the figure.

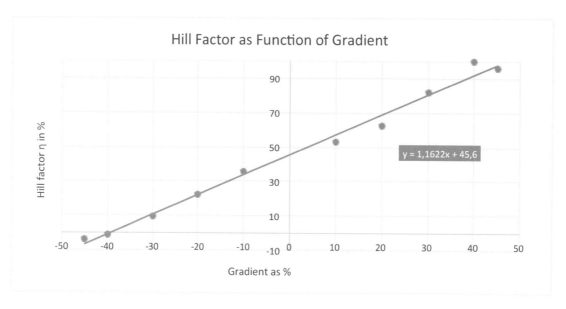

The results look reliable and reproducible. The hill factor is almost linearly dependent on the gradient. At extreme positive (uphill) gradients, the hill factor approaches 100%. At extreme negative (downhill) gradients, the hill factor even becomes negative! This means you have to use energy for braking without benefitting from the gain in altitude. We have concluded that these results are very useful, so we have included them in our running model, in accordance with the relationship of Minetti:

$\eta = 45.6 + 1.1622i$

The consequence is that the climbing resistance of the Marathon Man in the box is not 170 watts, but only $170*(45.6+1.1622*8.1)/100 = 98$ watts.

How Large Is the Climbing Resistance as a Function of the Gradient?

In the table below, we have calculated the climbing resistance (including the hill factor) for a speed of 15 km/h and as a function of the gradient. The total climbing resistance obviously is proportional to the body weight, so the specific climbing resistance is actually a better parameter. This is given in the figure as well. In real life, many runners will not be able to maintain a speed of 15 km/h uphill, as the sum of the running resistance, the air resistance and the climbing resistance will be larger than the available power of their human engine. In later chapters, we will calculate how fast you can run uphill and downhill, depending on the power of your human engine.

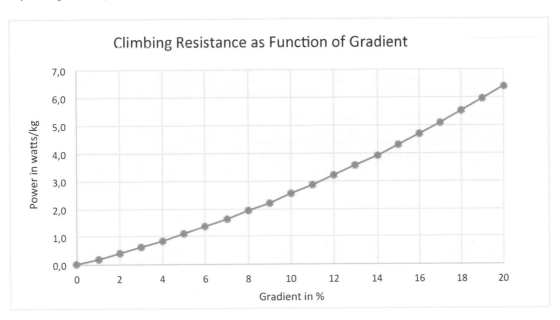

Climbing Resistance at 15 km/h			
Gradient	60 kg	70 kg	80 kg	
i	P	P	P	P/m
(%)	(watts)	(watts)	(watts)	(watts/kg)
0	0	0	0	0.0
1	12	14	15	0.2
2	24	28	32	0.4
3	37	43	50	0.6
4	51	60	68	0.9
5	66	77	88	1.1
6	81	95	109	1.4
7	98	114	130	1.6
8	115	134	153	1.9
9	133	155	177	2.2
10	152	177	202	2.5
11	171	200	228	2.9
12	191	223	255	3.2
13	213	248	283	3.5
14	235	274	313	3.9
15	257	300	343	4.3
16	281	328	374	4.7
17	305	356	407	5.1
18	330	385	440	5.5
19	356	415	475	5.9
20	383	447	510	6.4

The total climbing resistance is proportional to the body weight, so the specific climbing resistance is a better parameter.

15. THE RUNNING MODEL AND THE STANDARD CONDITIONS

In the previous chapters we derived the running formula, which we can use to calculate the achievable speed and race time as a function of the power of the human engine, as shown in the box:

$$P = cmv + 0.5\rho c_d A(v+v_w)^2 v + (i/100)mgv\eta$$

With the running formula, we can calculate the speed when all other parameters are known. We can also use it to make sensitivity analyses to see the impact of all the parameters. By doing this, we can answer many relevant questions, including:

» How much faster do you get when your power (P) increases as a result of training?
» How much slower do you get when you get older?
» How big is the advantage of pacemakers and running in the pack?
» How much do you lose in windy conditions?
» How much slower do you run uphill and how much faster downhill?
» How much faster do you get when you lose fat?
» How much can you gain from improving your running economy?
» How big is the advantage of lightweight running shoes?
» How big is the advantage of altitude training?
» What is the physiological limit of the world records?
» Is it possible to run the marathon in less than 2 hours?

In part IV of this book, we will systematically analyze all parameters and show the impact on the speed. But first we need to discuss how we have solved the running formula. This is not a trivial matter, as it is a third-degree equation of the speed (v).

The Solution of the Running Formula

In literature, several methods can be found to solve third-degree equations. We have chosen to use the universal solution given in the box below. Although it requires some elaborate calculations, it has the advantage of being robust and of giving the correct result in all possible conditions (including head wind and tail wind). We have programmed the solution in an Excel spreadsheet and into our calculator.

The Solution of the Running Formula

$$v = \sqrt[3]{\left(\frac{-b^3}{27a^3} + \frac{bc}{6a^2} - \frac{d}{2a}\right) + \sqrt{\left(\frac{-b^3}{27a^3} + \frac{bc}{6a^2} - \frac{d}{2a}\right)^2 + \left(\frac{c}{3a} - \frac{b^2}{9a^2}\right)^3}}$$

$$+ \sqrt[3]{\left(\frac{-b^3}{27a^3} + \frac{bc}{6a^2} - \frac{d}{2a}\right) - \sqrt{\left(\frac{-b^3}{27a^3} + \frac{bc}{6a^2} - \frac{d}{2a}\right)^2 + \left(\frac{c}{3a} - \frac{b^2}{9a^2}\right)^3}} - \frac{b}{3a}$$

$a = 0.5\rho c_d A$

$b = 2*0.5\rho c_d A\, v_w$

$c = 0.5\rho c_d A v_w{}^2 + cmcos(arctangent(i/100)) + \eta mgsins(arctangent(i/100))$

$d = P$

The Parameters of the Running Formula

The achievable speed depends on many parameters, including:

1. The available power (P) of the runner (in watts). This depends on many other factors, including talent, age, training, weight, duration and distance and specific aspects, such as preparation and tapering, altitude training, nutrition, etc.
2. The specific cost of running (c, in kJ/kg/km). This depends on running economy, which is influenced by body stature and running form.
3. The racing weight of the runner (m, in kg). This is influenced by his preparation (nutrition and training).
4. The temperature (T, in °K). Obviously, this depends on the weather conditions.

5. The air pressure (p_0, in Pa). This also depends on the weather conditions.
6. The altitude above sea level (in m). This is determined by the race location.
7. The air resistance factor ($c_d A$, in m^2). This depends on the presence of pacemakers and somewhat on the body stature of the runner.
8. The wind direction and speed (v_w, in m/s). This depends on the weather conditions and the race course.
9. The gradient (i, in %). Obviously, this depends on the race course.

Moreover, we should realize that the air density (ρ, in kg/m^3) depends on three parameters: the temperature, the air pressure and the altitude, as shown in the box below.

Calculation of Air Density

$\rho = (p*M)/(R*T)$

$p = p_0 * e^{(-Mgh/RT)}$

Example:
h = 0 m, p_0 = 101,300 Pa, R = 8.314 kJ/kmol/°K, T = 288 °K, M = 28.97 g/mol, g = 9.81 m/s^2
$p = 101,300*e^0 = 101,300$ Pa
$\rho = 101,300*28.97/(8,314*288) = 1.226$ kg/m^3

The Standard Conditions and Marathon Man

As many parameters play a role, we saw the need for a systematic analysis of the impact of all parameters. Consequently, we have chosen to use a set of standard conditions throughout the book. In later chapters, we will look at the impact of changing the parameters, one by one. Our standard conditions, including the data of our hypothetical runner Marathon Man, are shown in the table below:

Standard Conditions	Value	Unit	Clarification
P	235	watts	Marathon Man
c	0.98	kJ/kg/km	
m	70	kg	Marathon Man
T	15	°C	
p_0	101,300	Pa	
h	0	m	
c_dA	0.24	m^2	
i	0	%	
v_w	0	m/s	
ρ	1.226	kg/m3	Follows from T, p_o en h

With our calculator, we have calculated the race times of our Marathon Man at various distances and in the standard conditions. The results are given in the table below. These race times are the exact results of the running formula, contrary to the simplified calculations we used in previous chapters.

Results Marathon Man	
Distance	Time
(km)	(h:m:s)
0.8	00:03:04
1.5	00:05:59
3	00:12:32
5	00:21:37
10	00:45:15
15	01:09:43
20	01:34:46
21.1	01:40:20
25	02:00:13
30	02:26:02
42.195	03:30:00

In part III of this book, we will analyze how much faster or slower Marathon Man will run if the conditions change and the parameters deviate from the standard conditions.

But first, we will study the human engine in some more detail in part III. How does the human engine function and how can we determine the available power (P, in watts) and the specific power (P/m, in watts/kg)?

PART III

THE POWER OF THE HUMAN ENGINE

16. THE POWER–TIME RELATIONSHIP

I have never met a runner that did not want to run faster!

In order to calculate the performance at different distances, we first need to consider the power-time relationship. Everybody knows that marathon pace is less than 5K pace. As pace is determined by power, this means that the power of the human engine apparently decreases as time increases. In this chapter, we will analyze this power–time relationship in detail. How can we calculate the power decline as a function of time? And what is the cause for this decline? We will show that the power–time relationship is actually determined by the four energy systems of the human engine that we discussed in an earlier chapter. We will see that as time increases the fuel mix of the human engine gradually changes, which explains the decline of power with time.

Pete Riegel's Famous Formula

The relationship between speed and distance was first investigated by Pete Riegel. He was a mechanical engineer and marathon runner and, as he put it himself, nuts about numbers. He compared his race times at various distances with the world records and concluded that the speed declined exponentially as a function of the distance. He found the same exponential relationship for his own times as well as for the world records! He published his results on running in 1977[24]; later he published a paper on other sports as well[25]. Pete Riegel's formula is simple and straightforward:

$$v_2/v_1 = (d_2/d_1)^{-0.07}$$

In his formula *d* represents the distance and *v* is the speed. So the formula says quite simply that as the distance increases by a factor of two, the speed decreases by 5% ($2^{-0.07} = 0.95$).

Pete Riegel's formula is very powerful and is used in many running calculators on the internet. In Pete's papers and in literature by others, there has been some debate on the value of the exponent -0.07. Sometimes -0.06 or -0.08 is also mentioned. As we will see in a later chapter, these differences are related to the fatigue resistance. A runner with a very good fatigue resistance will have an exponent of -0.06, so his speed will only decline 4% as the distance doubles. However, for most runners -0.07 is the most realistic number. This exponent is also valid for the world records of both men and women, as can be seen in the graph below.

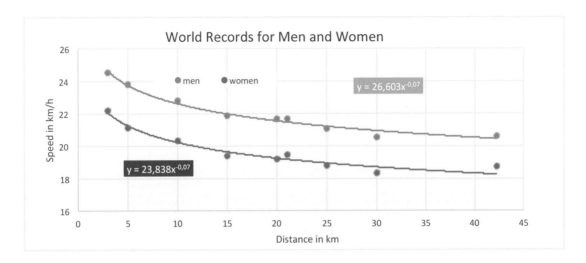

For both men and women the data points are quite close to the regression line with an exponent -0.07. As we will discuss later, Riegel's formula works less well for short distances (less than 1,500 meter), so we have excluded these from the graph.

As the running power depends linearly on the speed ($P_r = cmv$), we can use Riegel's formula to describe the power–distance relationship. Apparently, we can conclude that as the distance doubles, the power decreases by 5% ($2^{-0.07} = 0.95$) as well. As the distance is proportional with time, we can finally conclude that Riegel's formula can also be used to describe the power–time relationship.

How Should We Compare Performances at Different Distances?

In order to make an objective comparison of different performances, we should at least take into account the power–time relationship. A practical way of doing this, we use Riegel's formula to make a table of the power–time relationship. As the base for the table, we chose the power that can be maintained for one hour. We know from literature and experience that at this level the human engine is fueled virtually completely by the two aerobic energy systems, the aerobic conversion of glycogen and the aerobic conversion of fatty acids. These are the two primary energy systems for endurance sports. This level is called the functional threshold power or FTP (in watts/kg). The term *threshold* is used because at this level the anaerobic systems start to kick in. In a later chapter we will show that the maximum FTP of male world champions in various sports is around 6.4 watts/kg. We consider an FTP of 6.4 watts/kg the ultimate limit of the human performance. However, the FTP is not the maximum power output of the human engine. During a short period, everybody can mobilize more power than his FTP (as the FTP can be maintained for one hour). If you have to run for 10 minutes only, you can mobilize more power (i.e., $(10/60)^{-0.07}*100 = 113\%$ of your FTP). This means that during 10 minutes you can also run at a 13% higher speed than during one hour. The power–time relationship is given in the table.

Power Ratio With Time	
Time	% FTP
(min)	(%)
10 (= VO$_2$ max)	113
20	108
40	103
60 (= FTP)	100
120	95
240	91
300	89

We have set the lower limit of the table at 10 minutes, as during shorter times the anaerobic energy systems (the glycolysis and the conversion of ATP) become too important to be neglected. As we will see in a later chapter, the available power (in watts/kg) that can be maintained during 10 minutes is linearly proportional to the maximum oxygen uptake capacity, the VO$_2$ max. The table thus shows that the available power at the VO$_2$ max (duration 10 minutes) is 13% greater than at the power at the FTP (duration 60 minutes). We can say that the available power at the FTP is 100/113 = 88% of the power at the VO$_2$ max. Another well-known example is that the available power over two hours (which is the approximate marathon time for world-class runners) is equal to 95/113 = 84% of the VO$_2$ max. As the pace depends linearly on power, this means that world-class athletes can run the marathon at approximately 84% of the pace at their VO$_2$ max.

What Causes the Decline of Power With Time?

From literature it is well-known that the ratio of the aerobic conversion of glycogen and the aerobic conversion of fatty acids (i.e., the fuel mix) is not constant. During rest, the fuel mix consists primarily of fatty acids. When we start running, the share of glycogen in the fuel mix increases rapidly. At the pace of the VO$_2$ max, the share of glycogen has increased to 90%. The figure shows experimental findings on the relationship between the exercise intensity and the fuel mix[30]. Looking at the figure, you could also say that as you reduce your pace the share of the fatty acids in the fuel mix increases.

We wondered whether this could be the cause of the decline of power with time as expressed by Riegel's formula. To answer this question, we need to study the biochemistry of the human engine in some detail.

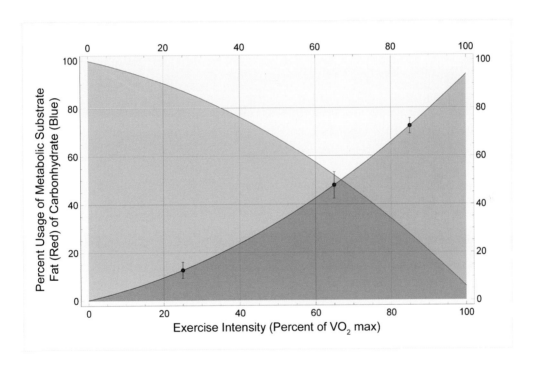

Fuel mix in muscles according to Rapaport[30].

The Power Output of the Four Energy Systems

We have reviewed literature on the biochemistry of the four energy systems of the human engine[31,32,33,34]. The table below gives the theoretical power output of the four energy systems, expressed in the conversion speed of ATP (in mmol/s). In the table we have set the conversion speed of glycogen at 100% and expressed the relative conversion speed of the other systems as a percentage of that of glycogen. From the table we can already see the cause of the phenomenon known as hitting the wall. This is the moment in the marathon (usually after some 30-35 kilometers) when your glycogen reserves are depleted. At this moment, the fuel mix in your muscles switches to fatty acids only. Unfortunately, fatty acids provide only 30% of the power of glycogen. Much to your despair, you will notice that instantly your legs feel empty. Puffing and stumbling, you have no choice but to reduce your speed to embarrassing levels as a result of the reduced power output of the fatty acids.

The Power Output of the Four Human Engines		
	P	Glycogen
	(mmol ATP/s)	(%)
ATP/CP		
ATP → ADP		
$C_{10}H_{16}N_5O_{13}P_3$ → $C_{10}H_{15}N_5O_{10}P_2$	73	317
Anaerobic conversion of glycogen		
$C_6H_{12}O_6$ + 3ADP → $2C_3H_6O_3$ + 3ATP	40	174
Aerobic conversion of glycogen		
$C_6H_{12}O_6$ + $6O_2$ + 38ADP → $6CO_2$ + $6H_2O$ + 38ATP	23	100
Aerobic conversion of fatty acids		
$CH_3(CH_2)_{14}COOH$ + $23O_2$ + 130ADP → $16CO_2$ + $16H_2O$ + 130ATP	7	30

Is the Decline in Power Caused by the Change in the Fuel Mix?

We have calculated the theoretical share of glycogen and fatty acids in the fuel mix that could explain the decline in power from Riegel's formula. We used the above table, setting the conversion speed of glycogen at 100% and of fatty acids at 30%. In accordance with literature, we set the share of glycogen at the VO_2 max at 90%. The table shows the results, which seem very convincing. The numbers match the experimental findings very well. As an example, we look at the world class athletes at the marathon. They run for approximately two hours, so their power output is 95/113 = 84% of the VO_2 max level and 95/100 = 95% of the FTP level. The share of fatty acids in their fuel mix thus becomes 31% according to the table. The same number was found experimentally, as can be seen in literature[30] and the earlier graph.

Calculated Share of Fatty Acids and Glycogen			
Time	% FTP	Glycogen	Fatty acids
(min)	(%)	(%)	(%)
10	113	90	10
20	108	84	16
40	103	78	22
60	100	75	25
120	95	69	31
240	91	64	36
300	89	62	38

And How About the Anaerobic Systems?

From the above, we believe we can conclude that the change in the fuel mix is indeed the cause of the decline of power with time as expressed by Riegel's formula; however this applies only to the aerobic systems, and thus for time periods of more than 10 minutes. But how about shorter time periods, when the anaerobic systems play a more important role and Riegel's formula is no longer as accurate? We believe that there the power—time relationship is also caused by the change in the fuel mix. Unfortunately, experimental data on the fuel mix during short periods are not readily available in literature. Therefore, we have only made the theoretical calculations of the below table. In the table we have just assumed a

certain share of the energy systems at different times and calculated the resulting available power (with the relevant data from biochemistry, so 317% - 174% - 100% - 30% of the power of glycogen). In later chapters, we will show that the calculated power output matches well with the results of the world records in athletics and the measured power profiles in cycling.

Calculated Power (Including Anaerobic Systems)				
Time	Glycogen	Glycolysis	ATP	FTP
(min)	(%)	(%)	(%)	(%)
5	90	8	2	125
1	50	40	10	201
0	0	0	100	385

Conclusions on the Power-Time Relationship

We conclude that the power–time relationship is expressed accurately by Riegel's formula for time periods of 10 minutes and above. For most runners and for the world records in athletics, an exponent of -0.07 best describes the results at different distances. The decline in power with time as expressed by Riegel's formula can be explained by the change in fuel mix. At the marathon, the pace is slower than at 5K, so the muscles automatically use a fuel mix with more fatty acids.

For time periods shorter than 10 minutes, the pace and the available power is higher than described by Riegel's formula. This is caused by the increasing share of the anaerobic systems in the fuel mix. Unfortunately, only limited experimental findings are available on this. We have calculated that the maximal available power is 385% of the FTP during a short burst, like the 100-meter sprint. In later chapters, we will show that the calculated power values match well with the world records.

Finally, we note that some deviations from the exponent of -0.07 can occur in practice, in particular for:

» Sprinters with a limited fatigue resistance (in this case the exponent can be -0.08 or -0.09)
» Ultra-runners with exceptional fatigue resistance (in this case the exponent can be -0.06 or 0.05)

In the chapter on fatigue resistance, we will discuss this in more detail and show the impact on the running times at different distances.

Haile Gebreselassie (number 86) ran world records at many distances. His records fit Riegel's formula with exponent -0.07 perfectly.

17. THE LIMITS OF HUMAN POWER

The human body is centuries ahead of the physiologist.
—Sir Roger Bannister

Quite regularly, the media speculate on the limits of human power in sports. Is it humanly possible to run 100 meters in less than nine seconds or the marathon in less than two hours? This often also involves debates on doping. Which performances are considered clean and which are suspect? In this chapter, we will analyze this topic. Can we calculate the power output during the world record races? And can we calculate the equivalent FTP of the world records at different distances? Does this match Riegel's formula and our theory on the change in fuel mix? And do our calculations provide a sufficient base to come to a conclusion on the ultimate physiological limits of the power of the human engine?

The Power Output at the World Record Races

With our theory we can calculate the required power to run any pace, including the world records. At a flat track or road race, the power required to overcome the running resistance is equal to:

$$P_r/m = cv = 0.98*v$$

Usually, we express v in km/h, so we have to divide by a factor of 3.6. The result thus becomes:

$$P_r/m = 0.272*v.$$

The air resistance at 15°C and in windless conditions is equal to:

$$P_a = 0.5*1.226*c_dA*v^3$$

As world records are always run with pacemakers, we have set the c_dA value at 0.20 m², except for the sprint events, where we have used the standard value of 0.24 m².

Finally, we can calculate the total power output as:

$$P_t = P_r + P_a$$

With these assumptions, we have calculated the required power to run the world records, both for men and women. We used a standard body weight for the men of 60 kg and for the women of 50 kg, in both cases with the exception of the sprint distances. Sprinters are usually significantly heavier, so we surfed the internet to find their real body weight. The results of our calculations are given in the table below.

World Records of the Men

World Records of the Men								
			v	P_r/m	P_a/m	P_t/m	$P_t/$ FTP	% FTP Riegel
Distance	Time	Name	(km/h)	(watts/ kg)	(watts/ kg)	(watts/ kg)	(%)	(%)
100 m	0:09.58	Usain Bolt	37.58	10.24	1.78	12.02	189	151
200 m	0:19.19	Usain Bolt	37.52	10.22	1.77	12.00	189	144
400 m	0:43.03	Wayde van Niekerk	33.47	9.12	1.53	10.65	168	136
800 m	1:40.91	David Rudisha	28.54	7.78	1.03	8.81	139	128
1,500 m	3:26.00	Hicham El Guerrouj	26.21	7.14	0.79	7.93	125	122
3,000 m	7:20.67	Daniel Komen	24.51	6.68	0.64	7.32	115	116
5,000 m	12:37.35	Kenenisa Bekele	23.77	6.48	0.59	7.06	111	112
10,000 m	26:17.53	Kenenisa Bekele	22.82	6.22	0.52	6.74	106	106
15 km	00:41:13	Leonard Komon	21.84	5.95	0.46	6.41	101	103
20 km	00:55:21	Zersenay Tadese	21.68	5.91	0.45	6.35	100	101
21.1 km	00:58:23	Zersenay Tadese	21.68	5.91	0.45	6.36	100	100
25 km	01:11:18	Dennis Kimetto	21.04	5.73	0.41	6.14	97	99
30 km	01:27:38	Emmanuel Mutai	20.54	5.60	0.38	5.98	94	97
42.2 km	02:02:57	Dennis Kimetto	20.59	5.61	0.38	5.99	94	95
100 km	06:13:33	Takahiro Sunada	16.06	4.38	0.18	4.56	72	88

The table shows a consistent decrease of both total power and the percentage of the FTP as the distance increases. We draw the following conclusions from the table:

1. The limit of the FTP (the power that can be maintained for one hour) is 6.36 watts/kg, as shown by the value of Zersenay Tadese at the half marathon.

2. The percentages of the FTP as calculated with Riegel's formula are quite close to the real percentages as determined from the calculated total power divided by 6.36. The only exceptions are the 100-kilometer races (which are run much less frequently, the record is not very strong) and the 100-800-meter races (in which the anaerobic systems contribute significantly to the power output).

3. When we use the total power at the world records from 5,000 meters up to the marathon to calculate the equivalent FTP of the world record holder with Riegel's formula, we get the figure below. This shows that the equivalent FTP of all world record holders is actually quite close to the value of 6.36 watts/kg. Apparently, the records at 25 and 30 kilometers are somewhat less strong, which is probably caused by the fact that these distances are run less frequently.

4. The maximum calculated power was produced by Usain Bolt at the 100 meter and was calculated at 12.02 watts/kg or 189% of an FTP of 6.36 watts/kg. This 189% is much lower than the maximum output of the ATP system (385%) that we calculated in the last chapter. The difference can be explained by the additional power that Bolt needed to accelerate from the start. In a later chapter, we will show that this acceleration requires an additional 11 watts/kg, bringing his total power output to 23 watts/kg or 363% of an FTP of 6.36 watts/kg.

5. The share of the air resistance in the total required power is 6% at the marathon and even 15% at the 100 meter! This confirms the importance of pacemakers that can reduce the air resistance. For sprinters, this confirms the advantage of running at altitude, where the air resistance is lower.

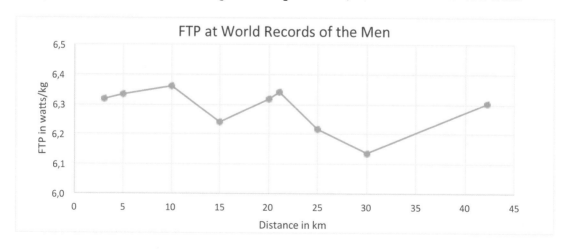

World Records of the Women

World Records of the Women								
			v	P_r/m	P_a/m	P_t/m	$P_t/$ FTP	% FTP Riegel
Distance	Time	Name	(km/h)	(Watts/ kg)	(Watts/ kg)	(Watts/ kg)	(%)	(%)
100 m	0:10.49	Florence Griffith Joyner	34.32	9.35	2.16	11.51	203	150
200 m	0:21.34	Florence Griffith Joyner	33.74	9.19	2.05	11.25	198	143
400 m	0:47.60	Marita Koch	30.25	8.24	1.41	9.65	170	135
800 m	1:53.28	Jarmila Kratochvilova	25.42	6.93	0.76	7.69	136	127
1,500 m	3:50.07	Genzebe Dibaba	23.48	6.40	0.68	7.08	125	121
3,000 m	8:06.11	Wang Junxia	22.22	6.06	0.58	6.63	117	115
5,000 m	14:11.15	Tirunesh Dibaba	21.15	5.76	0.50	6.26	110	111
10,000 m	29:17.45	Almaz Ayana	20.48	5.58	0.45	6.03	106	105
15 km	0:46:14	Florence Kiplagat	19.47	5.30	0.39	5.69	100	102
20 km	01:01:54	Florence Kiplagat	19.39	5.28	0.38	5.67	100	100
21.1 km	01:05:09	Florence Kiplagat	19.43	5.30	0.39	5.68	100	99
25 km	01:19:53	Mary Keitany	18.78	5.12	0.35	5.46	96	98
30 km	01:38:49	Mizuki Noguchi	18.22	4.96	0.32	5.28	93	97
42.2 km	02:15:25	Paula Radcliffe	18.70	5.09	0.34	5.44	96	94
100 km	06:33:11	Tomoe Abe	15.26	4.16	0.19	4.35	77	88

The table shows a similar consistent decrease of both total power and the percentage of the FTP as the distance increases. We draw the following conclusions from the table:

1. The limit of the FTP (the power that can be maintained for one hour) is 5.67 watts/kg, as shown by the value of Florence Kiplagat at the 20 kilometer.

2. The percentages of the FTP as calculated with Riegel's formula are quite close to the real percentages as determined from the calculated total power divided by 5.67. The only exceptions are the 100 kilometer (which is run much less frequently, the record is not very strong) and the 100-800 meter (in which the anaerobic systems contribute significantly to the power output).

3. When we use the total power at the world records from 5,000 meters up to the marathon to calculate the equivalent FTP of the world record holder with Riegel's formula, we get the figure below. This shows that the equivalent FTP of all world record holders is actually quite close to the value of 5.67 watts/kg. Apparently, the records at 25 and 30 kilometers are somewhat less strong, which is probably caused by the fact that these distances are run less frequently. Paula Radcliffe's world record at the marathon was apparently run with an impressive FTP of 5.76 watts/kg! Also Almaz Ayana ran her 10,000 meters world record at this impressive FTP.

4. The maximum calculated power was produced by Florence Griffith-Joyner at the 100 meter and was 11.51 watts/kg or 203% of an FTP of 5.67 watts/kg. The same remarks as with Bolt apply here.

5. The share of the air resistance in the total required power is 6% at the marathon and even 19% at the 100 meter! The percentages are slightly higher than for the men as the women have a lower body weight. The total air resistance in watts is independent of the weight, so the specific air resistance in watts/kg is higher for lightweight women.

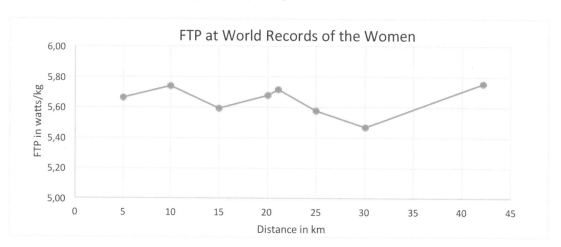

The Limits of the Power of the Human Engine

History has taught us that records are there to be broken, so we need to be humble in our understanding of the limits of human performances. Nevertheless, we feel confident to conclude that the present ultimate limits of the human power are close to an FTP of 6.40 watts/kg for men and 5.70 watts/kg for women. In addition to the above tables and figures, we submit the following arguments to support our bold statement:

1. Athletics is the mother of sports and practiced worldwide by millions. In spite of this, the current world records are broken only rarely and marginally and only in orchestrated races with pacemakers and in ideal conditions. Of course, we cannot rule out that humans will develop further in the future (perhaps as a result of improved training, nutrition or gear or even as a result of DNA engineering). However, we feel that in the foreseeable future significant advances beyond these levels are not to be expected.
2. In cycling, much more data on power output are available as a result of the widespread use of power meters. These data have been analyzed statistically which resulted in the well-known Power Profiles[2]. These data are quite consistent with our numbers. Also in cycling an FTP of 6.40 watts/kg for men and 5.70 watts/kg for women is considered the ultimate limit of human power.
3. We have made many calculations on various world-class performances, including the Tour de France, the climb to the Alpe d'Huez, the world hour record in cycling and also in speed skating. The results always confirmed the FTP values of 6.40 watts/kg and 5.70 watts/kg as the ultimate limits.

What Are the Limits of Human Power According to Biochemistry?

We were curious to see whether the FTP limit of 6.40 watts/kg can also be explained from the power output of the four energy systems of the human motor. Can we calculate the FTP limit from the biochemical data in literature? Therefore, we prepared the table below. In the table, for all four systems we multiplied the conversion speed in mmol ATP/s with the energy value of ATP (81 kJ/mol) and the metabolic efficiency of 0.25 and finally divided the result by 60 kg (which we considered a relevant body weight for a lean athlete with almost no body fat).

Power Output of the Four Human Engines		P	P/m
		(mmol ATP/s)	(watts/kg)
ATP/CP			
ATP → ADP			
$C_{10}H_{16}N_5O_{13}P_3$ → $C_{10}H_{15}N_5O_{10}P_2$		73	24.64
Anaerobic conversion of glycogen			
$C_6H_{12}O_6 + 3ADP$ → $2C_3H_6O_3 + 3ATP$		40	13.50
Aerobic conversion of glycogen			
$C_6H_{12}O_6 + 6O_2 + 38ADP$ → $6CO_2 + 6H_2O + 38ATP$		23	7.76
Aerobic conversion of fatty acids			
$CH_3(CH_2)_{14}COOH + 23O_2 + 130ADP$ → $16CO_2 + 16H_2O + 130ATP$		7	2.36

The table shows that the power output of the ATP system is 24.64 watts/kg. This should be considered the limit to human power during a very short burst. This number is confirmed by the 5-second value of the power profiles and the data on Usain Bolt.

In the previous chapter, we showed that the fuel mix in our muscles at the FTP level (during one hour) consists of 75% glycogen and 25% fatty acids. This means that the power output can be calculated from the table as 0.75*7.76+0.25*2.36 = 6.41 watts/kg! This matches very well with the limit of 6.40 watts/kg! Of course, we should note that some of our assumptions, such as the metabolic efficiency and the body weight, can also be somewhat higher or lower.

We believe we can explain the lower limit of the women (5.70 watts/kg) by the fact that they have a 10% higher body fat content. Obviously, 10% more body fat will lead to a 10% lower FTP (and also to a 10% slower pace in running).

Conclusions on the Limits of the Power of the Human Engine

We conclude that all four approaches (the world records in athletics, the power profiles in cycling, the calculation of world-class performances in various sports and the biochemical data) lead to the same result: the present ultimate limit of the FTP is close to 6.40 watts/kg for men and 5.70 watts/kg for women. In a later chapter we will show that these values are equivalent to a VO_2 max of $6.40/0.072 = 88.8$ ml/kg/min and $5.70/0.072 = 79.2$ ml/kg/min.

Farewell of the legendary Ethiopian middle and long-distance runner Haile Gebrselassie (1973) to competitive running in the 2015 Great Ethiopian Run. Gebrselassie broke a total of 27 world records on track and road. His FTP is around 6.30 watts/kg.

18. THE VO$_2$ MAX

To be a great runner, you have to select your parents carefully.

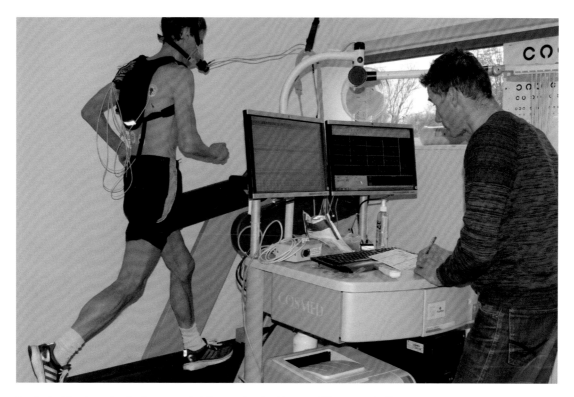

Sports physician Bernard te Boekhorst tests the VO$_2$ max of author Hans van Dijk on a treadmill.

Back in 1923, the English physiologist and Nobel Prize laureate A.V. Hill found that the oxygen consumption of runners increased with the speed up to a maximum value that could be maintained for a limited time only. Consequently, he postulated that the performance in running is determined primarily by the oxygen uptake capacity of the cardiovascular system. He labeled this maximum oxygen uptake as the VO$_2$ max. In the past century, many researchers have confirmed that the VO$_2$ max is indeed a very important parameter for the performance in running and other endurance sports like cycling. As we have seen before, this is caused by the fact that oxygen is needed for the aerobic conversion of glycogen and fatty acids, the two main fuel sources for endurance sports.

The VO$_2$ max is defined as the maximum volume (V) of oxygen (O$_2$) that can be taken up by the human body during exercise at sea level. The VO$_2$ max is expressed as the amount of milliliters of oxygen per kilogram of body weight and per minute (ml O$_2$/kg/min). From literature and experience it is known that you can maintain exercising at the intensity of the VO$_2$ max for no more than 10 minutes.

How Can the VO$_2$ max Be Determined?

In a laboratory, the VO$_2$ max can be determined experimentally by measuring the oxygen uptake during prolonged and intensive exercise. The VO$_2$ max is reached when the oxygen uptake does not increase any more in spite of increasing the exercise intensity. The VO$_2$ max can be measured while running on a treadmill or while cycling on a bicycle ergometer. These tests should be done under medical supervision (e.g., at a sports medical advice center). The authors of this book have taken such tests regularly in the past years. The picture shows author Hans, the treadmill, the breathing measuring equipment and the ECG.

The box[35,36] gives the formulas that can be used to calculate the VO$_2$ max. In the physiological lab, the oxygen uptake is determined from the oxygen balance of the breathing air. During a bicycle test the VO$_2$ max can also be estimated from the measured maximum power in watts. For a runner, a bicycle test is less suitable as it is less specific.

As these laboratory tests cannot be performed easily, several field tests have been developed to estimate the VO$_2$ max. The box gives two of those, including a very simple and crude method to estimate the VO$_2$ max, based solely on the maximal heart rate (MHR) and the resting heart rate (RHR). This method seems too simple to be true, but it has a certain logic as fit people usually have a high VO$_2$ max and a low RHR. The second method is frequently used and consists of running as far as you can during 12 minutes (the Cooper test). The distance (d, in meters) can then be used to estimate the VO$_2$ max.

Methods to Determine the VO$_2$ max

Lab tests

Oxygen balance:	VO$_2$ max = Q*(c$_a$-c$_v$)/m
Bike ergometer:	VO$_2$ max = (395+11.3W)/m

Field tests

Rough estimate:	VO$_2$ max = 15*(MHR/RHR)
Cooper test:	VO$_2$ max = (d-505)/45

Q is blood flow or cardiac output (in l/min), c$_a$ and c$_v$ are the concentrations of oxygen in the arterial and venous blood (in ml/l), m is the weight in kg, d is the distance in meters covered in 12 minutes, W is the maximal wattage during a bike test.

Which Factors Determine Your VO$_2$ max?

In literature and in practice, it has been established that the VO$_2$ max mainly depends on:

» Talent (if you want to be a great runner, you have to choose your parents carefully)
» Sex (the VO$_2$ max of men is 10-15% higher than that of women)
» Age (the VO$_2$ max decreases approximately 0.5-1.0% per year over the age of 35)
» Training (the VO$_2$ max can be increased by some 5-25% as a result of training)
» Body weight (the VO$_2$ max is inversely proportional to the weight, so shedding excess body fat will increase your VO$_2$ max)

The VO$_2$ max of the world record holders is in the order of 88 ml/kg/min, as we will show in a later chapter. Athletes like Haile Gebreselassie and Mo Farrah reach these values as a result of a combination of talent and years of meticulous training. Normal values for young men are around 40-45, for young women the values are 30-35 ml/kg/min. Consequently, normal persons can never reach the values of Haile and Mo, not even with the most fanatical training.

VO$_2$ max Values in ml/kg/min						
Men						
Age	Very poor	Poor	Fair	Good	Very good	Excellent
13 - 19	< 35.0	35.0 - 38.3	38.4 - 45.1	45.2 - 50.9	51.0 - 55.9	> 55.9
20 - 29	< 33.0	33.0 - 36.4	36.5 - 42.4	42.5 - 46.4	46.5 - 52.4	> 52.4
30 - 39	< 31.5	31.5 - 35.4	35.5 - 40.9	41.0 - 44.9	45.0 - 49.4	> 49.4
40 - 49	< 30.2	30.2 - 33.5	33.6 - 38.9	39.0 - 43.7	43.8 - 48.0	> 48.0
50 - 59	< 26.1	26.1 - 30.9	31.0 - 35.7	35.8 - 40.9	41.0 - 45.3	> 45.3
60+	< 20.5	20.5 - 26.0	26.1 - 32.2	32.3 - 36.4	36.5 - 44.2	> 44.2
Women						
Age	Very poor	Poor	Fair	Good	Very good	Excellent
13 - 19	< 25.0	25.0 - 30.9	31.0 - 34.9	35.0 - 38.9	39.0 - 41.9	> 41.9
20 - 29	< 23.6	23.6 - 28.9	29.0 - 32.9	33.0 - 36.9	37.0 - 41.0	> 41.0
30 - 39	< 22.8	22.8 - 26.9	27.0 - 31.4	31.5 - 35.6	35.7 - 40.0	> 40.0
40 - 49	< 21.0	21.0 - 24.4	24.5 - 28.9	29.0 - 32.8	32.9 - 36.9	> 36.9
50 - 59	< 20.2	20.2 - 22.7	22.8 - 26.9	27.0 - 31.4	31.5 - 35.7	> 35.7
60+	< 17.5	17.5 - 20.1	20.2 - 24.4	24.5 - 30.2	30.3 - 31.4	> 31.4

Above the age of 35, the VO$_2$ max decreases some 1% annually in untrained persons; with training this decline can be limited to 0.5% annually.

At a very high age, the VO$_2$ max could decline to such low levels that the life support functions become troublesome. At a level of 10 ml/kg/min or less, the heart is no longer capable of supplying the vital organs with sufficient oxygen. In literature predictions can be found of your lifespan based on your VO$_2$ max. Endurance runners don't have to worry about this, as we can show from the example of author Hans. His present (2015) VO$_2$ max is 60 ml/kg/min and his age is 61, so even if his VO$_2$ max decreased by 1% annually, it would still be 40 ml/kg/min by the time he celebrates his 100th birthday!

In the mountains, the air pressure is lower and consequently so is the VO$_2$ max. On top of Mount Everest the VO$_2$ max is only 27% of the value at sea level. When a normal person with a VO$_2$ max of 40 ml/kg/min tries to climb Mount Everest, his VO$_2$ max drops to 10.8 ml/kg/min, barely enough to survive. Without oxygen equipment, mountaineers can only progress some 50 meter per hour at great effort!

How Can Your VO$_2$ max Be Used to Predict Your Running Times?

On the internet there are many calculators that predict running times at various distances as a function of the VO$_2$ max. In later chapters, we will discuss this in more detail and show exactly what the relationship is between your VO$_2$ max and your running times.

For the moment, we will just give some examples. As we said earlier, the VO$_2$ max of the male world record holders is around 88 ml/kg/min. In 1984 the VO$_2$ max of author Hans was 74 ml/kg/min. At that time, he ran 31:55 at the 10K and 2:34:15 at the marathon. In 2010 his VO$_2$ max had reduced to 52 ml/kg/min and his times had gone up to 42:30 at the 10K and 3:35:30 at the marathon. In 2012, Hans managed to increase his VO$_2$ max to 60 ml/kg/min as a result of losing weight and improved training. His times improved to 36:25 at the 10K and 3:01:06 at the marathon.

Another perspective on the VO$_2$ max is given by the fact that some antelopes are known to have a VO$_2$ max of 300 ml/kg/min! These antelopes can easily maintain a speed of 65 km/h. Greyhounds and thoroughbred horses also have a very high VO$_2$ max (respectively 90 and 150 ml/kg/min) so they can easily beat Haile and Mo!

19. THE FTP

Ask yourself, can I give more? The answer is usually YES!
—Paul Tergat

In long-distance running, the functional threshold power (FTP) is one of the most important factors in determining your performance. The FTP is defined as the power output that can be maintained for one hour and is expressed in watts per kg of body weight. The term *functional threshold* is used because above this level lactate (lactic acid) starts to accumulate in your muscles. This means that if you go beyond the FTP intensity level, your muscles will start to acidify and you will not be able to maintain your speed. This also means that at the FTP level, your muscles will still produce power with the aerobic energy systems. In practice, the fuel mix at the FTP level will be about 75% glycogen and 25% fatty acids. Consequently, the share of glycogen will be less than at the VO_2 max level, where it is 90%. This also means that your power output and speed will be less than at the VO_2 max level. This makes sense as you can maintain the VO_2 max level for no more than 10 minutes. In the next chapter we will show that there is a fixed relationship between the FTP and the VO_2 max.

How Can the FTP Be Determined?

Traditionally the FTP is determined in cycling. Bikes can be equipped with power meters that enable the determination of the FTP, both in the field and in the lab. A practical problem is that it is not easy to go all out for one hour. This is not something you want to do regularly. Fortunately, we can estimate the FTP from a shorter test as well. As we saw in an earlier chapter, the FTP is equal to 93% of the power that can be maintained for 20 minutes or 88% of the power that can be maintained for 10 minutes. An all-out test of 10 or 20 minutes can be incorporated in most training programs. When executed in the lab (e.g., a sports medical advice center), the FTP test can be combined with additional tests and measurements, like the oxygen uptake and the lactate production, which will give a more complete picture of your fitness and performance level.

How Can the FTP Be Determined in Running?

Until recently, it was not possible to measure the power while running. However, presently the first running power meters are being produced and marketed. These power meters actually measure the acceleration in three dimensions by means of accelerometers. These data are then used to calculate the power by means of advanced software. This is based on the same theory as explained in this book. In a later chapter we will give more details of the running power meters, including our own test results. Also, in a later chapter, we will show how you can use a power meter to determine your FTP in the field.

In the present chapter, we will discuss how you can calculate your FTP based on your race times at different distances, both in the field and on a treadmill. As we saw earlier, your specific running resistance in watts/kg is directly proportional to your speed:

$P_r/m = cv$

This formula is valid in a situation without air resistance, as on a treadmill.

With c = 0.98 kJ/kg/km and v expressed in km/h, the formula becomes:

$P_r/m = 0.27*v$

This relationship is shown in the figure.

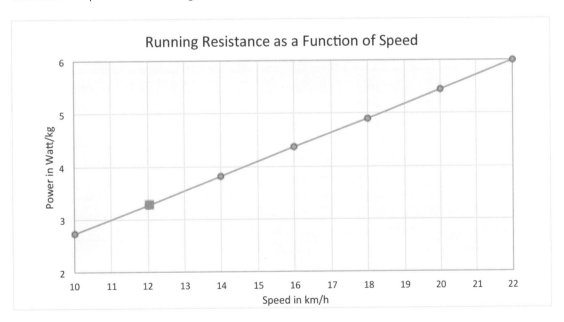

Now all you have to do is to correct for the duration of the test, as the FTP is equivalent to a one-hour test. As an example, we use a test of five minutes only. The correction factor should then be $(5/60)^{-0.07} = 0.84$. Let's say you run 15 km/h during these five minutes. According to the formula, your specific power at 15 km/h is 0.27*15 = 4.05 watts/kg. Your FTP thus becomes 0.84*4.05 = 3.40 watts/kg. We note that it is better to do the test during a somewhat longer period—10 or 20 minutes—to limit the impact of the anaerobic systems.

Which Factors Determine Your FTP?

In literature and in practice, it has been established that the FTP depends on the same factors as the VO_2 max:

- » Talent (if you want to be a great runner, you should choose your parents carefully)
- » Sex (the FTP of men is 10-15% higher than that of women)
- » Age (the FTP decreases approximately 0.5-1.0% per year over the age of 35)
- » Training (the FTP can be increased by some 5-25% as a result of training)
- » Weight (the FTP is inversely proportional to body weight, so shedding excess body fat will increase your FTP)

World top cyclist Chris Froome in the Grand Départ of the Tour de France 2015 (Utrecht, the Netherlands). In cycling, the FTP is commonly used to determine and optimize the performance in training and races.

The FTP of the world record holders is in the order of 6.4 watts/kg, as we have shown in an earlier chapter. Athletes like Haile Gebrselassie and Mo Farrah reach these values as a result of a combination of talent and years of meticulous training. Normal values for young man are around 3.1-4.2; for young women these values are 2.6-3.6 watts/kg. Consequently, normal persons can never reach the values of Haile and Mo, not even with the most fanatical training. The table below gives a classification of FTP levels that is used frequently in cycling.

Classification	FTP Men (watts/kg)	FTP Women (watts/kg)
World top	6.4	5.7
International	5.8	5.1
National	5.1	4.6
Regional	4.5	4.0
Tourist	3.8	3.4
Fair	3.2	2.8
Untrained	2.6	2.3
Poor	1.9	1.7
Very poor	1.4	1.1

How Can You Use Your FTP to Predict Your Running Times?

On the internet many calculators can be found that predict cycling times at various distances as a function of the FTP. For running, such calculators do not yet exist. However, in later chapters, we will show exactly what the relationship is between your FTP and your running times. We have also developed a calculator which can be used to assess your FTP and predict your running times at different distances and in various conditions.

20. THE RELATIONSHIP BETWEEN FTP AND VO₂ MAX

There is no luck in running. —Tim Noakes

In the previous chapter we saw that the FTP is defined as the specific power output (in watts/kg) that can be maintained for one hour. The VO_2 max is defined as the maximum specific amount of oxygen that can be taken up by the body per unit of time (in ml O_2/kg/min). In practice, exercising at the level of the VO_2 max can be maintained for no longer than 10 minutes. Oxygen is used in our muscles to produce energy from the conversion of glycogen and fatty acids. This means that the VO_2 max is actually also a measure of power, as power is the amount of energy per unit of time. So how can we relate the FTP and the VO_2 max? How can we calculate one from the other? In order to understand this, we have to look at the biochemistry of the energy systems of the human engine once more.

The Energy Production of the Human Engine

In an earlier chapter, we discussed the four energy systems of the human engine. The table specifies the amount of energy (in kJ/mol) that can be produced by the four systems.

Energy produced by the four human engines	ΔG
	(kJ/mol)
ATP/CP	
ATP → ADP	
$C_{10}H_{16}N_5O_{13}P_3 \rightarrow C_{10}H_{15}N_5O_{10}P_2$	81
Anaerobic conversion of glycogen	
$C_6H_{12}O_6 + 3ADP \rightarrow 2C_3H_6O_3 + 3ATP$	227
Aerobic conversion of glycogen	
$C_6H_{12}O_6 + 6O_2 + 38ADP \rightarrow 6CO_2 + 6H_2O + 38ATP$	2,880
Aerobic conversion of fatty acids	
$CH_3(CH_2)_{14}COOH + 23O_2 + 130ADP \rightarrow 16CO_2 + 16H_2O + 130ATP$	9,853

We can convert the amount of energy in kJ/mol to the equivalent amount in kcal/gram by dividing by the molecular weight of the compound and then by 4.184 (the amount of kJ equivalent to 1 kcal). When we do this for the aerobic conversion of glycogen and fatty acids, the result is 3.82 and 9.18 kcal/gram respectively. In the literature on nutrition, these energy values are usually rounded off to 4 and 9 kcal/gram respectively.

The Energy Production Per Liter of O$_2$

If we want to calculate the power equivalence of the VO$_2$ max, we first need to determine how much energy is produced per liter of O$_2$. We have done this for both aerobic processes: the aerobic conversion of glycogen and the aerobic conversion of fatty acids. Consequently, we have divided the numbers from the above table by the stoichiometric number of moles of O$_2$ in the equation (6 for glycogen and 23 for fatty acids) and then by the molar volume of O$_2$ (24.3 l/mole at 25°C). The result is given in the table.

Energy Production Per Liter of O$_2$	ΔG
	(kJ/l O$_2$)
Aerobic conversion of glycogen	
$C_6H_{12}O_6 + 6O_2 + 38ADP \rightarrow 6CO_2 + 6H_2O + 38ATP$	19.76
Aerobic conversion of fatty acids	
$CH_3(CH_2)_{14}COOH + 23O_2 + 130ADP \rightarrow 16CO_2 + 16H_2O + 130ATP$	17.64

The table shows that the amount of energy produced per liter of O$_2$ is less for fatty acids than for glycogen. You might think that this is the explanation for the phenomenon of hitting the wall, but it is not. As we saw in an earlier chapter, the correct explanation for this is the fact that the conversion speed and consequently the power produced is much less for fatty acids than for glycogen.

The Power Output at the VO_2 max

> **Power Output at VO_2 max**
>
> **watts/kg = 0.25*VO_2 max*19.55/60**
>
> Example = 51 ml/kg/min
>
> watts/kg = 0.082*51 = 4.18 watts/kg

From literature we know that at the VO_2 max level, the fuel mix consists of 90% glycogen and 10% fatty acids. Consequently, we can calculate the energy production at the VO_2 max as 0.9*19.76+0.1*17.64 = 19.55 kJ/l O_2. Next, in order to calculate the power output at the VO_2 max (in watts/kg), all we have to do is to multiply the VO_2 max (in ml/kg/min) by 19.55 (kJ/l), then divide the result by 60 (conversion of minutes to seconds) and finally multiply the outcome with the metabolic efficiency of 25%. The box gives the formula and an example.

The example is again valid for our Marathon Man, who has a VO_2 max of 51 ml/kg/min. We remark that the specific power (4.18 watts/kg) at his VO_2 max is obviously higher than his FTP (3.67 watts/kg), as the FTP can be maintained for one hour.

The Relationship Between FTP and VO_2 max

As we saw earlier the power output during one hour (the FTP) is equal to 88% of the power output at 10 minutes (the VO_2 max). Consequently, there is a fixed relationship between FTP and VO_2 max, which can be easily calculated, as shown in the box.

> **Relationship Between FTP and VO_2 max**
>
> **FTP = 0.88*0.25*VO_2 max*19.55/60**
>
> FTP = 0.072*VO_2 max
>
> Example: VO_2 max = 51 ml/kg/min
>
> FTP = 0.072*51 = 3.67 watts/kg

The figure below finally shows the relationship between FTP and VO$_2$ max for all relevant values of FTP (between 2.4 and 6.4 watts/kg) and VO$_2$ max (between 33 and 89 ml/kg/min). As we saw earlier the present ultimate limits of the power of the human engine are 6.4 watts/kg and 88 ml/kg/min. These numbers are valid for men; for women the limits are 5.7 watts/kg and 79 ml/kg/min.

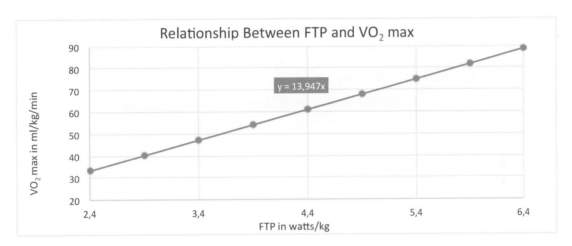

Marathon Man runs the marathon in 3:30. His VO$_2$ max of 51 ml/kg/min equals an FTP of 3.67 watts/kg.

PART IV

HOW FAST CAN YOU RUN?

21. THE IMPACT OF YOUR FTP

To give anything less than your best is to sacrifice the gift.
—Steve Prefontaine

Your race time is determined by the power of your human engine and the sum of the running resistance, the air resistance and the climbing resistance. In the following chapters, we will calculate how fast you can run with your human engine in different conditions. We will start elementary: how fast can you run at a flat course and in ideal conditions, like running on the track in windless weather? Later on, we will also look into the effect of more harsh conditions like wind, hills or trail runs.

The Simplified Running Formula

Obviously, the climbing resistance is zero at a flat course and the wind speed is zero in windless conditions. In this case, we can simplify the running formula to:

$$P = P_r + P_a = cmv + 0{,}5\rho c_d Av^3$$

This result is an unambiguous relationship (albeit cubic) between the attainable speed (v, in m/s) and the power (P, in watts) of your human engine. However, we should realize that the power of your human engine itself is not constant. It depends on the running time and distance, in accordance with Riegel's formula.

Therefore, we will first investigate the attainable speed at your FTP. As we saw earlier, this is the power that you can maintain for one hour. During shorter periods, you can mobilize more power. As an example, the power during 10 minutes will be $(10/60)^{-0{,}07} = 13\%$ higher than your FTP. This also means that your attainable speed during 10 minutes is roughly 13% higher than your speed during one hour.

Using our standard conditions (c = 0.98 kJ/kg/km, ρ = 1.226 kg/m³ and c_dA = 0.24 m²), we have calculated the relationship between the FTP (in watts/kg) and the attainable speed (in km/h). Obviously, this is the speed that can be maintained for one hour. The results for a standard body weight of 60 kg are given in the figure and table below. For the convenience of the readers who are used to the VO₂ max, we have also included the equivalent values of the VO_2 max in the table (as we saw earlier, the relationship is FTP = 0.072*VO_2 max).

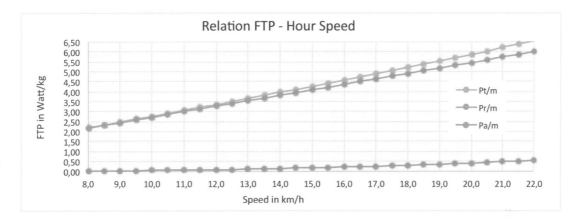

We see that there is a very straightforward relationship between the FTP and the attainable (hour) speed. To run at a speed of 10 km/h, your human engine needs to have an FTP of 2.78 watts/kg. A person who can run 15 km/h will have an FTP of at least 4.26 watts/kg. The maximum hour speed in our table of 21.5 km/h (which is slightly higher than the present world record of 21.285 km of Haile Gebrselassie) is equivalent to an FTP of 6.38 watts/kg. Our Marathon Man deviates a little from the data of the table, as he weighs 70 kg. His hour speed is 13.09 km/h and his FTP is 3.67 watts/kg.

Relation Between Speed and Power				
Speed	Specific power and FTP			
	P_r/m	P_a/m	P_t/m	VO_2 max
(km/h)	(watts/kg)	(watts/kg)	(watts/kg)	(ml/kg/min)
8.0	2.18	0.03	2.21	30.9
8.5	2.32	0.03	2.35	32.8
9.0	2.45	0.04	2.49	34.8
9.5	2.59	0.05	2.63	36.8
10.0	2.73	0.05	2.78	38.8
10.5	2.86	0.06	2.92	40.9
11.0	3.00	0.07	3.07	42.9
11.5	3.13	0.08	3.21	44.9
12.0	3.27	0.09	3.36	47.0
12.5	3.41	0.10	3.51	49.1
13.0	3.54	0.12	3.66	51.2
13.5	3.68	0.13	3.81	53.3
14.0	3.82	0.14	3.96	55.4
14.5	3.95	0.16	4.11	57.5
15.0	4.09	0.18	4.26	59.6
15.5	4.22	0.20	4.42	61.8
16.0	4.36	0.22	4.58	64.0
16.5	4.50	0.24	4.73	66.2
17.0	4.63	0.26	4.89	68.4
17.5	4.77	0.28	5.05	70.6
18.0	4.91	0.31	5.21	72.9
18.5	5.04	0.33	5.37	75.2
19.0	5.18	0.36	5.54	77.5
19.5	5.31	0.39	5.70	79.8
20.0	5.45	0.42	5.87	82.1
20.5	5.59	0.45	6.04	84.5
21.0	5.72	0.49	6.21	86.8
21.5	5.86	0.52	6.38	89.2

Which Race Times Could You Run With Your FTP?

Most runners will be less interested in their hour speed than in the race times they can run at the classic track and road distances. This means we have to calculate the power (P) at the different distances from the FTP, using Riegel's formula. Next, we can then calculate the attainable speed from the power (P) with the running formula. Finally, we can determine the race time from the distance and the speed. We have made these calculations with our computer program, as explained in the chapter on the running formula. The results are given in the table and figures below for distances between 1,500 meter and the marathon and for FTP values between 2.00 and 6.50 watts/kg.

The table and figures show a very straightforward and useful relationship between the FTP and the attainable race times at various distances. As an example, author Hans has an FTP of 4.50 watts/kg and his PRs at the various distances match the calculations very well. The same applies to author Ron, who has an FTP of 3.75 watts/kg.

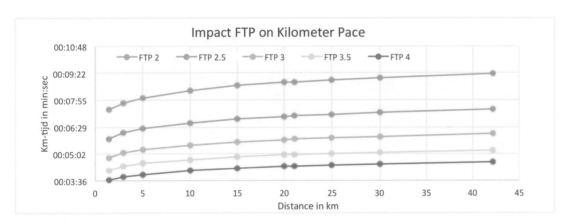

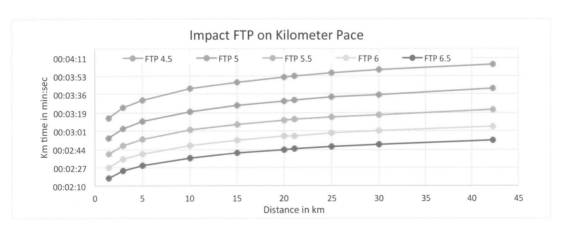

FTP-Speed-Time With Air Resistance						
FTP	Achievable time					
(Watt/kg)	1.500 m	3.000 m	5.000 m	10.000 m	15 km	20 km
2,00	00:11:05	00:23:16	00:40:12	01:24:24	2:10:14	02:57:11
2,25	00:09:49	00:20:36	00:35:34	01:14:41	01:55:15	02:46:02
2,50	00:08:47	00:18:27	00:31:53	01:06:55	01:43:16	02:20:30
2,75	00:07:58	00:16:43	00:28:53	01:00:39	01:33:36	02:07:20
3,00	00:07:15	00:15:14	00:26:19	00:55:01	01:25:16	01:56:16
3,25	00:06:43	00:14:04	00:24:20	00:51:06	01:18:51	01:47:16
3,50	00:06:13	00:13:04	00:22:34	00:47:23	01:13:07	01:39:28
3,75	00:05:48	00:12:12	00:21:04	00:44:13	01:08:14	01:32:50
4,00	00:05:27	00:11:26	00:19:45	00:41:27	01:03:58	01:27:01
4,25	00:05:08	00:10:46	00:18:35	00:39:01	01:00:13	01:21:55
4,50	00:04:51	0:10:10	00:17:34	00:36:53	00:56:55	01:17:25
4,75	00:04:36	00:09:39	00:16:40	00:34:58	00:53:58	01:13:26
5,00	00:04:22	00:09:11	00:15:52	00:33:18	00:51:23	01:09:54
5,25	00:04:10	00:08:46	00:15:08	00:31:46	00:49:01	01:06:41
5,50	00:04:00	00:08:23	00:14:29	00:30:24	00:46:54	01:03:49
5,75	00:03:50	00:08:02	00:13:53	00:29:08	00:44:58	01:01:11
6,00	00:03:41	00:07:43	00:13:20	00:28:01	00:43:13	00:58:48
6,25	00:03:32	00:07:26	00:12:51	00:26:58	00:41:36	00:56:36
6,50	00:03:25	00:07:10	00:12:23	00:26:01	00:40:08	00:54:36

	21,1 km	25 km	30 km	42,195 km	Hour run (km)	VO$_2$ max (ml/kg/min)
	00:07:38	03:44:58	04:33:25	06:33:51	7,27	28,0
	02:46:02	03:19:04	04:01:57	05:48:32	8:15	31,5
	02:28:47	02:58:23	03:36:49	05:12:19	9,03	35,0
	02:14:50	02:41:40	03:16:29	04:43:03	9,90	38,5
	02:02:51	02:27:18	02:59:01	04:17:53	10,80	42,0
	01:53:36	02:16:12	02:45:32	03:58:27	11,62	45,5
	01:45:20	02:06:17	02:33:30	03:41:06	12,47	49,0
	01:38:19	01:57:53	02:23:16	03:26:23	13,30	52,4
	01:32:09	01:50:29	02:14:17	03:13:26	14:13	55,9
	01:26:45	01:44:01	02:06:25	03:02:06	14,95	59,4
	01:21:59	01:38:18	01:59:29	02:52:06	15,76	62,9
	01:17:45	01:33:14	01:53:19	02:43:13	16,56	66,4
	01:14:01	01:28:45	01:47:52	02:35:23	17,34	69,9
	01:10:37	01:24:40	01:42:54	02:28:14	18,12	73,4
	01:07:35	01:21:02	01:38:29	02:21:52	18,88	76,9
	01:04:47	01:17:41	01:34:24	02:16:00	19,64	80,4
	01:02:16	01:14:40	01:30:45	02:10:43	20,38	83,9
	00:59:56	01:11:52	01:27:21	02:05:49	21,12	87,4
	00:57:50	01:09:20	01:24:16	02:01:23	21:84	90,9

Finally, we have calculated the attainable race times and the kilometer pace for our Marathon Man. For the standard condition, these are given in the table and figure. In the next chapters, we will see how much slower or faster he will run when the conditions change.

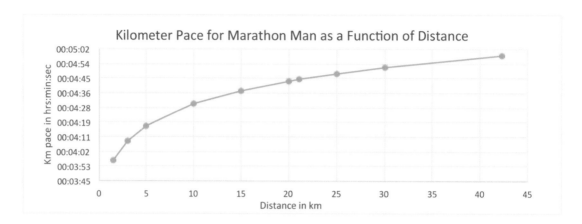

Impact Distance for Marathon Man	
Distance	Time
(km)	(hrs:min:sec)
0.8	3:04
1.5	5:59
3.0	12:32
5.0	21:37
10.0	45:15
15.0	1:09:43
20.0	1:34:46
21.1	1:40:20
25.0	2:00:13
30.0	2:26:02
42.2	3:30:00

In summary, we conclude that the FTP can be used to calculate the attainable race times at various distances in a very straightforward manner. The results are very useful, as we will show in the next chapters. We end this chapter with some comments:

1. Just like the FTP, the VO_2 max can also be used to calculate the race times at the various distances. Both parameters offer the possibility to compare race results. The advantage of the FTP is that it allows us to calculate exactly how big the impact is of all assumptions and conditions, like the body weight, the wind, the running surface, hills, and so on. Both parameters should not be used for comparison with a laboratory test of the VO_2 max. In the laboratory, the conditions differ from practice. The absence of air resistance on a treadmill will lead to an overestimation of the performance in practice. Also, a low running economy (RE) may lead to race times which are less than could be expected based on a laboratory test of the VO_2 max.

2. The calculated results are valid for normal runners with a standard fatigue resistance (Riegel's exponent of -0.07) and standard running economy (c-value of 0.98 kJ/kg/km, equivalent to an RE of 201 ml O_2/kg/km). We will show the impact of these factors in later chapters.

3. The calculated results are valid for the aerobic energy systems only. This means that the performance at the shorter distances of 400 and 800 meter are underestimated. At these distances, the anaerobic energy systems give a significant boost to the power output. Consequently, we did not include these distances in the table and figures.

Author Ron (No. 6186) in the 10,000 m track at the WMA Outdoor Championship 2015 in Lyon, France. Attainable race times are very predictable from your FTP.

22. THE WORLD RECORDS OF MEN AND WOMEN

Believe in your dreams and anything is possible. —Usain Bolt

What better way to compare our own race performances than with those of the world records on the track and on the road? The unparalleled performances of Kenenisa Bekele, Tirunesh Dibaba, Almaz Ayana and Paula Radcliffe and their impressive running form are a source of inspiration for the legion of common runners. The IAAF (International Association of Athletic Federations) acknowledges and administers the official world records[37].

How High Is the FTP of the World Record Holders?

We have calculated the equivalent FTP of the September 2016 world records from 800 meters to 100 kilometers. First, we calculated the total power required to run the speed of the world records. We used a standard body weight of 60 kg for the men and 50 kg for the women (except for Rudisha and Kratochvilova, for whom we used their actual body weight of 71 and 68 kg respectively). Next, we converted the power values to the FTP with Riegel's formula. The results are given in the tables below.

From the tables, we notice immediately that the FTP values of the 800-meter record holders are way too high. This is not surprising as the anaerobic energy systems give an additional power boost at the shorter distances. To a lesser extent, the same applies to the 1,500 meter.

The records at the 100 kilometer are relatively weak, as can be seen from the rather low FTP values. These distances are run much less frequently, which probably explains this. To a lesser extent, the same applies to the records at 25 and 30 kilometers. For all other world records between 3,000 meter and the marathon, we conclude that the equivalent FTP values of the world record holders are quite comparable. Apparently, all male world record holders have an equivalent FTP of around 6.33 watts/kg and all female record holders an FTP of around 5.70 watts/kg. We found the highest equivalent FTP values at the 10,000 meter record of Kenenisa Bekele and the marathon record of Paula Radcliffe. This means that these records are the strongest and the most difficult to beat.

World Records: Men			FTP
Distance	Time	Name	(Watt/kg)
800 m	1:40.91	David Rudisha	6.86
1,500 m	3:26.00	Hicham El Guerrouj	6.50
3,000 m	7:20.67	Daniel Komen	6.32
5,000 m	12:37.35	Kenenisa Bekele	6.33
10,000 m	26:17.53	Kenenisa Bekele	6.36
15 km	00:41:13	Leonard Komon	6.24
20 km	00:55:21	Zersenay Tadese	6.32
21.1 km	00:58:23	Zersenay Tadese	6.34
25 km	01:11:18	Dennis Kimetto	6.22
30 km	01:27:38	Emmanuel Mutai	6.14
42.2 km	02:02:57	Dennis Kimetto	6.30
100 km	06:13:33	Takahiro Sunada	5.18

World Records: Women			FTP
Distance	Time	Name	(Watt/kg)
800 m	1:53.28	Jarmila Kratochvilova	6.04
1,500 m	3:50.07	Genzebe Dibaba	5.83
3,000 m	8:06.11	Wang Junxia	5.76
5,000 m	14:11.15	Tirunesh Dibaba	5.66
10,000 m	29:31.78	Almaz Ayana	5.76
15 km	0:46:14	Florence Kiplagat	5.56
20 km	01:01:54	Florence Kiplagat	5.68
21.1 km	01:05:09	Florence Kiplagat	5.71
25 km	01:19:53	Mary Keitany	5.58
30 km	01:38:49	Mizuki Noguchi	5.49
42.2 km	02:15:25	Paula Radcliffe	5.76
100 km	06:33:11	Tomoe Abe	4.96

The tables also show clearly that the FTP (and thus the speed) of the women are 10% lower than the FTP of the men. This is well known; we believe it can be explained by the higher body fat percentage (BFP) of the women.

Finally, we can conclude from the tables that it is not likely that Kenenisa Bekele could run a sub 2-hour marathon. Some popular media have predicted this, but we feel such expectations are not supported by his FTP of 6.36 watts/kg. According to our calculations, an FTP of 6.36 watts/kg will lead to a marathon race time of 2:01:57. An impressive new world record of course, but still two minutes over the magical two hours!

How Much Slower Would the World Records Be Without the Assistance of Pacemakers?

Nowadays, world records are run almost exclusively in orchestrated races with pacemakers. The pacemakers may reduce the air resistance of the world class athletes by some 33%. In practice the impact will be somewhat less as the world class athletes still have to run the final part of the race solo. Consequently, in our calculations we used a 20% reduction in air resistance for the world record races (a c_dA value of 0.20 m^2 instead of the standard value of 0.24 m^2).

How much time did the world record holders gain from the assistance of the pacemakers? To answer this question, we have made an alternative calculation. We used the FTP of the world record holders from the table above to calculate their race time in a solo race with a c_dA value of 0.24 m^2. The results are given in the tables and figures below. As an example, we conclude that the world record of the men's marathon in a race without pacemakers would be only 2:04:21, 1.5 minutes slower than the present world record of 2:02:57!

How Much Faster Would the World Records Be Without Air Resistance?

As we saw earlier, anybody can run faster on a treadmill than in the outside world. The reason is that on a treadmill you do not have to overcome any air resistance, as you are not moving. In the real world, you always face air resistance, even in windless weather, as you are moving with a certain speed. Therefore, we thought it would be interesting to make another alternative calculation. This time we used the FTP of the world record holders from the above table to calculate their race time on a treadmill, with a c_dA value of just 0.01 m^2. The results are given in the tables and figures below. As an example, Paula Radcliffe could theoretically have run the marathon on a treadmill in an unbelievable 2:07:21! According to our calculations, the advantage of running without any air resistance for the world class athletes is around 10 seconds per kilometer!

World Records: Men				
Distance	Time	Name	Calculated time without pacers	Calculated time on treadmill
1,500 m	00:03:26	Hicham El Guerrouj	00:03:29	00:03:07
3,000 m	00:07:21	Daniel Komen	00:07:27	00:06:44
5,000 m	00:12:37	Kenenisa Bekele	00:12:48	00:11:38
10,000 m	00:26:17	Kenenisa Bekele	00:26:38	00:24:23
15 km	00:41:13	Leonard Komon	00:41:41	00:38:26
20 km	00:55:21	Zersenay Tadese	00:56:03	00:51:43
21.1 km	00:58:23	Zersenay Tadese	00:59:03	00:54:30
25 km	01:11:18	Dennis Kimetto	01:12:07	01:06:51
30 km	01:27:38	Emmanuel Mutai	01:28:32	01:22:21
42.2 km	02:02:57	Dennis Kimetto	02:04:21	01:55:39
100 km	06:13:33	Takahiro Sunada	06:35:47	05:59:17

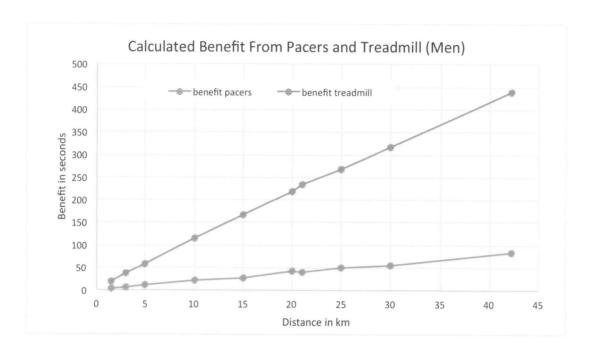

Calculated Benefit From Pacers and Treadmill (Men)

World Records: Women				
Distance	Time	Name	Calculated time without pacers	Calculated time on treadmill
1,500 m	00:03:50	Genzebe Dibaba	00:03:54	00:03:29
3,000 m	00:08:06	Wang Junxia	00:08:13	00:07:26
5,000 m	00:14:11	Tirunesh Dibaba	00:14:22	00:13:08
10,000 m	00:29:17	Almaz Ayana	00:29:54	00:27:28
15 km	00:46:28	Tirunesh Dibaba	00:47:00	00:43:31
20 km	01:01:54	Florence Kiplagat	01:02:34	00:57:55
21.1 km	01:05:09	Florence Kiplagat	01:05:54	01:01:01
25 km	01:19:53	Mary Keitany	01:20:49	01:15:09
30 km	01:38:49	Mizuki Noguchi	01:39:24	01:32:44
42.2 km	02:15:25	Paula Radcliffe	02:16:51	02:07:21
100 km	06:33:11	Tomoe Abe	06:36:02	06:16:53

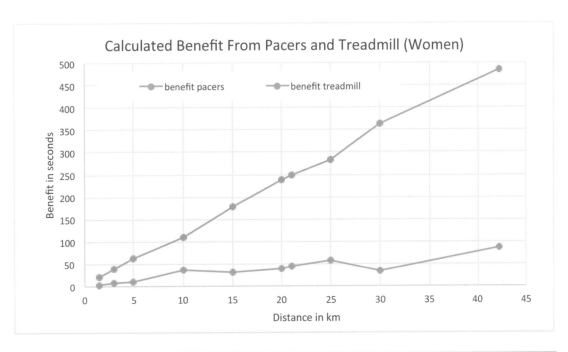

Genzebe Dibaba of Ethiopia celebrates after winning the women's 1,500-meter race during the Beijing 2015 IAAF World Championships.

23. THE IMPACT OF YOUR AGE

You don't give up running because you get old; you get old because you give up running.

Unfortunately, we all have to face the fact that our performance declines as we grow older. Long-distance runners peak at an age between 25 and 35 years. Above the age of 35, the performances inevitably decline slowly. Consequently, the World Master Athletics (WMA) uses age-grading tables[38] to compare performances of year classes. These tables show in general an annual decline in performance of some 0.8%.

The Statistical Analysis of Elmer Sterken

Professor Elmer Sterken is the rector of the University of Groningen, the Netherlands. His field of expertise is monetary economics, but he is also a committed long-distance runner and an expert on sports statistics. In 2003, he published a paper on age grading[39], which included a detailed statistical analysis of the performance as a function of age. He studied the extensive statistical database of the US Long Distance Running Association that contains many tens of thousands of race times. Using this database, he found a clear relationship between age and performance for both men and women. The figure shows the resulting age-grading factors at the 5K for men between the ages of 5 and 95.

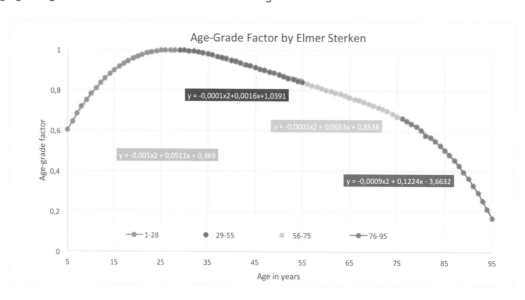

What Does This Mean for the Performance at Different Ages?

We have devided the tables from Sterken's paper into four segments and determined the regression equations as shown in the figure. Some interesting conclusions are:

1. The peak performance is found around the age of 30 years (age-grading factor 1.0).
2. The performance decreases gradually above the age of 35 years. Initially, the annual decline is 0.8%. At an age of 45, the resulting age-grade factor is 0.9. At 60 years, the age grade factor is 0.80.
3. Above the age of 75 years, the annual decline increases more rapidly, even beyond 5% at 85 years and more.
4. In general the performance decline at higher ages is somewhat higher than in accordance with the WMA tables. Apparently, the WMA is too optimistic on the attainable performance by the elder masters.

Obviously, the impact of age is substantial and irreversible. This is the reason for the age-grading system in the masters athletics. Internationally, masters are classified in 5-year age classes (35-39, 40-44, 45-49 and so on). Even with these age classes, the younger master has a significant advantage over his elder peers. Within a 5-year class, this advantage is $(1.008)^5$, which is equivalent to 4%.

Of course, these statistical relationships do not hold for everybody. The annual decline of 0.8% is an average for masters who train and race seriously. Less serious runners may face an annual decline of 1.0% or more. On the other hand, exceptional talents like the famous Canadian multiple world record holder Ed Whitlock managed to limit the annual decline to levels of 0.6% or even less up to a high age.

What Is the Impact of Age on the FTP and Race Times?

We have used Sterken's equations to calculate the impact of age on the FTP. As the FTP of our Marathon Man is 3.67 watts/kg at the age of 30, we could calculate his equivalent FTP at other ages. Next we calculated the marathon race times at these other ages from the equivalent FTP. The results are shown in the figure and table.

Age	FTP	Hour speed	Marathon
(year)	(watts/kg)	(km/h)	time (hrs:min:sec)
15	3.24	11.61	03:58:41
20	3.51	12.62	03:38:18
25	3.58	12.87	03:33:46
30	3.67	13.10	03:30:00
35	3.57	12.74	03:36:06
40	3.46	12.37	03:43:01
45	3.33	11.99	03:50:36
50	3.22	11.61	03:58:41
55	3.09	11.11	04:10:11
60	2.98	10.72	04:19:56
65	2.85	10.34	04:30:10
70	2.70	9.70	04:49:17
75	2.53	9.18	05:06:52
80	2.30	8.40	05:37:27
85	1.94	7.09	06:44:34

Although these calculations are somewhat hypothetical, they show a very clear picture. Good marathon times are possible in a broad age range, roughly between 15-55 years. Beyond the age of 60, and in particular beyond 80, the decline becomes much more progressive.

The start of the 200 m indoor M85 at the 2014 WMACi in Budapest, Hungary.

24. THE WORLD RECORDS OF THE MASTERS

Age for me is just a number. —Haile Gebrselassie

In the previous chapter, we saw that even long-distance runners have to face the fact that their performances decline with age. To compare performances of different ages, the World Masters Athletics (WMA) uses age-grading tables. The WMA also administers and publishes the official world records for the masters[40]. This is an interesting database which we have used to validate our models.

The World Records of the 5-Year Age Groups

The table below shows the world records for the distances from 800 meter up to the marathon and for the age groups of 35-100 years by September 2016. We have indicated the many world records of the famous Ed Whitlock in bold digits. This Canadian distance runner holds an impressive string of world records at many distances and in many age classes.

World Records: Masters (35-100 years)						
	800 m	1,500 m	3,000 m	5,000 m	10,000 m	42.2 km
M35	1:43.36	3:32.51	7:29.00	12:53.60	26:51.20	02:03:59
M40	1:48.22	3:41.87	7:42.75	13:06.78	28:30.88	02:08:46
M45	1:54.18	3:51.22	8:15.58	14:23.60	30:02.56	02:15:51
M50	1:58.65	3:58.26	8:41.20	14:53.20	30:55.16	02:19:29
M55	2:02.92	4:12.35	8:56.80	15:29.70	31:51.86	02:25:56
M60	2:08.56	4:24.00	9:29.47	16:12.57	33:57.60	02:36:30
M65	2:14.33	4:39.87	9:47.40	16:38.80	34:42.20	02:41:57
M70	2:20.52	4:52.95	10:42.40	18:15.53	**38:04.13**	**02:54:48**
M75	2:34.30	5:22.40	**11:10.43**	**19:07.02**	**39:25.16**	**03:04:54**
M80	2:48.95	**5:48.93**	12:13.56	20:58.12	42:39.95	03:15:54

World Records: Masters (35-100 years) (continued)						
	800 m	1,500 m	3,000 m	5,000 m	10,000 m	42.2 km
M85	3:09.10	6:51.32	**13:41.96**	**24:03.99**	**51:07.53**	**03:56:38**
M90	03:39.3	7:37.08	16:42.01	29:59.94	69:27.50	06:46:34
M95	6:02.94	12:57.70	26:17.40	50:10.56		
M100		16:46.41				

Impact of Distance

The figure below shows the kilometer pace as a function of the distance. We have validated that for all age groups this relationship complies perfectly to Riegel's formula:

$$v_2/v_1 = (d_2/d_1)^{-0,07}$$

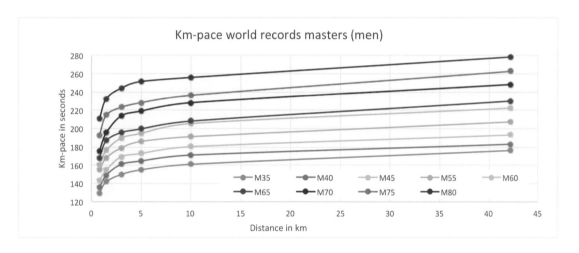

How Much Slower Do We Get as We Grow Older?

For the marathon, we have indicated the world record in a more detailed way (per one-year age class) in the figure below. The amazing streak of Ed Whitlock is shown in purple. The figure confirms that:

» For masters between the ages of 35-54, the annual decline is 0.8%
» For masters between the ages of 55-74, the annual decline is 1.0%
» For masters over 75 years, the annual decline is 5.0% or more!

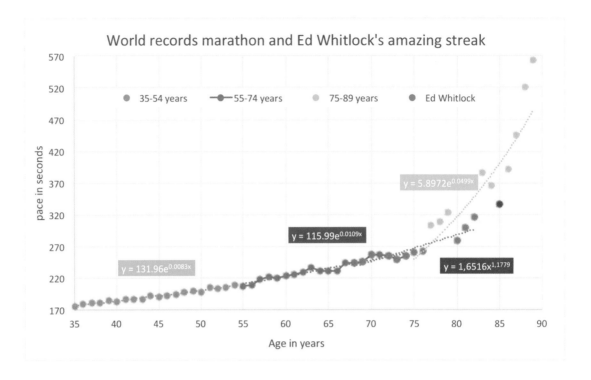

Consequently, we conclude once again that the age-grading tables of the WMA underestimate the actual annual decline for the elder masters. For ages beyond 55 years, the annual decline is more than 0.8%.

Do the World Records Match Our Theoretical Calculations?

In an earlier chapter, we concluded that the ultimate limit of human power is an FTP of 6.4 watts/kg. Obviously, this value is valid for a man of around 30 years. We have calculated the maximum FTP at other ages, using Sterken's equations. The results are shown in the figure below.

Next, we have calculated the marathon race times for the various age groups, based on these FTP values and using our model. The results are given in the table below, along with the current world records for the various age groups. We see that the times match pretty well! The most striking differences can be seen at the world record of the M35 (Haile Gebrselassie's very strong performance of 2:03:59) and the world record of the M90 (which appears to be very weak and will be hopefully improved by Ed Whitlock, by the time he reaches 90 years.).

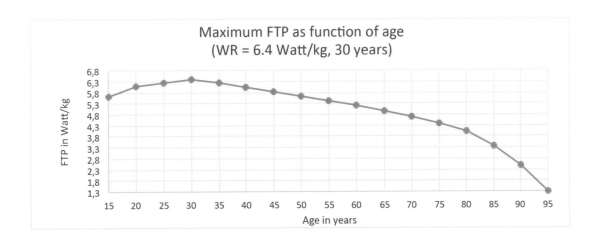

Maximum FTP as function of age
(WR = 6.4 Watt/kg, 30 years)

Age	FTP	Marathon	World record	
(year)	(watts/kg)	time (calculated)	Time	Name
15	5.64	02:18:15		
20	6.11	02:07:14		
25	6.25	02:04:45		
30	6.35	02:02:28	02:02:57	Dennis Kimetto
35	6.22	02:06:01	02:03:59	Haile Gebrselassie
40	6.03	02:09:46	02:08:46	Andres Espinoza
45	5.81	02:13:53	02:15:51	Kjell-Erik Stahl
50	5.62	02:18:15	02:19:29	Titus Mamabolo
55	5.39	02:24:34	02:25:56	Piet van Alphen
60	5.20	02:29:44	02:36:30	Yoshihisa Hosaka
65	4.97	02:35:29	02:41:57	Derek Turnull
70	4.70	02:45:54	02:54:48	Ed Whitlock
75	4.41	02:55:26	03:04:53	Ed Whitlock
80	4.01	03:12:07	03:15:54	Ed Whitlock
85	3.38	03:48:57	03:56:38	Ed Whitlock
90	2.48	05:14:33	06:46:34	Ernest van Leeuwen
95	1.31	10:35:20		

25. THE PERFORMANCE OF THE LADIES

In the marathon anything can happen. —Paula Radcliffe

On social media, some people state that women are superior to men regarding the fatigue resistance. The longer the distance, the better the relative performance of women is believed to be. Some people hypothesize that the higher body fat percentage (BFP) of women is the reason for this. In this chapter, we will review these aspects.

Are Women Really Superior to Men at the Ultra-Long Distances?

Is it really true that women have a superior fatigue resistance? We have calculated the equivalent FTP from the September 2016 world records of men and women at distances from 800 meters to 100 kilometers (see the table below). These data do not support the hypothesis that women are superior at the longer distances. As can be seen from the figure below, the ratio of the equivalent FTP of women and men is 89-90% for most distances. The exceptions are:

» the record of Junxia Wang at the 3,000 m (91%, this record has been associated with doping).

» the record of Paula Radcliffe at the marathon (91%, this record has been praised worldwide as being exceptionally strong).

» the record of Tomoe Abe at the 100 km (96%, this is probably due to the fact that the official men's record is relatively weak).

World Records: Men			FTP
Distance	Time	Name	(watts/kg)
800 m	1:40.91	David Rudisha	6.86
1,500 m	3:26.00	Hicham El Guerrouj	6.50
3,000 m	7:20.67	Daniel Komen	6.32
5,000 m	12:37.35	Kenenisa Bekele	6.33
10,000 m	26:17.53	Kenenisa Bekele	6.36
15 km	00:41:13	Leonard Komon	6.24
20 km	00:55:21	Zersenay Tadese	6.32
21.1 km	00:58:23	Zersenay Tadese	6.34
25 km	01:11:18	Dennis Kimetto	6.22
30 km	01:27:38	Emmanuel Mutai	6.14
42.2 km	02:02:57	Dennis Kimetto	6.30
100 km	06:13:33	Takahiro Sunada	5.18

World Records: Women			FTP
Distance	Time	Name	(watts/kg)
800 m	1:53.28	Jarmila Kratochvilova	6.04
1,500 m	3:50.07	Genzebe Dibaba	5.83
3,000 m	8:06.11	Wang Junxia	5.76
5,000 m	14:11.15	Tirunesh Dibaba	5.66
10,000 m	29:17.45	Almaz Ayana	5.76
15 km	0:46:14	Florence Kiplagat	5.59
20 km	01:01:54	Florence Kiplagat	5.68
21.1 km	01:05:09	Florence Kiplagat	5.71
25 km	01:19:53	Mary Keitany	5.58
30 km	01:38:49	Mizuki Noguchi	5.49
42.2 km	02:15:25	Paula Radcliffe	5.76
100 km	06:33:11	Tomoe Abe	4.96

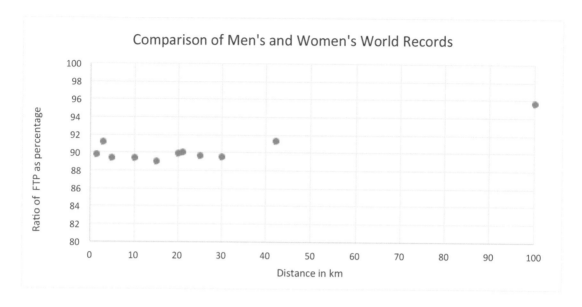

Although the data are not conclusive, we believe that at present there is insufficient evidence to support the hypothesis that women are superior in the ultra-long distance. The differences between men and women are around 9-10% for almost all distances.

Are Women Masters Superior to Men Masters?

The WMA publishes the world records masters for 5-year age classes, both for men and women. The records for the women per 31 December 2015 are presented in the table below. The results for the men are shown in an earlier chapter.

World Records: Women (35-85 Years)						
Distance	W35	W40	W45	W50	W55	W60
0.8	1:56.53	1:59.25	2:02.82	2:16.05	2:21.98	2:33.09
1.5	3:57.73	3:59.78	4:05.44	4:36.79	4:51.26	5:06.65
3	8:27.83	9:11.2	9:17.27	9:47.20	10:03.908	10:54.04
5	14:33.84	15:04.87	15:55.71	16:51.17	17:29.28	18:48.62
10	30:53.20	31:40.97	32:34.06	35:05.7	36:53.81	39:04.23
42.2	2:21.29	2:22:27	2:29:00	2:31:05	2:52:14	3:02.50

We see that the records of the women follow a similar decline with age as the men's records. We have printed in bold the relatively weak records in the class W85; apparently few women run at an elite level in this class.

We have calculated the decline with age in some more detail for the 5,000 meter in the figure below. Similar to the men we see that the annual decline increases with age:

» For women between the ages of 35-54, the annual decline is 1.0% (slightly more than the 0.8% of the men).

» For women between the ages of 55-74, the annual decline is 1.6% (again higher than the 1.1% of the men).

» For women over 75 years, the annual decline is 2.9% (less than the 5.0% of the men).

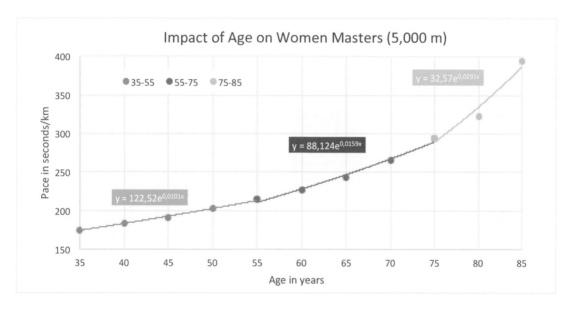

Distance	W65	W70	W75	W80	W85
World Records: Women (35-85 Years) (continued)					
0.8	2:41.81	2:59.55	3:07.35	3:43.62	4:15.99
1.5	5:29.85	6:00.50	6:34.22	7:25.50	**8:50.42**
3	11:48.2	12:53.03	13:55.58	15:34.64	**24:08.62**
5	20:10.09	21:34.08	24:03.90	26:33.60	**32:51.05**
10	41:40.27	44:43.27	50:00.93	55:26.46	**86:15.07**
42.2	3:12:57	3:35:29	3:53:42	4:12:44	**5:14:26**

The Phenomenal Performances of Merlene Ottey

We end this chapter with a figure that illustrates that statistics can be significantly influenced by exceptional performances. The figure below shows the impact of age on the world record of the 100 m women masters. We see that the annual decline in the age classes up to 50 years is very small, only 0.5%. Above 50 years, this percentage increases significantly to 2.4%! The reason is simple: all records up to 50 years have been set by the phenomenal Merlene Ottey. If she continues running at the elite level, she will probably smash the other age records in the future as well!

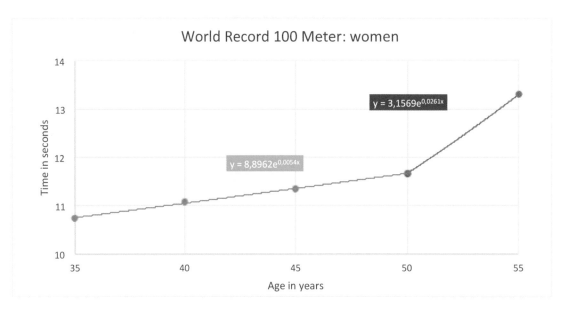

Silke Schmidt (F55, Germany) takes the lead in her golden 1.500 m at the 2015 World Masters Championships in Lyon, France

The German athlete Silke Schmidt (F55) holds world records at the 1,500 meter, 1 mile, 3,000 meter, 5,000 meter and 10,000 meter.

26. THE PERFORMANCE INDEX

Competitive running offers never-ending challenges!

Let's say you have run the marathon in 3 hours and 30 minutes, just like our Marathon Man. How good or how bad is this actually? How should you compare your performance with that of others?

Calculate Your FTP

Obviously, the first thing you should do is to correct your performance for the conditions of the race, like the weather (temperature, wind, rain), the distance and the running course (hills, footing). This is where you can use the concept of the FTP. The FTP is an objective parameter that can be used to compare one performance with another, as it is corrected for the conditions of the race. In a previous chapter, we have shown how you can use the running formula to calculate your FTP from the race result. Your FTP will tell you how good your performance has been, taking into account the conditions of the race.

Compare Your FTP to World-Class Level

Let's suppose that you have run your 3:30 marathon in ideal conditions. In that case your FTP will be the same as our Marathon Man, 3.67 watts/kg. When we compare this value to the world-class level of 6.40 watts/kg, the ratio is 3.67/6.40= 57%. What does this number tell you? In a previous chapter, we have shown that runners can be classified in accordance with the table below:

Power Levels of Men		FTP
Classification		(watts/kg)
World class	100%	6.4
International	90%	5.8
National	80%	5.1
Regional	70%	4.5
Recreational	60%	3.8

Power Levels of Men (continued)		FTP
Classification		(watts/kg)
Fair	50%	3.2
Untrained	40%	2.6
Poor	30%	1.9
Very poor	20%	1.4

Consequently, the performance of our Marathon Man (and of you) can be classified as fair. The performance index is defined as the ratio of your FTP and world-class level, so in this case your performance index would be 57%.

Correct for Your Age

As we saw earlier, age has a big impact on the performance. So, when a 60 year old runs the marathon in 3:30, his performance index should be higher than the one for a 30 year old with the same time. In order to make a fair comparison, we should correct for the age. We will do this using Sterken's equations from an earlier chapter. We have prepared the table and figure below for this purpose. In the table, the first column gives the maximum value of the FTP as a function of age (the world-class level). The other columns give the classes of international, national, regional, recreational and fair level. We can see that when someone runs a 3:30 marathon at the age of 60, his performance index would be 3.67/5.20 = 71%. A 75-year-old runner with a 3:30 marathon would even have a performance index of 83%, so this runner would be in the class of national level!

Performance Index as a Function of Age and Class						
Age	Max. FTP	FTP 90%	FTP 80%	FTP 70%	FTP 60%	FTP 50%
(years)	(watts/kg)	(watts/kg)	(watts/kg)	(watts/kg)	(watts/kg)	(watts/kg)
10	4.84	4.35	3.87	3.39	2.90	2.42
15	5.64	5.08	4.51	3.95	3.38	2.82
20	6.11	5.50	4.89	4.28	3.67	3.06

Performance Index as a Function of Age and Class (continued)						
Age	Max. FTP	FTP 90%	FTP 80%	FTP 70%	FTP 60%	FTP 50%
(years)	(watts/kg)	(watts/kg)	(watts/kg)	(watts/kg)	(watts/kg)	(watts/kg)
25	6.25	5.62	5.00	4.37	3.75	3.12
30	6.40	5.76	5.12	4.48	3.84	3.20
35	6.22	5.60	4.98	4.35	3.73	3.11
40	6.03	5.43	4.82	4.22	3.62	3.02
45	5.81	5.23	4.65	4.07	3.49	2.90
50	5.56	5.00	4.44	3.89	3.33	2.78
55	5.39	4.85	4.32	3.78	3.24	2.70
60	5.20	4.68	4.16	3.64	3.12	2.60
65	4.97	4.47	3.97	3.48	2.98	2.48
70	4.70	4.23	3.76	3.29	2.82	2.35
75	4.41	3.97	3.53	3.09	2.64	2.20
80	4.01	3.61	3.21	2.80	2.40	2.00

Final of the 400 meter indoor M60 at the European Masters Athletics Championships 2016 in Ancona, Italy. The German Reinhard Michelchen wins with a split-second difference from the Dutchman Marcel Scholten (58:97). Their performance index is 94%.

27. THE IMPACT OF YOUR BODY WEIGHT

Here's where less is more!

Runners are usually skinny, which can easily be understood. Once you start running, you will lose body fat; once you lose body fat, your running will improve. You will become better and faster as a result of the training and as a result of losing weight. You will experience a positive flow. More or less automatically, you will run lighter and get better and leaner. Runners congratulate each other on their racing weight. However, non-runners among your family or friends might inquire whether you are feeling okay!

How Big Is the Impact of Your Body Weight?

The mathematics of the impact of your body weight on your running performance is quite simple. In principle, your human engine has a more or less fixed power output (P, in watts). As we saw earlier, at a flat course your power output will be equal to the sum of the running resistance and the air resistance:

$$P = P_r + P_a = cmv + 0.5 \rho c_d A(v+v_w)^2 v$$

Normally, when you start losing weight, your body fat percentage (BFP) will decrease but your power output (P) remains constant. As your body weight (m) decreases, the running resistance ($P_r = cmv$) decreases proportionally. Consequently, the result is that you can run at a higher speed! As the air resistance is only a small percentage of the running resistance, it is safe to say that your speed will increase by almost one percent for every percent of weight loss. So, the speed you can maintain at a certain distance is inversely proportional to your weight. You can also say that it will be easier to run at a certain speed when you lose weight. This makes sense as you have to spend less energy as a result of your reduced weight, whereas the power of your human engine has remained the same. Of course, all this is true when you avoid excessive weight loss, so your muscle mass is not compromised.

The inverse relationship between your body weight and your running performance can also be seen immediately from the definition of the FTP in watts/kg body weight. The lower your body weight is, the higher your FTP becomes and thus the better your running performance. Next to talent and training, your body weight is actually the main factor determining your racing times.

As an example, we have calculated the impact of the body weight on the performance of the Marathon Man. The results are presented in the table and figure. We see that indeed his speed increases by almost 10% if he manages to lose 10% of his body weight. On the other hand, his speed will drop by 10% if he gains 10% of body weight. The latter is actually one of the reasons why the performance drops with age. Most people gain weight as they get older.

Impact of Body Weight on Speed and Time for Marathon Man		
Body weight	Hour speed	Marathon time
(kg)	(km/h)	(hrs:min:sec)
60	15.05	03:00:45
62	14.62	03:06:28
64	14.21	03:12:15
66	13.82	03:18:03
68	13.45	03:23:55
70	13.10	03:30:00
72	12.76	03:35:44
74	12.44	03:41:42
76	12.13	03:47:41
78	11.84	03:53:43
80	11.56	03:59:46

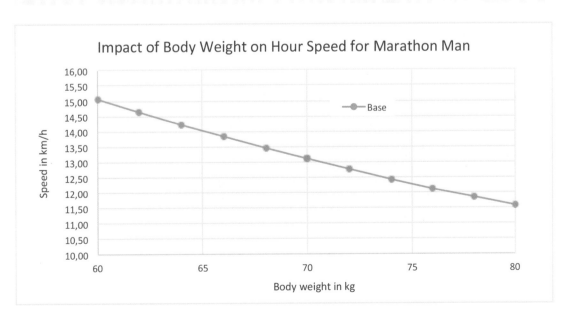

An Example of the Impact in Practice

Author Hans experienced the positive impact of weight loss in 2012. He started managing his diet, eating less calories and in particular less fat and sugar. As a result his body weight decreased from 67.5 kg to 57.5 kg (by 10 kg or 15%). It is noted that Hans was 58 years in 2012 and his weight had slowly increased over a period of 30 years by the same 10 kg. It should also be noted that Hans had been running on a daily basis during those 30 years. His performances had declined slowly during those years, which he had attributed to his age. But in 2012, he experienced a sudden and spectacular performance improvement that can only be explained by the weight loss as his training remained more or less the same. The significant improvement in his race results during 2012 are shown in the table and figure below.

Race Results of Hans van Dijk in 2012				
	Date	Body weight	Distance	Race time
		(kg)	(km)	(hrs:min:sec)
Lenteloop Eerbeek	18-3-2012	67.5	21.2	1:32:43
Rotterdam	15-4-2012	66.0	42.2	3:23:54
Hoogland	9-5-2012	63.8	7.6	0:27:53
Zeebodemloop	2-6-2012	62.6	21.1	1:28:40
Maarn	16-6-2012	61.9	21.1	1:29:40
Panbosloop	1-7-2012	61.5	15	1:04:25
Utrecht baan	13-7-2012	61.0	3	0:10:56
Dalfsen	3-8-2012	60.3	10	0:39:09
Utrecht baan	10-8-2012	59.6	1.5	0:05:10
Waterleidingloop	25-8-2012	59.0	15	1:02:12
Tilburg	2-9-2012	58.7	16.1	1:03:55
Hoogland	16-9-2012	58.3	21.1	1:25:33
NK10 km Utrecht	30-9-2012	58.0	10	0:37:57
Essen	14-10-2012	57.8	41.2	3:01:07
Renswoude	3-11-2012	57.5	21.1	1:21:34
Zevenheuvelen	18-11-2012	57.5	15.1	0:57:54

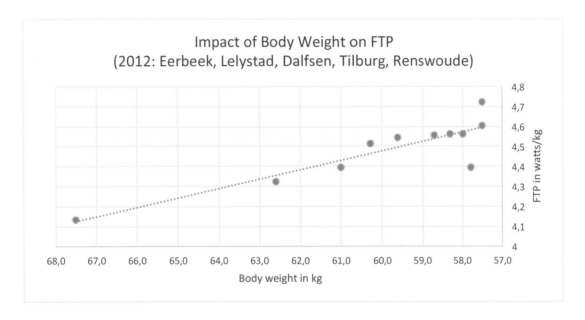

The data show a clear and continuous improvement of his FTP and race results as his body weight dropped during the year. The relationship between his weight loss and his increase in FTP and race times strongly supports the expectations from theory. We remark that the outlier in the figure (the point to the right, which is much lower than the regression line) is based on his results in the marathon. Throughout his running career, Hans experienced that his marathon performance was usually less good than could be expected. Apparently, his fatigue resistance is less than average.

In short, we conclude that for our Marathon Man, losing weight is a promising strategy if he wants to improve his performance. How much weight he can lose depends mainly on his body fat percentage. This will be discussed in the next chapter. Of course, it may not be easy for him to eat and drink less. Also, he may have to pay attention to the composition of his diet, to prevent deficiencies and optimize his health. This will also be dealt with in the other chapters.

28. BMI, BODY FAT PERCENTAGE AND RACING WEIGHT

With self-discipline all things are possible. —Theodore Roosevelt

In the previous chapter, we saw that your body weight is one of the main factors determining your performance in running. We cannot influence our talent and we cannot change the fact that we grow older, but we can manage our diet and prevent gaining weight! For most of us, it will even be possible to shed some body fat and reduce our body weight. This requires willpower, as we will have to eat and drink less and train more! Earlier we saw that our FTP is inversely proportional to our body weight, so our performance will definitely benefit from losing weight. But how far can we go? What is the optimal racing weight?

Body Mass Index (BMI)

Most people will be familiar with the concept of the BMI as an indicator of weight. The BMI is defined as:

BMI = m/L^2

In this formula, the body weight (m) is expressed in kg and the length (L) in meters. So, if you are 1.75 meter tall and your body weight is 65 kg, your BMI is $65/(1.75)^2$ = 21.2. This is considered a normal weight, according to the table and figure below.

Body Mass Index	BMI
Underweight	< 18.5
Normal (healthy weight)	18.5-25
Overweight	25-30
Obese	30-40
Very severely obese	> 40

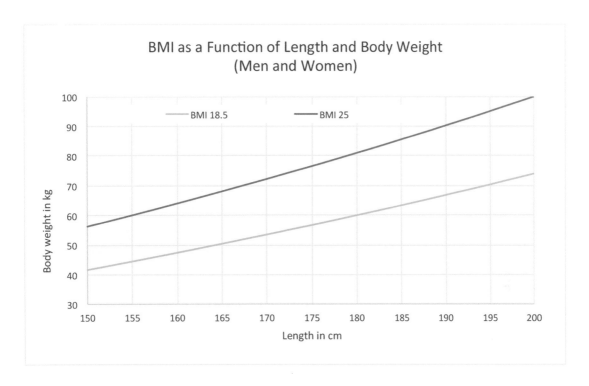

We note that the classification of the BMI is valid for normal people. Runners are usually skinny and may have a BMI of less than 18.5. For runners the BMI is actually a less meaningful index as compared to the body fat percentage (BFP). We will explain this below.

Lean Body Mass

Our body is composed of fat and fat-free body mass. The latter include the bones and muscles and is usually denoted as lean body mass (LBM). In the literature[41], the following formula has been presented to approximate the LBM as a function of body weight and length:

For men: **LBM = 0,32810*m+33,929*L-29,5336**

For women: **LBM = 0,29569*m+41,813*L-43,29335**

As an example we use a man of 65 kg and 1.75 meter; his LBM thus becomes 51.2 kg.

Body Fat Percentage

The body fat percentage (BFP) is defined as:

BFP = (m-LBM)/m

This means our man of 65 kg and 1.75 meter has a BFP of (65-51.2)/65 = 21.1%

There are several ways to determine your BFP. These include skin fold measurements, bioelectric impedance scales, hydrostatic weighing and a DEXA full-body scan. All of these measurements should be preferred over the abovementioned formulas, as large individual differences do exist between people. Nevertheless, we used the formulas to prepare the figure below. These figures should be used as a first indication only, so don't be alarmed if your data deviate from the lines! To be sure, you should have your BFP determined in a sports medical center.

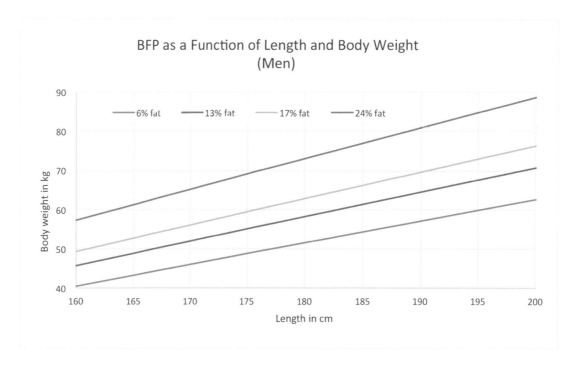

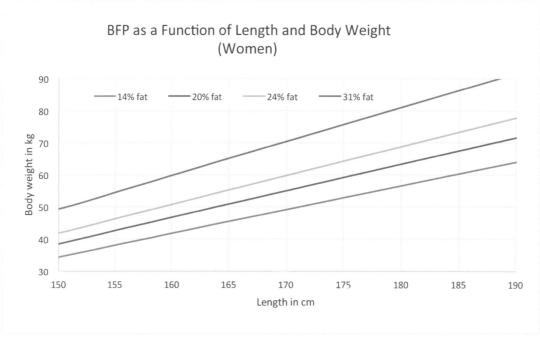

Your body weight has a big impact on your performance. For this reason top athletes try to reduce their body fat percentage as much as possible.

Optimal Racing Weight

So what is your optimal racing weight? For an optimal performance in running, you should try to reduce your BFP. By shedding body fat, your body weight will decrease and your performance in running will increase. Obviously, you should not go so far as to compromise the power and mass of your leg muscles. Also it is generally believed that some essential fat is required in our organs and other parts of the body. We have summarized the literature recommendations regarding BFP in the table below.

Recommendations for BFP (%)		
	Women	Men
Essential fat	10-15	2-5
Athletes	14-20	6-13
Fitness	21-24	14-17
Average	25-31	18-24
Overweight	> 32	> 25

The table shows that women generally have about 10% more body fat than men. We believe that this explains the 10% lower FTP and performance of women in running.

We note that we should consider our BFP as a kind of reserve that our body has stocked up for emergencies. In the past this function was essential to cope with times of food shortages. However, nowadays we live in a time of abundance with the result that most of us stock up too much fat, so we gain too much weight. If you want to perform as well as possible, you should make sure that you get rid of the surplus fat and lower your BFP as much as possible. Of course, it may not be easy to eat and drink less and avoid those snacks and sodas. Also, you will have to pay attention to eating healthy and varied food as explained in other chapters (with lots of vegetables and fruits). Finally you should take ample time to reduce your BFP and avoid extreme weight loss and unhealthy effects, such as *anorexia athletica*.

Jogging in New York's Central Park is fun. Losing some body fat increases your performance, health and the quality of your life.

29. HOW TO LOSE BODY FAT AND GAIN FITNESS

Be the change you want to see in the world. —Mahatma Gandhi

Your body weight does not only determine your performance in running, it is also one of the most important factors in your physical and mental well-being. In this chapter, we will discuss the personal experiences of author Hans. We note that Ron had similar experiences. We will describe how they managed to shed body fat. Also we will describe the positive impact this had on their health, performance and quality of life.

The Experiences of Author Hans

Hans first realized the importance of his body weight in 2011, when he cleaned up his attic and found an old running logbook from 1980. In this he read that in 1980 his body weight had been 57.5 kg, whereas by 2011 this had increased (slowly and unnoticed) to 68.5 kg. At that moment he decided to try to shed the additional body fat and get back to his earlier body weight. He started to limit his daily calorie intake, abandoning snacks and sodas. He paid attention to a healthy and varied nutrition: lots of vegetables and fruits, less meat and fat, no sugar in the tea and coffee and drinking lots of water. At first this was tough. He felt hungry all day, but he was motivated and persevered. After some time, it became easier and he actually started to enjoy his new low-fat diet. And with success, as can be seen from the table below! Since the end of 2012 his body weight is back at the 1980 level of 57.5 kg.

Body Weight of Hans van Dijk	
	(kg)
1980	57.5
1990	63.0
2003	64.5
2009	67.0
2011	68.5
2012	57.5

How to Lose Body Fat

The mathematics of losing weight is very simple: you just have to make sure that on a daily basis your energy (calorie) balance is (slightly) negative. So your daily energy use has to exceed the energy intake with your food. In an earlier chapter, we saw that the energy value of body fat is 37.6 kJ/gram. This means that you can calculate your daily weight loss from your daily energy balance as shown in the box.

Weight loss (in g/day) = (Energy use (in kJ/day)-Energy intake (in kJ/day))/37.6

The daily energy use is comprised of the base metabolism and the energy used for running. The daily metabolism of Hans uses around 6,500 kJ and his daily one-hour training around 2,500 kJ. He managed to reduce the energy intake with his food to some 6,700 kJ, so his daily energy balance was negative by 2,300 kJ. This resulted in a daily weight loss of 2,300/37.6 = 60 grams of body fat. This theoretical calculation matched perfectly well with the actual weight loss that Hans experienced in 2012, as can be seen in the figure.

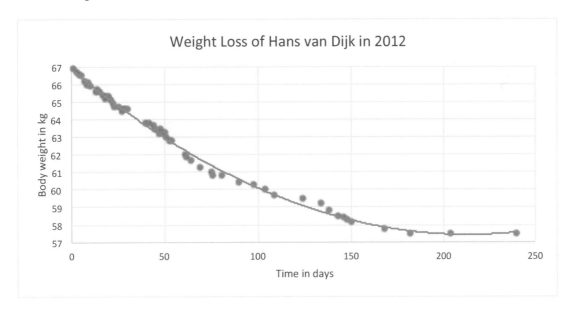

As could be expected, the weight loss gradually decreased. As his weight decreased, both his base metabolism and the energy used for running also decreased. So his energy balance became less negative and his weight automatically approached the equilibrium value of 57.5 kg. This took a period of 6 months

for a total weight loss of 11 kg. In this period his waist size decreased from 82 to 69 cm. His clothing did not fit anymore and even his calf size reduced from 36 to 33 cm!

Impact on Body Fat Percentage (BFP)

Hans had his BFP determined by means of skin fold measurements at the end of 2011, when his body weight was still 68 kg. His BFP turned out to be 22%, which means that he had a total of 0.22*68 = 15 kg of body fat. As we saw in an earlier chapter, we can calculate that his lean body mass (LBM) was 68-15 = 53 kg. Hans realized that he could lose the majority of the 15 kg of body fat, thus improving his fitness. When we presume that his LBM remained constant at 53 kg, we can calculate his BFP as a function of his body weight, as shown in the table below.

BFP Hans van Dijk	
Body weight	BFP
(kg)	%
68	22
66	20
64	17
60	12
58	9
56	5

The table shows that theoretically Hans could go as far as 56 kg, before reaching the critical level of 5% BFP. In literature this is the lower limit for athletes and thought to be the amount of essential body fat necessary to support body and organ functions. In practice the weight of Hans stabilized at 57.5 kg, so he could not reach the 56 kg (without severely restricting his diet). At the end of 2012, Hans had his BFP determined once more, this time with an EDAX full-body scan. The result was that his BFP was 6.5%, so this was close to the calculations. Also it was so low that Hans concluded that he had done enough and he should not strive for additional weight loss. The advantage of losing another kg would be small and would not outweigh the possible risk of compromising his body functions.

Impact on Cholesterol Levels

One important side effect of his weight loss in 2012 was that Hans experienced a dramatic improvement in his cholesterol levels, as shown in the table below.

Cholesterol Data for Hans van Dijk					
Date	Total	Triglycerides	HDL	LDL	Ratio Total/HDL
Normal ranges	<5 *	2.1	> 0.9	2.5-3.5	<5
23-1-1990	5.7				
6-10-2003	6.8	2.2	1.4	4.4	4.9
2-2-2005	6.6				
11-4-2007	6.1	2.0	1.4	3.9	4.5
11-8-2010	7.2	1.9	1.6	4.8	4.6
6-1-2011	7.7	3.1	1.5	4.8	5.0
17-5-2011	6.8	1.6	1.5	4.7	4.5
30-11-2011	7.3		1.4		5.2
24-7-2012	5.5	0.9	1.9	3.1	2.9
6-11-2012	4.6		2.2		2.1

An elevated level of cholesterol (in particular the LDL and the ratio total/HDL) is considered to be an important risk factor for cardiovascular diseases. Before 2012, the levels of Hans were higher than recommended. In 2012 they dropped by some 30% or more and at the end of 2012 all data complied to all recommended levels!

Impact on Fitness

The fitness level of Hans increased spectacularly during 2012. His resting heart rate dropped from 45 to 40, he felt reborn and had lots of energy. Before and after his weight loss, he took a physical fitness test (including a running test on a treadmill with breathing gas analysis and ECG) at the Dutch Olympic Sports Center Papendal. The results are shown in the table.

Fitness Tests for Hans at Papendal 2011-2012			
	2011	2012	Improvement (%)
Body weight in kg	68.5	58	18
VO$_2$ max in ml/kg/min	51	60	18
Speed at FTP in km/h	13.5	16	19
HR at FTP in bpm	153	157	3
Maximum speed in km/h	17.5	19	9
Vital capacity in ml	4,500	4,860	8
BFP in %	14	6.9	51
Waist size in cm	82	69	19
Total cholesterol in mmol/l	7.3	4.6	37
HDL in mmol/l	1.4	2.2	36
Cholesterol ratio	5.2	2.1	60

As can be seen from the table, all parameters showed a very significant improvement. His VO$_2$ max increased from 51 to 60 ml/kg/min, so by 18%. This means that his FTP increased from 3.7 to 4.3 watts/kg.

Impact on Running Performance

The details on the spectacular improvement of his race times were already given in an earlier chapter. In 2012, his performance at all distances improved by some 15%, more or less equivalent to his weight loss.

Impact on Quality of Life

Both Hans and Ron feel that this is probably the most rewarding advantage of losing body fat. They both feel reborn and more fit and healthy. They are cheerful, feel young and enjoy life. They sleep well, have lots of energy all day and enjoy their less-fat meals. They run as light as a feather and have delight in their daily runs in the great outdoors!

Hans van Dijk between the Russians Alexandr Kaplenko (207) and winner Leonid Tikhonov (1120) at the 5,000-meter M55 final of the World Master Games 2013 in Turin, Italy. Hans benefitted from his weight loss and won the silver medal.

30. THE IMPACT OF TRAINING

The single greatest cause of improvement is staying injury-free.

For most people, training will lead to an increase of the FTP. This means that the attainable speed at most distances will also increase. However, at short distances the impact on speed will usually not be so big. Sprinters are born, although they should train as well.

Possible Effects of Training

From most textbooks and papers on training[7,8,9,10,43], the following conclusions on the impact of training can be drawn:

1. The attainable speed for most distances can be improved by some 10-20% (maximum 30%). The time to exhaustion can even be improved by a factor of 10!
2. The effect of training can be reached rather quickly, in some weeks or months. The training effect is also lost quickly when the athlete stops training.
3. The intensity of the training is the most important factor determining the effect. In order to get the biggest improvement, it is vital to train at a high intensity. This means close to the maximum heart rate (MHR) and close to or above the FTP. Consequently, interval training is the most effective method.

In an earlier chapter, we have already discussed the different training methods, including interval training. In the next chapters we will discuss how fast you should run in training and give some examples and tips on how to get the best training results, including the use of heart rate meters and running watches. The use of power meters will be discussed separately in part V of this book.

Limitations of Research

We note that in practice it is quite difficult to optimize your training and get the best results. Consequently, the impact of training is less predictable than other factors, such as the impact of distance, body weight or age. The variability of the impact of training is caused by the following factors:

1. Most research into the impact of training is limited to a period of some weeks or months only. Consequently, it is not possible to predict the long-term impact (in which many runners are interested).
2. Most research is done on a limited group of runners, both in numbers and in level. Consequently, it is difficult or even impossible to draw statistically sound conclusions.
3. In practice, many factors change simultaneously, such as the body weight, the training program, the physical fitness, the conditions of training and racing and so on.

This means we should be more humble in predicting the impact of training on the attainable race times. In this chapter, we will just illustrate the potential impact by assuming that our Marathon Man can increase his FTP by 10% or 20% as a result of training. The table and figure give the impact of this increase of his FTP on his race times.

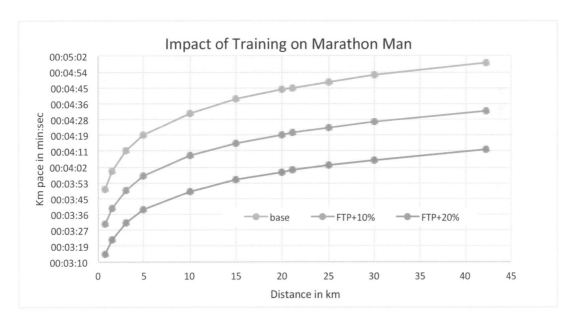

Impact of Training on Marathon Man			
Distance	Base FTP	FTP +10%	FTP +20%
(km)	(hrs:min:sec)	(hrs:min:sec)	(hrs:min:sec)
0.8	00:03:04	00:02:48	00:02:36
1.5	00:05:59	00:05:29	00:05:04
3	00:12:32	00:11:28	00:10:35
5	00:21:36	00:19:45	00:18:13
10	00:45:13	00:41:20	00:38:07
15	01:09:41	01:03:41	00:58:42
20	01:34:42	01:26:32	01:19:45
21.1	01:40:16	01:31:37	01:24:26
25	02:00:09	01:49:46	01:41:09
30	02:25:57	02:13:19	02:02:51
42.195	03:30:00	03:11:48	02:56:42

The table and figure show that the race time for our Marathon Man could theoretically be improved from 3:30 to sub 3 hours. Of course, this will require meticulous training! Not everybody will be able to get such an improvement.

The Dutchmen Cees Stolwijk started with recreational running when he was 45 years old. The impact of his training was unparalleled. Gradually, his performance improved until he became a multiple Dutch champion and multiple Dutch record holder. Finally, at the age of 65, he won 3 European and 3 World Championship titles and broke the world records for the 1,500 meter indoor M65 (4:43.01) and the 3,000 meter indoor M65 (10:02.51).

31. HOW FAST SHOULD YOU RUN IN TRAINING?

Success is one percent inspiration, ninety-nine percent perspiration.

Once you know your FTP, you can use it for many applications. In a previous chapter, we saw that the FTP is the best parameter to compare race results run in different conditions or by different runners. Your FTP is also the best parameter that you can use to determine your optimal training pace.

As we discussed in an earlier chapter, an optimal training program should always contain the following components:

1. **Easy aerobic endurance runs**
    These are meant to train your leg muscles and your fatigue resistance. The pace should be easy, around 80% or less of the pace of your FTP. The daily volume should be moderate, around 10-15 kilometers, but once a week a long run of 30 kilometers is recommended while preparing for a marathon.

2. **Brisk endurance runs or tempo blocks**
    These are meant to increase your pace feel and fatigue resistance. The pace should be that of the marathon, so around 90 % of your FTP. The volume is moderate, 5 kilometers per block and 10-15 kilometers per training.

3. **Threshold blocks**
    These are meant to increase your FTP and lactate resistance. The pace should be such that you can maintain it for one hour, around 100% of your FTP. The volume is around 2-5 kilometers per block and 10 kilometers per training.

4. **Interval training**
    These are meant to increase your VO_2 max. The pace should be that of the 5,000 meter, so around 110% of your FTP. These are the long intervals of around one kilometer each. The volume is around six kilometers per training.

5. **Speed training**

    These are meant to increase your anaerobic capacity, speed and running economy (RE).The pace should be that of the 1,500 meter, so around 120% of the FTP. These are the short intervals of 200-400 meters. The volume should be less than six kilometers.

Using our program, we have calculated the best training pace for the different training components and for different values of the FTP. The results are given in the table below.

FTP Km Pace in Training					
FTP	Training pace in time/km				
(watts/kg)	Easy	Brisk	Threshold	Interval	Speed
2.00	10:23	08:40	08:16	07:30	06:52
2.25	09:16	07:44	07:23	06:42	06:08
2.50	08:21	06:59	06:40	06:03	05:32
2.75	07:37	06:22	06:05	05:31	05:03
3.00	06:59	05:50	05:34	05:03	04:37
3.25	06:30	05:25	05:11	04:42	04:18
3.50	06:03	05:03	04:49	04:23	04:00
3.75	05:40	04:44	04:31	04:06	03:45
4.00	05:20	04:28	04:15	03:52	03:32
4.25	05:03	04:13	04:01	03:39	03:20
4.50	04:47	04:00	03:49	03:28	03:10
4.75	04:33	03:48	03:38	03:18	03:01
5.00	04:21	03:38	03:28	03:09	02:53
5.25	04:10	03:29	03:19	03:01	02:45
5.50	04:00	03:20	03:11	02:53	02:39
5.75	03:51	03:12	03:04	02:47	02:33
6.00	03:42	03:06	02:57	02:41	02:27
6.25	03:34	02:59	02:51	02:35	02:22
6.50	03:27	02:53	02:45	02:30	02:17

In your daily training you can easily incorporate the well-known training adage "Keep varying your training program." With the help of a running watch, you can easily do an interval workout by yourself.

The table clearly shows that a wide range of paces is necessary to train all systems, including fatigue resistance (easy pace), pace feel (brisk pace), FTP and lactate resistance (threshold pace), VO_2 max (interval pace), speed and anaerobic capacity and runnning economy (speed pace). This confirms the well-known training adage "Keep varying your training program." The popular easy endurance runs will have to be complemented by the other components to get the best results!

Easy aerobic endurance run early in the morning.

32. THE IMPACT OF YOUR HEART RATE

Running gives us the evidence we are well.

We can envisage the human heart as a pump. When we want to increase the flow of a pump, we need to increase the number of revolutions per minute. Similarly, the heart rate (HR, in number of beats per minute) needs to increase in order to provide a higher blood flow (and consequently more oxygen) to the muscles. The capacity of a pump is usually defined in l/h. Similarly, the capacity of the cardiovascular system is defined by the oxygen transport capacity, the VO_2 max (in l O_2/min, or more usually in ml O_2/min/kg body weight).

MHR and RHR

As stated above, the HR will increase with the pace in order to provide the muscles with more blood and more oxygen. The relationship between HR and VO_2 is more or less linear between two limits:

1. The upper limit is the maximum heart rate (MHR).
   The human heart has a natural upper limit, which protects the heart from overloading. For most people, the MHR is in the order of 150-200 beats per minute. It declines with age. The following formulas can be found in literature[43]:

   - MHR = 220-age (in years)
   - MHR = 205.8-0.685*age (men)
   - MHR = 206-0.88*age (women)

   The first formula is believed to be more appropriate for sedentary people, whereas the other formulas are thought to better describe the HR of athletes, who stay active and fit. The figure gives the relationship according to the formulas.

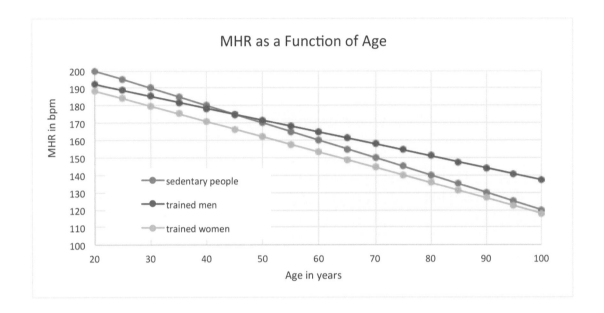

2. The lower limit is the resting heart rate (RHR).

    The resting heart rate is the most distinctive difference between trained athletes and inactive persons. The RHR of trained athletes is always low, certainly below 50 and sometimes below 40 bpm. Five-time Tour de France winner Eddy Merckx had a RHR of just 33 bpm! The RHR of sedentary people is significantly higher, over 60 and sometimes over 70 bpm. Although individual differences and exceptions to the rule may occur, the RHR is a very useful indicator of your fitness.

    The reason for the low RHR in trained athletes is that the sports heart has a higher stroke volume. Consequently, in order to provide the same blood flow, the RHR can be lower. This means that the heart has an easy job providing the blood flow required during rest and for the base metabolism. This also explains why trained athletes feel fit and energetic all day.

The Capacity of the Heart as a Function of the Difference Between MHR and RHR

Obviously, the difference between MHR and RHR is an important factor determining the capacity of the heart. As we age, the MHR declines and consequently so does the VO_2 max and our performance. In an earlier chapter, we learned that the decline in performance of master athletes is around 0.8% per year. A large part of this decline can be explained by the annual decline in MHR (0.685 bpm for men, see the above formula). As an example, we use a person with an MHR of 160 and an RHR of 45. The decline of MHR by 0.685 bpm corresponds to a decline in VO_2 of (160-45)/(159.315-45) = 1.006 or 0.6% per year. The above figure also shows that on average the MHR of women is around 10% lower than the MHR of men. This corresponds more or less to the difference in performance between men and women. As an example, we use the data for the age of 55. At this age the average MHR for men is 168 bpm, for women it is 158 bpm. Assuming the RHR is 45 in both cases, the difference in heart capacity becomes (168-45)/(158-45) = 1.088 or 8.8%.

How to Estimate Your VO_2 max and FTP From Your MHR and RHR

In an earlier chapter, we learned that we can use the following formula to get a rough estimate of the VO_2 max:

VO_2 max = 15*MHR/RHR

Also, we know that there is a fixed relationship between the VO_2 max and the FTP:

FTP = 0.072*VO_2 max

These formulas are almost too good to be true, because they enable us to estimate the FTP, based solely on the MHR (and thus on the age) and the RHR. The figures below give this relationship both for men and for women.

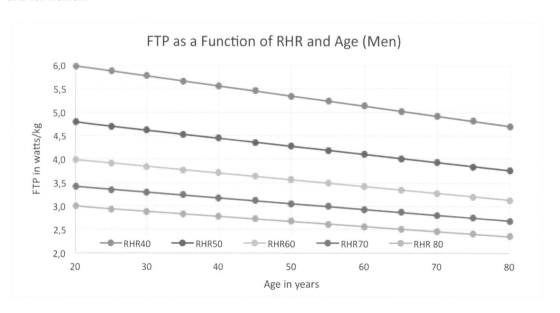

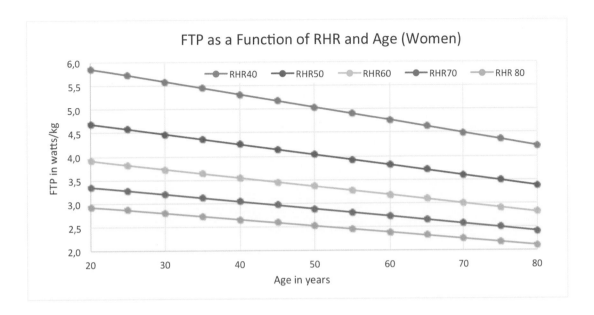

It gets even better when we realize that the FTP enables us to calculate the attainable marathon race time, just like we have done in the other chapters. So, with these formulas it is possible to make a rough estimate of your marathon race time based solely on your age and your RHR. The figures below give the results for men and women.

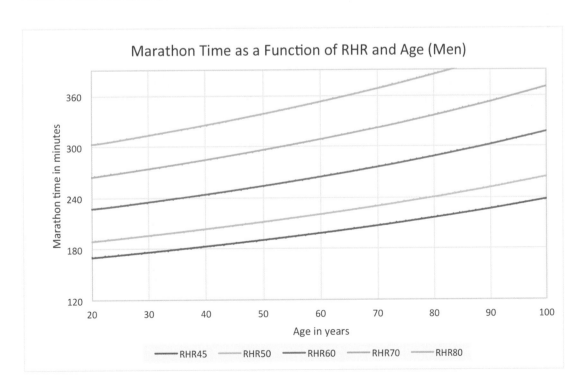

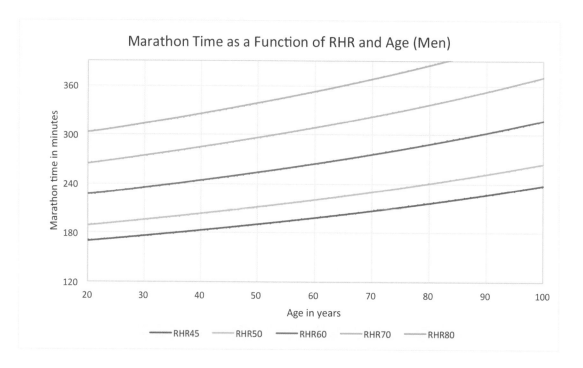

The figures clearly show the decline in performance as a function of age. They also show the distinct impact of the RHR.

We end this chapter with some cautionary notes. Obviously, these formulas should only be used as a first indication of your FTP and running performance. It is quite possible that your results will differ from the estimates. Furthermore, we feel that the predicted performances are rather optimistic, in particular for low values of the RHR. When we use the data of author Hans (61 years, RHR 42), an FTP of around 4.5 watts/kg and a marathon race time of 2:52 are predicted. In real life, Hans does have an FTP of 4.5 watt/kg, but his marathon time is a little off with 3:01.

Finally, it should be noted that the results are only possible if you have trained well to fully mobilize your potential.

The Women's Marathon of the London 2012 Olympic Games in front of Buckingham Palace.

33. THE RELATIONSHIP BETWEEN HR AND PACE

The body never lies. —Martha Graham

Most runners use a running watch or app on their smart phone to record the data of their workouts and races. Both have access to GPS systems, so you can see real-time data of the distance and pace of your run. In addition you can use a heart rate monitor (either a chest strap model or a strapless model built into your watch) to keep track of your heart rate (HR, in beats per minute). After your workout, you can upload the data on your computer and analyze the results. In this chapter, we will discuss the relationship between HR and pace, which we found to be a very useful indicator of our fitness and performance.

The Relationship Between HR and Pace During Training

The reader will not be surprised to learn that your HR increases when you run faster. As you run faster, the muscles require more oxygen, so the heart needs to supply a higher blood flow by increasing the HR. As we saw in the previous chapter, theoretically the blood flow and thus the VO_2 is determined by the difference between the actual HR and the RHR (HR-RHR). The maximum capacity or VO_2 max is determined by the difference between the MHR and the RHR (MHR-RHR). As your RHR will be more or less constant, you will notice a more or less linear relationship between the actual HR and the pace. We have found that this relationship is very important, as it indicates your fitness. Once you know this relationship, you can easily detect whether you are in good shape or not. By studying your HR—pace relationship, you can also accurately predict your performance in races.

An Example: The Experiences of Author Hans

Author Hans keeps track of the HR—pace relationship of his workouts on a daily basis. He runs the same course (of 12 kilometers) at least a couple of times per week to get comparable and reproducible results. He found a very clear and reproducible linear relationship between the average HR and the average pace during this workout. No matter how fast or slow he runs or what type of workout he does (endurance run, tempo run, climax run, intervals), all data points are quite close to the linear relationship. The figure below gives some data illustrating the HR–pace relationship for Hans.

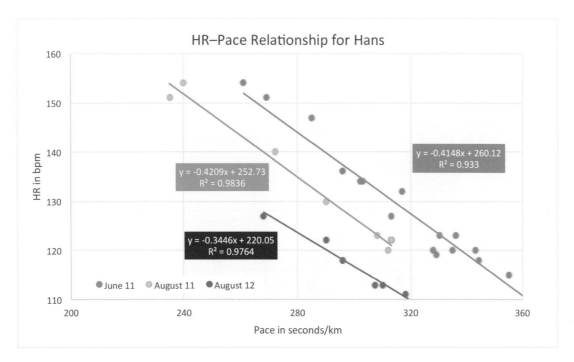

We can elucidate the figure by the following:

1. The data of June 2011 (the blue line) represent the first of Hans' workouts after his retirement. This is when he noted that all the data points were quite close to the blue line, irrespective of how fast or slow he ran or whether he included intervals or ran at a constant pace. He was not very fit in this period and his body weight had increased over the years from 58 kg to 68 kg.

2. The data of August 2011 (the green line) represent an improved state of fitness that he achieved after two months of serious training, including interval workouts. He noticed a significant improvement, as he ran better and more easily and his HR was some 10 bpm lower than in the earlier period (the green line is some 10 bpm below the blue line).

3. The data of August 2012 (the red line) represent the optimal fitness that Hans achieved after reducing his body weight from 68 kg to 58 kg (while maintaining his serious training). This led to the dramatic improvement of his fitness and performance, described earlier in this book. He ran feather light, felt strong and his HR was up to 20 bpm below the blue line. His race results were very good in this period; he ran PBs at the 5K (17:43) and the 10K (36:25). Since this time, Hans knows that when his HR is 20 bpm below the blue line, he is in good shape and he can run fast race times.

We conclude that your HR–pace relationship in training provides a very powerful tool to determine your fitness. Once you know this relationship, you can easily see whether you are in top shape and can run fast race times. We highly recommend that our readers take the trouble to record the required data, so they can put a number on their fitness. Obviously, you should take care to use the data of a standard course to limit the impact of incomparable aspects such as the presence of hills or a rough footing.

In 2012 Hans van Dijk achieved optimal fitness after reducing body weight and optimal training.

The Impact of a Cold or Disease

The HR–pace relationship will not only tell you whether you are in shape, but it will also show very clearly the impact of a cold or disease. In those cases, you will immediately notice a significant and sometimes dramatic increase of the HR as compared to your standard line. The figure below illustrates the impact of a cold on the fitness of Hans.

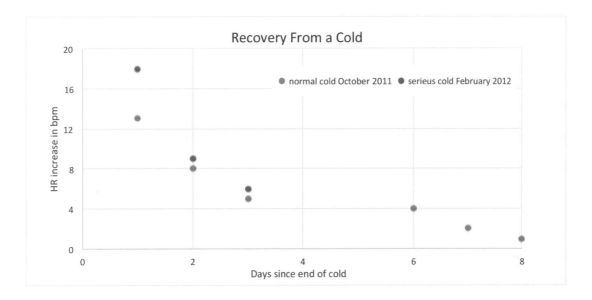

He defined day 1 as the day he felt well enough to run again after some days of being ill. Obviously, this was several days after his fever had broken. As the figure shows, his HR was some 13-18 bpm higher than what it should have been at the pace of the workout. It took 10 days for the HR to return to normal, so this clearly illustrates that you should be careful not to race too soon after a cold! Since these experiences, Hans monitors his HR carefully after any disease to make sure that he is sufficiently recovered before he plans serious workouts or races.

The Impact of the Heat and the Wind

Obviously, the HR—pace relationship can and will be influenced by extreme conditions, such as high temperatures. In such conditions, more blood is needed, causing the skin blood vessels to dilate, which will lead to increased blood flow to the skin where it may release part of the heat produced by running. However, it means that less blood is available for other functions, including the leg muscles. In effect your cardiovascular capacity is reduced and so is your running capacity. You can note this from the cardiac drift of your HR: at the same pace your HR becomes higher. Author Hans noted this on the hot morning of July 19th 2014; at a temperature of 25°C his HR turned out to be 6 bpm higher than the normal value for his pace. As the MHR of Hans is 172 bpm and his RHR is 42 bpm, this means that his performance capacity was reduced by 6/(172-42) = 4.6%!

Strong winds can also have a noticeable impact on the HR—pace relationship. Obviously, the energy cost of running against a head wind is significant, so your HR will be increased. As we saw earlier, this is only partly compensated by the advantage of a tail wind. Consequently, the combined impact of head wind and tail wind is always negative (i.e., your HR will be increased). For this reason, Hans always notes strong winds in his running diary and excludes these data points from his normal analysis.

The HR-Pace Relationship in Races

Experienced runners know that the pace in races is usually higher than in training. During a race, you are capable of digging deeper and running faster than in training. In particular, long-distance runners find it hard to attain race speeds during training. This also applies to author Hans. In training he rarely runs faster than 4:00/km, but in a 1,500 meter race he may run faster than 3:15/km! Obviously, during these shorter races the anaerobic energy systems play an important role, which will have an impact on the HR-pace relationship. For these reasons, Hans monitors a separate HR-pace relationship with the data points from his races. The figure below gives this relationship, which covers the full range from the 1,500 meter (HR 170, pace 188 sec/km) to the marathon (HR 150, pace 256 sec/km).

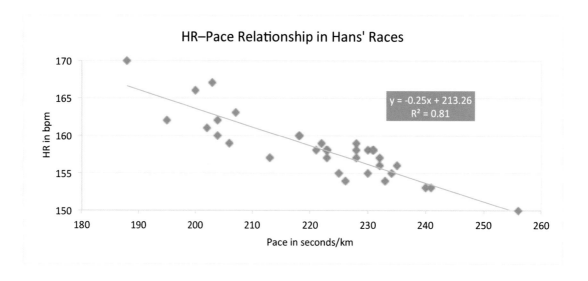

We end this chapter by noting that your HR is also a good indicator of whether you train at the proper pace and intensity. As we discussed earlier, your training program should be composed of many workouts at different paces and intensities. Your HR will tell you whether you are working out in the proper zone. It does a better job at this than running at a specific pace, as the HR shows the impact of the workout on your body. This will be discussed further in the next chapter.

Author Hans (2nd from right) in the 5,000 m at the 2014 Netherlands Masters Championships (M60).

34. HOW TO TRAIN AND RACE WITH HEART RATE METERS

If you train hard, you'll be hard to beat. —Herschel Walker

The theory and practice of running both indicate that you should train fast in order to get fast. This seems logical, but what is fast? Remember that you should ensure that all energy systems are adequately stimulated by training at race pace. For middle and long distance runners, this means the following:

» Training of endurance (easy pace, long duration)
» Training of aerobic capacity (around anaerobic threshold pace, short duration)
» Training of anaerobic capacity (pace around MHR, very short duration)

Endurance is very trainable. Sedentary people already get tired after a few kilometers, whereas trained athletes easily run 30 kilometers or more in a training. This means that an improvement in endurance by a factor of 10 is feasible. Consequently, the training of many long-distance runners consists mainly of endurance training at an easy pace. Although this is an enjoyable workout and it can be fun to run at an easy pace by yourself or with a group in the forest or along the fields, this is not recommended as the sole form of training. This way your body gets used to running slowly and not to running fast. Remember that in training your HR and pace are much lower than in races. The impact of easy running on your HR and aerobic capacity is limited and the impact on your anaerobic capacity is zero. This cannot be good, so you need to complement your training with fast running. This is where training zones come into the picture.

Training Zones

All training plans should contain a wide variety of intensities. In most training handbooks[8,9,10,42] training zones are defined to describe the intensity of the workout. The table below gives an example of this. In this case six zones of increasing intensity are used. For each training zone, a specific training goal is defined and examples of training forms are given as well as the HR in the zone as a percentage of the MHR. These training zones are frequently used as a basis to develop or modify a training plan, depending on the ambitions of the athlete and the race plans.

Zone	Training goal	Training form	HR (% of MHR)
0	Circulation in muscles	Warming up, cooling down, technical exercise, recovery from race or heavy training	60-70
1	Improvement of aerobic capacity and efficiency	Aerobic endurance training	70-75
2	Improvement of transition from aerobic to anaerobic system	Tempo endurance with long tempo blocks	75-80
3	Improvement of lactate threshold power and anaerobic efficiency	Interval training with blocks between 3 and 30 minutes with relatively short breaks	80-85
4	Improvement of lactate tolerance and VO_2 max	Interval training with short blocks of fast pace and high intensity (1-6 minutes)	85-100
5	Improvement of anaerobic capacity	Short intense intervals (30 seconds-3 minutes)	90-100
6	Improvement of explosive power	Full sprint (5-30 seconds)	95-100

With the HR–pace relationship that we discussed in the previous chapter, the training zones can be translated into pace. The table below presents an example of training paces, HRs and training forms that author Hans frequently uses.

Author Hans' HR and Pace During Training				
	HR	Pace	HR	Pace
	(%MHR)		(bpm)	(min:sec/km)
Endurance runs				
Recovery	60-70		105-123	5:30
Base	70-75		123-131	4:50
Brisk	75-85	marathon	131-149	4:15
Tempo runs				
Tempo	85-90	half marathon	149-158	3:50
Intervals				
Intervals 1,000 m	90-93	10K	158-161	3:40
Intervals 400 m	93-95	5K	161-166	3:30
Intervals 200 m	95-98	3K	166-172	3:20
Speedwork	95-100	1,500 m	166-175	3:10

Interval Training for Better Results

It is essential to approach your race pace and HR in the training. Because this is very hard, you can only maintain such an effort for a short time. This is why interval training is such a proven success. In intervals you can reach high values of HR and pace. During the periods between the intervals, your body can recover. Because the HR decreases exponentially within 10 to 20 seconds, the recovery is fast, so you can start the next interval quickly. By doing many intervals, you can maintain the high intensity during a considerable amount of time during the workout.

In interval training it is very important to find a good balance between high intensity and sufficient recovery. When the workout is very hard, a recovery of at least two days is needed. Muscle damage and the washout of lactic acid especially take time to recover. In practice, this often means that a schedule is maintained with no more than two interval workouts per week, alternated with recovery training at a lower HR and pace.

As we discussed earlier, it is difficult, if not impossible, to achieve the same HR and pace in training as in racing. During a race, you can always find something extra and dig a little deeper than in training. This is illustrated in the figure below, that gives the results of a 5,000-meter track race of author Hans. As you can see, he ran the entire race at almost MHR (167 bpm) and very high pace (3:35/K).

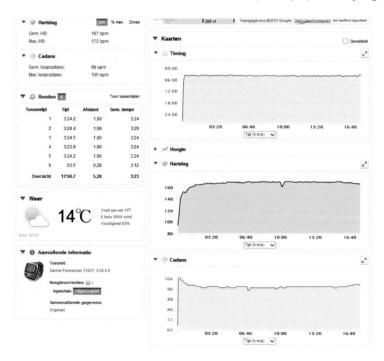

Results from a 5,000-meter track race.

Intervals, High-Intensity Training (HIT) and Relaxed Intervals

Your aerobic capacity and your anaerobic capacity can best be stimulated and developed by working out close to your MHR. Obviously, next to races, intervals are the most appropriate methods to achieve this. You could run 5 x 1,000 meters or 3 x 2,000 meters for the longer intervals. This way you will run at between 90-100% of your MHR and stimulate your aerobic capacity. During the shorter intervals, (e.g., 10 x 400 meters or 200 meters) your HR may reach 95-100% of your MHR, so you provide a good stimulus for your anaerobic capacity.

A popular, alternative form for short, fast intervals is to alternate 20 seconds of sprinting with 10 or 20 seconds of easy running. With this high-intensity training (HIT) very good results have been reported: an increase of the VO_2 max by 13% and of the anaerobic capacity by 28% in six weeks. You can easily optimize this training for yourself based on your HR. Adjust the duration of the interval and the recovery in such a way that you are approaching the MHR during the interval. During the recovery, your HR should drop to 85% of the MHR.

It's also a good idea—and even recommended—to run relaxed intervals, for example 200 meters, 400 meters or 1,000 meters, but at a lower HR, around the anaerobic threshold (85% MHR). Former multiple Dutch champion Klaas Lok even recommends to do this on a daily basis and to refrain from endurance runs altogether.

Climax Run and Races

Finally, the climax run is an attractive alternative. This means you start your workout at an easy pace and low HR, but gradually you increase the pace and HR. At the end of the workout, you approach the pace and HR of a 10K race. This way your daily training does not become too hard, but you still provide some stimulus for all your energy systems.

Obviously, races can be considered as the best training method, as you will run at an even higher pace and for a longer time than in training. However, running too many races is not advised as this will wear you down.

Races can be considered the best training method, as you will run at an even higher pace and for a longer time than in training. You can easily check your pace and heart rate with your running watch.

Create Your Own Training Plan

With the information in this chapter, you can now make a plan that suits your own training goals. As a result of the necessity to alternate hard and easy training days, this will look somewhat like the example below:

- » Monday   Short intervals (e.g., 10 x 400 meters)
- » Tuesday   Climax run (around 10 km) or relaxed intervals
- » Wednesday   Long intervals (e.g., 5 x 1,000 meters)
- » Thursday   Climax run (around 10 kilometers) or relaxed intervals
- » Friday   Endurance run (around 10 kilometers, easy pace)
- » Saturday   Race or hill training or climax run
- » Sunday   Long endurance run (approximately 20-30 kilometers, easy pace, combined with a number of accelerations and hill sprints)

Keep a Daily Training Diary

We highly recommend that you maintain a daily training diary in which you record all relevant data, such as pace, distance, HR, weather conditions and so on. As mentioned in the previous chapter, we also recommend that you regularly run a standard course and use the data points of this run to determine your HR–pace relationship. By doing this, you will learn many things about yourself and your running, including your fitness and your performance capability.

Examples of Running Data for Various Workouts and Races

Below we have presented some examples of relevant data from various workouts and races of author Hans. The examples clearly illustrate the wide range of intensities, paces and HRs.

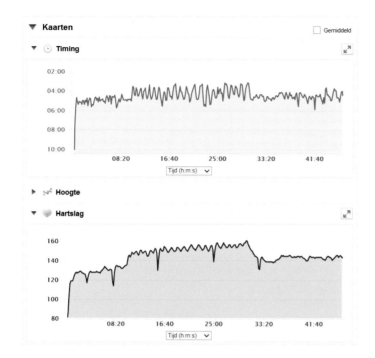

Interval training: 15 × 15 seconds.

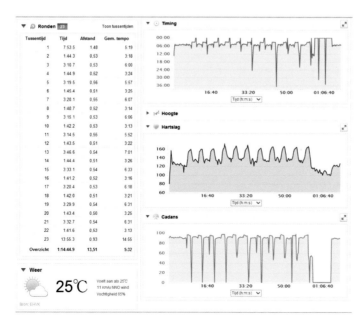

Interval training (12 × 500 meters) on a track.

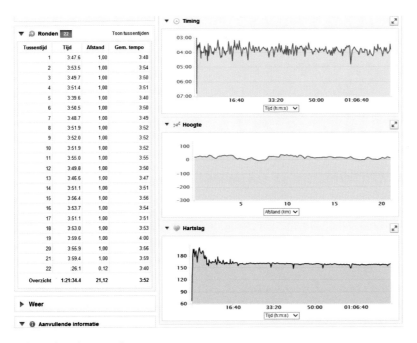

Tussentijd	Tijd	Afstand	Gem. tempo
1	3:47.6	1,00	3:48
2	3:53.5	1,00	3:54
3	3:49.7	1,00	3:50
4	3:51.4	1,00	3:51
5	3:39.6	1,00	3:40
6	3:50.5	1,00	3:50
7	3:48.7	1,00	3:49
8	3:51.9	1,00	3:52
9	3:52.0	1,00	3:52
10	3:51.9	1,00	3:52
11	3:55.0	1,00	3:55
12	3:49.8	1,00	3:50
13	3:46.6	1,00	3:47
14	3:51.1	1,00	3:51
15	3:56.4	1,00	3:56
16	3:53.7	1,00	3:54
17	3:51.1	1,00	3:51
18	3:53.0	1,00	3:53
19	3:59.6	1,00	4:00
20	3:55.9	1,00	3:56
21	3:59.4	1,00	3:59
22	:26.1	0,12	3:40
Overzicht	1:21:34.4	21,12	3:52

Half marathon of Renswoude.

35. HOW USEFUL IS THE SOFTWARE OF YOUR RUNNING WATCH?

The only source of knowledge is experience. —Albert Einstein

Each year, new types and models of running watches are being developed and introduced to the market. They provide us with new options and new information, next to the traditional data on distance, time, speed and heart rate. Over the past few years, authors Hans and Ron have tested and used the Garmin Forerunner types 620, 630 and 920. In this chapter, we will discuss their experiences and the possibilities that the new watches and software provide to help you in optimizing your training and race performance.

Which New Data Are Available?

Modern watches are equipped with an accelerometer, along with the GPS and heart rate sensors. The accelerometer is used to measure the running dynamics (cadence, stride length, ground contact time (GCT) and vertical oscillation). The Garmin watches use the sophisticated software of Firstbeat Technologies[44,45,46,47,48] to analyze the heart rate data. Firstbeat Technologies is a spin-off company of the Olympic Research Institute, based at the University of Jyväskylä, Finland. They have developed the software to calculate your breathing frequency, VO_2 max and anaerobic threshold (or lactate threshold) from the heart rate data. The Garmin 620, 630 and 920 provide you with the following new data (along with the traditional distance, time, pace and heart rate):

1. Cadence (number of strides per minute)
2. Stride length (in meter)
3. GCT (in milliseconds)
4. Vertical oscillation (in centimeters)
5. VO_2 max (in ml/kg/min)
6. Race predictor (prediction of your race times at various distances)
7. Recovery advisor (number of hours)
8. Lactate threshold (both as heart rate and as pace)

How Useful Are the New Data?

As is the case with all new technologies, it takes some time before you are familiar with the options and the benefits. Authors Hans and Ron like to quantify their running, so they have analyzed all the options. How good and reliable are the data and how useful are they in the pursuit of optimizing our training and racing performances? We will discuss the running dynamics (cadence, stride length, vertical oscillation and GCT) in three separate chapters. In this chapter we will focus on the VO_2 max and the race predictor.

The VO_2 max and the Race Predictor

These are very interesting and useful data for any competitive runner. The software uses your pace and heart rate (and indirectly your breathing frequency) as input to determine your current VO_2 max and to predict your attainable race performance at different distances. Obviously, the software needs to know your MHR, which you need to enter in one of the data fields. The results are quite sensitive to the MHR as author Hans once experienced. His new watch gave an unrealistically high VO_2 max of 64 ml/kg/min. After checking the data, Hans discovered that the MHR was set at 192 bpm instead of his real value of 172 bpm. Once this was corrected, the watch gave a lower and more realistic VO_2 max of 61 ml/kg/ml.

How Good and How Reliable Are the Software Predictions?

We have found the software predictions to be quite good and reliable. Apparently, the software is also self-learning so that the quality of the results improves with time. As an example, Hans once experienced that the VO_2 max result given by his new watch increased from a very low value of 50 to a more realistic value of 61 ml/kg/min in some five or six weeks. Also the VO_2 max goes up and down with your fitness. When you return from a cold or disease the VO_2 max is much lower than before. When your fitness increases as a result of proper and consistent training, the VO_2 max increases accordingly.

During periods of optimal fitness, the VO_2 max of author Hans is 61 ml/kg/min, according to his Garmin 630 watch. This value is quite accurate according to the physiological tests that he regularly takes at sports medical centers. When Hans is out of shape (due to disease, reduced training or even overtraining), his watch immediately reduces his VO_2 max to values as low as 56 ml/kg/min. So all in all, we are quite impressed by the quality of the software and the VO_2 max data calculated!

The market for running watches is huge. Nearly everybody in a marathon takes advantage of such a watch.

Most runners will find the race predictor function even more interesting than the VO_2 max calculator. In the table below we have compared the results of the race predictor function with the real race times of author Hans. We have noted that the race predictor function is a bit optimistic; in general the predicted race times are a bit too fast. Perhaps the Garmin people are trying to stimulate us with these fast times!

Race Predictor (VO_2 max 61 ml/kg/min)		
Distance	Predicted time	Real time
5 km	17:41	17:43
10 km	34:50	36:25
21.1 km	01:16:57	01:21:34
42.2 km	02:40:55	03:01:30

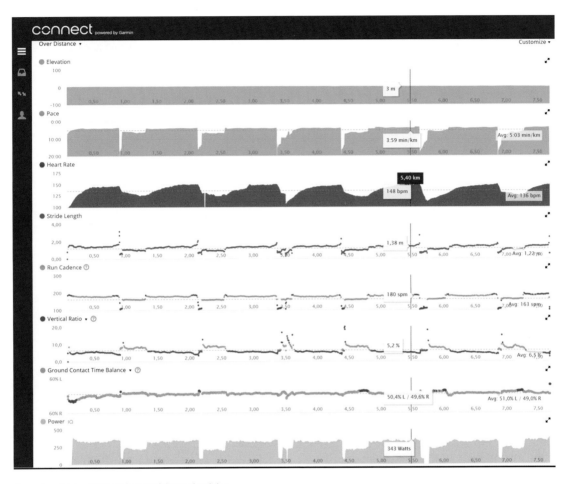

Examples of data measured in a track interval training.

36. THE IMPACT OF YOUR RUNNING ECONOMY (RE)

Running has taught me humility to realize my limitations and to accept them with pride!

In an earlier chapter, we saw that we can determine the power required to overcome the running resistance with the formula:

$P_r = cmv$

Our Marathon Man runs the marathon in 3 hours and 30 minutes, with a speed (v) of 42.195/3.5 = 12.06 km/h. As his body weight m is 70 kg and the specific energy cost of running (c) is 0.98 kJ/kg/km, the value for his running resistance P_r is 0.98*70*12.06/3.6 = 230 watts.

In this chapter we will look into the impact of the specific energy cost of running (c, in kJ/kg/km). We can also express the specific energy cost of running in terms of the specific oxygen uptake (in ml O_2/kg/km). This parameter can be determined in the laboratory with a treadmill test. Usually, it is called the running economy (RE). As the energy value of 1 ml of O_2 is equal to 19.5 J and the muscle efficiency can be set at 25%, the following relationship holds:

$c = (19.5*0.25/1000)*RE$

This means an RE of 201 ml O_2/kg/km is equivalent to our standard value for c of 0.98 kJ/kg/km.

Obviously, the c and the RE are not the same for all runners and in all conditions. Many papers have been published on the values of c and RE[49,50,51,52,53,54,55,56]. Some authors state that some distance runners, in particular the Kenyans and Ethiopians, run more economically than the average athlete. This means that they use less oxygen, so their RE is low (and so is their c). However, it is not known exactly which factors influence the RE and c in practice and what you can do to optimize it.

The Theory

According to the literature, the RE is influenced by our body posture and our running form. From biomechanical theory, the following aspects of body posture seem to be relevant:

» Weight of the legs (slim calves are better)
» Length of the legs (long legs are favorable)
» Lever of the Achilles tendon (small feet are better)
» Hip angle (narrow and flexible hips give an advantage)

Of course, we cannot control these aspects. They are determined by our DNA. At best, we can try to get rid of too much body fat in our calves. We can and should try to keep our hip, knee and ankle joints as flexible as possible through exercise and training.

The Impact of Our Running Form

The most concrete factor we can influence by training is our running form. This includes aspects such as having a short and spring-loaded ground contact, avoiding a heel strike pattern, using the arms to support the movement and stretching your toes at takeoff. Many runners and coaches have a different opinion on what constitutes the most economical running form.

The most practical factors that we can influence are the stride frequency (or cadence), the stride length and the vertical movement or oscillation. In the next chapters, we will investigate the impact of these factors more closely to see what you can do to try to improve your RE.

How Big Is the Impact of Your RE?

In this chapter, we will calculate the potential impact of a lower or higher RE. Next to the standard value of 201 ml O_2/kg/km (equivalent to a c-value of 0.98 kJ/kg/km), we have calculated the impact of two alternatives:

1. a 10% higher RE of 220 ml O_2/kg/km (this higher value means that the runner uses more O_2, so he is less efficient)
2. a 10% lower RE of 180 ml O_2/kg/km (this is the lowest value reported in literature for an extremely efficient Kenyan runner)

The figure and table below show the impact of these alternatives. It is clear that the RE has a big impact on your race times. It is very important to try to decrease your RE. In the next chapters, we will discuss what you can do in training to achieve this.

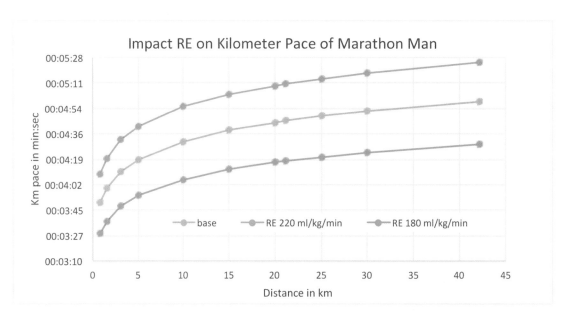

Impact RE Marathon Man			
Distance	Base	RE 220	RE 180
(km)	(hrs:min:sec)	(hrs:min:sec)	(hrs:min:sec)
0.8	00:03:04	00:03:20	00:02:47
1.5	00:05:59	00:06:30	00:05:26
3	00:12:32	00:13:37	00:11:21
5	00:21:36	00:23:28	00:19:33
10	00:45:13	00:49:11	00:40:55
15	01:09:41	01:15:48	01:03:01
20	01:34:42	01:43:03	01:25:37
21.1	01:40:16	01:49:06	01:30:38
25	02:00:09	02:10:45	01:48:35
30	02:25:57	02:38:51	02:11:52
42.195	03:30:00	03:48:37	03:09:41

Ethiopian and Kenyan runners have some genetically favorable body features: slim calves, long legs, small feet and narrow and flexible hips.

37. RUNNING DYNAMICS I: RUNNING STYLE

Running provides relaxation and creativity. —Tim Noakes

The ideal running form is one of the myths of running. We see a huge difference between the smooth strides of world champions like Haile Gebrselassie and Tirunush Dibaba and the gasping and wobbling of some joggers. But what is the secret of an optimal running form? In the next three chapters, we will look more closely into the impact of the four parameters that we can now determine with our running watch or smart phone:

» The stride length (in m)
» The stride rate of cadence (the number of strides per minute or spm)
» The ground contact time or GCT (in millisecond)
» The vertical movement or oscillation of your upper body (in cm)

Together, these four parameters are called the running dynamics. We will investigate which values of these running dynamics you should try to achieve. Which running dynamics will improve your running form, running speed and running economy?

Running Dynamics: Which Numbers Are Best?

This is a much debated topic. In literature[49-56], the following recommendations can be found:

1. The stride length should be long as long strides lead to a higher speed.
2. The cadence should be high, preferably more than 180 spm.
3. The GCT should be small, preferably less than 200 msec.
4. The oscillation should be small.

Consequently, you should try to run with a high cadence, making long strides with a small vertical oscillation. The GCT will then automatically be small. In practice, many runners find it difficult to maintain such a running form. It is one thing to make long strides at a 800 m race, but quite another to maintain these long strides during the marathon! Body length also influences the running dynamics: tall runners usually run with a longer strides, lower cadence, larger oscillation and longer GCT.

In general we can distinguish two extreme running styles:

1. The shuffle

   This style is used by many marathon runners and can be characterized by a heel strike, low cadence, short strides, small oscillation and high GCT.

2. The power stride

   This style is used by many sprinters and middle distance runners and can be characterized by a toe strike, high cadence, long strides, large oscillation and small GCT.

Producers of running watches, like Garmin, have apparently struggled with the running dynamics, as they do not give clear recommendations which values of the four parameters are best. They limit themselves to a color coding as presented below.

Running Dynamics Color Codes (Garmin)			
Color	Cadence	Oscillation	GCT
	(ppm)	(cm)	(ms)
	>185	<6.7	<208
	174-185	6.7-8.3	208-240
	163-173	8.4-10	241-272
	151-162	10.1-11.8	273-305
	<151	>11.8	>305

We see that the purple code for cadence and GCT is in accordance with the recommendations from literature. We conclude that this probably means that Garmin considers the purple code to represent the best running form. We also suspect that they have used the green code to represent the values of the average runner. The red code will probably indicate a bad running form; these runners should try to improve their running dynamics, by increasing their cadence and decreasing their GCT and oscillation.

Two Practical Examples: The Authors Hans and Ron

The authors of this book represent the two extreme running styles. Hans runs with the power stride and Ron is a typical shuffle runner, as the pictures illustrate.

Hans (third in the row) running with the power stride.

We have analyzed the running dynamics of Hans and Ron during the Dutch Championship for Masters in Zierikzee on the 13th and 14th of June 2015. The results are summarized in the table.

Running Dynamics of Hans and Ron at the NC Masters 2015 in Zierikzee					
	Hans	Hans	Ron	Ron	
Distance	5,000	10,000	5,000	10,000	m
Time	18:05	38:42	22:04	46:09	min:sec
Speed	16.6	15.5	13.6	13.0	km/h
Stride length	1.47	1.39	1.27	1.24	m
Cadence	188	186	180	174	spm
GCT	198	198	256	259	msec
Oscillation	9.4	9.2	7.1	7.3	cm

Ron with the shuffle at the Dutch Masters Championship in Zierikzee.

The differences between Hans and Ron are striking. As an example we take the 5,000 meter. The power stride of Hans results in a longer strides (1.47 meters vs 1.27 meters for Ron), a higher cadence (188 vs 180 spm), a lower GCT (198 msec vs 256 msec) and a higher oscillation (9.4 centimeters vs 7.1 centimeters). The final result is that Hans attained a higher speed and a better race time. But how can we relate this final result to the running dynamics? What is the impact of the various parameters and what is the optimal value for each parameter?

Which Running Style Is the Fastest?

Obviously, the first question that interests us is how we can run as fast as possible. The running speed follows directly from the stride length and the cadence, according to the following formula:

Speed (in km/h) = stride length (in m)*cadence (in spm)*60/1000

As an example, we use a stride length of 1.20 meters and a cadence of 180 spm, so the speed is 1.20*180*60/1000 = 12.96 km/h. The formula shows clearly the importance of stride length to your speed. Of course, in theory the cadence is equally important. In practice however, the cadence of most runners is near 180 spm, and it is not so easy to increase this by a significant amount. Consequently, elite runners always make very long strides. Mo Farah runs the 5,000 and 1,000 meter with giant strides of around 2.20 meters and a cadence of around 180 spm. His speed thus becomes 2.20*180*60/1000 = 23.8 km/h (60.6 seconds laps). During his phenomenal finishing kick, he manages to increase his cadence to 200 spm, while maintaining his stride length. This increases his speed to 26.2 km/h (final lap in 54 seconds). Another impressive example is that of Ethiopian Kenenisa Bekele, who ran the marathon of Paris with an average stride length of 1.85 meters and an average cadence of 182 spm (his race time was 2:05:03, so his speed was 20.2 km/h). The figure and table give the speed as a function of stride length and cadence. They show clearly that it is vital to increase your stride length if you want to run fast. This is a strong argument in favor of the power stride as this enables longer strides. Consequently, elite runners always use the power stride, even at the marathon.

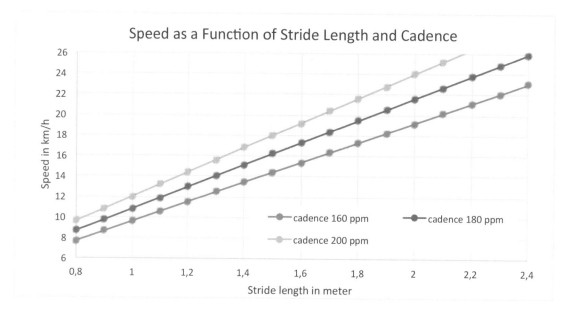

How to Increase Your Stride Length?

Obviously, your stride length depends on your running style: do you use the shuffle or the power stride? As the power stride requires more effort, most runners switch automatically to the shuffle during long runs, like the marathon. At shorter distances, particularly on the track, many runners will use the power stride to increase their stride length and their speed. Of course, your stride length will also depend on your leg length, the strength of your leg muscles and the takeoff push. Try to drive the takeoff forward and limit the vertical takeoff. Support the forward movement with your arms and lean somewhat forward.

Analyze Your Running Dynamics

Nowadays, our running watch or mobile phone can give us the data on our running dynamics. After your training session or race, you can analyze the data on your computer or use web applications such as Garmin Connect for this purpose. Of course, the authors Hans and Ron have done this. Some interesting results are given in the figures below:

Speed as a Function of Stride Length and Cadence			
Cadence:	160 ppm	180 ppm	200 ppm
Stride length	Speed	Speed	Speed
(m)	(km/h)	(km/h)	(km/h)
0.80	7.7	8.6	9.6
0.90	8.6	9.7	10.8
1.00	9.6	10.8	12.0
1.10	10.6	11.9	13.2
1.20	11.5	13.0	14.4
1.30	12.5	14.0	15.6
1.40	13.4	15.1	16.8
1.50	14.4	16.2	18.0
1.60	15.4	17.3	19.2
1.70	16.3	18.4	20.4
1.80	17.3	19.4	21.6
1.90	18.2	20.5	22.8
2.00	19.2	21.6	24.0
2.10	20.2	22.7	25.2
2.20	21.1	23.8	26.4
2.30	22.1	24.8	27.6
2.40	23.0	25.9	28.8

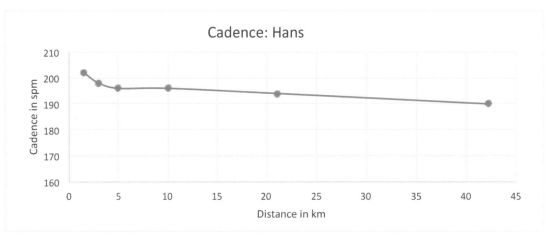

The figures lead to the following conclusions:

1. The stride length depends strongly on the distance. For Hans the stride length is 1.58 meters at the 1,500 meter, but only 1.22 meters at the marathon!

2. The cadence depends much less on the distance. For Hans the cadence at the 1,500 meter is 202 spm and still 190 spm at the marathon.

3. The speed is determined mainly by the stride length. At the 1,500 meter Hans is able to run with much longer strides and thus at a much higher speed compared to the marathon.

4. We have not shown the results of Ron, but they are similar. The main differences are that he has a lower cadence, a shorter stride and a larger GCT. Consequently, his speed is significantly lower. At first we were surprised to find that his stride length is smaller, as Ron is taller than Hans (1.91 meters vs 1.76 meters). Apparently, his forward takeoff is insufficient. This will certainly be influenced by his running style, as Ron uses the shuffle, even during short distance track races.

Train Your Cadence and Your Stride Length!

So far, we conclude that it is important to try to increase both your cadence and stride length, as the product of these parameters determines your speed. The former is relatively easy to achieve: anybody can train his cadence using a metronome or otherwise. Make sure that you increase your cadence to at least 180 spm! Training to increase your stride length is more difficult. This requires sufficient strength in your leg muscles and attention to your running style. Try to run with the power stride, use the arm swing to support the forward movement and lean slightly forward. Start with short training sessions to prevent injuries. Try to develop your strength by means of hill training. Run track races regularly, as this will develop your stride length and running technique.

Which Running Style Is the Most Economical?

This is not so easily said. At first sight, you might think that Ron with his shuffle uses less energy for the vertical oscillation, so his running economy might be higher. This reasoning is in line with the fact that many runners automatically use the shuffle during long endurance runs at an easy pace. On the other hand, many runners switch automatically to the power stride during track races at higher speed. However, there is much more to be said on this topic. Therefore, in the next two chapters, we will study the impact of the running dynamics on the energy cost of running and the running economy.

38. RUNNING DYNAMICS II: STRIDE LENGTH AND CADENCE

We may train or peak for a certain race, but running is a lifetime sport. —Alberto Salazar

In the previous chapter, we saw that nowadays our running watches and smart phones enable us to measure the four parameters, that together are called the running dynamics:

» The stride length (in meters)
» The stride rate or cadence (the number of strides per minute or spm)
» The ground contact time or GCT (in milliseconds)
» The vertical movement of oscillation of your upper body (in centimeters)

Also we learned that it is important to run with long strides and at a high cadence as the product of both determines your speed, according to the formula:

Speed (in km/h) = stride length (in m)*cadence (in spm)*60/1000

But what is the exact impact of these four parameters? Are they interconnected? And more importantly, what values of the four parameters are the best? And what is the best, fastest speed or the best running economy?

To answer these questions, we will investigate the running motion more fundamentally. First, we will make a distinction between the stance phase (during which your foot is in contact with the ground) and the flight phase (during which both feet are off the ground). The stance phase is sometimes also called the support phase to accentuate the fact that one foot is on the ground continuously during this phase. A stride consists of the stance phase and the flight phase combined, so the stride length is equal to the step length plus the flight length. During race walking, one foot must be in contact with the ground at all times, so there is no flight phase. This means that the stride length is equal to the step length.

The Stance Phase and the Step Length

During the stance phase, your foot is in contact with the ground continuously. However, the center of gravity of your body moves with the speed v, so during the GCT the center of gravity of your body moves forward with a distance GCT*v. We call this the step length:

d_{step} (in meter) = GCT (in msec)*v (in km/h)/3600

The stance phase begins at the moment of touchdown and ends at the moment of takeoff. As your foot is continuously in contact with the ground, your leg and hip move like a pendulum around the ground contact point. At the center of this pendulum, your body is exactly erect and vertical. During touchdown and takeoff, your hip bends somewhat, so we have an negative vertical oscillation. We can describe the pendulum movement of your leg with the following formulas:

$d_{step} = 2*L*sin\Phi$

$osci = L*(1-cos(\Phi))$

In these formulas L is the leg length, which is on average 50% of your body length. As an example, we use someone who is 1.80 meters tall and has a hip angle (Φ) of 25°, so his step length will be 2*0.5*1.80*sin(25°) = 0.76 meter and his oscillation will be 0.5*1.80*(1-cos(25°))/100 = 0.08 meter or 8 centimeters. The figure below gives the step length as a function of the body length and the hip angle. We clearly see that both body length and hip angle influence step length. Tall people make bigger steps and older people (with stiff hips) make smaller steps. Therefore, we can conclude that it makes sense to maintain the hip flexibility by means of regular exercises and core stability training.

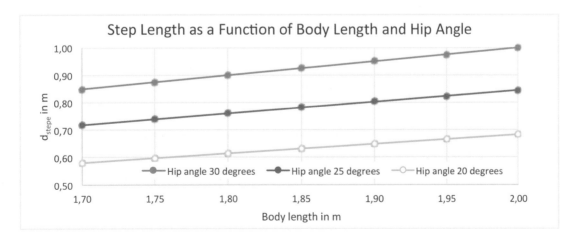

The GCT in Relation to the Step Length

Before we start analyzing the important flight phase, we will first look at the relationship between GCT and d_{step}. This can be described by the inverse of the earlier formula:

GCT (in msec) = d_{step} (in m)/v (in km/h)*3600

As an example, we use a very reasonable step length of 0.8 meter and a speed of 12 km/h, so the GCT becomes 0.8/12*(3600) = 240 msec. Therefore, we can conclude that the recommendation by Garmin that your GCT should be lower than 208 msec, actually means that your speed should be higher than (3600*0.8)/208 = 13.8 km/h! This has very little to do with your running form!

The figure below gives the relationship between GCT, step length and speed.

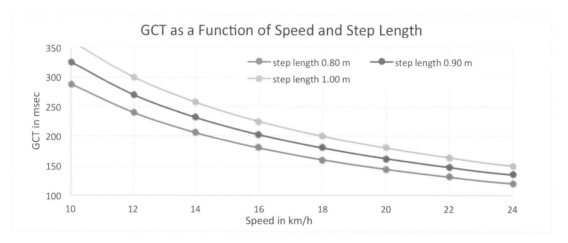

The figure clearly illustrates that your GCT is mainly determined by your speed. This relationship is very strong, in particular as the step length for most runners is around 0.80 meter.

The Flight Phase

The flight phase is the most important part of the running motion, as it increases the step length by the flight length. Consequently, your stride length becomes much larger and so does your speed, as the speed depends linearly on the stride length which of course is the sum of the step length and the flight length.

During the flight phase, your body follows a parabolic trajectory. At takeoff, a small part of your horizontal speed is transferred into a vertical motion. Consequently, during the first half of the flight phase, you move in the upward direction and your oscillation increases. During the second half of the flight phase, your body falls down from the maximum height as a result of gravity. We can describe the flight phase exactly with the formulas of a parabolic trajectory.

The Flight Time

It is convenient to start the analysis with the flight time. This can be calculated easily from the GCT and cadence:

t_{flight} (in msec) = (60/cadence (in spm)- GCT (in msec)/1000)*1000

Earlier we saw that the GCT itself is equal to d_{step}/v*3600. As an example, we use again a step length of 0.8 m and a speed of 12 km/h. Thus, the GCT is 0.8/12*3600 = 240 msec. With a cadence of 160 spm, the flight time then becomes (60/160-240/1000)*1000 = 135 msec.

The relationship between the flight time, the cadence and the speed are given in the figure.

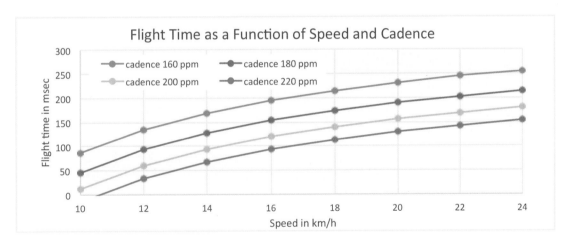

From the formula and figure, we can conclude that the flight time:

» Increases with speed
» Decreases with cadence

Both relationships are logical. In order to achieve a higher speed, you need to increase your stride length and thus your flight length and flight time. When you increase your cadence, your foot contacts the ground more often, so your flight time decreases.

The Flight Length

Once we know the flight time, we can calculate the flight length easily. During the flight phase, our body moves a distance that is equal to the product of flight time and speed:

$$d_{flight} \text{ (in m)} = t_{flight} \text{ (in msec)} * v \text{ (in km/h)}/(3600)$$

As an example, we use again our runner with a step length of 0.8 meter and a speed of 12 km/h. Earlier, we saw that with a cadence of 160 spm, his flight time is 135 msec. This means that his flight length becomes 135*12/(3600) = 0.45 meter. Therefore, his stride length is 0.80+0.45 = 1.25 meters. The relationship between flight length, cadence and speed is given in the figure below.

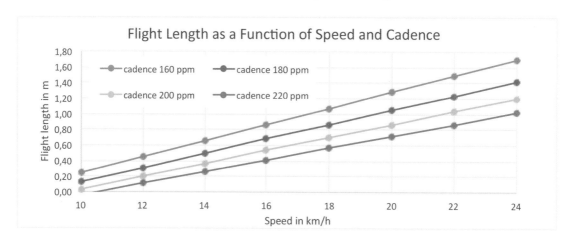

From the formula and figure, we can conclude that the flight length and consequently the stride length, which is equal to the sum of the flight length and the step length:

» Increases with speed
» Decreases with cadence

Both relationships are logical. In order to achieve a higher speed, you need to increase your stride length and thus your flight length. When you increase your cadence, your foot contacts the ground more often, so your flight time and flight length decrease.

The Relationship Between the Running Dynamics in Numbers

All in all many factors influence each other in the running dynamics. To clarify this further, we have prepared the four tables below for four different values of the cadence (i.e., 160, 180, 200 and 220 spm). We did this because the cadence is the factor that you can purposely change rather easily.

As an example, we use the same runner again. In the base case, he runs at 12 km/h with a cadence of 160 spm. If he increased his cadence to 180 spm, while maintaining his speed, the numbers of his running dynamics would change as follows:

» His GCT would remain at 240 msec (the GCT depends only on d_{step} and v).

» His t_{flight} would decrease from 135 to 93 msec.

» His d_{flight} would decrease from 0.45 to 0.31 meter.

» His d_{stride} would drop from 1.25 to 1.11 meter.

This may occur at the end of a race, when our runner no longer has the strength to maintain his stride length. He could then maintain his speed by increasing his cadence. A more positive example would be if he manages to increase his cadence *and* his speed. If he could increase his speed to 16 km/h, the numbers of his running dynamics would change as follows:

» His GCT would now drop to 180 msec.

» His t_{flight} would now increase to 153 msec.

» His d_{flight} would increase to 0.68 meter.

» His dstride would increase to 1.48 meters.

In summary, the tables and figures show a clear picture that enables us to draw the following conclusions:

1. The GCT depends only on the speed and decreases linearly with speed.
2. The time of flight increases with speed and decreases with cadence.
3. The flight length and stride length increase linearly with speed and decrease with cadence.

Running Dynamics at Cadence 160 ppm and Step Length 0.80 m				
v	GCT	t_{flight}	d_{flight}	d_{stride}
(km/h)	(msec)	(msec)	(m)	(m)
10	288	87	0.24	1.04
12	240	135	0.45	1.25
14	206	169	0.66	1.46
16	180	195	0.87	1.67
18	160	215	1.08	1.88
20	144	231	1.28	2.08
22	131	244	1.49	2.29
24	120	255	1.70	2.50

Running Dynamics at Cadence 180 ppm and Step Length 0.80 m				
v	GCT	t_{flight}	d_{flight}	d_{stride}
(km/h)	(msec)	(msec)	(m)	(m)
10	288	45	0.13	0.93
12	240	93	0.31	1.11
14	206	128	0.50	1.30
16	180	153	0.68	1.48
18	160	173	0.87	1.67
20	144	189	1.05	1.85
22	131	202	1.24	2.04
24	120	213	1.42	2.22

The last conclusion is vital. As your speed is determined by the product of stride length and cadence, it means that in theory it does not matter which one you increase, your stride length or your cadence. In practice some runners prefer to increase their stride length, whereas others prefer to increase their cadence. However, it is impractical to increase the cadence to very high numbers, 220 spm is already extreme. This means that elite runners have to run with very long strides in order to achieve a very high speed. Also, large differences exist between runners. As an example, author Ron has tried to switch from his natural shuffle to the power stride to try to increase his stride length and speed, but he still struggles with this.

Running Dynamics at Cadence 200 ppm and Step Length 0.80 m				
v	GCT	t_{flight}	d_{flight}	d_{stride}
(km/h)	(msec)	(msec)	(m)	(m)
10	288	12	0.03	0.83
12	240	60	0.20	1.00
14	206	94	0.37	1.17
16	180	120	0.53	1.33
18	160	140	0.70	1.50
20	144	156	0.87	1.67
22	131	169	1.03	1.83
24	120	180	1.20	2.00

Running Dynamics at Cadence 220 ppm and Step Length 0.80 m				
v	GCT	t_{flight}	d_{flight}	d_{stride}
(km/h)	(msec)	(msec)	(m)	(m)
10	288	-15	-0.04	0.76
12	240	33	0.11	0.91
14	206	67	0.26	1.06
16	180	93	0.41	1.21
18	160	113	0.56	1.36
20	144	129	0.72	1.52
22	131	142	0.87	1.67
24	120	153	1.02	1.82

So far, we have looked mainly at the impact of running dynamics on speed. But how about the energy cost of running? At which numbers of your running dynamics do you use the least amount for energy? Can you improve your running economy by optimizing your running dynamics? This will be analyzed in the next chapter.

39. RUNNING DYNAMICS III: RUNNING ECONOMY

If you do what you've always done, you will get what you've always gotten!

In the previous chapters, we saw that nowadays our running watches and smart phones enable us to measure the four parameters that together are called the running dynamics:

» The stride length (in meters)
» The stride rate or cadence (the number of strides per minute or spm)
» The ground contact time or GCT (in millisecond)
» The vertical movement or oscillation of your upper body (in centimeters)

Also we learned that it is important to run with long strides and at a high cadence as the product of both determines your speed, according to the formula:

Speed (in km/h) = stride length (in m)*cadence (in spm)*60/1000

In the previous chapter, we learned that if you want to increase your speed you have the choice to either increase or your stride length. But which one is the best for your running economy?

To answer this question, we will look more fundamentally into the energy cost of running and in particular the energy cost of the flight phase. During the flight phase you move upward, so your oscillation increases. How much energy does this cost and what is the impact on your RE?

The Flight Altitude

In the previous chapter, we learned that the flight time can be determined from the GCT and the cadence:

t_{flight} (in msec) = (60/cadence (in spm)-GCT (in msec)/1000)*1000

Earlier we saw that the GCT itself is equal to d_{step}/v*3600. As an example, we use again a step length of 0.8 m and a speed of 12 km/h. Thus, the GCT is 0.8/12*3600 = 240 msec. With a cadence of 160 spm, the flight time then becomes (60/160-240/1000)*1000 = 135 msec.

During the flight phase, your body follows a parabolic trajectory. At takeoff, a small part of your horizontal speed is transferred into a vertical motion. Consequently, during the first half of the flight phase, you move in the upward direction and your oscillation increases. During the second half of the flight phase, your body falls down from the maximum altitude as a result of gravity. So we can determine the flight altitude easily from half of the flight time:

$$h_{flight} = 0.5*g*(t_{flight}/2)^2$$

We use the same example as before with a flight time of 135 msec. With the gravity constant (g) being 9.81 m/s^2, the flight altitude thus becomes $0.5*9.81*(135/2000)^2 = 0.022$ meter or 2.2 centimeters.

The relationship between flight time and flight altitude is given in the figure below.

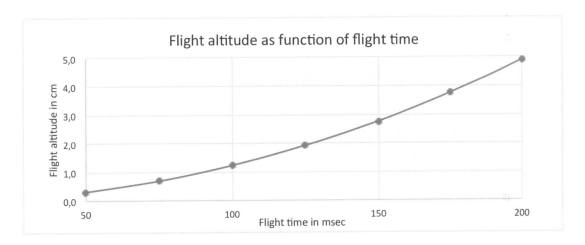

The formula and figure clearly show that the flight altitude increases with the flight time to the second degree. How much energy does this cost?

The Energy Cost of the Flight Phase

We have approached this topic analogous to the climbing resistance. In an earlier chapter, we saw that we can calculate the power required to overcome a difference in altitude with the formula:

$$P_c = (i/100)mgv$$

As an example, we used the climb to the top of the Alpe d'Huez with a gradient (i) of 7.4%. In order to run uphill with a speed (v) of 12.06 km/h, our Marathon Man with his body weight (m) of 70 kg, would thus use 7.4/100*70*9.81*12.06/3.6 = 170 watts. Also we learned from the research of Minetti et al. that in practice the required power is somewhat less, by a factor of (45.6+1.622i)/100. Minetti et al. explained the difference with theory by a somewhat higher muscle efficiency uphill.

We postulate that we can calculate the required power for the flight phase with the same formula, using an equivalent gradient (i):

$$i = h_{flight}/d_{flight}$$

As an example, we use again the flight altitude of 2.2 cm and the flight length of 0.45 meter; the equivalent gradient (i) thus becomes 0.022/0.45*100 = 5.0%. We should not confuse this gradient (i) with the vertical ratio, which is given by some running watches. This vertical ratio includes the stance phase. As the vertical oscillation during the stance phase is some 5 centimeters and the step length is 0.8 meter, the total vertical ratio of the stride would in the example be (0.022+0.050)/(0.45+0.80)*100 = 5.8%, so slightly different from the gradient (i).

From the required power we can finally calculate the specific energy cost of the vertical motion (in kJ/kg/km):

$$E_{vert} = P_c/mv = (i/100)*g*(45,6+1,266i)/100$$

We will compare this specific energy cost with the normal specific energy cost of running:

$$E_{hor} = c = P_r/mv$$

In the above example, E_{vert} is equal to 5.0/100*9.81*(45.6+1.266*5.0)/100 = 0.26 kJ/kg/km. When we compare this to the normal specific energy cost of running c = 0.98 kJ/kg/km, the ratio is 0.26/0.98*100 = 27%. So, it would seem that the energy cost of the flight phase is a substantial part of the total specific energy cost of running!

The Impact of Your Running Dynamics on the Energy Cost

All in all many factors influence each other in running dynamics. To clarify this further, we have prepared the four tables below for four different values of the cadence (i.e., 160, 180, 200 and 220 spm). We did this because the cadence is the factor that you can purposely change rather easily.

Ethiopia's Rio2016 10,000 meters Gold medalist Almaz Ayana demonstrates her flight fase.

As an example, we use the same runner again. In the base case, he runs at 12 km/h with a cadence of 160 spm. If he increased his cadence to 180 spm, while maintaining his speed, the numbers would change as follows:

» His flight altitude would drop from 2.23 centimeters to 1.07 centimeters.
» The equivalent gradient (i) of his flight phase would drop from 4.97% to 3.43%.
» The energy cost of the flight phase would drop from 0.26 kJ/kg/km to 0.17 kJ/kg/km. As a percentage of the total energy cost of running, it would decrease from 27% to 18%.

This case may occur at the end of a race, when our runner no longer has the strength to maintain his stride length. He could then maintain his speed by increasing his cadence, using less energy for the flight phase. A more positive example would be if he manages to increase his cadence *and* his speed. If he could increase his speed to 16 km/h, the numbers would change as follows:

» His flight altitude would increase to 2.88 centimeters.
» The equivalent gradient (i) would still drop to 4.23%.
» The energy cost of the flight phase would still drop to 0.22 kJ/kg/km. As a percentage of the total energy cost of running it would still drop to 22%.

Flight Altitude and Energy Cost at Cadence 160 spm				
v	h_{flight}	i	E_{vert}	E_{vert}/E_{hor}
(km/h)	(cm)	(%)	(kJ/kg/km)	(%)
10	0.93	3.84	0.20	20
12	2.23	4.97	0.26	27
14	3.51	5.34	0.28	29
16	4.66	5.38	0.29	29
18	5.67	5.27	0.28	29
20	6.54	5.10	0.27	27
22	7.31	4.90	0.26	26
24	7.97	4.69	0.24	25

Flight Altitude and Energy Cost at Cadence 180 spm				
v	h_{flight}	i	E_{vert}	E_{vert}/E_{hor}
(km/h)	(cm)	(%)	(kJ/kg/km)	(%)
10	0.25	2.00	0.10	10
12	1.07	3.43	0.17	18
14	2.00	4.02	0.21	21
16	2.88	4.23	0.22	22
18	3.68	4.25	0.22	22
20	4.40	4.18	0.21	22
22	5.02	4.06	0.21	21
24	5.58	3.92	0.20	20

Flight Altitude and Energy Cost at Cadence 200 spm				
v	h_{flight}	i	E_{vert}	E_{vert}/E_{hor}
(km/h)	(cm)	(%)	(kJ/kg/km)	(%)
10	0.02	0.53	0.02	2
12	0.44	2.21	0.11	11
14	1.09	2.97	0.15	15
16	1.77	3.31	0.17	17
18	2.40	3.43	0.17	18
20	2.98	3.44	0.17	18
22	3.51	3.39	0.17	17
24	3.97	3.31	0.17	17

Flight Altitude and Energy Cost at Cadence 220 spm				
v	h_{flight}	i	E_{vert}	E_{vert}/E_{hor}
(km/h)	(cm)	(%)	(kJ/kg/km)	(%)
10	0.03	-0.67	-0.03	-3
12	0.13	1.20	0.06	6
14	0.55	2.11	0.10	10
16	1.05	2.56	0.12	13
18	1.56	2.76	0.14	14
20	2.03	2.84	0.14	14
22	2.47	2.85	0.14	14
24	2.86	2.81	0.14	14

In summary, the tables and figures show a clear picture that enables us to draw the following conclusions:

1. The energy cost of the flight phase hardly increases at higher speeds! This is caused by the fact that the larger flight time is compensated by the larger flight length, so the equivalent gradient stays more or less the same.

2. The energy cost of the flight phase decreases with increasing cadence! This is caused by the fact that the flight altitude is reduced. Although the flight length also decreases somewhat, the equivalent gradient still becomes smaller.

The figures below confirm these findings. Consequently, it can be concluded that the energy cost can be reduced by running at a high cadence! This would therefore lead to a lower oxygen cost of running and a better running economy. However, we should remark that we did not yet include the required energy for the pendulum movement of the legs. This may influence the findings as at a higher cadence more energy will be required for this. On the other hand, we did also not yet include the energy recovery of the Achilles tendon and possibly the running shoes.

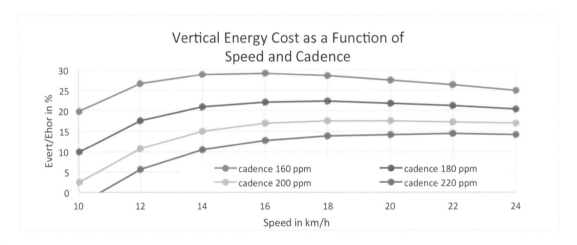

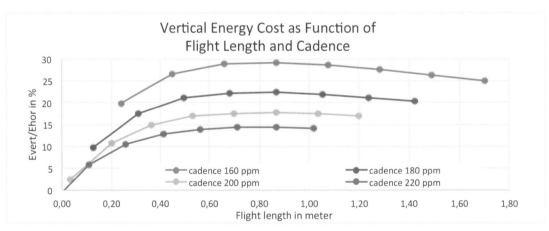

So How Should You Improve Your Running Dynamics?

It is clear that your speed is determined by the product of stride length and cadence. If you want to increase your speed, we can conclude that in theory it does not matter which one you increase, your stride length or your cadence. However, increasing your cadence reduces the energy cost of the flight phase, so this will have a positive impact on your running economy. Although we did neglect some aspects (the energy cost of the pendulum movement and the energy recovery in the Achilles tendon), this conclusion seems to corroborate the opinion of many runners and coaches who feel that an increase in cadence is vital. Also, increasing your cadence can be easily trained and the risk of injuries are low.

In practice most runners will want to increase both stride length and cadence to achieve the highest speed. Obviously, increasing your stride length is essential as increasing your cadence beyond 200 spm is not realistic (except during a short finishing kick). A runner with a natural cadence of 160 spm will find it hard to increase this to 180 spm, by some 10%. On the other hand, a runner with a natural stride length in training of one meter may manage to increase this to 1.50 meters during a middle distance race, by 50%.

Consequently, we conclude that increasing both your cadence and your stride length should be a goal of your training. Increasing your stride length is not easy in practice, as this requires leg strength and power. Unfortunately, it is not quite clear which training strategy is most effective for increasing your stride length. Various methods are being used for this, including hill training, interval training, strength training, plyometrics and track racing. Most likely all of these methods should be used and combined in a structured long-term training program. Finally, we warn our readers not to try to increase their stride length too fanatically, as this may lead to injuries.

Mo Farah celebrates after winning the men's 5,000 m final during the Beijing 2015 IAAF World Championships. He radically changed his running form after failing to qualify for the Beijing Olympics (2008).

40. THE IMPACT OF YOUR FATIGUE RESISTANCE

Pain is temporary, pride lasts forever!

On a number of occasions during a marathon, author Hans has been overtaken by other runners that he had beaten easily at shorter distances. How can we explain this? Is Hans less resistant to fatigue than other runners?

Fatigue resistance is a complicated phenomenon. It is influenced by factors such as body posture (small and slim runners have an advantage), physiology (using the fatty acid energy system is favorable), training (in particular the amount of long runs) and psychology (mental power to dig deep for a long time). In this chapter, we will analyze the impact of the fatigue resistance on your race times.

Riegel's Formula

Mathematically, we can simulate the fatigue resistance by the exponent in Riegel's formula:

$$v_2/v_1 = (d_2/d_1)^{-0.07}$$

As we saw earlier, for most people -0.07 is the correct exponent to be used in the formula. This is also valid for the speed–distance relationship of the world records of men and of women of all age classes. Nevertheless, the exponent is not necessarily the same for everybody and in all conditions. Some variations have been observed in practice. The results of sprinters and short-distance runners with a limited fatigue resistance can best be described by an exponent of -0.09. On the other hand, the results of ultra-runners with exceptional fatigue resistance can best be described by an exponent of -0.05. The figure and table below summarize the impact of the fatigue resistance on the results of the Marathon Man (normal means an exponent of -0.07, better is equivalent to -0.05 and less is equivalent to -0.09).

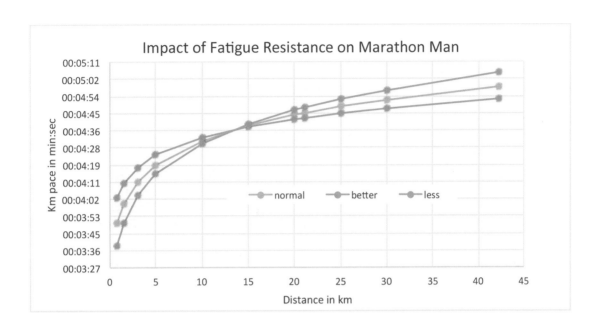

Impact of Fatigue Resistance			
Distance	Normal	Better	Less
(km)	(hrs:min:sec)	(hrs:min:sec)	(hrs:min:sec)
0.8	00:03:04	00:03:14	00:02:55
1.5	00:05:59	00:06:14	00:05:45
3	00:12:32	00:12:53	00:12:12
5	00:21:36	00:22:00	00:21:13
10	00:45:13	00:45:29	00:45:01
15	01:09:41	01:09:33	01:09:54
20	01:34:42	01:34:00	01:35:31
21.1	01:40:16	01:39:25	01:41:14
25	02:00:09	01:58:45	02:01:43
30	02:25:57	02:23:45	02:28:21
42.195	03:30:00	03:25:22	03:34:45

The figure and table show that the impact can be significant, particularly for the marathon. Runners with better fatigue resistance may gain 10 minutes or more in comparison to runners with less fatigue resistance. As the calculations were made for the same FTP (of 3.67 watts/kg), the results are the same for a one-hour period or 13.09 kilometers.

Faster at Short Distance or at Long Distance?

As all lines pass through the same point at 13.09 kilometers, we notice another phenomenon. Runners with a better fatigue resistance have an advantage at longer distances but a disadvantage at shorter distances. For runners with less fatigue resistance, the reverse is the case. This phenomenon is well-known from masters athletes, who usually gain strength in the long distance but lose their speed at short distances.

We conclude that differences in fatigue resistance can cause significant differences at the marathon. This is the reason for the disappointing experiences of author Hans at the marathon.

Just like Hans, our Marathon Man will try to improve his fatigue resistance by training. As he trains more, he will definitely improve as he will lose some body fat (very important as it decreases the energy cost for the marathon) and his fatty acid energy system will be stimulated. However, just like Hans, at some point he will also have to face his limitations. Fatigue resistance definitely can be improved by training, but not everyone has the fatigue resistance of an ultra-runner!

The 71 K Nepal Annapurna Ultratrail comprising 3,500 altitude meters presented no problems to Dutchman Jo Schoonbroodt. With an exponent of -0.05 Jo has the fatigue resistance of an ultra-runner.

41. THE IMPACT OF ALTITUDE TRAINING

Running has made me aware of my body and my responsibility to look after it. —Tim Noakes

This is one of the most debated aspects in the training program of elite athletes for the major championships. During a prolonged stay at altitude, the athlete's body adapts to the lower availability of oxygen in the thin mountain air. In practice, altitudes of between 2,500 and 4,000 meters are recommended for altitude training. Research has shown that at altitude the kidneys produce an increased amount of the hormone erythropoietin or EPO. This hormone stimulates the production of red blood cells. Consequently, the blood hemoglobin level and the oxygen transport capacity (VO_2 max) of the cardiovascular system increase. Upon return to sea level, the athlete will benefit for some time—about a month—from the increased oxygen transport capacity. His FTP will be slightly increased and accordingly his racing times will be somewhat better.

Altitude Training Regimes

The principle of altitude training has been known for many years, but many questions remain on the best regime and the results in practice. The most explicit opinion on the topic was voiced by Sir Roger Bannister (the first man to run a sub 4-minute mile). His answer to the question how one could best be adapted to altitude was: "There are two ways. Get born at altitude.... or train there for 25 years."

Often, the fact that Kenyans and Ethiopians live and train their entire lives at altitude is used to explain their dominance in long-distance running. For generations, their bodies have been adapted to the altitude, giving them an advantage at sea level.

Elite athletes living at sea level try to obtain a similar competitive edge by training at altitude for some weeks prior to the major championships. However, the results have not always been satisfactory. In part, this can be explained by the fact that it is difficult, if not impossible, to train at the same speed and intensity at altitude. During the first days at altitude, the athlete may even suffer from altitude disease. Also during the remaining time, the athlete will be forced to adapt his training program.

In practice, the following training regimes can be distinguished:

1. Live High, Train High (LHTH)

    This is the classic regime. Typically it involves a training block of 18 days at an altitude of 2,500 meters. As mentioned before, the results can be mixed and sometimes even not demonstrable. This may be attributed to the fact that the athlete will struggle to train as well as at sea level.

2. Live High, Train Low (LHTL)

    Nowadays, this is considered to be the best regime. Typically, it involves living for about one month at an altitude of 2,500-3,000 meters and training at an altitude of 1,250 meters. This will enable the athlete to maintain the same high-intensity training program as at sea level. Various studies have shown that an increase in the FTP of around 2.5% can be achieved in this way.

3. Artificial altitude in an altitude simulation tent or house

    These systems use equipment to reduce the oxygen level of the air from 21% to 15%, thus simulating the thin mountain air. In theory, this enables the athlete to carry out the LHTL regime, as he will sleep at artificial altitude and can carry out his training at sea level. In practice, the results are somewhat mixed. This may be caused by the fact that it is not easy to spend sufficient time in the altitude simulating tent or house.

How Big Is the Impact on Your Race Times?

As an example, we have calculated the impact of an increase of the FTP by 2.5%, which seems to be the most realistic number for an LHTL training regime. The results are shown in the table and figure below.

We see that altitude training may provide an interesting competitive edge. Our Marathon Man may gain five minutes at the marathon or one minute at a 10K race. Finally, we note that these results are not guaranteed. As discussed, the results may vary, depending on the training regime and the individual response of the athlete's body.

Impact of Altitude Training		
Distance	Base	Altitude training
(km)	(hrs:min:sec)	(hrs:min:sec)
0.8	00:03:04	00:03:00
1.5	00:05:59	00:05:51
3	00:12:32	00:12:15
5	00:21:37	00:21:06
10	00:45:15	00:44:11
15	01:09:43	01:08:04
20	01:34:46	01:32:30
21.1	01:40:20	01:37:57
25	02:00:13	01:57:22
30	02:26:02	02:22:33
42.195	03:30:00	03:25:07

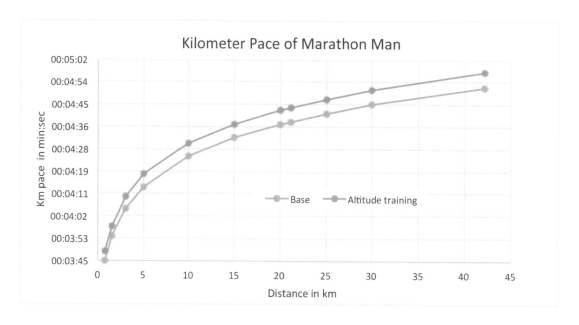

Runners from the Ethiopian rural town of Bekoji have won numerous Olympic gold medals and World championships. The training center of the Ethiopian Athletics Federation in this town of runners is situated at an altitude of 2,780 meters.

42. THE IMPACT OF THE RUNNING SURFACE

All great runners are humble, thoughtful and anxious to acquire new knowledge.

Most of us prefer to run our races on a fast course. Your race times will be fastest on a hard and flat surface, such as a concrete or asphalt road or a synthetic track. On these surfaces, your running feels smooth and the running resistance is minimal. For these surfaces, we can use the standard value for the specific energy cost c of 0.98 kJ/kg/km. But experienced runners also know that some bumpy parts with boulders can have a negative impact on your race time. This is even more so when the course contains many bends or when you have to cross through trails or sand. How big is the impact of the running surface on your race time? How much time do you lose when the conditions are not ideal?

Additional Running Resistance of Sand, Grass and Forest Trails

Several papers[57,58,59] have been published on the specific energy use of running on different surfaces. It was found that a forest trail may increase the energy use by some 3% or more. Crossing through sand requires up to 33% more energy than running on a hard and flat surface. These data do not surprise us, as we have experienced that it can be very tough to run trails or crosses.

Additional Energy Cost of Bends

This has not been a topic of research. Nevertheless, we can make an educated guess on the additional energy cost of bends and the impact on the race time. We estimate that both before and after a sharp bend we have to decrease our speed over 10 meters. Let's say our speed is reduced by 10% during these 2*10 = 20 meters. When we assume that a bendy course has one bend every 200 meters, we can calculate that the increase in race time as a result of the bends will be 20/200*10% = 1%. This is equivalent to an increase in the specific energy cost (c) of also 1%.

Impact on Race Time of a Non-Ideal Course

We have calculated the impact on the race time of the following cases:

1. Ideal course (asphalt road, synthetic track, c = 0.98 kJ/kg/km).
2. Bendy course or parts with boulders (c = 1% higher).
3. Forest trail (mix of cycle paths and grass, c = 3% higher).
4. Cross (mix of sand and grass, c = 6% higher).

Obviously, these cases are schematized and may differ from your course in practice. However, we do believe that they illustrate the possible impact. The results of the calculations for the Marathon Man are given in the table and figure below.

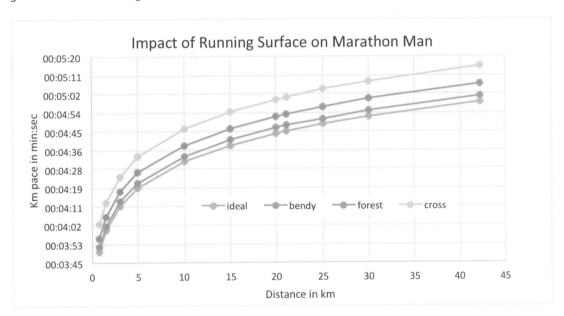

Impact of Running Surface on Marathon Man				
Distance	Ideal	Bendy	Forest	Cross
(km)	(hrs:min:sec)	(hrs:min:sec)	(hrs:min:sec)	(hrs:min:sec)
0.8	00:03:04	00:03:06	00:03:09	00:03:14
1.5	00:05:59	00:06:02	00:06:09	00:06:19
3	00:12:32	00:12:39	00:12:52	00:13:13
5	00:21:36	00:21:48	00:22:11	00:22:47
10	00:45:13	00:45:38	00:46:28	00:47:44
15	01:09:41	01:10:19	01:11:37	01:13:33
20	01:34:42	01:35:35	01:37:20	01:39:59
21.1	01:40:16	01:41:12	01:43:04	01:45:52
25	02:00:09	02:01:16	02:03:30	02:06:52
30	02:25:57	02:27:18	02:30:01	02:34:07
42.195	03:30:00	03:31:58	03:35:53	03:41:48

We see that in theory the impact of the running surface on the race times of the Marathon Man can be in the order of 1-2 minutes at the 10K and 2-10 minutes at the marathon. In practice, the differences will be somewhat less as most marathons are run on a proper running surface.

In summary, we can conclude the following:

1. At the marathon, the increase in race time due to a non-ideal course (containing parts with bends or boulders) will be around 2 minutes.
2. At crosses of 10K, the increase in race time may be up to 2.5 minutes.

Crossing through sand requires up to 33% more energy than running on a hard and flat surface.

43. THE IMPACT OF RACE SHOES

On the starting line, we are all cowards. —Alberto Salazar

Each year the producers of running shoes dazzle us with catalogues of new training and race models. The new models may incorporate technological developments such as new materials, which are lighter or have improved shock-absorbing capacities. Other features include improved energy recovery, extra cushioning or the even absence of these features as in minimalist shoes used in natural running. Often the producers state that their shoes will prevent injuries and improve your race time. As an example, Nike[60] claims that saving four ounces (113 grams) on the weight of your shoes will improve your marathon time by three minutes! For our Marathon Man this would be equivalent to a gain of 1.4%! For such an competitive edge, most runners surely won't mind paying the cost of a new pair of race shoes.

But are these claims valid? Is there any experimental proof for this? What research has been reported in the scientific literature? And what could we expect in theory, looking at the fundamental laws on the physics of running? In this chapter, we will try to answer these questions.

Literature Review

In the 1980s some authors have reported on experimental studies[61,62,63] from which they concluded that 100 grams of weight reduction in the shoes could lead to a gain of 1% in running speed. In those years, it was also claimed that the air sole of Nike would provide a gain of 1.6-2.8% in speed. However, more recently, it was shown[64] that these studies were not scientifically and statistically sound. In the past decade over 1,000 studies have been published in which the authors attempted to find the impact of such aspects as shoe weight, sole stiffness, shock absorbance, use of minimalist shoes and even running barefoot. Obviously, many of these studies were funded by producers of running shoes. In spite of the large number of studies, no paper has provided hard evidence of a positive impact on the speed or running economy. This could actually have been expected beforehand, as it is quite difficult to statistically prove a small impact in a comparative study.

Recently, a good systematical review of all the published papers on the impact of shoes has been made and reported by Fuller et. al[65]. They have evaluated and rejected many studies on the grounds of insufficient scientific quality (e.g., methodology, statistical analysis, peer review and verifiable data). They have concluded that the better studies have shown a small positive impact of shoes that provide more sole stiffness, shock absorbance and comfort. Also they saw a small advantage from lightweight race shoes and minimalist shoes as compared to the more heavy training shoes. They have derived a statistical relationship showing a gain of 0.25% per 100 grams of weight reduction. Finally, they concluded that below a weight of 220 grams per shoe no further gain can be achieved.

Lightweight race shoes may improve your race time by 0.25-0.50% per 100 grams of weight reduction.

How Big Is the Theoretical Gain From a Lighter Shoe?

Based on the laws of physics, we can analyze the potential gain of lightweight race shoes. Obviously, lightweight shoes will have a positive impact, as the total weight of your body plus shoes will be reduced (slightly). As the power of your human engine (in watts) remains constant, your specific power (in watts/kg) increases slightly. This will lead to a slight increase in the attainable speed. In principle, the gain is directly proportional to the reduction in total weight. As an example, let's compare regular training shoes of 300 grams each to lightweight race shoes of 200 grams each. For our Marathon Man of 70 kg, the reduction in weight is (2*0.1)/(70+0.6)*100 = 0.28%. As the gain is linearly proportional to the weight reduction, we can say that the gain is 0.14 % per 100 grams of weight reduction. This is much less than the claims of the shoes producers and even less than the findings of the review of Fuller et. al. Our example of 0.28% (two shoes each weighing 100 grams less) will give the Marathon Man a gain of 36 seconds on his race time of 3:30 at the marathon. We note that he could get the same gain by losing 200 gram of body fat!

But How About the Energy Cost of Moving Your Legs?

Of course, the above analysis is too simple. In practice, running with 100 fewer grams of weight at your feet will save more energy than the same weight reduction around your waist. This is caused by the fact that your feet make a pendulum motion (moving upward and downward). The energy cost of this pendulum motion is higher than the energy cost of the horizontal motion of the center of gravity of your body. This is one of the reasons for the high running economy (RE) of the Kenyan runners, who are famous for their slender and lightweight calves. Moreover, your shoes are located underneath your feet, so the lever to the knee and the hip is maximal. We can expect that the gain will be bigger than the above 0.14% per 100 grams, which was based merely on the total weight decrease.

How Big Is the Additional Gain as a Result of the Pendulum Motion of Your Feet?

We have calculated this using a theoretical model that was first published by Herman Pontzer[66]. He derived the following formula for the power required for the pendulum motion of the legs:

$$P = 2kfgmM_lD\varphi(1-f^2/f_0^2)$$

This rather complex formula contains several parameters, that describe the pendulum motion. These include the pendulum frequency (f, in s^{-1}, this is equal to the cadence/120), the resonance frequency (f_0) of the lower leg (this depends on the length of the leg and the lever), the hip angle (φ) and the ratio (M_l) of the weight of the leg as compared to the body weight.

We have first used the model to see how big the required power for the pendulum motion is as compared to the total power required for running. The results are given in the figure.

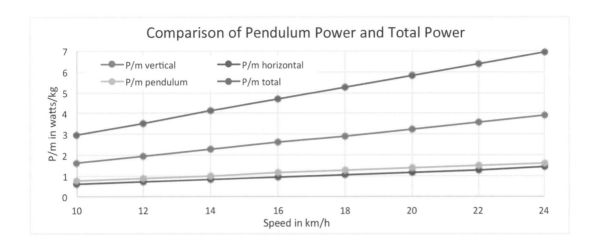

The figure shows that the required power for the pendulum motion is in the order of 25% of the total power required for running. This result seems realistic and the total power as calculated with Pontzer's model matches the results of our own model.

Next, we have calculated how much additional power is required when 100 grams of shoes are connected at the bottom of the feet (with the maximum lever). The results are given in the figure.

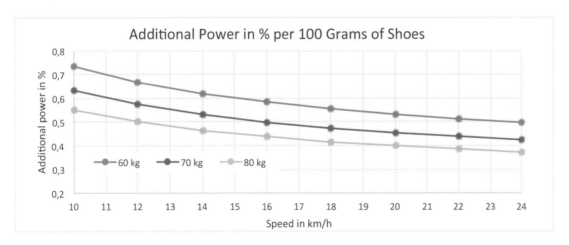

We see that the additional required power is in the order of 0.5% per 100 grams of shoes. This is significantly higher than the 0.14% that we calculated earlier, based merely on the total weight. It is even higher than the 0.25% that was found in the review by Fuller et. al.

So, we think we can conclude that the pendulum motion of the legs increases the gain that we may expect from lightweight race shoes. The gain also depends on the weight and the FTP of the runner, as the figure shows. This is logical, as the gain from 100 grams is bigger for a 60-kg runner than for a 80-kg runner. Also a runner with a higher FTP and consequently higher speed will be less affected. This confirms the result that we have found throughout this book: when the conditions get tougher, the differences between elite runners and normal runners increase.

But How About the Energy Recovery of the Shoes?

Producers of running shoes often mention that their shoe is designed to recover part of the energy at touchdown. From the literature of biomechanics[53] it is indeed known that a significant energy recovery (up to 50%) may occur in the Achilles tendon and the arch of the foot. So, it is not impossible that this percentage could be increased by shoe design. Obviously, an increased energy recovery would lead to a lower specific energy cost of running and thus to faster race times.

We have not been able to calculate the impact of this aspect, as concrete data on the energy recovery of shoes are lacking. However, we feel that the impact cannot be large as the review of Fuller et. al. found a total impact of just 0.25%, and this was mainly due to the weight effect.

Conclusions

All in all, we conclude that in practice the gain of using lightweight race shoes will be in the order of 0.25-0.50% per 100 grams of weight reduction. As a reduction of 200 grams is realistic (training shoes weigh 300 grams each, race shoes 200 grams each), this means that the total gain can be 0.5-1.0% or 1-2 minutes at the marathon for our Marathon Man. Many runners will be keen to get this additional edge!

However, we feel we should end this chapter with a cautionary note. The primary function of running shoes is to prevent injuries! Modern shoes can provide all the required shock absorbance, cushioning and comfort. We should be aware that our desire to reduce the weight does not compromise this primary function. Also, feeling good and comfortable in your shoes is an important aspect to many runners. Authors Hans and Ron do use lightweight race shoes in the majority of their races, but in the marathon they cautiously wear their training shoes to limit the risk of injuries.

Haile Gebrselassie and Patrick Makau from Kenia make fun with light weight running shoes during the press conference of the 2011 Berlin Marathon.

44. THE IMPACT OF (NO) AIR RESISTANCE

I love the feeling of freedom in running, the fresh air, the feeling that the only person I'm competing against is me.
—Wilma Rudolph

The treadmill test is often regarded as the holy grail of physiological research. With this test, you can have your VO_2 max determined at a sports medical advice center. You will run on a treadmill with a breathing cap, so your oxygen uptake from the air can be calculated. In practice, you will start with a low velocity (e.g., 10 km/h), and thus at a low VO_2. Every three minutes the speed of the treadmill is increased (e.g., by 1 km/h), until you cannot go any faster. During the test your VO_2 will increase until it reaches a maximum value, the VO_2 max. The authors of this book have taken such tests regularly in the past years. The picture shows author Hans, the treadmill and the breathing measuring equipment.

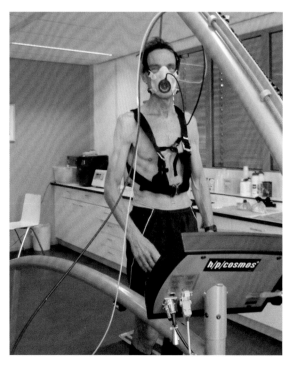

Author Hans at the treadmill with breathing measuring equipment.

What Does the Result of the Test Tell You?

The test will give you a good indication of how fit you are. As an example, we mention that author Hans took the test in November 2011 (when his weight was 68.5 kg) and again in November 2012 (when his weight had dropped to 57.5 kg). The impact of his weight loss on his fitness was impressive, as can be seen in the figure. His VO_2 max increased from 51 ml O_2/kg/min in 2011 to 60 ml O_2/kg/min in 2012! These numbers are equivalent to an FTP of resp. 3.7 and 4.3 watts/kg.

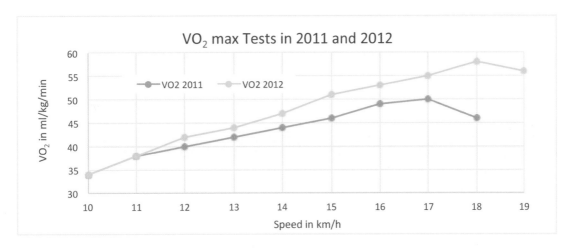

But Does It Tell You How Fast You Can Run?

The treadmill test is a good method to determine the VO_2 max as it is measured while you run. Therefore, it is more suitable than a bicycle ergometer test (which is less specific to running) and the other methods we described in an earlier chapter. Nevertheless, the treadmill test has one inherent and serious drawback: on a treadmill you run without any air resistance! In practice, we always have to deal with air resistance! Even in windless conditions, we face a head wind which is equal to our own running speed. This own wind creates an air resistance that we have to overcome. This means that we have to use part of the power of our human engine for this. Consequently, less power is available for the running resistance, so our speed is reduced.

How Big Is the Air Resistance of Your Own Wind?

We have calculated the air resistance of your own wind with the formula:

$P_a = 0.5\rho c_d A v^3$

For the standard conditions (ρ = 1.226 kg/m³, $c_d A$ = 0.24 m²), the results are given in the figure below.

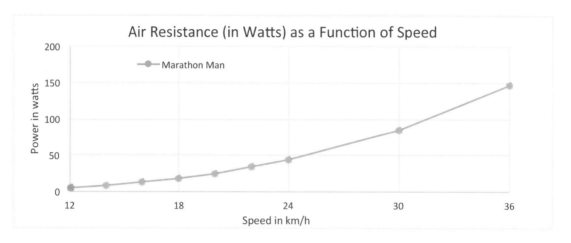

We see that the air resistance of your own wind cannot be neglected, particularly at a higher speed.

The share of the air resistance in the total power required increases from less than 2% at 10 km/h to more than 9% at 22 km/h, as shown in the figure below!

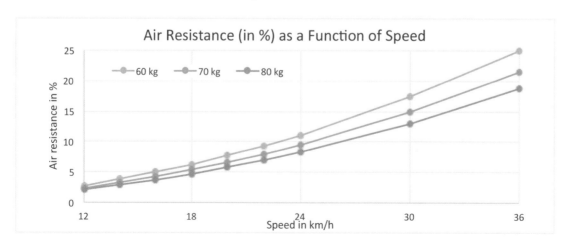

What Is the Impact of (No) Air Resistance on Your Speed?

On a treadmill you do not move, so there is no own wind. This means that your air resistance is zero, so your power can be used to overcome the running resistance. Consequently, depending on your FTP and speed, you can run 2-9% faster on a treadmill than in the real world (both outdoors and indoors). We have calculated how fast you could run on a treadmill as a function of your FTP. For these calculations, we reduced the air resistance (c_dA) from the standard value of 0.24 m² to a negligible value of 0.01 m². The results are given in the table.

When we compare the table without air resistance to the one that includes the standard air resistance, we see that the impact is very significant, particularly for the world-class elites.

We see that world-class athletes could theoretically run the marathon well within two hours on a treadmill! Of course, this would be a very dull marathon and we hope they don't stumble and fall off the treadmill. In practice, many runners struggle somewhat with running on the treadmill. Apparently, our brains are programmed for the forward motion, so stationary running is difficult. To illustrate the impact of running with and without air resistance, we have prepared the following figure showing the pace for world-class athletes. As they always run with pacemakers, we have used a c_dA value of 0.20 m² for the base case.

For our Marathon Man the impact of the air resistance is much smaller, as his speed is lower. Still, he could gain six minutes on his marathon race time, as shown below.

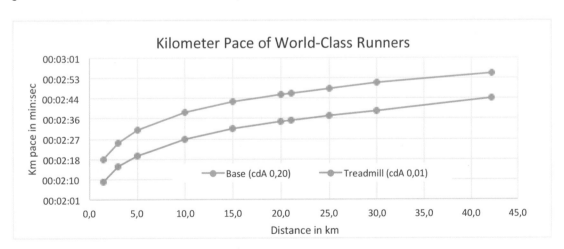

FTP, Speed and Race Time Without Air Resistance ($c_dA = 0.01$ m²)					
FTP	Attainable race time				
(watts/kg)	1,500 m	3,000 m	5,000 m	10,000 m	15 km
2.00	00:10:58	00:23:02	00:39:47	01:23:32	02:08:54
2.25	00:09:41	00:20:20	00:35:07	01:13:43	01:53:45
2.50	00:08:39	00:18:09	00:31:21	01:05:50	01:41:35
2.75	00:07:49	00:16:24	00:28:20	00:59:29	01:31:48
3.00	00:07:07	00:14:56	00:25:48	00:54:11	01:23:37
3.25	00:06:32	00:13:43	00:23:42	00:49:46	01:16:48
3.50	00:06:02	00:12:40	00:21:53	00:45:57	01:10:55
3.75	00:05:37	00:11:47	00:20:21	00:42:42	01:05:54
4.00	00:05:14	00:11:00	00:19:00	00:39:53	01:01:32
4.25	00:04:54	00:10:18	00:17:48	00:37:22	00:57:39
4.50	00:04:37	00:09:42	00:16:45	00:35:09	00:54:15
4.75	00:04:22	00:09:09	00:15:49	00:33:12	00:51:13
5.00	00:04:08	00:08:40	00:14:58	00:31:26	00:48:30
5.25	00:03:55	00:08:14	00:14:13	00:29:50	00:46:03
5.50	00:03:44	00:07:50	00:13:32	00:28:24	00:43:49
5.75	00:03:33	00:07:28	00:12:54	00:27:05	00:41:48
6.00	00:03:24	00:07:08	00:12:20	00:25:54	00:39:58
6.25	00:03:15	00:06:50	00:11:49	00:24:48	00:38:16
6.50	00:03:07	00:06:33	00:11:20	00:23:47	00:36:42

20 km	21.1 km	25 km	30 km	42,195 km
02:55:22	03:05:43	03:42:40	04:30:38	06:29:50
02:34:45	02:43:53	03:16:29	03:58:49	05:44:01
02:18:12	02:26:21	02:55:28	03:33:16	05:07:13
02:04:54	02:12:16	02:38:35	03:12:44	04:37:38
01:53:45	02:00:28	02:24:26	02:55:33	04:12:52
01:44:29	01:50:38	02:12:39	02:41:14	03:52:15
01:36:29	01:42:10	02:02:30	02:28:53	03:34:29
01:29:40	01:34:57	01:53:51	02:18:22	03:19:19
01:23:43	01:28:39	01:46:18	02:09:11	03:06:06
01:18:26	01:23:04	01:39:35	02:01:02	02:54:21
01:13:49	01:18:10	01:33:43	01:53:54	02:44:04
01:09:41	01:13:48	01:28:29	01:47:32	02:34:54
01:05:59	01:09:52	01:23:47	01:41:49	02:26:41
01:02:39	01:06:20	01:19:32	01:36:40	02:19:15
00:59:37	01:03:08	01:15:42	01:32:00	02:12:32
00:56:52	01:00:13	01:12:12	01:27:45	02:06:24
00:54:22	00:57:34	01:09:02	01:23:54	02:00:51
00:52:03	00:55:07	01:06:05	01:20:20	01:55:43
00:49:55	00:52:52	01:03:23	01:17:02	01:50:58

FTP, Speed and Race Time With Air Resistance ($c_dA = 0.24$ m^2)					
FTP	Attainable race time				
(watts/kg)	1,500 m	3,000 m	5,000 m	10,000 m	15 km
2.00	00:11:05	00:23:16	00:40:12	01:24:24	02:10:14
2.25	00:09:49	00:20:36	00:35:34	01:14:41	01:55:15
2.50	00:08:47	00:18:27	00:31:53	01:06:55	01:43:16
2.75	00:07:58	00:16:43	00:28:53	01:00:39	01:33:36
3.00	00:07:15	00:15:14	00:26:19	00:55:15	01:25:16
3.25	00:06:43	00:14:05	00:24:20	00:51:06	01:18:51
3.50	00:06:13	00:13:04	00:22:34	00:47:23	01:13:07
3.75	00:05:48	00:12:12	00:21:04	00:44:13	01:08:14
4.00	00:05:27	00:11:26	00:19:45	00:41:27	01:03:58
4.25	00:05:08	00:10:46	00:18:35	00:39:01	01:00:13
4.50	00:04:51	00:10:10	00:17:34	00:36:53	00:56:55
4.75	00:04:36	00:09:39	00:16:40	00:34:58	00:53:58
5.00	00:04:22	00:09:11	00:15:52	00:33:18	00:51:23
5.25	00:04:10	00:08:46	00:15:08	00:31:46	00:49:01
5.50	00:04:00	00:08:23	00:14:29	00:30:24	00:46:54
5.75	00:03:50	00:08:02	00:13:53	00:29:08	00:44:58
6.00	00:03:41	00:07:43	00:13:20	00:28:01	00:43:13
6.25	00:03:32	00:07:26	00:12:51	00:26:58	00:41:36
6.50	00:03:25	00:07:10	00:12:23	00:26:01	00:40:08

20 km	21.1 km	25 km	30 km	42,195 km
02:57:11	03:07:38	03:44:58	04:33:25	06:33:51
02:36:47	02:46:02	03:19:04	04:01:57	05:48:32
02:20:30	02:28:47	02:58:23	03:36:49	05:12:19
02:07:20	02:14:50	02:41:40	03:16:29	04:43:03
01:56:01	02:02:51	02:27:18	02:59:01	04:17:53
01:47:16	01:53:36	02:16:12	02:45:32	03:58:27
01:39:28	01:45:20	02:06:17	02:33:30	03:41:06
01:32:50	01:38:19	01:57:53	02:23:16	03:26:23
01:27:01	01:32:09	01:50:29	02:14:17	03:13:26
01:21:55	01:26:45	01:44:01	02:06:25	03:02:06
01:17:25	01:21:59	01:38:18	01:59:29	02:52:06
01:13:26	01:17:45	01:33:14	01:53:19	02:43:13
01:09:54	01:14:01	01:28:45	01:47:52	02:35:23
01:06:41	01:10:37	01:24:40	01:42:54	02:28:14
01:03:49	01:07:35	01:21:02	01:38:29	02:21:52
01:01:11	01:04:47	01:17:41	01:34:24	02:16:00
00:58:48	01:02:16	01:14:40	01:30:45	02:10:43
00:56:36	00:59:56	01:11:52	01:27:21	02:05:49
00:54:36	00:57:50	01:09:20	01:24:16	02:01:23

Impact of Air Resistance on Marathon Man		
Distance	With air resistance time	Without air resistance time
(km)	(hrs:min:sec)	(hrs:min:sec)
0.8	00:03:04	00:02:56
1.5	00:05:59	00:05:44
3	00:12:32	00:12:03
5	00:21:37	00:20:49
10	00:45:15	00:43:41
15	01:09:43	01:07:25
20	01:34:46	01:31:43
21.1	01:40:20	01:37:08
25	02:00:13	01:56:28
30	02:26:02	02:21:33
42.195	03:30:00	03:23:54

Worldwide the most marathon world records for men and women have been set in Berlin, known for its flat profile, even surface, and its mild autumn weather conditions. In 2016 the balance is 6 marathon world records for men and 3 for women.

45. HOW FAST COULD USAIN BOLT RUN THE 100 METER IN MEXICO?

Don't think about the start of the race, think about the ending. —Usain Bolt

Usain Bolt set his unparalleled 100-meter world record on the 16th of August 2009 at the IAAF World Championships in Berlin. He crossed the finish line in an awesome 9.58 seconds. Consequently, his average speed was 37.57 km/h! In an earlier chapter, we calculated that at this speed the air resistance amounts to more than 15% of the total power required. So, we thought it would be interesting to calculate how much faster Bolt could run if he could benefit from a lower air resistance by running at altitude in Mexico City.

Which Factors Determine the Air Resistance?

In an earlier chapter, we learned the formula that describes the air resistance:

$$P_a = 0,5 \rho c_d A(v+v_w)^2 v$$

Accordingly, the air resistance (P_a, in Watt) depends on the following factors:

1. The density of the air (ρ)

2. The air resistance coefficient ($c_d A$)

3. The wind speed (v_w)

Obviously, the attainable speed (v) becomes less at a higher air resistance (P_a). This can be understood as the total power your human engine (P) has to be divided over the running resistance (P_r) and the air resistance (P_a). In this chapter, we will look more closely into the three factors that determine the air resistance. What could Bolt do to reduce the air resistance and increase his speed?

The Density of the Air

At sea level, the density of the air (ρ, in kg/m³) is determined by the air pressure and the temperature, according to the ideal gas law:

$$\rho = (p*M)/(R*T)$$

In this formula, M is the molecular weight of the gas (for air this is 28.97 g/mole) and R is the molar gas constant (8,314 J/mole/°K). Consequently, at the standard temperature of 15°C (288°K) and the standard air pressure of 101,300 Pa, the air density is 101,300*28.97/8,314/288/1000 = 1.226 kg/m³. We have made our calculations using this value.

During a depression, the air pressure will be less than 101,300 Pa (1013 mbar), so Usain should be able to run faster. The reverse is the case during a high. We have calculated how big the impact of a low or a high could be on the race times of Bolt. We have assumed that Bolt set his world record at the standard air pressure of 1,013 mbar and made alternative calculations for a low of 963 mbar and a high of 1,053 mbar. The results are given in the table and show that, according to theory, Bolt could run 0.04 second faster during a depression.

Impact of air pressure	Time	Speed
(mbar)	(sec)	(km/h)
963	9.54	37.74
1013 (= WR)	9.58	37.57
1053	9.62	37.41

We have made similar calculations into the effect of the temperature. We assumed that Bolt set the world record at a temperature of 20°C and made alternative calculations for a low temperature of 10°C and a high temperature of 25°C. The results are given in the table and show that theoretically Bolt could gain 0.01 second at 25°C.

Impact of temperature	Time	Speed
(°C)	(sec)	(km/h)
25	9.57	37.62
20 (= WR)	9.58	37.57
10	9.62	37.43

We do note that these calculations are based solely on the impact of the temperature on the density of the air and the air resistance. We did not yet look into the impact of the temperature on the performance and power output of the human engine. This will be discussed in a later chapter.

How Big Is the Advantage of the Thin Air at Altitude?

At altitude, the air pressure reduces in accordance with the following formula:

$$p = p_0 e^{(-Mgh/RT)}$$

As an example, in Mexico City (altitude h = 2,250 meter), the air pressure becomes $101,300 * e^{(-28.97*9.81*2,250/1,000)/(8,314*288)}$ = 77,559 Pa or 76.6 % of the standard air pressure at sea level. The lower air pressure brings about an equivalent lower air density and an equivalent lower air resistance. We have calculated how fast Bolt could run at altitude, using these relationships. The results are given in the table below and show that theoretically at Mexico City he could finish in 9.36 seconds, so he would beat his current world record by 0.22 seconds.

Impact of altitude	Time	Speed
(meter)	(sec)	(km/h)
0 (= WR)	9.58	37.57
1000	9.48	37.97
2000	9.38	38.37
2250	9.36	38.46

We do note that these calculations are based solely on the impact of the altitude on the density of the air and the air resistance. We did not yet look into the impact of the altitude on the performance and power output of the human engine. For sprinters, this impact is small, as will be discussed in a later chapter. Also we have changed just one parameter at a time, so the calculation for Mexico City is valid for a temperature of 20°C. In Mexico it may often be warmer, which will enable Usain to run even a little faster than we calculated.

How Big Is the Impact of the Air Resistance Coefficient (c_dA)?

The air resistance is linearly proportional to this coeffcient, so theoretically it could have a big impact. However, in practice Bolt cannot do much to reduce this parameter. Shaving off body hair and optimizing running wear may save only a percent or so. In an earlier chapter, we concluded that the standard value for the c_dA of runners should be set at at 0.24 m². This value matches best with the experimental findings in literature. We could expect that the air resistance of a tall runner like Bolt will be somewhat higher than that of a smaller person. As only limited experimental data are available to verify the impact of body size, we have not yet included this aspect in our model.

We have shown in earlier chapters that drafting behind pacemakers can reduce the c_dA- value for elite runners to 0.20 m².

The ultimate reduction can be achieved on a treadmill, where the air resistance and thus the c_dA value is virtually zero. To illustrate the impact of the c_dA , we have calculated the impact of different values. The results are shown in the table and show that theoretically the impact is very big indeed! Of course, these calculations are not very relevant to the real world, as we cannot image the 100 meter being run on a treadmill or with pacemakers (quite apart from the fact that no pacemaker could keep up with Usain, of course)!

Impact of c_dA	Time	Speed
(m²)	(sec)	(km/h)
0.24 (= WR)	9.58	37.57
0.20	9.42	38.20
0.01	8.46	42.57

How Big Is the Impact of the Wind?

In practice, the impact of the wind is very important. This is the reason that records on the 100 and 200 meter are only recognized by the IAAF when the tailwind does not exceed 2 m/s. Bolt was already lucky to benefit from a tailwind of 0.9 m/s at Berlin, so we included this in our calculations. We made alternative calculations for the impact of the wind, up to a maximum tailwind of 2 m/s, and also of a head wind of -2 m/s. The results are given in the table below and show that Bolt could gain another 0.20 second with a tailwind of 2 m/s.

Impact of wind speed	Time	Speed
(m/s)	(sec)	(km/h)
2	9.38	38.38
0.9 (= WR)	9.58	37.57
0	9.77	36.85
-2	10.22	35.23

In summary, we conclude that the impact of air resistance on the speed and race time at the 100 meter is quite significant. The impact of temperature and air pressure is in the order of a few hundreds of a second, but the impact of wind and altitude is in the order of a few tenth of a second.

Finally, we have calculated the ultimate 100-meter world record: the race time of Bolt at Mexico City with a tailwind of 2 m/s and a temperature of 25°C. The result is that theoretically he could cross the 100-meter finish line in a phenomenal 9.18 seconds!

We end this chapter with the note that these calculations were all based on the equilibrium situation only ($P = P_r + P_a$). Consequently, we did not yet include the power required for the acceleration from the start. For the sprinting events, this is a significant aspect, as will be shown in another chapter.

Usain Bolt wins the 200-meter final ahead of Justin Gatlin at the Beijing 2015 IAAF World Championships.

46. THE IMPACT OF PACEMAKERS AND RUNNING IN A PACK

If you are losing faith in human nature, go out and watch a marathon. —Katherine Switzer

Nowadays, all big city marathons use pacemakers to assist the elite athletes in running fast times. The same applies to the major international track races, most of all when elite runners attempt to break world records. In all of these races, the pacemakers have the job of maintaining a steady and very high pace during the earlier part of the race. The elite athletes run in the wake of the pacemakers, so they are drafted and have to spend less energy overcoming the air resistance. Normal runners will not have the luxury of pacemakers, but they may find a similar advantage by running in a pack. In cycling, the advantage of drafting is so big that it is almost impossible for an individual cyclist to stay away from the pack at a flat course. In this chapter, we will investigate how big the impact is in running and what it could mean for your race times.

How Big Is the Air Resistance?

In the previous chapter, we saw the formula for the air resistance:

$$P_a = 0.5\rho c_d A(v+v_w)^2 v$$

At the standard conditions (15°C, 1013 mbar), ρ is equal to 1.226 kg/m^3. During windless conditions, v_w is 0 m/s. Earlier we learned that the standard value of $c_d A$ can be set at 0.24 m^2. Consequently, we can calculate the air resistance as a function of the running speed (v) as seen in the figure.

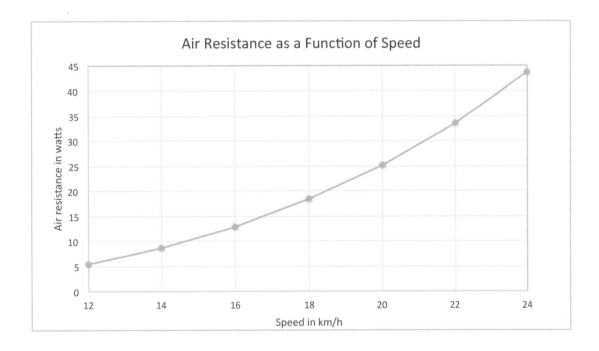

Our Marathon Man runs the marathon is 3:30, with a speed of 42.195/3.5 = 12.06 km/h. From the formula and the figure, we can see that the air resistance due to his own wind is 5.5 watts. This is a small, but not negligible, part of the total power of his human engine (which is 235 watts). In races over shorter distances, the share of the air resistance will be somewhat higher than at the marathon. This is caused by the fact that the speed increases as the distance decreases. The air resistance is determined by the speed to the 3rd exponent, so it increases substantially as the race distance decreases.

How Much Benefit Can Marathon Man Get From Running in a Pack?

As we saw earlier, the elite runners run in the wake of pacemakers. This reduces their c_dA value to 0.20 m^2. Therefore, the air resistance due to their own wind is reduced by 20% and they can run faster. Marathon Man can try to achieve the same reduction in his c_dA value by shielding behing other runners in a pack. We have calculated how much he could gain from this tactic in the various classic distances. The results are shown in the figure and table. For comparison purposes, we have also indicated the results that he could obtain on a treadmill with no air resistance at all.

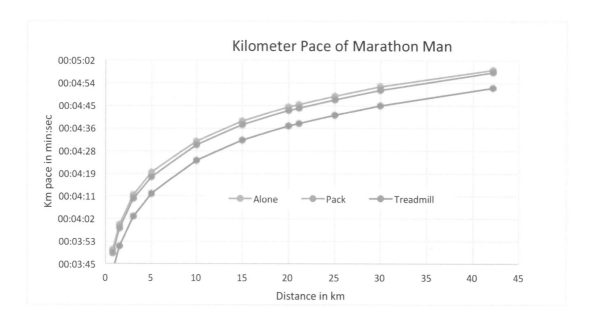

Benefit of Drafting for Marathon Man		
Distance	Alone	Pack
(km)	(hrs:min:sec)	(hrs:min:sec)
0.8	00:03:04	00:03:03
1.5	00:05:59	00:05:57
3	00:12:32	00:12:28
5	00:21:37	00:21:30
10	00:45:15	00:45:01
15	01:09:43	01:09:23
20	01:34:46	01:34:19
21.1	01:40:20	01:39:51
25	02:00:13	01:59:40
30	02:26:02	02:25:22
42.195	03:30:00	03:29:13

The table shows that Marathon Man could shave almost one minute off his marathon time if he uses the tactic of running in the pack. This is a very wise tactic, not just for himself but also for the other members of the pack. Research has shown that even the front runner of a pack faces a slightly lower air resistance as compared to running alone. This can be understood by the fact that the other runners in the pack push the air forward slightly by their own wind. All in all, everybody wins in the pack, so you should try to stay there! Of course, some runners may feel strong in the early part of the race and may be tempted to pass the pack. Remember that this will cost additional energy, so you may regret it in the later stages!

The Ethiopian 10,000 meter women's Olympic selection trials for the 2016 Rio Olympic Games in Hengelo (the Netherlands) with pacers at the front. The later Olympic champion Almaz Ayana (third from the left) won the selection trial in 30:07.00. In the Rio 2016 Olympics she ran a new 10,000 meters world record in 29:17.45.

How Much Do World-Class Runners Benefit From Their Pacemakers?

The speed of world-class runners is much higher than that of Marathon Man, so the air resistance due to their own wind is much higher too. We have calculated how much they have benefitted from their pacemakers. We have done this by comparing the time they could race solo (c_dA value of 0.24 m²) with their actual world records (with pacemakers, c_dA value of 0.20 m²). The table below shows the results. It appears that Dennis Kimetto would have run his marathon 1.5 minute slower without the assistance of his pacemakers! Also at the track races, the impact of the pacemakers is substantial. We see that Kenenisa Bekele owes 20 seconds of his 10,000-meter world record to his pacemakers! The results of our calculations match well with the rule of thumb that the benefit of pacemakers is in the order of one second per 400-meter lap.

Benefit of Drafting Among World-Class Athletes		
Distance	Alone	Pacemakers
(km)	(hrs:min:sec)	(hrs:min:sec)
0.8	00:01:43	00:01:41
1.5	00:03:30	00:03:26
3	00:07:28	00:07:21
5	00:12:49	00:12:38
10	00:26:40	00:26:20
15	00:41:46	00:41:16
20	00:56:06	00:55:26
21.1	00:59:10	00:58:28
25	01:12:13	01:11:24
30	01:28:43	01:27:45
42.195	02:04:21	02:02:57

In summary, we conclude that both Marathon Man and world-class athletes can gain an interesting edge by using pacemakers or shielding in a pack. In our model, we calculated a reduction in the air resistance of 20% (c_dA 0.20 m² vs 0.24 m²). Theoretically, the benefit could be even bigger, up to 80% at a perfect position in the wake of the front runner. In cycling, it is well known that shielding in the pack provides a 40% reduction in air resistance. However, in running practice, it is not easy to maintain an ideal position throughout the race.

Finally, we note that in practice, the impact of your own wind and the real wind will influence each other continuously. Other aspects complicate matters as well, such as local shelter from trees and buildings, changes in the wind direction and wind force and bends in the course. Experienced athletes will try to select an optimal strategy in which they seek maximum shelter against a head wind (in the midst of the pack, behind trees and walls) and profit as much as possible from a tail wind. These aspects will be discussed further in the next chapter.

On March 12, 2006 Haile Gebrselassie beat the world record at the 25K in the Dutch city of Alphen aan den Rijn. However, his time of 1:11:37 was not recognized by the IAAF. After the initial 5K Haile joined the official 20K race with a second group of fresh pacers.

47. THE IMPACT OF THE WIND

May the road rise up to meet you. May the wind be always at your back. —Irish proverb

Most runners will have experienced the impact of wind in practice, in training or during races. On occasions, your pace may drop to that of a pedestrian when you have to battle against a strong head wind. On the other hand, you may feel like you are flying like Haile Gebrselassie when you are blessed with a strong tail wind. So, how can we calculate the impact of the wind on our speed and race times? In this chapter, we will analyze this.

How Big Is the Wind Resistance?

In an earlier chapter, we learned the formula to calculate the air resistance:

$$P_a = 0.5 r c_d A (v+v_w)^2 v$$

At the standard conditions (15°C, 1,013 mbar), ρ is equal to 1.226 kg/m³. Earlier, we saw that $c_d A$ can be set at 0.24 m² for the standard runner. Consequently, we can calculate the air resistance of Marathon Man (who runs with a speed (v) of 12.06 km/h) as a function of the wind speed (v_w, in m/s). The result is given in the figure below for a head wind. In this case v_w is positive; in case of a tail wind v_w is negative. This means that with a strong tail wind, the air resistance can even become negative. In this situation, the wind literally pushes you forward and supports the power of your human engine.

As the figure shows, the air resistance of a head wind can become quite large. At a wind speed of 66 km/h (equivalent to wind force 8 at the Beaufort scale[67], see the table), the air resistance (P_a) would become equal to the total available power of Marathon Man (235 watts). Obviously, this is impossible as the running resistance (P_r = cmv) also requires part of the power. Consequently, Marathon Man will have to slow down to the speed where the sum of the running resistance and the air resistance becomes equal to the power of his human engine: $P = P_r + P_a$.

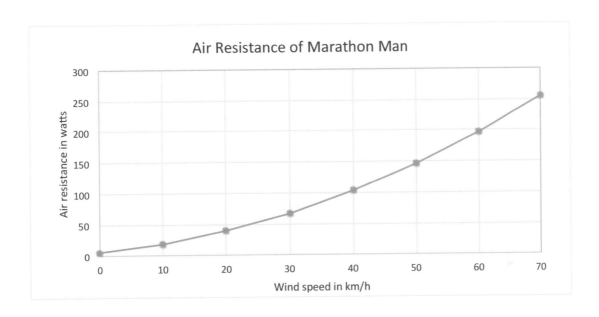

Wind force	Description	Wind speed
(Beaufort)		(km/h)
0	Calm	0-1
1	Light air	1-5
2	Light breeze	6-11
3	Gentle breeze	12-19
4	Moderate breeze	20-28
5	Fresh breeze	29-38
6	Strong breeze	39-49
7	High wind	50-61
8	Gale	62-74
9	Strong gale	75-88
10	Storm	89-102

How Big Is the Impact of Wind on the Speed of Marathon Man?

In order to calculate how fast you can run at a certain wind speed, we need to solve the complete running formula. As we saw earlier, this is a cubic equation of the speed. Using our program, we have calculated the attainable running speed of Marathon Man as a function of the wind speed. We made the calculations for the standard conditions and the FTP of Marathon Man (3.67 watts/kg). This means that the result is the speed which he can maintain for one hour. This is presented in the figure.

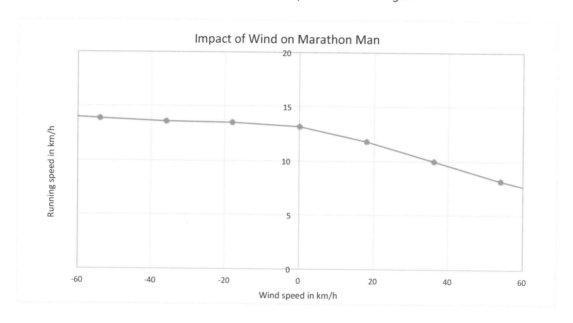

The figure illustrates the big impact of the wind on the attainable running speed. At a head wind of 36 km/h, his speed drops from 13.1 km/h to a mere 10.0 km/h. Unfortunately, a tail wind of 36 km/h provides a much smaller advantage as his speed then increases to 13.6 km/h only. The phenomenon that the advantage of a tail wind is much smaller than the disadvantage of a head wind is well known from literature. Both Davies[28] and Pugh[26,27] found that the difference was 50%. They reasoned that with a tail wind the muscle efficiency was somewhat reduced, partly as a result of the depressing effect of the tail wind. This can be compared to the lifting effect of a head wind as we know it from the takeoff of airplanes. We have taken this effect into account by using a 50% lower c_dA value in case of a tail wind. The impact can be seen in the figure by the change in the gradient at a wind speed of zero.

How Much Time Do You Lose as a Result of Wind?

You always lose time as a result of wind. This is caused by two aspects:

1. The fact that the advantage of a tail wind is only 50% of the disadvantage of a head wind, as we discussed above.
2. The fact that you always lose more time in the slowest section than you may gain in a faster section.

We will illustrate this last aspect by the example of a 10K race. If Marathon Man ran this race without wind at a speed of 13.1 km/h, his race time would be 45:58. Now, let's compare this with the case of a wind speed of 36 km/h and let's say that the 10K is divided into a 5K with a head wind and a 5K with a tail wind. He would then run the tail wind part in 5/13.6 hours (22:04) and the head wind part in 5/10.0 hours (30:00). Consequently, he would lose more than 7 minutes on the head wind part, whereas he would gain a mere 50 seconds on the tail wind part!

From Which Wind Force Do We Notice an Impact on the Race Time?

The above figure shows that already a quite low wind speed can have a substantial impact on the attainable speed and the race time. The example of 36 km/h is equivalent to a wind force 5, a fresh breeze. But already at wind force 3 (a gentle breeze), the attainable speed of Marathon Man drops from 13.1 km/h to 12.4 km/h! So, we can say that already from wind force 3 onwards, there will be a noticeable impact on the race time. This is also the reason why records at the sprinting events are only recognized at a tail wind speed of less than 2 m/s. This is equivalent to 7.2 km/h or wind force 2 (light breeze).

In practice, the real impact on the race time depends a lot on the conditions on the race course. Usually, there will be some parts with head wind, some with tail wind and some with crosswind. Crosswind can be tough as well, because you are running diagonally against the wind. It also depends on whether you can find shelter from the wind by trees or behind buildings. Seeking shelter against a head wind in the pack is always advantageous and will have a favorable impact on your race time.

Theoretically, the air resistance (in watts) is independent of the weight. This means that lightweight runners have a small disadvantage, as their specific air resistance (in watts/kg) will be slightly higher. However, this disadvantage will probably be compensated by the fact that smaller runners will have a slightly lower $c_d A$ value.

How Big Is the Impact of Wind on the Speed of World-Class Athletes?

As world-class athletes have a more powerful human engine, they run faster than normal people and they have more power available to cope with the wind. Consequently, in windy conditions the time differences between world class athletes and normal people will increase. On the other hand, the high speed of the world-class athletes leads to a higher air resistance. We have calculated the total impact of the wind on the speed of the world-class athletes at the standard conditions, and at an FTP of 6.35 watts/kg. The results are given in the figure.

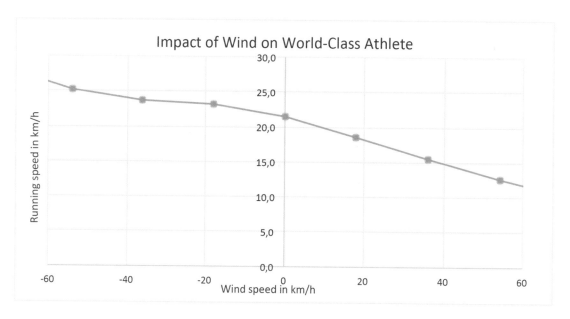

From the gradient of the figure, we see that the speed of the world-class athletes reduces by 16% of the wind speed in case of a head wind. In case of a tail wind, their speed increases only by 6%. At a tail wind of 50 km/h (wind force 7), their speed increases to over 25 km/h! This advantage is one of the reasons why records at the Boston Marathon are not recognized. The start and the finish of the Boston Marathon are not at the same location and the race course runs in a general northeasterly direction. This means that it is possible that the runners enjoy a tail wind for a large part of the race. Theoretically, a northeast wind with force 3 could already shave 9 minutes off the race time of elite athletes!

Kenyan Purity Cherotich (F4) had to battle a strong head wind to win the 2015 PWN Egmond Half Marathon. As a result, her race time of 1:11:40 was much slower than she had hoped.

48.THE IMPACT OF HILLS

It's a hill. Get over it. —Nike

In an earlier chapter, we learned that theoretically we can calculate the power required to overcome an altitude difference with the formula:

$P_c = (i/100)mgv$

As an example, we used the climb to the Alpe d'Huez with a gradient (i) of 7.4%. In order to run the climb with a speed of 12.06 km/h, Marathon Man would require a climbing power (P_c) of 7.4/100*70*9.81*12.06/3.6 = 170 watts. This climbing resistance would come on top of his running resistance of 230 watts (P_r = cmv = 0.98*70*12.06/3.6). As the total power of his human engine is only 235 watts, he will have to slow down as compared to his speed at the flat of 12.06 km/h. Theoretically, his speed will thus drop to 12.06*(235/(230+170) = 7.1 km/h.

We have also learned from the research of Minetti et al.[29] that in practice the results are somewhat more favorable. They found that the power required to overcome an altitude is somewhat lower than according to theory by a factor $\eta = (45.6+1.622i)/100$. They reasoned that the difference is caused by the fact that uphill the muscle efficiency is higher. We have included their factor in our model.

What are the options available to Marathon Man to limit his climbing resistance? As we can see from the formula, he has just one option, to reduce his body weight (m). We have discussed the impact of the body weight already in an earlier chapter, both for flat and hilly courses. There, we concluded that shedding body fat has a favorable impact on the specific power (P/m, in watt/kg) of your human engine. This specific power determines your speed, both on the flat (P/m = cv) and on a hilly course (P/m = (i/100)gv). Consequently, losing 1% of your body weight will increase your speed by 1% also, both at the flat and uphill.

In this chapter, we will study the impact of the gradient percentage (i). Obviously, Marathon Man cannot change this, but the gradient does have a huge impact on his speed.

The Impact of the Gradient on the Speed of Marathon Man

Once again, we have made the calculations for the standard conditions (ρ = 1.226 kg/m^3, m = 70 kg, c_dA = 0.24 m^2, v_w = 0 m/s). In this case, we varied the gradient percentage (i) between the extreme values of -45% and +45%. We used the FTP of Marathon Man (3.67 watts/kg), so the results are the speed that he can maintain for one hour. We refer to the figure and table for the results of the calculations.

Impact of Gradient on Marathon Man	
i	v
(%)	(km/h)
-45	6.1
-40	7.6
-30	12.1
-20	17.2
-15	18.3
-10	17.8
-5	15.8
0	13.1
5	10.5
10	8.3
15	6.6
20	5.3
25	4.4
30	3.7
35	3.1
40	2.7
45	2.4

We see that at normal uphill gradients (between 0 and 10%) the speed decreases more or less proportionally to the gradient. At a gradient of 5% the speed is reduced from 13.1 km/h to 10.5 km/h, so by 20%. Downhill the speed also increases more or less proportionally to the gradient. At a gradient of -5% (downhill) the speed has increased to 15.8 km/h, also by 20%.

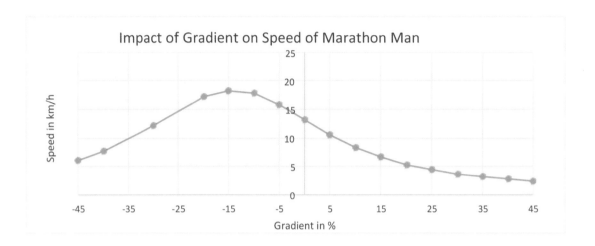

How Much Time Do You Lose as a Result of Hills?

You always lose time as a result of hills. This is caused by the fact that you always lose more time uphill than you gain downhill. This is a similar phenomenon as the one we saw earlier in the case of wind: you always lose more time on the slower part than you gain on the faster part. We can illustrate this by calculating the race time of Marathon Man on a 10K at a flat course: 10/13.1 = 45:48. Now let's compare this with a 5K uphill (+5%) and a 5K downhill (-5%). According to the table, the uphill section will take him 5/10.5 = 28:34 and the downhill section will take him 5/15.8 = 18:59. So we see that he loses 5:40 on the uphill section and he gains only 3:55 on the downhill section!

What Happens at Extreme Gradients?

At extreme positive gradients, the curve deviates more and more from a straight line. This is because the factor representing the muscle efficiency approaches one. Consequently, the climbing resistance approaches the theoretical value.

At extreme negative gradients, the curve even reverses and Marathon Man no longer increases in speed, but slows down! This is caused by the fact that at these extreme downhill sections, the muscle efficiency becomes negative due to the braking forces.

Contrary to popular opinion, heavyweights and lightweights suffer equally from hills. Both slow down just as much uphill. Obviously, heavyweights will run slower as a result of the impact of the weight on the specific power (P/m). However, this lower specific power reduces their speed both at the flat and uphill! Of course, heavyweights would do well to lose body fat as this will increase their speed, both at the flat and uphill.

The Impact of the Gradient on the Speed of World-Class Athletes

Finally, we have made the same calculations for the world-class athletes, using an FTP of 6.4 watts/kg. The results are given in the figure and table below.

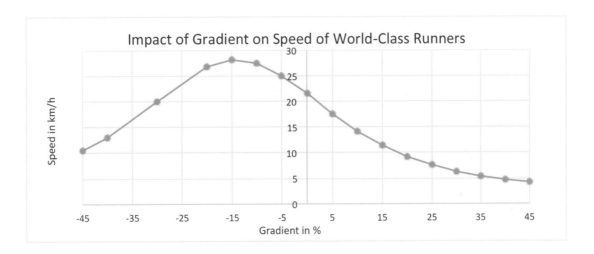

As expected, we see similar results, but with higher values. At an uphill gradient of 5%, the speed of the world-class athletes is reduced from 21.6 km/h to 17.7 km/h, so by 18%. At a downhill gradient of 5%, their speed increases to 25.1 km/h, by 16%. At an extreme uphill gradient of 35%, even the world-class athletes have slowed down to the pedestrian speed of 5.4 km/h!

The time gap between world-class athletes and normal runners increases on hilly terrain. This is similar to the impact of other harsh conditions, such as wind, heat and rough footing. Again this can be explained by the fact that you lose relatively more time as the speed gets lower. Your race time is equal to the distance divided by the speed. At a very low speed, this fraction increases exponentially.

In summary, we conclude that the impact of differences in altitude is very significant. Uphill, you lose a lot of time, which you can never regain completely downhill. No wonder the organizers of record races do their utmost to design a fast course with minimal altitude differences. Even a few viaducts can already have some impact on the race time.

Impact of Gradient on World-Class Runners	
i	v
(%)	(km/h)
-45	10.5
-40	13.1
-30	20.1
-20	26.8
-15	28.2
-10	27.6
-5	25.1
0	21.6
5	17.7
10	14.2
15	11.4
20	9.2
25	7.6
30	6.4
35	5.4
40	4.7
45	4.2

Extreme cases are the races to the top of a mountain, such as the Mont Blanc Marathon or the climb to the top of the Alpe d'Huez. The latter will be discussed in a separate chapter.

As the finish of the Boston Marathon is 140 meters lower than the start, records cannot be recognized there. This 140-meter altitude gain is equivalent to a gradient of -0.3% over 42.2 km, which would theoretically give a time benefit of 2.5 minutes!

We end this chapter with some supplementary notes. As we mentioned, the calculations were made for the standard conditions. This means we did not yet take into account two aspects, which will be relevant in mountain races:

1. The positive impact of the altitude on the air pressure and the air density. The thin mountain air has the advantage of reducing the air resistance. In running, the impact of this is limited as the air resistance is much smaller than the running resistance and the climbing resistance.

2. The negative impact of the thin mountain air on the performance of the human engine. The lower availability of oxygen leads to a reduced oxygen uptake capacity of your cardiovascular system. As a result, your FTP is reduced. In practice, this negative impact is decisive, so endurance running performance at altitude is always compromised. This aspect will be discussed in a separate chapter as well.

Uphill, you lose a lot of time, which you can never regain completely downhill.

49. THE IMPACT OF ALTITUDE

What does not destroy me makes me strong. —Friedrich Nietzsche

The Mexico Olympic Games

The general public became aware of the negative impact of altitude on the performance of endurance runners at the 1968 Mexico Olympic Games. The Kenyan athlete Naftali Temu won the 10,000 meter in a very modest 29:27. Ethiopian runner Mamu Wolde won the marathon in an equally slow 2:20:26. Both race times were about 7% slower that the world records at the time. Obviously, the most important explanation for these slow times is the fact that Mexico City is located at an altitude of 2,250 meters above sea level. At such an altitude, the air pressure and the air density are much lower, which compromises the ability of our blood to transport oxygen to the muscles. Consequently, the performance of the human engine is reduced at altitude.

How can we calculate the effect of the altitude? What is the impact at different altitudes? We will answer these questions in this chapter.

How Can We Calculate the Air Density?

At sea level, the air density (ρ, in kg/m^3) is determined by the air pressure and the temperature, according to the formula:

$$\rho = (p*M)/(R*T)$$

In this formula, M is the molecular weight of air (28.97 g/mole) and R is the molar gas constant (8,314 kJ/mole/°K). At the standard temperature of 15°C (288°K) and the standard air pressure of 101,300 Pa, the air density thus becomes (101,300*28.97(/(8,314/288) = 1.226 kg/m^3. In the previous chapters, we have used this value for our calculations.

At altitude, the air pressure is reduced, in accordance with the following formula:

$$p = p_0 * e^{(-Mgh/RT)}$$

Consequently, at Mexico City (altitude (h) = 2,250 meters), the air pressure is only $101,300 * e^{(-28.97*9.81*2,250)/(8,314*288)}$ = 77,559 Pa or 76.6% of the sea level air pressure.

What Are the Consequences of the Lower Air Density?

The lower air density at altitude has two bearings on the running performance:

1. The small advantage of a lower air resistance
   Earlier, we learned that in running the air resistance is relatively small as compared to the running resistance. The figure shows that at low speeds the share is only a few percent. However, for the world-class sprinters, this increases to more than 15%. Consequently, sprinters have a significant advantage from the lower air resistance at altitude. In an earlier chapter, we have already calculated that theoretically Usain Bolt could improve his Berlin 100-meter world record of 9.58 seconds by 0.22 second at the altitude of Mexico City. Endurance runners gain only a small benefit from the lower air pressure. With our model, we calculated that a world-class athlete with an FTP of 6.33 watts/kg could theoretically improve his sea level hour speed of 21.35 km/h to 21.70 km/h, so by 2% only.

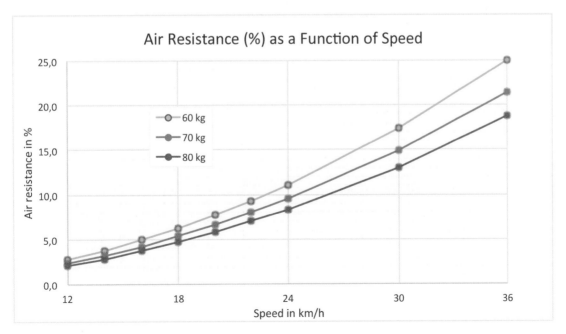

2. The significant disadvantage of a reduced performance of the human engine

   The solubility of oxygen in the blood is linearly proportional to the air pressure. This means that at Mexico City the blood of the athletes contains 23% less oxygen! As oxygen is essential for the aerobic oxidation of glycogen and fatty acids in the mitochondria, this leads to a significantly reduced power output by the muscles. Consequently, the performance of endurance runners at altitude is compromised significantly. Sprinters do not suffer from this phenomenon as they derive their power mainly from the anaerobic glycolysis and the direct conversion of ATP. Both processes do not require oxygen.

To What Extent Is the Performance at Altitude Reduced?

This depends on the adaptation process of the athlete's body. Upon arrival at altitude, the body will start to adapt to the lower availability of oxygen by producing more red blood cells. Obviously, the presence of more red blood cells will partly mitigate the impact of the lower solubility of oxygen. The level of hemoglobin may increase up to 10-15%, but this requires time. This process of adaptation is called acclimatization and usually requires about one month.

In the scientific literature[68,69,70,8], several formulas have been published to calculate the reduction of performance as a function of altitude. We have summarized these in the table below.

Performance at Altitude	
(h in km)	
Basset	Before acclimatization
	$\% = 100{,}352 - 4{,}307*h - 1{,}434*h^2 + 0{,}1781*h^3$
	After acclimatization
	$\% = 99{,}921 - 1{,}8991*h - 1{,}1219*h^2$
Cerretelli	$\% = 1 - 11{,}7*10\text{-}3h^2 - 4{,}01*10\text{-}3*h$
Daniels	No formula

As Daniels has not published an explicit formula, we have detailed an example based on a table from his book and compared this to the formulas of Basset and Cerretelli. The results are given in the figure. Based on this comparison, it seems to us that that Cerretelli and Daniels underestimate the impact of the altitude. Consequently, we have used Basset's formulas in our model.

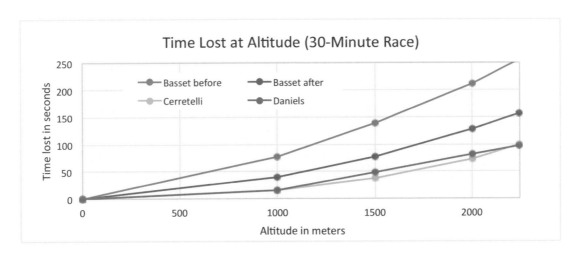

Using Basset's formulas, we have calculated the impact of the altitude on the performce (as FTP). The results are given in the figure below. At the altitude of Mexico City (2,250 meters), the predicted reduction in FTP is 10%.

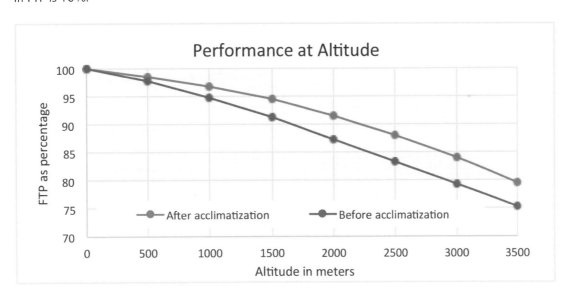

How Big Is the Impact on the Race Time of the World-Class Athletes?

We have calculated the example of the 10,000-meter race time for the world-class athletes. We thought it would be nice to simulate the performances at the Mexico Olympic Games. We did this by using realistic conditions for this case (altitude 2,250 meters, temperature 25°C, $c_dA = 0{,}20$ m^2, m = 60 kg, $v_w = 0$ m/s). As the 1968 world record was only 27:39 (set by the great Australian runner Ron Clarke), we used a slightly lower sea level FTP as compared to the present world-class athletes (6.0 watts/kg vs 6.35 watts/kg). The results after acclimatization are given in the figure below.

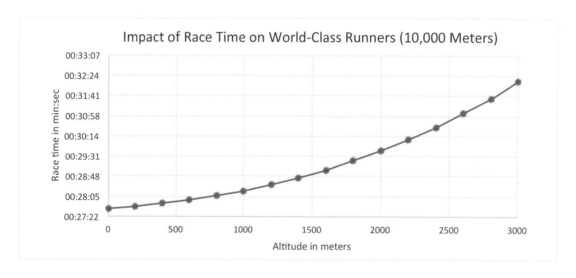

The calculated results match with the real performances in 1968:
» The calculated sea level world record at an FTP of 6.0 watts/kg is 27:38.
» The calculated Mexico race time is 30:10, slightly slower than Temu's race time of 29:27.

How Big Is the Impact of Altitude on the Race Time of Marathon Man?

Finally, we have made a similar calculation for the race time of Marathon Man. We used the same conditions as before, but with an FTP of 3.67 watts/kg and a c_dA value of 0.24 m^2 (as Marathon Man does not have pacemakers). The results are given in the figure. We see that at the altitude of Mexico City, Marathon Man would need almost four hours to complete the marathon, so he would lose 30 minutes as compared to his sea-level race time!

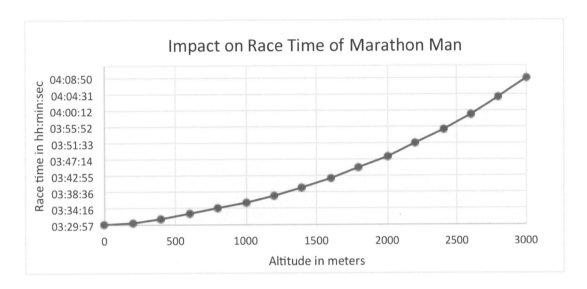

In summary, we conclude that the impact of altitude on the performance of endurance runners is substantial and negative. The small advantage of the lower air resistance is more than offset by the substantial disadvantage of the lower power output of the human engine as a result of the lower oxygen availability at altitude. We can calculate both aspects with our model. The results match the real results at the Mexico Olympic Games (i.e., a 2-minute slower race time at the 10,000 meters by the world-class athletes). Our Marathon Man will lose 30 minutes as compared to his sea-level race time if ran the marathon at Mexico City! In the next chapters, we will calculate exact results, taking into account both aspects of the altitude.

The 10K Great Ethiopian Run in Addis Ababa is at about the same altitude as Mexico City. Only few of the world's best elite athletes are faster than 29 minutes here. In 2015 it was the official farewell run for Haile Gebreselassie.

50. HOW FAST COULD YOU RUN THE CLIMB TO THE ALPE D'HUEZ?

Rewards in running, like in life, come in proportion to the amount of effort that we are willing to exert.

The Alpe d'Huez is one of the most famous cycling mountains of the Tour de France. So far, 27 times a stage of Le Grand Boucle finished at the Alpe d'Huez. The famous climb starts at the village of Le Bourg d'Oisans at an altitude of 744 meters above sea level. The climb includes a total of 21 officially numbered hairpin bends. Each bend is signaled by a plaque with the name of one or two past stage winners, including Dutch cyclists Hennie Kuiper and Joop Zoetemelk. The mythical image of the mountain attracts large crowds of spectators along the course, who feverishly cheer the professional cyclists each year.

How Fast Could You Run the Climb to the Alpe d'Huez?

We thought it would be fun to calculate how fast we could run the climb to the Alpe d'Huez. How much slower would we be than the professional cyclists? In our book The Secret of Cycling (Dutch edition)[2] we already had made the calculations for cycling, so comparing these with running would be interesting.

We have tried to make the calculations as realistic as possible. According to the website of the Alpe d'Huez, the official running course has a length of 13.8 km and an altitude difference of 1,020 meters, so the gradient is 7.4%. Next to this, we have used the following conditions:

m = 60 kg

c_dA = 0.24 m^2

T = 20°C

Maximum altitude is 1,815 meters

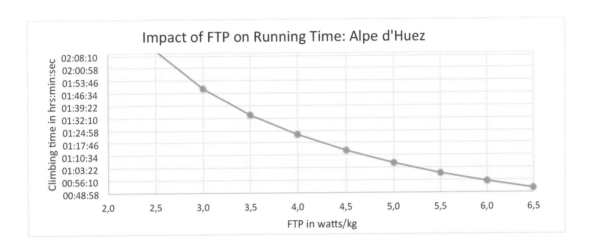

Furthermore, we have used Basset's formula (after acclimatization and calculating the average altitude) for the reduction of the FTP at altitude. Finally, we calculated the attainable speed and climbing time as a function of the FTP of the runner. The results are given in the figure and table below.

Running Speed and Climbing Time to Alpe d'Huez		
FTP	v	Time
(watts/kg)	(km/h)	(hrs:min:sec)
1.0	2.5	05:27:06
1.5	3.8	03:38:14
2.0	5.1	02:43:50
2.5	6.3	02:11:15
3.0	7.6	01:49:33
3.5	8.8	01:34:04
4.0	10.0	01:22:29
4.5	11.3	01:13:30
5.0	12.5	01:06:19
5.5	13.7	01:00:28
6.0	14.9	00:55:36
6.5	16.1	00:51:29

The results of our calculations seem very realistic when we compare them to the official records of the race:

» Men

The record was set at 53:43 by Jean Paul Payet in 1994.

» Women

The record was set at 65:05 by Fabiola Rueda in 1989.

These official records are equivalent to a sea level FTP of 6.2 watts/kg and 5.1 watts/kg, respectively. This means that Payet's performance is close to world-class level (6.4 watts/kg). The performance of Ruelda is of international level (world-class level for women would be 5.7 watts/kg).

The authors of this book want to verify experimentally as much as possible by themselves. Ron ran the climb to the Alpe d'Huez and checked his race time with our model.

How Do the Running Times Compare to the Records in Cycling?

We have used the official top 10 of the fastest cycling climbs[71] as a basis for the comparison. The famous Marco Pantani still holds the record with a climbing time of 37:35. This means he climbed 43% faster than Payet. Unfortunately, we now know that Pantani used EPO during his record climb. Actually, all cyclists from the top 10 of the fastest climbs have been associated with doping at some point in their career. Obviously, this sheds a different light on their record performances.

Fastest Climbs of Alpe d' Huez (Cycling)	
	Time
	(min:sec)
Marco Pantani (1997)	37:35
Lance Armstrong (2004)	37:36
Marco Pantani (1994)	38:00
Lance Armstrong (2001)	38:01
Marco Pantani (1995)	38:04
Jan Ullrich (1997)	38:23
Floyd Landis (2006)	38:34
Andreas Klöden (2006)	38:35
Jan Ullrich (2004)	38:37
Richard Virenque (1997)	39:02

How High Was the FTP of the Top 10 Cyclists?

We have calculated this with our cycling model, as explained further in The Secret of Cycling (Dutch edition)[2]. The table below shows how we have done this. First, we calculated the speed from the climbing time. From the speed and the body weight of the cyclist, we then calculated the specific power he has used to climb the mountain. Then we converted this specific power to his sea level specific power (using Basset's formula) and finally to his FTP (using Riegel's formula).

The results are painfully clear: the calculated FTP of all top 10 cyclists are near or even significantly above the maximum of 6.4 watts/kg, which we believe to be the highest possible value for a clean athlete. It seems logical that this is the result of doping. When we compare the maximum FTP of Pantani (6.85 watts/kg) with our limit of 6.4 Watt/kg, we might conclude that the impact of the EPO has been an increase in performance of 8% (100*(6.85/6.4-1)).

Fastest Climbs Alpe d'Huez (Cycling)								
	Time	v	m	P	P/m	FTP/m	$P_{sea\ level}$	$FTP/m_{sea\ level}$
	(min:sec)	(km/h)	(kg)	(Watt)	(Watt/kg)	(Watt/kg)	(Watt)	(Watt/kg)
Marco Pantani (1997)	37:35	23.07	57	375	6.58	6.36	404	6.85
Lance Armstrong (2004)	37:36	23.06	75	466	6.21	6.01	502	6.47
Marco Pantani (1994)	38:00	22.82	57	370	6.49	6.28	398	6.75
Lance Armstrong (2001)	38:01	22.81	75	460	6.13	5.93	495	6.38
Marco Pantani (1995)	38:04	22.78	57	369	6.47	6.26	397	6.74
Jan Ullrich (1997)	38:23	22.59	72	439	6.10	5.89	473	6.34
Floyd Landis (2006)	38:34	22.48	68	417	6.13	5.93	449	6.38
Andreas Klöden (2006)	38:35	22.47	63	393	6.24	6.03	423	6.49
Jan Ullrich (2004)	38:37	22.45	72	437	6.07	5.87	470	6.32
Richard Virenque (1997)	39:02	22.21	65	398	6.12	5.92	428	6.37

The Alpe d'Huez is one of the most famous cycling mountains of the Tour de France. The official running course has a length of 13.8 kilometers and an altitude difference of 1,020 meters.

51.WHICH IS THE TOUGHER RUN: UP ALPE D'HUEZ OR BATTLING WIND FORCE 7?

No pain, no gain!

Each year we see images of heroic actions of the Tour de France professional cyclists who hit the wall as they climb the Alpe d'Huez. Puffing and sweating they labor uphill, while their pace drops to a pedestrian level. These image are most inspiring to the fans, who consider this climb the most arduous effort imaginable.

In our daily training, most of us do not have the opportunity to run up Alpe d'Huez. However, most of us do have to face some pretty nasty weather, including strong breezes or even storms. We have experienced that a strong head wind can be very tough indeed. At severe wind gusts, you can almost come to a standstill! So, we were wondering which is actually the tougher effort: running up Alpe d'Huez or battling against a high wind force 7?

How Tough Is the Effort of Running Up Alpe d'Huez?

In the previous chapter on the Alpe d'Huez, we have already calculated the attainable speed uphill as a function of the FTP. The result for our Marathon Man was that he could maintain a speed of 9.2 km/h with his FTP of 3.67 watts/kg. At a flat course, Marathon Man can attain a speed of 13.1 km/h with his FTP. So, we have taken the speed reduction to 9.2 km/h as the criterion for how tough running up the Alpe d'Huez really is. Next, we will compare this with the speed reduction as a result of a head wind to see which effort is the toughest.

Training in windy flat countries is not necessarily easier than training in mountain areas.

How Tough Is Running Into a Head Wind?

In the earlier chapter on the impact of the wind, we have already calculated the attainable speed of Marathon Man as a function of the wind speed. From those data, we can conclude that his speed drops to 9.2 km/h at a head wind with a speed of 43 km/h. This is equivalent to wind force 6, a strong breeze. So, we think we can conclude that—perhaps surprisingly—running into a head wind with force 7 is tougher than running up the Alpe d'Huez!

Which Wind Speeds and Gradients Are Equally Tough?

We have also taken a more general approach to the topic by investigating at which conditions the air resistance is equal to the climbing resistance:

$$P_a = 0.5\rho c_d A(v+v_w)^2 v$$

$$P_c = (i/100)mgv\eta$$

In order to simplify matters, we have made some assumptions. We have used the standard conditions (m = 70 kg, p = 1.226 kg/m³, c_dA= 0,24 m²) and we have set v at 10 km/h. In these conditions, the figure below gives the wind speeds and gradients that fulfill the criterion that the air resistance and the climbing resistance are equal.

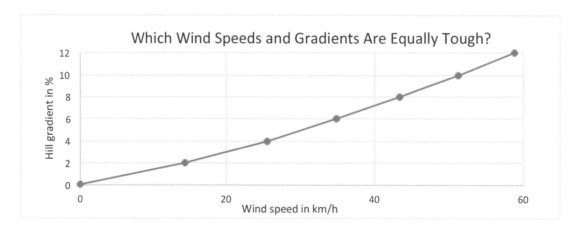

In summary, we conclude that a strong head wind can provide the same resistance as a steep gradient. A head wind of 25 km/h (wind force 4) already matches the resistance of a 4% gradient! So, training in flat countries is not necessarily easier than training in mountain areas. However, the wind conditions are far less stable and predictable. At times you almost come to a standstill in a head wind and at times you could be flying as a result of a tail wind. So all in all, the training conditions change continuously. The impact of such a training cannot easily be compared with that of a continuous climb.

Training in windy flat countries is not necessarily easier than training in mountain areas.

52. THE IMPACT OF PACE AND RACE STRATEGY

Last thought before a race: "Why am I doing this?"
First thought after a race: "When can I do this again?"

So far, we have limited our analysis to the equilibrium situation with constant power and constant speed. The only exception was the chapter on the 100-meter sprint, where we investigated the additional power required for the start and the initial acceleration during the first 40 meters.

However, in practice our power and speed are usually not constant. In training, we deliberately change both during interval sessions. In races, both may change as a result of pace increases, windy or hilly sections or the final kick to the finish. How should we analyze these variations? What is the impact of them on our training load and training effect? And finally, what pacing strategy should you adopt to get the best racing times?

Normalizing Power

As the reader will sense, variations in pace require additional energy and power. Consequently, running at a steady pace is usually the best strategy to save energy and minimize the required power. This is caused by the fact that accelerations and decelerations waste energy.

We can express the variations in power by the notion of the normalized power (P_n). This notion stems from cycling and indicates how much more power is required for variations in power as compared to the average power. The normalized power (P_n) is defined by the following formula:

$$P_n = ((1/t)*(\sum P_i^4 t_i))^{0.25}$$

In order to illustrate the formula, we use the example of an interval training of our Marathon Man. During this one-hour training, he alternates eight minutes of easy running at 10 km/h with five minutes of fast running at 16 km/h. Consequently, his running resistance ($P_r = cmv$) during the recovery sections is $0.98*70*10/3.6 = 190$ watts. During the intervals it is $0.98*70*16/3.6 = 305$ watts. The table and figure below show the values for P_n as compared to the average power P_{av}. The table shows that P_n is always higher than P_{av}, as expected. In the example, the ratio of the two is 1.08.

Interval Training (4 x 5 Minutes During One Hour, Eight Minutes Recovery)				
T	P	P_n	P_{av}	P_n/P_{av}
(sec)	(watts)	(watts)	(watt)	-
480	190	190.0	190.0	1.00
780	305	253.5	234.2	1.08
1260	190	235.1	217.4	1.08
1560	305	253.5	234.2	1.08
2040	190	242.6	223.8	1.08
2340	305	253.5	234.2	1.08
2820	190	245.8	226.7	1.08
3120	305	253.5	234.2	1.08
3600	190	247.5	228.3	1.08

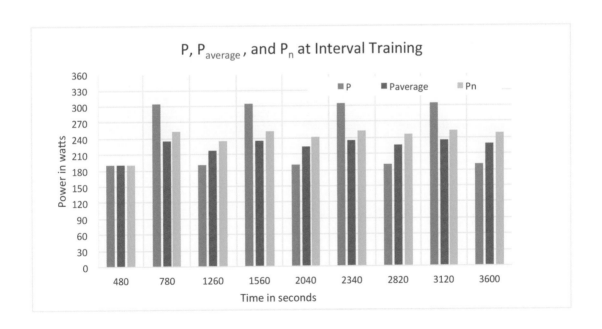

Normalizing Intensity

In earlier chapters, we learned the importance of training at a high intensity. The best way to express intensity is by comparing the normalized power with the FTP. Consequently, the normalized intensity (I_n) is defined by the following formula:

$$I_n = P_n / FTP$$

If you were to run an entire training or race with a P_n at the level of your FTP, your normalized intensity (I_n) would thus be one. The table and figure give the values of I_n as a function of the percentage of P_n. Obviously, a normalized intensity of one can be considered very tough, as it means that you have run at the level of your FTP.

In as a Function of %FTP and P_n			
%FTP	$P_n = 1$	$P_n = 1.2$	$P_n = 1.5$
30	0.3	0.36	0.45
40	0.4	0.48	0.6
50	0.5	0.6	0.75
60	0.6	0.72	0.9
70	0.7	0.84	1.05
80	0.8	0.96	1.2
90	0.9	1.08	1.35
100	1	1.2	1.5

In practice, the following classification is used for I_n:

» $I_n < 0.75$: easy, recovery training
» I_n 0.75-0.85: normal endurance training
» I_n 0.85-0.95: tempo training, long intervals, marathon race
» I_n 0.95-1.05: short intervals, road races of 10-21 kilometers
» I_n 1.05-1.15: speed training
» $I_n > 1.15$: short track races

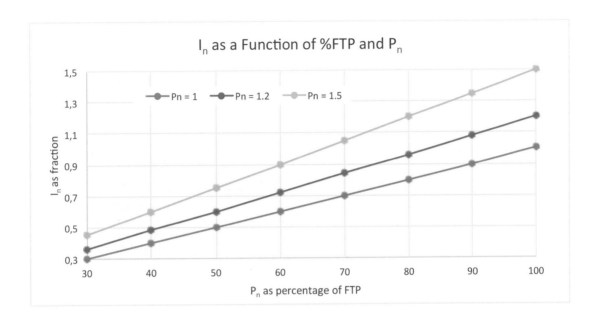

Normalizing Training Load

The stress that a training or race imposes on your body is not just determined by P_n and I_n, but also by a third factor i.e., the duration (t, in hours). The three parameters P_n, I_n and t can be combined in the total stress score (TSS), which is defined by the following formula:

TSS = 100*t*I_n^2

The table and figure below give the values for TSS as a function of I_n and t (in hours).

I_n	t = 1 hour	t = 2 hours	t = 4 hours	t = 6 hours
0.3	9	18	36	54
0.5	25	50	100	150
0.7	49	98	196	
0.9	81	162		
1.1	121			

TSS as a Function of I_n and t

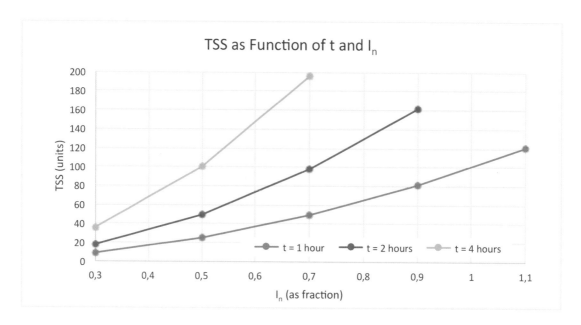

TSS values of more that 150 only occur at very hard training sessions or races. It goes without saying that it is physiologically impossible to maintain an I_n of one longer than one hour. In practice, the following classification for TSS is used:

» TSS < 50: light, recovery training
» TSS 50-100: normal training that can be done on a daily basis
» TSS 100-150: hard training or race that require recovery the next day
» TSS > 150: very hard races (marathon) that require longer recovery

Which Is the Best Racing Strategy?

From the theory of the human engine and the above, it follows that your race performance is determines primarily by two factors:

1. The duration of the race
   In a short track race, you can run at an I_n of 1.15, a power of 15% above your FTP. At a longer road race your power will drop to your FTP (at a one-hour race) or lower (0.88 FTP at a two-hour race). This means you will have to judge carefully the power and pace that you can maintain during the entire race. If you start too fast, you will pay the price in the latter part of the race! If you start too slow, you may not use your full potential.

2. The variations in pace and power

As we learned from the notion of normalized power, it is always best to limit variations in power as much as possible, so try to run with constant power throughout the race. At a flat course and in windless conditions, constant power also means constant pace. However, when the conditions change during the race (e.g., because of hills or wind), constant power is not equivalent to constant pace! Uphill constant power means you will slow down, just like everybody else around you. Don't worry about this! Just hold on to the strategy of keeping your power constant throughout the race.

So, what all of the above boils down to is that it is always the best strategy to judge the power and pace that you can maintain during the entire race. This will require self-knowledge, but you can also use the data of your power meter to your advantage!

The only exception to the above rule is determined by the fact that you always lose more time on the slower sections of the course. Consequently, it may be wise to use some additional power on the tough sections (e.g., uphill or against a headwind). You may gain valuable time there that you could use to recover in the easier sections. However, you should be prudent with this strategy as it may get you into the red zone. The last thing you would want is to get into trouble on account of an accumulation of lactic acid! So don't push it too far and use this strategy only just before a section where you can recover.

Kenyan Moses Mwarur wins the 2014 Antwerp marathon (Belgium). He managed to maintain a constant pace throughout the race.

53. THE IMPACT OF TEMPERATURE

There is no such thing as bad weather, just soft people.
—Bill Bowerman

Almost all distance runners will have experienced an ideal race: fast course, no hills, windless conditions and perfect weather. But what is actually the ideal temperature, how high or how low should it be to provide the best race times? And how big is the impact of non-ideal temperatures on the race times? In this chapter, we will answer these questions.

The impact of the temperature on the running performance is determined by at least three factors:

1. When the temperature gets too low, we need to wear additional clothing to protect us from the cold. Additional clothing increases our weight and consequently the energy cost of running. Moreover, it may hinder our motion.
2. When the temperature gets too high, it becomes more difficult to release the heat that our body produces. Consequently, we run the risk of overheating and dehydration from sweating. The processes of overheating and dehydration depend strongly on the distance. This will be discussed in detail in the next chapter.
3. As the solubility of oxygen is inversely dependent on the temperature, the alveoli of the lungs have a slightly easier job of taking up oxygen from cold air. However, this is a minor factor, also because the air is warmed up in the lungs.

Which Is the Ideal Temperature for Running?

Practical experience has revealed that the ideal temperature for distance running is around 5-10°C. This temperature is low enough to prevent problems with overheating and high enough so we don't need to wear additional clothing. It is noted that wind and rain may also have a big impact and cause hypothermia. This will be discussed in a later chapter. Finally, we note that the 5-10°C optimum is valid for world-class runners. As recreational runners produce much less heat than world-class runners, they may find temperatures around 15°C ideal.

The Impact of a High Temperature on the Body

We should differentiate between the increase of the body core temperature (hyperthermia) and the dehydration of the body. When we run, we almost invariably produce more heat than we use. Consequently, our body temperature will increase and we start to sweat in order to release the excess heat from our body. At a low temperature, we may lose a considerable amount of heat to the air by means of convection, so the need for sweating is reduced. At a high temperature, we need to sweat much more, which may lead to dehydration. At severe weather conditions (high temperature combined with high humidity), sweating can become increasingly difficult, so we cannot release the excess heat any more. This may lead to a sunstroke or collapse.

As a result of the increase in body temperature, the skin blood vessels will dilate, which will lead to increased blood flow to the skin where it may release heat. However, it means that less blood is available for other functions, including the leg muscles. In effect our cardiovascular capacity has been reduced and so has our running capacity. We may note this from the cardiac drift of our HR monitor; at the same HR we run more slowly or at the same speed our HR becomes higher. Author Hans noted this on the hot morning of July 19th 2014: at a temperature of 25°C his HR turned out to be 6 bpm higher than normal at the same speed. As the MHR of Hans is 172 bpm and his RHR is 42, this means that his performance was reduced by 6/(172-42)*100 = 4.6%!

The increase of the body core temperature also leads to a decrease in the fatigue resistance and an increase in the glycogen/fatty acids ratio in the fuel mix.

The sweat loss leads to a decrease in the blood (plasma) volume, as a result of which the stroke volume and the cardiac output decrease. Ultimately, this may even lead to extremely low pressures in the vena, which may endanger the return blood flow to the ventricles. When the body core temperature rises above 39.5°C, the symptoms of a sunstroke may occur (fainting, extreme fatigue, reduced sweating ability).

The Impact of the Temperature in Running a Marathon

Several studies[72,73,74] have been reported in literature on the statistical relationship between the temperature and the racing times in the marathon. We think the study of Helou et al.[73] is particularly useful. They have analyzed the results of over 1.7 million finishers of six big city marathons (Berlin, Boston, Chicago, London, New York and Paris) between 2001 and 2010. The temperature ranged between 1.7

and 25.2°C during these events. The authors found a statistically significant relationship between the finish times and the wet-bulb temperature[75]. In winter the wet-bulb temperature is almost equal to the normal air temperature. However, in summer the wet-bulb temperature can be much lower than the air temperature, particularly at low humidity. We will discuss this further in the next chapter.

The figure gives the impact of the wet-bulb temperature on the marathon race times of world-class runners and of normal runners like our Marathon Man.

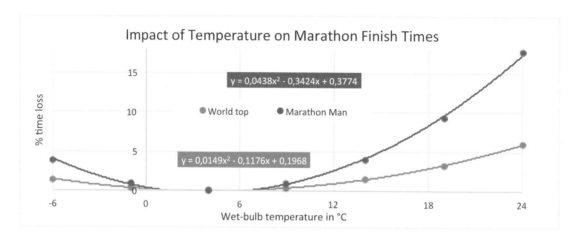

The results can be summarized as follows:

» The optimum temperature is around 5°C (world-class runners 4°C, normal runners 7°C).
» In the cold (-5°C) the speed is reduced by 3% (world-class runners 2%, normal runners 4%).
» In the heat (25°C) the speed is reduced by 6% (world-class runners) up to 18% (normal runners).
» For women the optimum temperature is slightly higher (9°C) and the speed loss is slightly smaller (13% at 27°C). Apparently, women are a little better resistant to the heat.

Which Is the Ideal Temperature at Shorter Distances?

It makes sense that runners suffer most from the heat at the marathon. Obviously, at a short distance, the problem of overheating will not manifest itself. On the other hand it is well-known that sprinters thrive best in warm conditions. They need some heat to warm up their muscles so they can mobilize maximum peak power in a few seconds. In literature, a study has reported the optimal temperature for various distances[72]. The results are given in the table and figure.

Optimum Temperature		
Distance	Men	Women
(km)	(°C)	(°C)
0.1	22.1	23.0
0.2	22.6	22.3
0.4	20.8	17.7
0.8	19.0	18.4
1.5	22.2	19.4
5	18.3	17.2
10	16.8	19.0
21.1	14.3	13.4
42.195	9.7	11.0

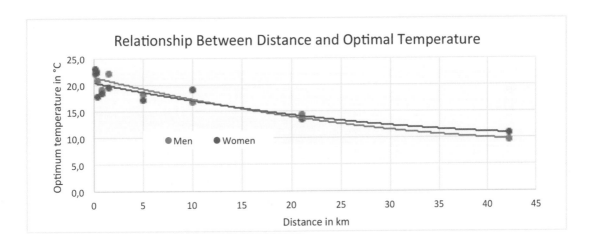

The relationship in the figure makes sense. Sprinters thrive in warm weather, whereas distance runners need cold weather to get rid of the excess heat that they produce. Too low temperatures should always be avoided as it increases the risk of hypothermia, particularly during rain and windy conditions.

How Big Is the Impact of Temperature on Race Times at Distances Other Than the Marathon?

We did not find concrete research in literature on the impact of temperature on the race times of distances other than the marathon. However, we were able to derive a relationship by ourselves. We based this on the research of Helou et al.[73] for the marathon and the following additional considerations:

1. We believe the impact of distance will be more than proportional, so at the half marathon the impact should be less than half of the marathon. Similarly, the impact at the 10K should be less than half the impact at the half marathon, and so on.
2. We believe the impact will be minimal below 3,000 meter; for the 3,000 meter we assumed a minimum impact of 1% at the highest temperature (24°C).

The table and figure below give the results of our reasoning. We see that Marathon Man may lose more than 37 minutes at the marathon (at a wet-bulb temperature of 24°C, which means very severe tropical conditions). At the half marathon he would lose 6 minutes and at a 10K less than 1 minute.

Impact of Temperature on Performances by Marathon Man						
T_{wb} (°C)	Marathon time	21.1 km Time	15 km Time	10 km Time	5 km Time	3 km Time
-6	03:37:55	01:27:38	01:09:33	00:45:02	00:21:26	00:12:25
-1	03:31:58	01:27:28	01:09:28	00:45:00	00:21:26	00:12:25
4	03:30:00	01:27:25	01:09:26	00:45:00	00:21:26	00:12:24
9	03:32:00	01:27:28	01:09:28	00:45:00	00:21:26	00:12:25
14	03:38:13	01:27:39	01:09:33	00:45:02	00:21:27	00:12:25
19	03:49:27	01:27:57	01:09:42	00:45:05	00:21:28	00:12:25
24	04:07:14	01:33:13	01:12:12	00:45:58	00:21:35	00:12:26

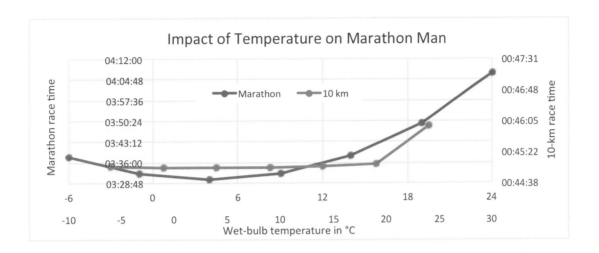

We end this chapter with the note that runners may know from experience that next to the temperature, the humidity is an important factor determining the severity of the conditions. This is implicitly accounted for in the wet-bulb temperature. As an example, the wet-bulb temperature may be more than 10°C lower than the air temperature at low humidity. These are the days of dry heat during which running is still very feasible. However, humid tropical days can be dangerous as will be discussed in the next chapter.

Winner Mare Dibaba of Ethiopia and others pass a mist station in the Women's Marathon race at the 2015 IAAF World Championships in Beijing. The race began early with the thermometer reading 28°C by the time the athletes finished.

54. THE DANGERS OF THE HEAT

There is no failure in running, or in life, as long as you keep moving. —Amby Burfoot

At the 1996 Olympic Games in Atlanta, the marathon was run in tropical conditions with a temperature of 25°C and a relative humidity of 70%. Many runners suffered from the heat. The race was won by the South African lightweight Josiah Thugwane (43 kg), whereas the South Korean lightweight Lee Bon Ju (45 kg) took second place. Was it just a coincidence that two extreme lightweight runners ran well under these tropical conditions or can this be explained by the laws of physics? In this chapter, we will answer this question.

The Wet-Bulb Temperature

In summer, we may experience one of those tropical, humid days when our clothing gets wet and sticky. Those days really bother us, much more than days with dry heat. This is caused by the fact that we cannot release excess heat to humid air. On such days, our problems are not so much related to high air temperatures, but to high wet-bulb temperatures.

What is the wet-bulb temperature[75]? When we expose water to the air, it starts to evaporate and so the humidity of the air increases. This continues until the air becomes saturated with water, so condensation may start. The wet-bulb temperature is defined as the temperature when condensation starts. This means that in humid air, the wet-bulb temperature can be equal to the air temperature. However, in dry air the wet-bulb temperature will be much lower than the air temperature. In practice, the conditions become severe at a wet-bulb temperature above 15°C. Sweating becomes more or less impossible and conditions become dangerous at a wet-bulb temperature above 22°C.

Obviously, the difference between the air temperature and the wet-bulb temperature depends on the relative humidity of the air. The wet-bulb temperature T_{wb} (in °C) can be calculated from the air temperature (T, in °C) and the relative humidity (RH, in %) with the following formula[76]:

T_{wb}=T*arctan(0.151977*(RH+8.313659)$^{0.5}$)+arctan(T+RH)-arctan(RH-1.676331)+0.00391838*RH 1.5*arctan(0.023101*RH)-4.686035

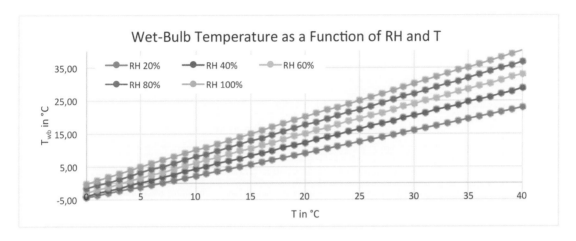

The figure gives the relationship between T, RH and T_{wb}. In winter, the RH is usually high, so the T_{wb} will not deviate much from T. However, in summer, on days with dry heat, RH will be low, so T_{wb} can be 10°C or more below T. The figure shows that the dangerous level of T_{wb} = 22°C may not even be reached on days with an air temperature of 40°C, provided the RH is sufficiently low! These are the hot dry days that are still quite tolerable.

Heat Balance for Running

In order to understand what happened at the Atlanta Marathon, we first need to draw up the heat balance for running. This heat balance is given in the box[77].

Heat Balance for Running

E = H-R-C

E is net heat production per unit of time (J/s = watts).

H is heat production by running in watts.

R is heat loss by radiation in watts.

C is heat loss by convection in watts.

The Heat Production by Running (H)

We can calculate the heat production by running easily from the FTP. As we learned earlier, we can maintain the FTP for about one hour. Our Marathon Man weighs 70 kg and has a specific FTP of 3.67 watts/kg, so he can run for about one hour with his FTP of 3.67*70 = 257 watts. As the muscle efficiency is 25%, this means that the total power produced by Marathon Man is 257/0.25 = 1,027 watts. It also means that 75% of his total power (or 770 watts) is transferred into excess heat! This excess heat has to be released from his body in order to prevent his body from overheating! As the heat production is linearly proportional to the body weight, heavyweights produce more heat and have more problems releasing the excess heat. This is illustrated in the table below.

Heat Production (H, in watts)			
FTP (watts/kg)	Weight 60 (kg)	70 (kg)	80 (kg)
1	180	210	240
2	360	420	480
3	540	630	720
4	720	840	960
5	900	1,050	1,200
6	1,080	1,260	1,440
6.4	1,152	1,344	1,536

The Heat Loss by Radiation (R)

From literature, it is known that we can calculate the heat loss by radiation (R) with the following formula[77]:

$$R = 9.1 * (T_{skin} - T_{wb})$$

The formula shows that R depends on T_{wb}. The table below gives the relationship for a skin temperature T_{skin} of 34°C. We see that in cold weather we may lose a lot of heat by radiation. However, at high wet-bulb temperatures the heat loss by radiation can be small or even negative. The formula also shows that R is independent of the body weight. This means that heavyweights, who produce more heat as we saw earlier, cannot release more heat by radiation.

Radiation (R, in watts)	
T_{wb}	R
(°C)	(watts)
0	309
5	264
10	218
15	173
20	127
25	82
30	36
35	-9

The Heat Loss by Convection (C)

From literature, it is known that we can calculate the heat loss by convection (C) with the following formula[77]:

$$C = 12.5 * v^{0.6} * (T_{skin} - T_{wb})$$

The formula shows that C does not only depend on T_{wb}, but also on the speed (v). This is the speed of the air flowing past our skin. When we run in windless conditions, v will be equal to our own running speed. As we saw earlier, our running speed is proportional to our FTP:

$$v = P_r/cm = FTP/c$$

This means that world-class runners with a superior FTP can release the excess heat by convection much more easily than recreational runners! The relationship between C, FTP and T_{wb} is given in the table below. The table confirms that the world-class athletes have much better air cooling! We also note that C gets very small at high wet-bulb temperatures, again confirming the problems of releasing excess heat during these conditions.

Convection (C, in watts)			
	T_{wb}		
FTP (watts/kg)	10 (°C)	20 (°C)	30 (°C)
1	303	177	51
2	460	268	77
3	587	342	98
4	697	407	116
5	797	465	133
6	889	519	148
6.4	924	539	154

The Net Heat Production (E)

Now that we have determined all the parameters of the heat balance, it is easy to calculate the net heat production from the balance:

E = H-R-C

Below we present three tables with the results at T_{wb} of 10, 20 and 30°C. We draw the following conclusions from the tables:

1. At a low T_{wb}, low FTP and low body weight, E can even become negative. These are the conditions during which we may face hypothermia. Of course, the remedy is simple: wear sufficient protective clothing and protective skin oil.
2. E increases strongly at higher T_{wb} and higher body weight. The impact of FTP is smaller as a result of the air cooling at higher FTP.

Net Heat Production (E) at 10°C (in watts)			
	Weight		
FTP (watts/kg)	60 (kg)	70 (kg)	80 (kg)
1	-342	-312	-282
2	-318	-258	-198
3	-265	-175	-85
4	-195	-75	45
5	-115	35	185
6	-27	153	333
6.4	9	201	393

Net Heat Production (E) at 20°C (in watts)			
	Weight		
FTP (watts/kg)	60 (kg)	70 (kg)	80 (kg)
1	-124	-94	-64
2	-36	24	84
3	70	160	250
4	186	306	426
5	308	458	608
6	434	614	794
6.4	486	678	870

Net Heat Production (E) 30°C (in watts)			
	Weight		
FTP	60	70	80
(watts/kg)	(kg)	(kg)	(kg)
1	93	123	153
2	247	307	367
3	406	496	586
4	567	687	807
5	731	881	1031
6	895	1075	1255
6.4	962	1154	1346

How Much Do You Need to Sweat in Order to Release the Excess Heat?

One of the reasons for calculating the heat balance is to determine how much you need to sweat in order to release the excess heat. As the heat of evaporation of water (sweat) is 2,249 kJ/l, we can calculate the sweat production (S, in liters per hour) from the heat balance with the following formula:

$S*2,249*1,000 = E*3,600$, or $S = 0.0016*E$

We have calculated the sweat production (S) as a function of FTP and body weight and for a T_{wb} of 20 and 30°C. The results are given in the figures.

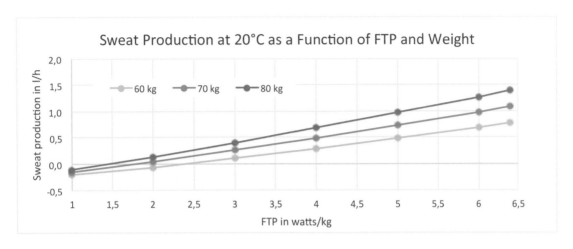

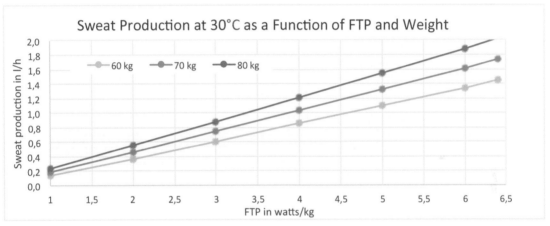

The results of the calculations on the heat balance, the net heat production (E) and the sweat production (S) are very clear:

1. E and S increase proportionally with the body weight (m).
2. E and S increase with FTP.
3. E and S depend strongly on T_{wb}.
4. E and S increase proportionally with the distance (d, this follows directly from the heat balance, so we have made the calculations for the FTP, the distance covered in one hour).

Consequently, we can now understand why the sweat loss may become a problem in the marathon and in particular for heavy runners. The sweat loss of our Marathon Man (FTP = 3.67 watts/kg) at a T_{wb} of 30°C becomes one liter per hour, a total of 3.5 liters during the marathon. Additionally, we should note that this is the net sweat loss. Part of the sweat will drip from the skin or is adsorbed by clothing. This means

the gross sweat loss will be even bigger. Depending on the RH this could be a factor of 2-3, so the gross sweat loss could be up to 10 liters! At such high sweat losses, the dangers of dehydration and sunstroke are imminent. As a rule of thumb, the sweat loss should definitely not exceed 5% of the body weight, so in the case of Marathon Man it should not exceed 0.05*70 = 3.5 liters.

The Heat Stress Index

Finally, we should look at one additional factor that is relevant in tropical conditions i.e., the fact that is can be hard or impossible to sweat in humid air. This means you lose the ability to release your excess heat and you could suffer from a heat collapse or a Foster collapse[78]. The symptoms of the Foster collapse will be discussed more closely in the next chapter. Here we will look at the risk of getting one, which is determined by the Heat Stress Index (HSI). The HSI can be calculated by the following formula:

$HSI = E/E_{max}$

In this formula E_{max} is the maximum amount of heat that can be released to the ambient air. Obviously, the HSI needs to be less than one to prevent the accumulation of heat and overheating. To illustrate the concept, we have calculated the HSI for a RH of 100% and a T_{wb} of 20 and 30°C. The results are given in the figures. The figures show clearly that at a wet-bulb temperature of 30°C extreme values for the HSI of 2-3 will occur. In such conditions many runners will succumb to the heat, so races should be banned!

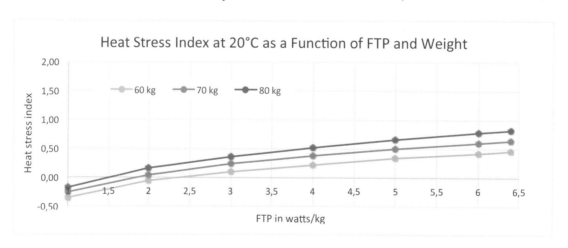

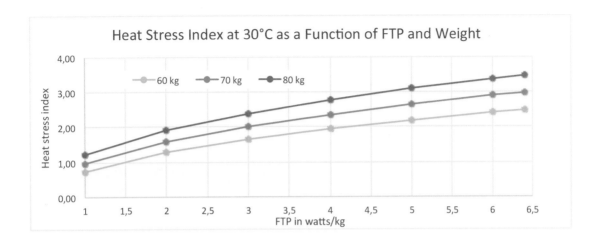

Conclusions on the Impact of Tropical Conditions (Such as the Atlanta Olympic Marathon)

During the Atlanta Olympic Marathon, the conditions were severe with an air temperature of 25°C and a relative humidity of 70%, so the wet-bulb temperature was around 20°C. In these conditions, the net sweat loss of a 60 kg world-class runner will be around 0.8 l/h. This means that the gross sweat loss during the marathon can be as high as 3*2*0.8 = 4.8 liters. A flyweight like Thugwane would lose only 3*2*0.55 = 3.3 liters, a significant advantage, which most likely has contributed to his success!

A heavy runner of 90 kg would have lost almost 10 liters of sweat during the same race. This is equivalent to a weight loss of 11% and will lead to an increase in rectal temperature of 2.2°C. In practice, severe dehydration phenomena can already occur at a weight loss of 5% and an increase of rectal temperature of 1.5°C. So, it is clear that the heavy runner runs a major risk of suffering from heat exhaustion, a sunstroke or even a Foster collapse.

Tim Noakes, the author of *The Lore of Running*,[6] summarized the impact of sweat loss on the performance of runners with the slogan "All great marathoners are small." We now understand this is particularly true in tropical conditions.

55. THE FOSTER COLLAPSE: CRAWLING TO THE FINISH

For me a day without training is a day without eating.
—Haile Gebrselassie

Occasionally, we see a runner that has become so exhausted that he literally crawls to the finish. How is this possible? What happens to your body at such a moment? Recently, a good review study on the topic was published in the literature[78]. We will summarize the results in this chapter that we wrote together with Karel Bos, MD (and long distance runner).

History

The most famous incident in recent history was the Swiss marathon runner Gabriela Andersen-Schiess, who collapsed in the final stretch of the 1984 Olympic Games in Los Angeles. In full view of millions of startled TV viewers, she literally crawled to the finish. Equally dramatic was the finish of American triathlete Julie Moss at the 1982 Hawaii Marathon. After leading throughout the race, she collapsed and crawled to the finish, where she was just passed by Kathy McCartney. Both Gabriela and Julie refused any assistance as they knew of the experiences of Italian Dorando Pietri. He was the first to cross the finish line at the 1908 Olympic Games in London, but he was carried to the finish by officials. The American team protested, Pietri got disqualified and American Johnny Hayes was declared the official winner.

Physiology of the Foster Collapse

Most runners manage to regulate their pace and to complete competitive endurance events without mishap. However, some runners do experience an exercise-induced collapse associated with postural hypotension, which in rare cases results in life-threatening conditions such as cardiac disorders and heat stroke. Despite the experience of either catastrophic system failure or extreme peripheral muscle fatigue, some runners persist in attempting to reach the finish line. This often results in a sequence of dynamic

Dorando Pietri at the 1908 Olympic Games.

changes in posture and gait that has been named after the American physiologist Carl Foster. The runners will sequentially show the following phenomena (see also the four figures):

1. Early Foster: the runner can no longer maintain an upright position and will stumble ahead, leaning forward.

3. Fall: the runner lies on the ground with both arms and legs down.

2. Half Foster: the torso is bent forward to a horizontal position.

4. Full Foster: the runner tries to crawl to the finish line.

Which Are the Causes?

Previously, it was thought that dehydration and hyperthermia caused the Foster collapse, but nowadays physicians believe that the real cause is an extremely low blood pressure in combination with a too low heart rate and insufficient blood return flow by the vena. As a result of this, the heart has insufficient capacity to pump blood to the brain. Therefore, the runner becomes dizzy, his legs start waddling and he cannot run any more. Consequently, most Foster collapses occur right after the finish, when the heart rate drops and the runner gets dizzy as a result. Obviously at that moment the air cooling is also lost, as we saw in the previous chapter!

Which Are the Consequences?

The Foster collapse should be regarded as a protective mechanism of the body. As the torso and the brain get closer to the ground, the heart can still manage to maintain the circulation and the supply of blood to the brain. Consequently, physicians and medics should not attempt to position victims upright, but instead treat them lying on the ground. The best treatment is to provide cooling and water. The victim should definitely not be encouraged to complete the race! In most cases, the body will recover after some time and the heart will be capable to maintain circulation. The runner may then slowly get up again and will not suffer any permanent damage.

Medical Risks

The Foster collapse should not be confused with the phenomenon of a cardiac arrest or silent death. Just like all people, athletes run a small risk (approximately 1 in 100,000) of dying from cardiac arrest while running. This can be caused by cardiac arrhythmia (often young people who suffer a hereditary heart condition), by a heart infarction (as a result of arteriosclerosis) and by hyperthermia. You can reduce the risks by regularly taking a physical exam in a sports medical center. A fatal cardiac arrhythmia can also be caused by a viral infection. Never run a race when you have the flu or a fever! In spite of the above risks, running should be regarded as a very healthy sport. The large majority of runners age healthy and fit!

The number of non-fatal Foster collapses cannot easily be estimated as they are not well reported. According to literature at least 99.9% of all runners complete the marathon without collapsing. 59% of all reported cases of Foster collapse occurred after the finish line!

Which Are the Risk Factors?

The large majority of runners are simply unable to dig so deep that these problems may occur. Most of us listen to our body and reduce our pace in time. Only the extremely motivated runners may get into problems as a result of the following factors:

» Deliberately ignoring the signs
» Not noticing the signs as a result of habit
» Malfunctioning of the body's control system

Conclusions

We hope that this information will encourage our readers to run wisely and avoid maintaining an excessive pace for too long. Listen to your body and avoid these excesses!

56. THE IMPACT OF THE RAIN, THE WIND AND THE COLD

If you want to be the best runner you can be, start now. Don't spend the rest of your life wondering if you can do it.

In winter, we regularly have to face the rain, the wind and the cold. In this chapter, we will look into the impact of these factors on your performance. We will study the experiences of authors Hans and Ron during the Dutch Masters Championship Marathon in November 2013 at Eindhoven, the Netherlands. The temperature was 8°C, so it looked fine. Nevertheless, Hans had to drop out of the race with hypothermia, whereas Ron did well and finsihed in a PB. What happened? How can the combination of rain, wind and cold cause hypothermia? How can we explain the different results of Hans and Ron? At least four factors play a role in hypothermia; they will be discussed in this chapter.

The Windchill

As a result of the wind, the perceived temperature at your skin can be much lower that the air temperature. This perceived decrease in temperature is called the windchill. It is caused by the fact that the wind blows away the insulating layer of air around your skin. The windchill temperature (T_{wc}) can be calculated with the following formula[79]:

$$T_{wc} = 13.12 + 0.6215T_a - 11.37v^{0.16} + 0.3965T_a v^{0.16}$$

In this formula T_a is the air temperature and v is the wind speed in km/h. The figure below gives T_{wc} as a function of the air temperature and the wind speed.

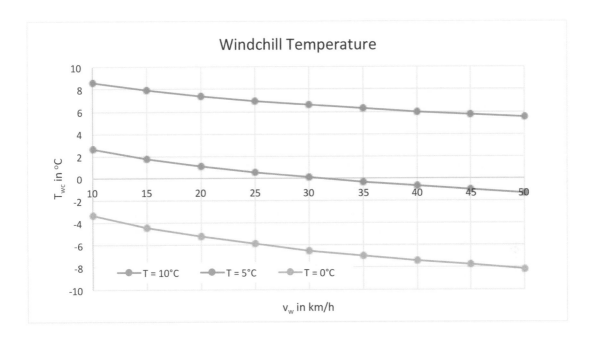

In pratice, the windchill temperaure can be as much as 10°C lower than the air temperature. In the conditions of the Eindhoven Marathon, the windchill temperature was around 3°C, close to freezing!

The Rain May Cause Hypothermia

In the rain, your skin gets wet. This prevents the insulating layer of air from forming around your skin. This is a very serious drawback, as air insulates 26 times better than water! In literature[6] experiences in rainy conditions during the Glasgow Marathon have been reported. The air temperature was 12°C and the wind speed 16-40 km/h (4-6 Beaufort). Many runners had to drop out with hypothermia, some of them with a rectal temperature as low as 34.3°C!

Wear Protective Clothing and Use Protective Skin Oil

A main function of running wear is to maintain the insulating layer of air around the skin. In cold conditions, it is wise to wear multiple layers of lightweight porous and breathable running wear that will not adsorb moisture and will ensure an optimal insulation. In literature[6], guidelines can be found on the number of insulating layers as a function of the windchill temperature and the running speed. At windchill temperatures around the freezing point at least two or three layers are required, in particular when the cloth can get wet and lose its insulating properties. When the running speed drops to pedestrian pace, even four layers are necessary! The impact of running speed is significant. At rest four times as many layers are required as compared to running at a speed of 16 km/h. An extreme example are the Inuit at the North pole; they need ten layers of insulating clothing!

Nowadays, you can also use protective skin oil. This will form a thin insulating layer on the skin, limiting the heat loss. This oil is also used by many cyclists, who are even more bothered by the cold than runners as a result of their higher speed. Be aware that the rain may wash off the oil, so the insulating properties are lost!

Small and Skinny Runners Are More Vulnerable to the Cold

The fourth and final factor is the sensitivity of the runner to the cold. Literature[6] states that small runners are more vulnerable. This is caused by the fact that they have more skin surface area as compared to their body weight. Consequently, their heat balance is less favorable. Runners with a low body fat level are also more vulnerable, as body fat has insulating properties. Tim Noakes, the author of The Lore of Running[6], concluded that the vulnerabilty to the cold is the reverse of the vulnerabilty to the heat. In the heat, small and skinny runners have an advantage, but in the cold the reverse is the case. Frank Shorter, the American winner of the 1972 Olympic Games, is an example of a runner that performed well in the heat and poorly in the cold.

Looking back at the experiences of authors Hans and Ron at the Eindhoven Marathon, we can now understand the differences. The conditions were severe, with a windchill temperature of 3°C in combination with the rain. Ron made the correct choice by wearing three layers of protective clothing. Hans was too ambitious and started the race without any protection, just wearing his singlet. Also Hans is much smaller and skinnier than Ron. The results confirm the above theory: Hans learned an expensive lesson as he dropped out with hypothermia and Ron ran a PB!

With a windchill temperature of 3 °C in combination with the rain Ron (5500) made the correct choice by wearing three layers of protective clothing. Hans (5501) was too ambitious, wearing just his singlet.

57.THE MARATHON I: HITTING THE WALL

If you want to win something, run 100 meter. If you want to experience something, run a marathon. —Emil Zatopek

Most long-distance runners consider the marathon to be the ultimate goal. Next to the illustrious fame of the distance and the thrill of running amidst cheering crowds in the big city centers, there is another good reason for this: the challenge of going to the limit of human endurance. Unfortunately, many runners go even beyond this point and they may experience the dreaded phenomenon of hitting the wall. In this first chapter on the marathon, we will study this phenomenon and learn what you can do to avoid it.

What Happens When Tou Hit the Wall?

Many marathoners will hit the wall around the 30K point. Suddenly your legs feel completely empty and from one moment to the other your power stride disintegrates into a cumbersome stumble. Author Hans remembers his first encounter with the wall very well. In the 1983 Rotterdam Marathon, he ran easily at a pace of 3:30/km and around 30K he was confident he could finish sub 2:30. But all of a sudden, his legs gave out, he started puffing and gasping and his pace dropped to 4:30/km. He was overtaken by hundreds of other runners and had to master all of his will power to keep moving and avoid the disaster of dropping out. To this day, he vividly remembers the agony of the last 10K and the exhilarating relief when he crossed the finish line and his legs were allowed to stop moving! Looking back now, his final race time of 2:43 does not seem bad, but at the time he was bitterly disappointed.

What Can You Do to Avoid Hitting the Wall?

The mathematics of hitting the wall consist of three factors:

1. As we saw in an earlier chapter, the energy cost of running is linearly proportional to the body weight and the distance:

   E = cmd

   In the formula c is the specific energy cost of running (0.98 kJ/kg/km), m is the body weight (in kg) and d is the distance (in kilometers). As an example, the energy cost for our Marathon Man becomes 0.98*70*42.2 = 2895 kJ. We also note that when Marathon Man would gain 10 kg in body weight, his energy use would increase to 0.98*80*42.2 = 3308 kJ!

2. When we compare this energy use with the amount of energy stored in our body (in the blood, the liver and the muscles) in the form of glucose and glycogen, we find that there is a deficit. In the table, the energy balance is given. We see that Marathon Man will face a deficit of some 28%. If his weight increased to 80 kg, the deficit would increase to 37%!

Energy Balance in a Marathon (kJ)				
	Marathon Man (70 kg)			
	weight 70 kg		weight 80 kg	
Energy use in a marathon		2895		3308
Glucose storage in blood	21		21	
Glycogen storage in liver	366		366	
Glycogen storage in muscles	1308		1308	
Glucose intake during running	395		395	
	2090	2090	2090	2090
Deficit		805		1219
Percentage deficit = percentage fatty acids		28%		37%

3. When the stores of glucose and glycogen are exhausted, our body will switch over to using fatty acids as fuel. However, as we saw earlier, the conversion of fatty acids requires more oxygen and produces far less power. This is what happens when we hit the wall. The stores of glucose and glycogen are

exhausted and suddenly we need to breath much more heavily to supply the additional required oxygen and the power in our legs is strongly reduced. From the data of the table, you might conclude that Marathon Man will hit the wall after 0.72*42.2 = 30K. In reality, the situation is somewhat more favorable. This is caused by the fact that in the initial part of the marathon your muscles do not derive their energy solely from glucose and glycogen, but from a fuel mix that also contains fatty acids. The exact fuel mix depends on your pace. The amount of fatty acids in the fuel mix is higher at a low pace. Normal runners will run the marathon at about 94% of their FTP, as we saw earlier. At this pace, the amount of fatty acids in the fuel mix will be about 30%. This slightly exceeds the deficit of 28% that we calculated above. Consequently, Marathon Man might just avoid hitting the wall. However, if his weight increased to 80 kg, he would definitely hit the wall, as his calculated deficit of 37% is significantly higher than the 30% share of the fatty acids. We note that in reality the results depend somewhat on the individual characteristics of the runners. Runners with exceptional fatigue resistance can maintain a higher percentage of their FTP during the marathon. However, as a result of their higher pace, they use less fatty acids in their fuel mix, as shown in the table below.

Pace and Fuel Mix		
	Pace	Fuel Mix
Fatigue resistance	(% FTP max)	(% fatty acids)
Exceptional	100	26
Good	97	28
Normal	94	30
Less good	92	32
Limited	90	34

Which Are the Conclusions?

Based on the energy balance, the following conclusions are quite clear:

1. Additional body weight leads to a higher energy cost of running, so it increases the risk of hitting the wall.
2. A high initial pace leads to a higher share of glucose and glycogen in the fuel mix, so it increases the risk of hitting the wall.

In the figure we have illustrated these conclusions for our Marathon Man. In the standard situation, his body weight is 70 kg and he runs a 3:30 marathon, so he would run at 94% of his FTP. At this pace, his

Your body weight and your initial pace are important factors in determining the risk of hitting the wall during the marathon.

fuel mix would contain 30% fatty acids, so he could just avoid hitting the wall. However, if his weight would increase to 80 kg, he would have to run at 104% of his (new and lower) FTP at the same 3:30 marathon pace. At 104% of his FTP, the fuel mix would contain only 22% of fatty acids, so he would definitely hit the wall early in the race. At 80 kg, he would be wise to limit his initial pace to a 4:00 marathon. At this pace, he would run at around 91% of his FTP and with 33% fatty acids in his fuel mix. Although he would still face a deficit at the end of the race, this strategy will buy him time and may postpone the wall to the final kilometers.

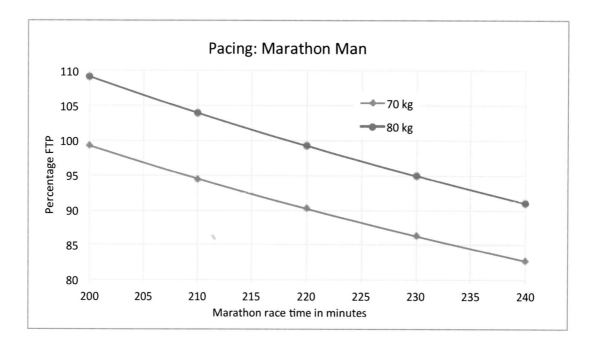

In summary, we conclude that reducing your body weight and your initial pace are the most important strategies you can use to minimize the risk of hitting the wall. We note that the above calculations are valid for normal runners with average supplies of glucose and glycogen. In the next chapters, we will investigate what you can do to optimize the stock of glycogen by means of carbo-loading and how you may optimize the intake of glucose with sports drinks during the race.

A well chosen initial pace is one of the most important ingredients in your strategy to minimize the risk of hitting the wall.

58. THE MARATHON II: THE IMPACT OF CARBO-LOADING

When you run a marathon, the things happen after 20K.
—Haile Gebrselassie

In the 1970s, the Swedish researcher B. Saltin[6,80] was the first to observe that the glycogen level in the muscles of athletes could be increased by eating food with a high amount of carbohydrates for a few days. This was the origin of the marathon diet, or carbo-loading as it is now practiced by many marathon runners worldwide. The majority of the big city marathons nowadays have a traditional pasta party on the eve of the marathon.

How Does Carbo-Loading Affect the Energy Balance?

Carbo-loading comprises of changing the diet during the last 2-3 days before the race in such a way as to increase the level of carbohydrates to some 70%. Normally athletes will have a diet containing only 50% of carbohydrates. In practice, it means that the consumption of fats and to some extent also proteins has to be reduced greatly. Instead, products rich in carbohydrates have to be eaten, like vegetables, fruits, whole-wheat bread, potatoes, pasta, honey, figs, and so on. During these final days, you should avoid products like butter, cheese, fat meat, chocolate, cake and fried snacks. This carbo-loading will lead to an increase in the glycogen level in your muscles and the liver (also known as super compensation). This effect will be strengthened by the fact that you will reduce the training significantly during these final days (known as tapering).

The table shows the average impact of carbo-loading on the energy balance of Marathon Man[6,7,80]. We see that the glycogen stores in the liver and the muscles may increase to such a level that there is no longer a deficit in the energy balance. This means that Marathon Man could avoid hitting the wall, provided he does not start at an excessive pace.

Energy Balance During a Marathon (kJ) and the Impact of Carbo-Loading				
	Marathon Man (70 kg) weight 70 kg		Carbo-loaded weight 70 kg	
Energy use during marathon		2895		2895
Glucose storage in blood	21		21	
Glycogen storage in liver	366		549	
Glycogen storage in muscles	1308		2092	
Glucose intake during running	395		395	
	2090	2090	3057	3057
Deficit		805		-162
Percentage deficit = percentage fatty acids		28%		-6%

Body Weight Increase From Carbo-Loading

The above confirms the advantages of carbo-loading, so we can understand and support the widespread application of this practice by marathoners around the world. As a matter of fact, carbo-loading has psychological advantages as well. Most runners relish these last days of rest and eating large amounts of sweet carbohydrates!

However, we note that you should be careful not to overdo it and eat too much. This will lead to an undesirable increase in your body weight as each gram of glycogen will chemically bind three grams of water as well. Author Hans noted a significant increase in his body weight during the final days before the Rotterdam Marathon of 2012. As the figure shows, he gained 2.2 kg and it took five days before his weight had returned to normal.

According to theory, the weight increase of 2.2 kg is equivalent to an additonal intake of carbohydrates of 2.2/4 = 550 grams. This matched well with the additional amount of honey, bananes, pasta and sweets that Hans ate the last days before the marathon. He concluded that he had overdone the carbo-loading! In later marathons, he reduced the carbo-loading somewhat (including limiting the carbo-loading to the final two days instead of three) and was able to manage his weight increase to 1 kg.

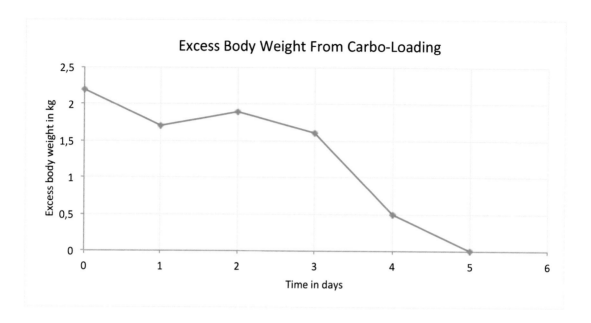

Excess Body Weight From Carbo-Loading

Marathon Breakfast

Finally, we note that you should take an alimentary breakfast on the morning of the marathon, some three hours before the start. This will stock up the glycogen stores in the liver. During the night, these stores are reduced, so it is neccesary to complement them. The stores in the muscles are not reduced during the night, so you don't have to worry about this and you can dream of a PB!

Carbo-loading comprises increasing the amount of carbohydrates in your diet to 70% during the last 2-3 days before the marathon. However, avoid eating too much, because it will increase your body weight and subsequently negatively affect your race time.

59. THE MARATHON III: THE IMPACT OF SPORTS DRINKS

And finally I run, because there is no better way to see the sun rise and set. —Amby Burfoot

In the previous chapters, we learned that the glucose and glycogen stores are quite critical in the marathon. When the available stores become exhausted, the muscles have to switch to fatty acids as fuel. Fatty acids require more oxygen and produce much less power than glucose and glycogen. This is the moment you suddenly feel your legs are empty: you are hitting the wall.

Most marathon runners experience hitting the wall around 30K. Effective strategies to postpone or even avoid hitting the wall are:

1. Reduce your body weight as this will reduce the energy cost of running.
2. Reduce your initial pace as this will reduce the share of carbohydrates in the fuel mix.
3. Stock up the stores of glycogen by carbo-loading in the last few days before the race (in combination with tapering).
4. Complement the use of carbohydrates during the race by eating gels or drinking sports drinks.

The table shows the impact to the energy balance of our Marathon Man should he choose not to complement carbohydrates during the race. We see that the result will be that his deficit will increase from 28 to 41%! Obviously, this deficit is so large that he will definitely hit the wall and collapse early in the race!

Energy Balance During a Marathon (kJ) and the Impact of Sports Drinks				
	Marathon Man (70 kg)			
	With sports drinks		Without sports drinks	
Energy use during marathon		2895		2895
Glucose storage in blood	21		21	
Glycogen storage in liver	366		366	
Glycogen storage in muscles	1308		1308	
Glucose intake during running	395		0	
	2090	2090	1695	1695
Deficit		805		1200
Percentage deficit = percentage fatty acids		28%		41%

Sports Drinks Supplement the Energy Use in the Marathon!

The calculations show that you should always supplement the use of carbohydrates during the marathon! Fortunately, all big city marathons nowadays have hydration stations with sports drinks and water every 5K. These sports drinks contain 70 gram/liter of carbohydrates. Such drinks are isotonic, which means they have the same osmotic pressure as the blood plasm. As a result of this, the carbohydrates will be quickly transferred to the blood. When a runner drinks 150 ml every 5K and an additional 150 ml at the starting line, he will boost his glucose level by 9*0.15*70 = 95 gram. As the energy value of glucose is 16.7 kJ/g and the muscle efficiency can be set at 25%, this will add 395 kJ to his energy balance. This is the amount with which we have calculated so far. As we saw, for Marathon Man, this should just be sufficient to avoid hitting the wall.

As we saw in the calculations, drinking sports drinks can make all the difference in the energy balance of the marathon. At first sight, this may seems surprising as theoretically the 395 kJ is equivalent to the energy cost of running 395/(70*0.98) = 5.8 km. Nevertheless, for our Marathon Man, the makeup of 395 kJ will mean that he can avoid hitting the wall. Also in this respect lightweight runners have an advantage, as the same amount of drinks will have a relatively bigger impact on their energy balance.

Sports Drinks Also Supplement the Liquid Loss

Another good reason to use sports drinks in the marathon is to partly compensate the sweat loss and avoid dehydration. As we saw in an earlier chapter, the sweat loss of Marathon Man could be as high as five liters in severe weather conditions. His weight loss would be 5/70*100 = 7% and his rectal temperature would increase by 7*0.2 = 1.4°C. Both would exceed the recommended limits (5% and 1°C, respectively), which means that severe dehydration phenomena could occur, including heat exhaustion, sunstroke and Foster collapse. However, if Marathon Man drank as specified above, he would consume 1.35 liters of water, so his liquid loss would be limited to 3.65 liters. Although still severe, this would limit his weight loss of 3.6/70*100 = 5% and the increase of his rectal temperature of 5*0.2 = 1°C. Both values would just remain at the critical limits, so he might make it without severe dehydration.

Use Sponges in Hot Conditions

In tropical conditions, it is essential to use the sponge posts as well! Sponge your skin regularly to assist in cooling and limit the temperature increase resulting from the heat produced by running. Research has shown that any increase in rectal temperature will have a negative impact on the running performance[6].

Sports Drinks Are Necessary, But Only During the Marathon

We often see runners taking in large amounts of sports drinks or gels during a 10K or half marathon. They may gain a psychological advantage from these practices, but it is really unnecessary from the point of view of the energy or fluid balance. In these shorter distances, the glycogen supplies are never critical. Also the liquid loss will not likely be a problem, unless the conditions are extremely tropical. You should be cautious in habituating yourself to sports drinks as these provide additional calories, which are unnecessary and undesirable. This applies even more to energy drinks that contain much more calories. They are only meaningful to extreme sports like the Tour de France, where the cyclists use close to 10,000 kJ of energy on a daily basis.

Composition of Sports Drinks Is Not Very Critical

Despite all the advertisements, the composition of the sports drinks is not very critical. The main factor is the amount of carbohydrates which should be around 70 gram/liter. A mixture of glucose and fructose is recommended as this has the quickest rate of absorption. Other additives are unnecessary or at most relevant for reasons of taste. The salt content is also irrelevant as the salt loss by sweating is small. Preparing your own drink from some fruit juice or sugar mixed with water is also possible. It is always wise to test the composition of the drink in training to make sure you digest it well.

Except during the marathon, sports drinks are not really necessary from the point of view of the energy or fluid balance.

60. THE MARATHON IV: TIPS AND TRICKS

When you run a marathon, you run against the distance, not against the other runners and not against the time.
—*Haile Gebrselassie*

The marathon is the ultimate goal of most distance runners and for good reasons:

1. The marathon is the culmination of a long period of meticulous preparations.
   Consistent and extensive training is required as the marathon poses a challenge at or beyond the limit of human endurance. During these many months, your fitness improves to optimal levels. Your mental fitness also improves and you become more and more anxious to meet the ultimate challenge. Particularly during the final weeks, you feel strong and confident. Those are the moments you dream of crossing the finish line in a PB!

2. The marathon itself is a unique and exhilarating happening.
   The thrill of big city marathons is very special indeed. You get the opportunity to start amidst the elite Kenyan and Ethiopian runners. TV helicopters are circling over your head and a gun marks the start of the race. Many thousands of spectators are cheering you on while you run along historic landmarks in the big city centers. You feel that the city belongs to you and your fellow runners that day!

3. The marathon is the ultimate human challenge.
   Triathletes may challenge this, but we consider the marathon the toughest sporting event as a result of the combination of the distance and the pace. For most people, running a marathon at the peak of their performance cannot be completed without protracted and extreme suffering. From a physiological point of view, it can be stated that running a marathon at peak performance requires going to the edge or beyond the limit of human endurance. That is why so many runners hit the wall around the 30K mark and are forced to resort to stumbling, walking or even dropping out. Even the elite Kenyans and Ethiopians can only perform to the best of their abilities if all goes well on that particular day.

In this chapter, we will give some tips and tricks for the marathon. These are based on our own views and experiences. We have included some aspects that have already been discussed in earlier chapters, such as the energy cost of running a marathon, the impact of carbo-loading and the impact of sports drinks during the marathon.

Training

Don't start unless you have run consistently and regularly! You should be able to run a half marathon without any difficulties! For the marathon itself, you should specifically prepare during a period of three months. Don't run more than two or three marathons per year. Build a sufficient base by including a weekly long endurance run (25-30K) at an easy, conversational pace. This will stimulate your fatty acid system and improve your fatigue resistance. During the other days of the week, you should include the other training elements: tempo runs, climax runs, hill training, fartlek, intervals and speed work. Be sure to include sufficient speed training to increase your FTP, VO_2 max, speed and running economy. Participate regularly in races at shorter distances (3K, 5K, 10K, 15K, 21.1K). It is recommended to train almost every day (for about one hour) and reach a total volume of at least 80K per week. Make sure you plan a gradual buildup in the training, with the maximum volume around three weeks before the marathon. For more details on training, we refer to the earlier chapters.

Tapering

During the last two weeks before the marathon, you should substantially reduce the volume of the training, so you arrive at the start fresh and hungry. Let's say you have trained 100K in the third week before the marathon. It would be good to reduce the volume to 60K in the second week and 30K or even less in the final week before the marathon. Try to do as little as possible in the final three days. Research has shown that tapering will improve your performance by 1.5%. However, it is important that you maintain your speed in these final weeks by doing a few intervals or short tempo runs.

Nutrition

Try to eat as healthy as possible in the months before the marathon. This means eating lean products, with a substantial base of vegetables and fruit and avoiding snacks and sodas. You will probably lose some body fat as a result of the improved nutrition and training. This is fine and will contribute to your performance!

During the final 2-3 days before the marathon, you should apply the carbo-loading diet. This means you need to increase the share of carbohydrates to 70%. Consequently, you should eat even less meat and fat. On these days, you should eat even more vegetables, fruit, honey, raisins and pasta. Don't overdo it, as this may lead to an undesirable increase in weight! However, do enjoy these final days of resting and eating tasty carbohydrates, including the pasta party on the eve of the marathon! You have earned these days of relaxing and can be confident that you will perform well.

On the morning of the marathon day, you should consume an alimentary breakfast three hours before the race to complement the nightly decrease of the glycogen level in your liver. Take two cups of strong coffee en route to the marathon to benefit from the ergogenic effect of caffeine. This will stimulate the fatty acid system and has a positive impact on the nervous system. When the start is more than three hours after breakfast, you can eat some refreshment (whole-wheat bread or bananas) up to two hours before the race.

Mental Preparation

Make sure you prepare a good race plan, based on your training and earlier performances in races. As an example, in 2011 author Hans had run a 10M race at a pace of 3:58/km. Based on this, he calculated that he should be able to run the marathon at a pace of 4:15/km. From his training data, he knew that this pace would be equivalent to a HR of around 145-150 bpm. As his threshold level was 153, he figured he should be able to maintain this pace throughout the marathon. The race plan proved to be perfect as in reality he finished the Essen Marathon in 3:01:07 with an average HR of 150!

Try to make a similar plan for your own race and stick to it during the race! Many are tempted to increase the pace in the early part of the marathon. This is understandable as you are fit, rested and eager to run a PB. However, you will certainly regret this in the later stages when your legs give out! The only realistic strategy for the marathon is to attempt to maintain an even pace. Starting too fast is the most common error. You may win a few minutes early on, but you will lose many more in the second half!

You should visualize the race course beforehand and prepare yourself for any predicaments, like the thrill of the start and the fatigue in the later stages. Be calm and confident: when you have done the training, you can do it! Commit yourself to avoid dropping out, even when your legs give out; you will surely regret this! Of course, this does not apply to serious problems, such as dehydration or injuries. Your health is more important than your performance.

The Start

Be sure to arrive early, but don't hang around many hours before the start. Enjoy the moment, the happening and the fact you are fit enough to participate. A warming up is not required, save your strength for the 42 km. Bring along an old sweater you can throw away after the start. Wear this over your race shirt in the starting section, so you don't get cold.

Drink some 200 ml of sports drink a few minutes before the start. This will ensure that the glucose level in your blood will be supplemented already in the first 5K. Start at a relaxed pace and don't let yourself get carried away by the mass of unexperienced runners starting too fast. Look at your running watch so you know your pace already during the first kilometer. Stick to your race plan and don't be tempted to win some seconds in the early stages. A high pace will increase the consumption of glucose and glycogen, so you will face a deficit later on. This will definitely increase the risk of hitting the wall! Run carefully and alert during the first kilometers. Unfortunately, stumbles and falls regularly happen in the crowd.

During the Race

Try to get into a good pack of runners. This can be a big help, as it will reduce the air resistance and also provide moral support. Stick to the race plan! Drink 150 ml of sports drink at every refreshment post (usually every 5K). In training you will have practiced drinking, so you can run and drink at the same time. Also use the sponges to cool your legs and the back of your head in hot conditions. Enjoy the race and the crowds! Remember your plans and evaluate your pace, your HR and how your legs feel. Consider whether it is necessary to change the plan, but don' t do this too soon. In the marathon good and bad moments can alternate, so stick to the plan as long as possible. After all, you have prepared the race plan carefully, so don't throw it away rashly.

As the race progresses, you can start the count down and consider whether you have something left in the tank for a final pace increase. Don't do this before the 30-35K point. The marathon remains unpredictable and you may easily lose one minute per kilometer when you hit the wall! Watch the other runners around you; when you regularly overtake others, you are probably still strong and may take a chance. When the going gets tough, you may try to surmount this by changing your rhythm or by reducing your stride length and increasing your cadence.

During the marathon take sports drinks for extra energy and rehydration. When you like you can also eat bananas or take an energy gel or bar.

The Finish

Give it all you've got in the final 2K and if nothing is left in the tank, try to at least keep the pace going. Your legs will feel empty, but after the finish this will momentarily be forgotten! Your pack will probably have disintegrated, but if you still have a companion you can stimulate each other to push to the limit in these final moments. The cheers of the spectators and your fans will surely help as well. Watch for the finish and the finish photo. Be sure to raise your arms, so you will get a memorable photo. Enjoy the finish and the euphoria of reaching it. You will feel a sense of great relief, just by allowing your legs to stop moving! Chat with your fellow runners on how great the experience has been. Rehydrate by drinking water and sports drinks and eat some bananas, oranges or apples. Embrace your loved ones and be proud that you did it!

After the Marathon

The next day, you will notice that you feel like an old man who cannot climb down the stairs. The pain in your muscles will stay for a few days. Rest and don't resume training for at least four days. Then slowly and gradually you can build up the training again.

Many runners will find that they can run PBs at shorter distances in the months after the marathon. This is the super compensation effect of the marathon and is caused by the training and the body fat loss. Enjoy your fitness and the flow that you may experience! With a proper program, you can utilize your increased fitness and start planning for a new target.

61. HOW FAST COULD YOU CYCLE, ICE SKATE AND CLIMB STAIRS?

Everything you need is already inside. —Bill Bowerman

In this chapter, we will illustrate a fun application of our models—to calculate how well you could perform in other sports besides running. We can do this using the FTP as the amount of power that your human engine can maintain for one hour. For other durations, we can calculate the power from the FTP with Riegel's formula.

In an earlier chapter, we saw that our Marathon Man has an FTP of 3.67 watts/kg. As his body weight is 70 kg, his human engine can maintain a power output of 3.67*70 = 257 watts during one hour of running. In this chapter, we will assume that he can mobilize the same amount of power for other sports as well. Next to running, we will study the examples of cycling, ice skating and stair climbing. The laws of physics apply to all of these sports, so we can easily modify the running equation and calculate the performance in these sports as well. Of course, our Marathon Man is a runner and he will have to train sufficiently in order to master these other sports as well. Also, he might be more talented in running than in these other sports. Nevertheless, we believe that our method can be used to predict his potential performance in other sports as the power of the human engine is the driving force in all sports.

Running

In running, obviously the total power of the human engine should be equal to the sum of the running resistance, the air resistance and the climbing resistance ($P = P_r + P_a + P_c$). As an example, the figure gives the race time at the 10,000 meters as a function of the specific power (in watts/kg) in ideal (windless) conditions. We see that Kenenisa Bekela ran with a specific power of 7.04 watts/kg to set his world record of 26:17. Marathon Man can run a time of 45:13 with his specific power of 3.75 watts/kg (which is slightly more than his FTP of 3.67 watts/kg as the duration is less than one hour).

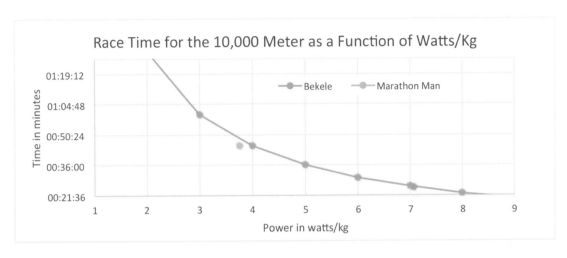

The Ethiopian 10,000-meter men's Olympic selection trials for the 2016 Rio Olympic Games in Hengelo (the Netherlands). Kenenisa Bekele ran with #1.

Cycling

In cycling, we use the cycling equation[2], which says that the total power of the human engine should be equal to the sum of the rolling resistance, the air-resistance, the climbing resistance and the mechanical resistance ($P/\eta = P_r + P_a + P_c$). The rolling resistance in cycling is 33 times smaller than the running resistance, so the wheel was really an amazing invention! The c_dA value of a streamlined time-trial specialist is somewhat lower than that of a runner. We have prepared the two figures below, which illustrate the potential performance of Marathon Man in cycling:

1. The attainable distance in one hour

    Bradley Wiggins improved the world hour record to 54.5 kilometers in 2015. According to our calculations, he needed 468 watts to do this. Our Marathon Man can cycle 44.5 kilometers in one hour with his FTP of 257 watts, provided of course that he can cycle with similar skill and streamlining as Bradley.

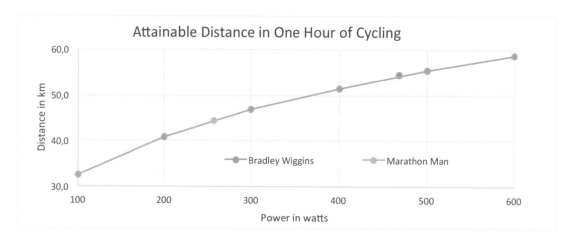

2. The climbing time to the top of Alpe d'Huez

    Pantani holds the record with a time of 37:35. According to our calculations, he needed a specific power of 6.52 watts/kg, which is suspiciously high in view of the thin mountain air. Our Marathon Man could reach the top in 57 minutes with his specific power of 3.67 watts/kg, provided he can cycle with the same skill and gear as Marco.

A young Bradley Wiggins wins Gold in the 4000 m pursuit at the 2004 Athens Olympic Games.

Ice Skating

In ice skating, we equate the total power of the human engine to the sum of the gliding resistance and the air resistance ($P = P_g + P_a$). The gliding resistance is five times higher than the rolling resistance in cycling and 6.6 times lower than the running resistance[3]. The c_dA value in ice skating is somewhat higher than in running on account of the sliding motion in skating. Using these data and some results in practice, we have prepared the below figure of the race time at the 10,000 meter as a function of the total power. According to our calculations, multiple world champion Sven Kramer needed a total power of 580 watts for his Heerenveen track record of 12:40. Marathon Man can skate a time of 16:17 with his total power of 281 watts (somewhat higher than 257 watts as the duration is only 17 minutes).

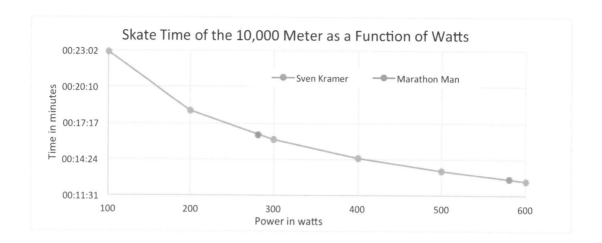

Skate Time of the 10,000 Meter as a Function of Watts

Climbing the Stairs of the Empire State Building

In stair climbing, the climbing resistance is decisive (P_c = mgv). Consequently, how fast you can climb follows directly from the power (P). As an example, we use the Empire State Building Run-Up (height (h) = 320 meters). The attainable race time follows from:

$$t = E/P = mgh/P = m*9.81*320/P = 3139/(P/m)$$

So far, we have neglected the power required for the running resistance. To compensate for this, we have added 25% to the climbing resistance. The figure shows the resulting relationship between the climbing time and the specific power.

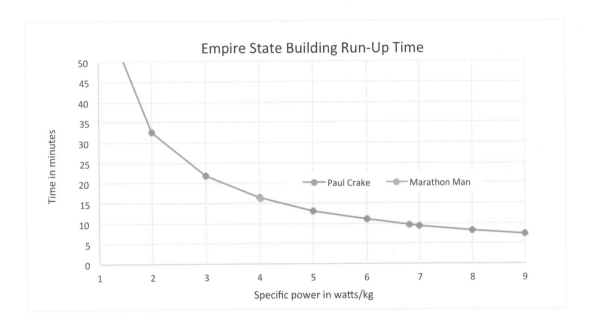

The record time of 9:33 by Paul Crake means that his specific power (P/m) must have been 6.8 watts/kg. According to our calculations, Marathon Man could reach the top in 16 minutes with a specific power of 4.0 watts/kg (somewhat higher than 3.67 watts/kg as the duration is only 16 minutes).

In summary, we conclude that the laws of physics enable us to calculate the performance in many endurance sports, including running, cycling, ice skating and stair climbing. Of course, these calculations are just theory. In practice, you will have to train well to develop the muscles and skills required for the different sports. Also, you might be more talented in one sport than in another. Nevertheless, we believe these calculations will give a good estimate of the potential performance with your human engine.

62. THE MAXIMUM POWER OF SPRINTERS AND DISTANCE RUNNERS

We all have dreams. But in order to make dreams come into reality, it takes an awful lot of determination, dedication, self-discipline and effort. —Jesse Owens

So far, we have calculated a lot with the FTP, the specific power (in watts/kg) that you can maintain for one hour. We have shown the FTP provides a good base to compare performance in different conditions and in different sports. Furthermore, we saw that the ultimate limit of human power can be set at an FTP of 6.40 watts/kg for men and 5.70 watts/kg for women.

Now that we are approaching the end of this book, we want to look more closely at the maximum limit of human power for performances with a different time span, from short explosions in sprinting to protractive endurance power.

How Big Is the Maximum Power of the Four Energy Systems?

In an earlier chapter, we showed the table below that gives the biochemical limits of the specific power (in watts/kg) of the four energy systems of the human engine. We note that we have prepared this table with data from the thermodynamic literature, using the muscle efficiency of 25% and an athletic body weight of 60 kg. The table clearly shows that the maximum power is very different for the four systems. On the one hand, the ATP/CP system can supply a lot of power, but it can only sustain this for a brief explosion like the 100-meter sprint. On the other hand, the conversion of fatty acids supplies much less power, but it can maintain this for a very long time (many hours, even days).

Power Output of the Four Human Engines	
	P/m
	(watts/kg)
ATP/CP	
ATP $\rightarrow$ ADP	
$C_{10}H_{16}N_5O_{13}P_3 \rightarrow C_{10}H_{15}N_5O_{10}P_2$	24.64
Anaerobic conversion of glycogen	
$C_6H_{12}O_6 + 3ADP \rightarrow 2C_3H_6O_3 + 3ATP$	13.50
Aerobic conversion of glycogen	
$C_6H_{12}O_6 + 6O_2 + 38ADP \rightarrow 6CO_2 + 6H_2O + 38ATP$	7.76
Aerobic conversion of fatty acids	
$CH_3(CH_2)_{14}COOH + 23O_2 + 130ADP \rightarrow 16CO_2 + 16H_2O + 130ATP$	2.36

Which Fuel Mix Is Used by Sprinters and Distance Runners?

Earlier, we saw that the human engine more or less automatically adapts the fuel mix. In rest and at relative low exercise intensity, mainly fatty acids are used. As more power is required (e.g., at a higher pace in running), more and more glycogen is used in the fuel mix. At intensities above the FTP, the anaerobic breakdown of glycogen starts to kick in. Finally, near full power (e.g., sprinting), ATP becomes the main fuel in the mix. Obviously, you cannot maintain high paces for a long time, so the fuel mix depends also on the duration of the exercise. Sprinters use mainly ATP and distance runners rely on a mix of glycogen and fatty acids. Earlier, we also learned that the gradual change in the fuel mix is the reason for the gradual decline of power with time, as described by Riegel's formula. The table and figure below summarize the composition of the fuel mix as a function of the time in minutes.

Fuel Mix				
	Anaerobic	Anaerobic	Aerobic	Aerobic
Time	ATP	glycolysis	glycogen	fatty acids
(minutes)	(%)	(%)	(%)	(%)
0	100	0	0	0
1	10	65	20	5
5	2	8	80	10
10	0	0	90	10
20	0	0	84	16
40	0	0	78	22
60	0	0	75	25
120	0	0	69	31
240	0	0	64	36

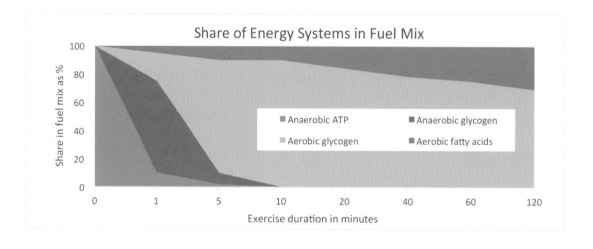

How Big Is the Maximum Human Power as a Function of Time?

When we multiply the share of the four energy systems with the specific power from the first table, we can calculate the maximum human power as a function of time. The result is given in the table and figure.

Limits of Human Power	
Time	Specific power
(minuten)	(watts/kg)
0	24.64
1	12.91
5	8.02
10	7.22
20	6.90
40	6.57
60	6.41
120	6.09
240	5.82

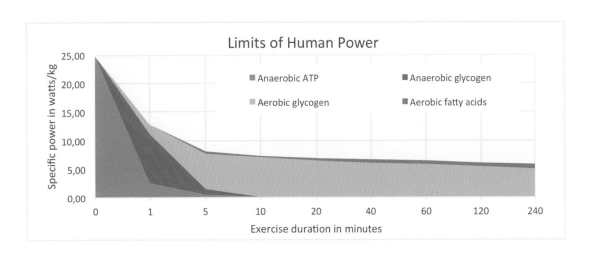

Can These Limits Be Confirmed in the Real World?

Earlier, we confirmed that the maximum level of the FTP (the specific power that can be maintained for one hour) is indeed 6.4 watts/kg for elite male athletes. This value is corroborated by the power profiles in cycling and we also found that the current world records in athletics are equivalent to an FTP of 6.35 watts/kg.

We have also calculated the equivalent specific power for times other than one hour. The table gives the results of our calculations on various world records. Almost all calculated power values are based on our model, which is based on the equilibrium situation without the power required to accelerate from the start. The exceptions in the table are the data on the 100-400 meter, where we obviously had to include the additional power for the acceleration from 0 to 10 m/s during the first four seconds from the start. This is equivalent to an acceleration of 2.5 m/s^2. This acceleration requires an additional power (P/m = av) of 25 watts/kg. As the acceleration lasts only four seconds, the impact on the average power of Usain Bolt is 4/9.58*25 = 10.5 watts/kg. We have added this value to the equilibrium power of 12.0 watts/kg. For Michael Johnson the average acceleration power comes down to 4/43*25 = 2.3 watts/kg, which we have added to his equilibrium power of 10.6 watts/kg. All in all the results of the calculations match the theoretical limits very well.

Relevant Performances and Equivalent Power	
Time (minutes)	Examples
0	Bolt 100 m 22.5 watts/kg, power profiles 25 watts/kg
1	Van Niekerk 400 m, 12.9 watts/kg
5	Daniel Koomen 3000 m, 7.32 watts/kg
10	Bekele 5000 m, 7.06 watts/kg
20	Bekele 10,000 m, 6.74 watts/kg
40	Koomen 15 km, 6.41 watts/kg
60	Tadese 21.1 km, 6.36 watts/kg
120	Kimetto 42.2 km, 5.99 watts/kg

In summary, we conclude that the limits of human power can be based on the biochemical maximum values of the power of the four energy systems. The result is that the maximum power for a short explosion such as the 100-meter sprint is 24.6 watts/kg. The maximum power that can be maintained for one hour (the FTP) is 6.4 watts/kg. These data are confirmed by our analysis of the performances of elite athletes in running, cycling and ice skating. The values are valid for male athletes; the values for women are some 11% lower at 5.7 watts/kg. We believe that this difference is caused primarily by the higher body fat percentage of women.

The maximum power for a short explosion such as the 100-meter sprint is 24.6 watts/kg. The photo shows Usain Bolt of Jamaica on his way to win the men's 4x100 m relay final of the Rio 2016 Olympic Games.

PART V

RUNNING WITH POWER METERS

63. POWER METERS: THE GAME CHANGER IN RUNNING!

Any day I am too busy to run is a day I am too busy.
—John Bryant

In earlier chapters we explained the theory of running power and the running model. Summarized we can state that the power (P) of your human engine should be equal to the sum of the power required to overcome the running resistance (P_r), the air resistance (P_a) and the climbing resistance (P_c), as shown in the figure.

$$P = P_r + P_a + P_c$$

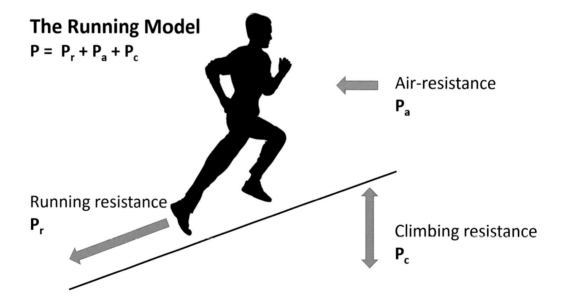

The Running Model
$$P = P_r + P_a + P_c$$

Air-resistance P_a

Running resistance P_r

Climbing resistance P_c

The running model.

In the next chapters we will discuss how you can measure your running power in practice. Recently, the first power meters for running were developed[81,82,83,84]. This means that you now have the ability to measure your running power in real time each and every day! Using these data you can start to optimize your daily training and your races. Also, it is now finally possible to quantitatively determine your running economy (RE), as we will show in a later chapter. You can now really start to optimize your RE (e.g., by changing your cadence and seeing the impact on the specific energy cost of your running).

We have described our experiences with power meters in the following eight chapters:

1. The breakthrough of power meters
2. How good and how reliable are power meters?
3. Measure and improve your running economy!
4. Determine your functional threshold power (FTP) and your training zones.
5. Why should you train with a power meter?
6. Why should you race with a power meter?
7. Tips and tricks for everyday use
8. Laboratory testing

We wrote part V together with Guido Vroemen, sports physician, coach and co-author of our book *The Secret of Cycling*[2] (in Dutch).

The Experiences in Cycling

Power meters are well-known and are often used in cycling. A famous example is Chris Froome, who cycles uphill the major climbs of the Tour de France, based on the readings of his power meter. He does not try to follow Alberto Contador in his breakaways, but pushes exactly the amount of wattsage that he knows he can maintain. The widespread use of power meters is not limited to the professional cyclists; performance-oriented national or regional cyclists and even cycling tourists use them nowadays as it helps them to optimize their training and their races.

In cycling, the measuring principle of the power meter is based on using strain gauges to determine the force (F) delivered to the crank shaft. This force multiplied by the speed (v, which depends on the cadence), results in the power output: $P = F*v$.

Both in theory and in practice, a very strong relation is found between the power output and the performance in cycling. In *The Secret of Cycling*[2] we have shown that on a flat track the performance is

determined by the total power output (in watts). Contrary, in the mountains the performance is determined by the specific power (in watts/kg).

The use of power meters in training and in races offers great advantages. With a power meter you measure your effort exactly, so you can optimize your workout and can keep the right pace in the race. Without a power meter you have to rely on your speed or your heart rate (HR). However, these strongly depend on the conditions. Facing a headwind or cycling uphill your speed is much less, while pushing the same wattsage! At the same speed your HR is higher. Your HR is also related to the temperature and your physical fitness.

The Breakthrough of Power Meters in Running

Because of the proven value of power meters in cycling, the search for a power meter in running has been going on for years. Obviously, it is difficult—if not impossible—to directly measure the power provided by the legs of a runner. Consequently, another measuring principle has been developed. The breakthrough came with the use of accelerometers. These are small chips, containing crystals that exhibit a piezo-electric effect at an acceleration. This piezo-electric effect produces a voltage, which can be measured and transferred to the acceleration. Accelerometers are now very cheap, very accurate and have already been applied in many devices, such as smartphones, tablets, cars, pedometers and running watches. As a result of accelerometers your smartphone knows if you hold it horizontally or vertically. Accelerometers in your running watch are able to measure your vertical oscillation, cadence and the number of strides.

The Stryd: A Revolution in Running?

Very recently, a practical running power meter has been developed by the Stryd firm in Boulder, Colorado[81,82,83,84]. The beta version has been tested by Guido Vroemen. Early 2016 the Stryd Pioneer became available to the general public. Late 2016 Stryd brought a foot pod version on the market.

The Stryd Pioneer power meter is a simple pod (similar to a foot pod), which also features a chest band to measure your heart rate. The sensor includes three accelerometers. These measure the acceleration of your body while running in three directions: horizontally, vertically and laterally or sideways. Obviously, it is important to restrict the vertical and lateral movements to optimize your running economy (RE). With an app you can adjust your body weight. During the training or race you can see the real-time data of your running power (in watts) on your running watch or smart phone. After the training or race, you can analyze all the data on your computer.

The power (P) is calculated from your body weight (m, kg), the acceleration (a, in m/s²) and the speed (v, in m/s) with the formulas we have used earlier:

P = F*v

F = m*a

The breakthrough of Stryd is obviously their software, which allows the real-time calculation of the running power from all the 3D-acceleration data. The basic formulas are simple, but it requires a complex algorithm to integrate the accelerations in all directions in a correct and stable manner. One of the advantages of the Stryd is that it provides you with accurate and real-time information on the power that you are producing in your workout. This gives a much better representation of your real effort than your pace or your HR alone.

The original Stryd Pioneer power meter attached to a chest band.

The Potential Benefits

At the time we were writing this book we found many enthusiastic reviews on the possibilities of using a Stryd on the internet[82,83,84]. We have critically reviewed this information and also tested the Stryd ourselves, as will be discussed in the next chapter. Based on all of this, we are very pleased with this new tool that offers the potential to optimize our running.

It seems to us that power meters in general—and the Stryd in particular—may provide a historical and revolutionary breakthrough in running. The use of accelerometers combined with advanced software seems to have paved the way for runners to get realistic and reliable data on their running power. Many potential benefits have already been identified. We believe the following to be the most promising:

1. Optimizing your running economy
    A power meter will tell you how much power you are using and thus how economically you are running. By changing your running form (e.g., cadence, stride length and so on) you can measure whether or not your RE improves.
2. Measuring your fitness and shape
    You can now measure your FTP and your VO_2 max without the need to have yourself tested in a sports medical center. This means you can now determine how your fitness evolves.
3. Measuring the exact effort of your workout
    A power meter provides realistic and reliable information better than pace and HR. This means you can prevent overtraining, adjust your training and optimize your tapering.

4. Maintaining the optimal pace in a race
    Obviously, changing conditions such as wind and hills will affect your pace. Power data will help you to maintain a constant effort, so you have something left in the tank at the finish.
5. Optimizing the communication with your coach
    Daily exchange of the data on your workout, power, RE and so on will be of great value, not just to yourself but also to your coach.

Obviously, it is early days yet with the application of running power meters. In practice, these potential advantages still have to be proven. Also, other advantages may materialize in the coming years. We have already started our own experiments and hope that many other runners will join us in this quest to optimize our running!

A Stryd foot pod is available since late 2016.

64. HOW GOOD AND HOW RELIABLE ARE POWER METERS?

I don't run to add days to my life, I run to add life to my days. —Ronald Rook

We have explained the breakthrough of running power meters in the previous chapter. We elaborated on the measuring principles of the Stryd running power meter and the potential benefits for optimizing your training and your races. In this chapter we will discuss the tests that we have done ourselves to see how good and how reliable the data of the Stryd are.

How Good and How Reliable Is the Stryd?

Physician Guido Vroemen tested the Stryd Pioneer in his physiological laboratory. A total of 14 runners (including authors Hans and Ron, who are test persons 13 and 14) performed a standard VO_2 max exercise test on a treadmill. During this test, a runner starts at a relatively low speed (e.g., 10 km/h). The speed is gradually increased until the maximum value that can be maintained for three minutes is reached. During the test, heart rate, oxygen uptake, carbon dioxide production, ventilation and many more parameters are measured. The runners also wore a Stryd power meter, so we could make a good comparison between the power data of the Stryd and the oxygen uptake VO_2. The results of the Stryd were impressive and will be explained below in more detail.

Author Hans testing the Stryd running power meter at sports medical centre SMA Midden Nederland. Behind the desk, sports physician Guido Vroemen can be seen.

Results of the Standard Exercise Test (VO$_2$)

In a standard exercise test, the oxygen consumption (VO$_2$, in ml/kg/min) is the most important parameter. In the table and graph below, we have summarized the results. We see the measured values for the VO$_2$ (in ml/kg/min) of the 14 test persons (including their body weight) at various speeds. As could be expected, the oxygen consumption increases as the speed nears a maximum value (VO$_2$ max, in kg/ml/min). Obviously, the VO$_2$ max is an important parameter for predicting the attainable speed and race times at different distances.

Relation Between Speed and VO$_2$

v (km/h)	Theory RE 201	1 65 kg	2 50 kg	3 59 kg	4 85 kg	5 81 kg	6 69 kg	7 69 kg
7	24							
8	27							
9	30	40						
10	34	42			39	41	39	38
11	37	44			42	43	42	40
12	40	46	48	44	46	46	44	44
13	44	46		47	48	49	47	47
14	47	51	59	52	51	51	51	51
15	50		62	58	54	55	54	54
16	54		65	60				
17	57			65				
18	61			68				
RE	201	233	245	224	223	227	221	218

The results are quite normal:

1. For all test persons the VO$_2$ increases almost proportionally with the speed.
2. The numerical values of the VO$_2$ are not exactly the same for all persons at the same speed. The values are close to each other, but there are notable differences.

It is well known that this latter phenomenon is caused by running economy (RE), which can differ from person to person. As we learned earlier, the RE indicates how much oxygen you use to run one kilometer (per kg of body weight, the unit of the RE is ml O$_2$/kg/km). Apparently, our test persons did not have the same RE, as they did not use exactly the same amount of oxygen at the same speed. So, the RE is a measure of how economically you are running. It also means that if you run economically (i.e., at a low RE), you can run faster at the same VO$_2$ max!

	8	9	10	11	12	13	14	Average
	71 kg	57 kg	104 kg	83 kg	78 kg	58 kg	80 kg	
					28			28
					33			33
			35		38			38
	40	39	37		42	40		40
	43	43	41	43		44	43	43
	47	46	43	46		47	47	46
	52	49	45	49		49	48	48
	55	53	48	53		52	50	52
	60	58	51	56		54		56
		63		62				63
		66						66
								68
	237	231	213	227	248	228	216	228

In an earlier chapter we gave an overview of the literature on the RE. There we concluded that the average value of the RE in literature was 201 ml/kg/km. This is also the value that we used for the calculations in this book. In the table and figure below, this value of 201 is referred to as "Theory."

Note that all 14 test persons had a relatively high value for the RE. The average was 228 ml/kg/km, the minimum value and the maximum value were 213 and 248 ml/kg/min respectively. Remember that a high value of the RE means that the person is NOT running economically. He uses a relatively large amount of oxygen (and therefore energy) to run one kilometer. Such a runner will also run slower at the same VO_2 max than another runner with a lower RE.

In the first instance, we were somewhat surprised at the relatively high value of the RE of the 14 runners in comparison. We believe the explanation is that in the literature above average quality runners were tested. As an example Guido Vroemen once tested world-class athlete Wilson Kipsang and measured a very low RE of 180 ml/kg/min! So at the same speed Kipsang uses only 180/228 = 79% of the amount of O_2 as our average test runners. This means he is running much more economically—by 21%!

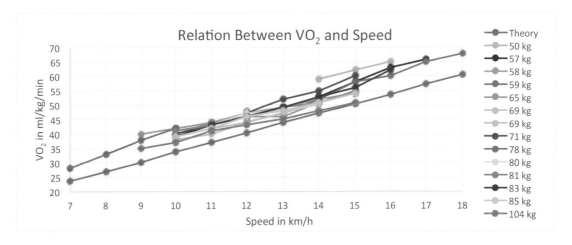

Results of the Stryd Meter (Watt/Kg)

In running, the specific power (in watts/kg) is the most important factor predicting the attainable speed and race times at different distances. In the table and graph below, we have summarized the results of the specific power data of the test persons at different speeds. As could be expected, the specific power increased with the speed, just like the VO_2.

We can even determine the theoretical relationship between the specific power and the VO_2. The energy value of 1 ml O_2 is 19.5 J and the metabolic efficiency is 25%, so the following applies:

P/m (in watts/kg) = 19.5*0.25/60*VO_2 (in ml/kg/min), or

P/m = 0.08125*VO_2

Just like the VO_2 data, the specific power data were also quite normal:

1. For all test persons the specific power (in watts/kg) increases almost proportionally to the speed.
2. The numerical values of the specific power are exactly the same for all persons at the same speed. The values are close to each other, but there are notable differences.

Obviously, this latter phenomenon is also caused by difference in RE. For the Stryd the running economy can best be expressed as the specific energy consumption (c, in kJ/kg/km). In accordance with the theory:

P = c*m*v, so

P/m = c*v

The c value indicates how much energy you use to run one kilometer (per kg body weight, the unit is kJ/kg/km). Just like the RE, it is a parameter which indicates how economically you run. Just like the RE, it means that if you have a lower c value, you can run faster with the same amount of power!

In an earlier chapter we provided an overview of the literature on the c value. There we concluded that the average value in literature was 0.98 kJ/kg/km. This is also the value that we used for the calculations in this book. It corresponds to an RE of 201 ml/kg/km. In the following table and figure this value of 0.98 is referred to as "Theory."

As could be expected, we found that our 14 test persons also had a fairly high value for the c. The average was 1.06 kJ/kg/km, the minimum value and the maximum value were 0.87 and 1.25 kJ/kg/min respectively. Remember that a high value of c indicates that the runner is NOT running economically. Such a runner will also run slower at the same power than someone with a low value of c. So once again we see that our test runners were running less economically than has been reported in the literature; the explanation will be the same as mentioned before.

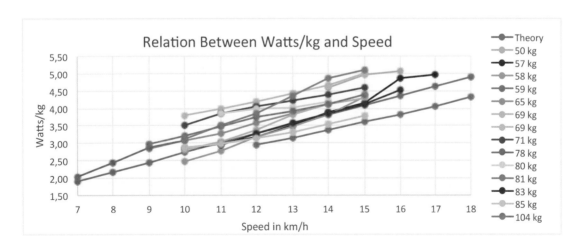

Relation Between Speed and Power								
v	Watt/kg	1	2	3	4	5	6	7
(km/h)	c = 0.98	65 kg	50 kg	59 kg	85 kg	81 kg	69 kg	69 kg
7	1.91							
8	2.18							
9	2.45	2.83						
10	2.73	3.08			2.86	3.12	2.80	3.80
11	3.00	3.28			2.98	3.52	3.04	4.00
12	3.27	3.57	4.10	2.95	3.15	3.84	3.39	4.20
13	3.54	3.85		3.15	3.32	4.35	3.83	4.43
14	3.82	4.11	4.58	3.37	3.54	4.86	4.12	4.65
15	4.09		4.98	3.61	3.79	5.10	4.30	5.00
16	4.36		5.08	3.83				
17	4.63			4.07				
18	4.91			4.34				
c	0.98	1.08	1.17	0.87	0.94	1.19	1.03	1.25

Comparison of Stryd Data With VO_2 Data

When comparing the data of the Stryd with the VO_2 data, we were impressed to see how well they matched. Looking at all the tables and graphs, we concluded that all results were as could be expected from theory and the quality of the Stryd data was just as good as the VO_2 data. Also, we did not see any outliers, so apparently the data from the Stryd were both correct and reliable! We were really surprised by these findings as the VO_2 has always been considered to be the gold standard of physiological research.

We finally made the ultimate comparison in the table and graph below. For all runners and for all speeds, we determined the ratio of the specific power data (in watts/kg) and the VO_2 (in ml O_2/kg/min). According to the theory that we discussed earlier, this ratio should be 0.081.

The table and graph clearly show that there is indeed a very clear relationship:

8	9	10	11	12	13	14	Average
71 kg	57 kg	104 kg	83 kg	78 kg	58 kg	80 kg	
				2.04			2.04
				2.42			2.42
		2.97		2.88			2.89
3.51	2.84	3.20		3.08	2.46		3.08
3.85	2.98	3.47	2.94		2.79	3.85	3.34
4.06	3.19	3.74	3.27		3.17	3.98	3.59
4.23	3.51	3.92	3.58		3.48	4.03	3.81
4.38	3.88	4.13	3.84		3.81	4.19	4.11
4.59	4.14	4.39	4.12		4.34		4.40
	4.85		4.52				4.57
	4.96						4.52
							4.34
1.18	1.01	1.11	0.99	1.10	0.94	1.02	1.06

1.   The ratio averaged 0.078, very close to the theoretical value of 0.081.
2.   The ratio varied between 0.067 and 0.096; this is a limited range around the theoretical value.

The small differences may be related to individual differences between the test persons regarding the following aspects:
1.   The metabolic efficiency (if this is higher you will produce more watts/kg at the same amount of O_2)
2.   The ratio of fatty acids/glycogen in the fuel mix (when your muscles burn relatively more glycogen relatively more watts/kg is produced at the same amount of O_2)

Relation Between Stryd and VO$_2$								
v	Theory	1	2	3	4	5	6	7
(km/h)		65 kg	50 kg	59 kg	85 kg	81 kg	69 kg	69 kg
7	0.081							
8	0.081							
9	0.081	0.071						
10	0.081	0.073			0.073	0.076	0.072	0.100
11	0.081	0.075			0.071	0.082	0.072	0.100
12	0.081	0.078	0.085	0.067	0.068	0.083	0.077	0.095
13	0.081	0.084		0.067	0.069	0.089	0.081	0.094
14	0.081	0.081	0.078	0.065	0.069	0.095	0.081	0.091
15	0.081		0.080	0.062	0.070	0.093	0.080	0.093
16	0.081		0.078	0.064				
17	0.081			0.063				
18	0.081			0.064				
Average	0.081	0.077	0.082	0.066	0.070	0.085	0.077	0.096

	8	9	10	11	12	13	14	Average
	71 kg	57 kg	104 kg	83 kg	78 kg	58 kg	80 kg	
					0.073			0.073
					0.073			0.073
			0.085		0.076			0.077
	0.088	0.073	0.086		0.073	0.062		0.078
	0.090	0.069	0.085	0.068		0.063	0.090	0.079
	0.086	0.069	0.087	0.071		0.067	0.085	0.078
	0.081	0.072	0.087	0.073		0.071	0.084	0.079
	0.080	0.073	0.086	0.072		0.073	0.084	0.079
	0.077	0.071	0.086	0.074		0.080		0.079
		0.077		0.073				0.073
		0.075						0.069
								0.064
	0.085	0.071	0.086	0.071	0.075	0.067	0.085	0.078

Conclusions

Although this is a first test only, we find the results very impressing. Beforehand, we had not expected that the Stryd would be able to produce results as good and reliable as VO_2, which has always been considered to be the gold standard of the physiological research!

We have come to the following conclusions:

1. The data of the Stryd are very realistic, accurate and reliable.
2. The data are close to expectations from theory and in good agreement with the VO_2.
3. The data provide very useful additional information relative to the VO_2.
4. Combining the Stryd and the VO_2 data gives more insight into aspects such as the metabolic efficiency and the fuel mix.
5. For daily use the Stryd provides a wealth of additional information. Every day you can get data which you could otherwise obtain only from a physiological laboratory test.

Obviously, it is early days yet. The potential advantages of power meters still have to be proven in practice. However, we believe power meters hold the promise of improving our running results. Besides the known advantages of power meters (such as optimization of training and races), we expect especially a lot from the daily measurement of the RE or c value. This allows all of us to quantify our running form and to work systematically towards optimizing it.

Winner Mo Farah (C) laps Germany's Arne Gabius (L) in the Men's 10,000 m final at the 15th IAAF Athletics World Championships in Beijing.

65. MEASURING AND IMPROVING YOUR RUNNING ECONOMY!

You can't be miserable when you run. It's such a simple and pure way to feel alive. —Veronica Rossi

In previous chapters we have discussed the breakthrough of running power meters and the results of the first tests in the sports medical center SMA Midden Nederland. We concluded that the Stryd power data are as good and reliable as the VO_2 data from a physiological lab. During our research we noted that the running economy (RE) of the 14 test runners was quite different. This lead us to conclude that measuring and improving the RE could be a promising application of the Stryd. In this chapter we elaborate on this and explain how you could use a power meter to measure and improve your RE.

Which Factors Determine Your Running Economy?

There is almost no topic that runners and coaches discuss more than the running economy. Almost everyone has an opinion on it. At athletics clubs much attention is paid to exercises and training to improve the running technique, which is supposed to improve your RE. Yet the question remains how we can understand this? What can science tell us about the running economy?

Studying the literature we noticed that usually this topic is discussed only in broad and general terms. Quantitative information on the influence of various factors on the RE is lacking. Our literature survey [49-59] revealed that the following aspects are believed to influence the RE:

1. Body posture
   A low body fat percentage, long legs, slim calves, small feet and narrow and flexible hips are associated with an improved RE.

2. Fuel mix
   A higher percentage of glycogen produces more power, so it improves the RE.

3. Running form

   Many factors are thought to have an impact on the RE, including cadence, GCT, stride length, oscillation, arm drive, foot strike, hip angle, knee lift, leg stretching, calf lift and ankle angle. However, opinions differ on exactly what constitutes the best running form.

That these factors will play a role seems logical. Obviously, it takes less energy to run with the slim calves of the Kenyan elite runners. Also it makes sense that glycogen produces more power than fatty acids. And it also makes sense that our running form will have an impact on our RE, as vertical and lateral movements cost energy and do not contribute to our forward speed.

Besides the fact that there is little quantitative information on the RE, we have to deal with another problem. This is the fact that we cannot control our body posture (except by reducing our body fat percentage) and the fuel mixture in our muscles (apart from carbo-loading before the marathon). So, the only factor that we can try to optimize is our running form.

The Impact of the Running Form

The ideal running form is one of the myths of running. On television we see a big difference between the smooth strides of elite athletes like Haile Gebrselassie or Tirunesh Dibaba and the puffing and gasping of some joggers. But what is the secret of a good running form? Factors that are often referred to are a short ground contact time, a high cadence, avoiding heel landing, a strong drive by the arms in support of the running motion, a good knee lift and the stretching of the toes at the take off.

We all know examples of runners with a smooth running form. Hans and Ron are always impressed by their teammate Willem de Ruijter (see the photo). But does that beautiful running form lead to a better RE, and which concrete steps should we take to improve our RE?

The smooth running style of Willem de Ruijter at the Dutch National Championships 3000 meter indoor.

How Can We Measure the RE?

The RE is defined as the amount of oxygen you use to run one kilometer (per kg of body weight, the RE is expressed in ml O_2/kg/km). Until now, the RE can only be measured in a sports physiological laboratory by dividing the oxygen consumption of a runner by the speed of the treadmill:

RE = VO_2/v

The VO_2 is expressed in ml O_2/kg/min and v in m/s. As an example we use a VO_2 of 50 ml/kg/min and a v of 15 km/h, then the RE is 50/(15/3.6) = 200 ml O_2/kg/km.

Very efficient Kenyan elite athletes like Wilson Kipsang have an RE of 180 ml/kg/min, whereas our 14 test runners had RE values varying from 213 to 248 ml O_2/kg/km. This means that our test runners use more oxygen at the same speed as compared to Kipsang. A high value of the RE means that you are NOT running economically. Consequently, you will run slower at the same value of the VO_2 max. Your VO_2 max and your RE together determine how fast you can run. We can calculate the maximum attainable speed with the formula:

v_{max} = VO_2 max/RE

The v_{max} is the speed that you can maintain for 10 minutes which corresponds to the duration of the VO_2 max. It is more interesting to calculate the speed corresponding to the functional threshold power (FTP) which you can maintain for an hour. As we saw earlier, this speed is equivalent to 88% of v_{max}. In the table and graph we have calculated this attainable hour speed as a function of your VO_2 max and your RE.

To illustrate the big impact of your RE, let's check the table for a speed of 15 km/h. If you are running very economically with an RE of 180 ml/kg/min, you need a VO_2 max of only 51 ml/kg/min to maintain this speed during an hour. If, on the other hand, you are an uneconomical runner with an RE of 240 ml/kg/km, you need a VO_2 max of no less than 68 ml/kg/min to maintain the same speed! As we have explained earlier, the maximum value of the VO_2 max of world class athletes is around 88 ml/kg/min, so the values beyond this level are not possible in practice.

Required VO$_2$ max (ml/kg/min)			
	RE	RE	RE
v_{hour}	180	210	240
km/h	ml/kg/km	ml/kg/km	ml/kg/km
10	34	40	45
11	38	44	50
12	41	48	55
13	44	52	59
14	48	56	64
15	51	60	68
16	55	64	73
17	58	68	77
18	61	72	82
19	65	76	86
20	68	80	91
21	72	84	95
22	75	88	100
23	78	91	105
24	82	95	109
25	85	99	114

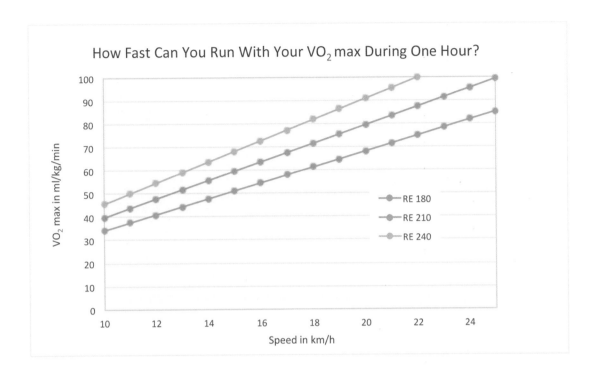

How Fast Can You Run With Your VO_2 max During One Hour?

How Can You Measure Your RE With the Stryd?

With the Stryd you can measure your specific power (P/m, in Watt/kg) at a certain speed. According to theory you can calculate your specific energy consumption (c, in kJ/kg/km) by dividing the specific power by the speed (v, in m/s):

c = (P/m)/v

As an example we use a specific power of 4.1 watts/kg and a speed of 15 km/h. The c value can then be calculated as 4.1/(15/3.6) = 0.98 kJ/kg/km. This c value corresponds to an RE of 201 ml O_2/kg/km, as we saw in the earlier chapter. Remember that the energy value of 1 ml O_2 is 19.5 J and the metabolic efficiency is 25%, so:

c = 19.5*0.25/1000*RE, or

c = 0.004875*RE

A high c value means the same as a high RE: you are using a lot of energy and you are NOT running economically. Now the challenge is to change your running form so that you are able to reduce your specific power at the same speed and thus your c value!

As we have previously derived a relation for the attainable speed as a function of VO_2 max and RE, we can now do the same for your speed as a function of the specific power (P/m) and the c value. The relation is:

v = (P/m)/c

For the sake of our readers who are more familiar with the RE, we have made a similar table and figure for the attainable speed as a function of the specific power and the RE. As an example, let's look once more to a speed of 15 km/h. With an RE of 180 ml/kg km you can already maintain that speed with a specific power of 3.66 watts/kg. If, on the other hand, you are an uneconomical runner with an RE of 240 ml/kg/km, you need a specific power of no less than 4.88 watts/kg to maintain the same speed. Remember that we consider a specific power of 6.4 watts/kg as the maximum limit of human performance. Values beyond this level are not possible in practice (we have marked these in red).

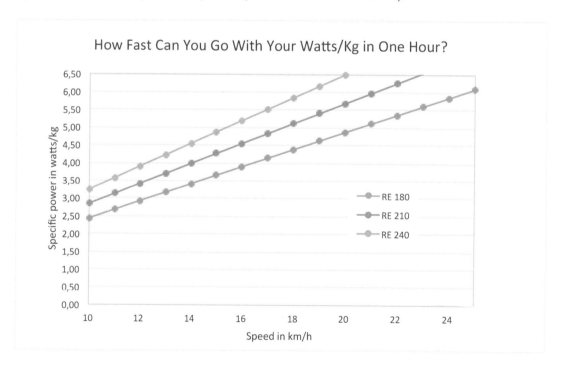

Required Watt/Kg			
		RE	
v	180	210	240
km/h	ml/kg/km	ml/kg/km	ml/kg/km
10	2.44	2.84	3.25
11	2.68	3.13	3.58
12	2.93	3.41	3.90
13	3.17	3.70	4.23
14	3.41	3.98	4.55
15	3.66	4.27	4.88
16	3.90	4.55	5.20
17	4.14	4.83	5.53
18	4.39	5.12	5.85
19	4.63	5.40	6.18
20	4.88	5.69	6.50
21	5.12	5.97	6.83
22	5.36	6.26	7.15
23	5.61	6.54	7.48
24	5.85	6.83	7.80
25	6.09	7.11	8.13

The Future: What Should You Do to Optimize Your RE?

The Stryd offers you the opportunity to measure your RE on a daily basis. It can be easily done by dividing your specific power (P/m, in watts/kg) by your speed (v, in m/s):

$$c = (P/m)/v$$

You can either use the c value directly or transfer it into the RE, with the formula RE = c/0.004875.

We suggest that you note the c value or RE every day in your running spreadsheet. Now you need to collect a lot of data and relate the values of c or RE with your running form, so cadence, GCT, oscillation, stride length and so on. Remember that the conditions of the run (e.g., weather, footing) may also have an impact. Therefore we recommend that you collect data regularly at a standard training course to get reproducible results. This should enable you to recognize the conditions in which you were able to run most economically (i.e., with the lowest value of c and RE).

We are very excited that power meters finally provide us with an opportunity to put a concrete number on the vague parameter of RE. We are sure that this will pave the way to concrete improvements in our RE. We realize that this will not be easy because for us—and for most people—our running form will be habituated in many years of running. We will not be able to change it overnight. But with time and concrete data, we are confident we will be able to get some improvement. We hope that many readers will join us in this effort. Let's share our data and conclusions on how we can measure and improve our RE!

Improving your running form and running economy requires specific training and a lot of patience.

66. DETERMINE YOUR FTP AND YOUR TRAINING ZONES

Train, don't strain. —Arthur Lydiard

One of the advantages of power meters such as the Stryd is that you can now determine your own functional threshold power (FTP, in watt/kg). Your FTP corresponds to an effort that you can maintain for one hour. It is a very important parameter to predict your attainable speed and race time at various distances. Before, you had to go to a sports medical center to get your FTP determined. Now you can do it yourself as frequently as you like. This means you can keep track of how your fitness evolves with time. The FTP is also an important parameter to determine your training zones, as we will explain in this chapter. You can easily adjust these zones when your FTP increases or decreases.

The Stryd Critical Power Test

Stryd uses a standard protocol to determine critical power (CP). Stryd defines the critical power for runners as the power at which an athlete transitions from aerobic to anaerobic respiration. Unfortunately, it is not entirely clear which algorithm they use and to which time period the CP corresponds. Consequently, it is not possible to relate the CP to the FTP, which corresponds to the power which an athlete can maintain for one hour.

Stryd recommends doing this test at a running track. You may also use an alternative measured course. The protocol is as follows:

1. Warm up for five minutes.
2. Run 800 meters at an easy pace.
3. Do another warm-up or easy run for five minutes.
4. Run 1,200 meters at your maximum effort.
5. Recover for 30 minutes by walking or doing some easy running.
6. Run 2,400 meters at your maximum effort.
7. Cool down for ten minutes.

Based on this test, the Stryd app calculates your critical power (CP) and personalized training zones. It is not entirely clear to what extent the results of the 2,400 meter are affected by some residual fatigue of the preceding 1,200 meter.

A Simple and Science-Based Test

Because it is not clear to which time period the CP corresponds and because we do not know the algorithm of the Stryd, we have developed a simple alternative method.

Our method is based on the physiological science of the time–power relationship as explained in this book. Remember that the FTP is the amount of power that you can maintain for one hour. Of course it is not very practical to perform a test of one hour as this would be too exhausting. But we know the time– relationship, as we discussed in an earlier chapter. Let's look at a test of ten minutes. The power output will obviously be higher than the FTP by a factor of $(10/60)^{-0.07} = 1.13$. You can determine your FTP by dividing the specific power output during a ten-minute test by 1.13. Such a test can be easily integrated in a training program, and is in fact a good pace training. We recommend doing this test once every six to eight weeks, so you keep track of your fitness and assess whether or not your progress proceeds as desired. The following protocol can be used:

1. Warm up for 10-20 minutes with some accelerations.
2. Run for ten minutes at your maximum effort.
3. Cool down for ten minutes.

By repeating this test regularly, you will get a better grip on how your fitness and performance level evolve over time.

Determining Your Training Zones

Now that you have determined your FTP, you can determine your own training zones. Based on the literature and our own experience, we have compiled the following table, detailing seven training zones to stimulate and improve the different energy systems of your human engine.

Zone	Training goal	Training form	%FTP
0	Improve circulation in muscles	Warm-up and recovery training	60-70
1	Improve aerobic capacity and aerobic efficiency	Endurance training (10-30 km)	70-80
2	Improve transition from aerobic to anaerobic system	Tempo endurance training with long tempo blocs (3-5 km)	80-90
3	Improve lactate threshold power and anaerobic efficiency	Extensive interval training with longer blocs (1,000 m)	90-100
4	Improve lactate tolerance and VO_2 max	Intensive interval training with shorter blocs (400 m)	100-110
5	Improve anaerobic capacity	Speed training (200 m intervals)	110-150
6	Improve explosive power	Sprint training (50-100 m)	>>150

Explanation

Zone 0: Active Recovery

This zone includes a warm-up and easy runs with a duration of 30-90 minutes and an intensity of less than 70% of your FTP. The goal is to recover from previous hard training sessions or races. Warming up and cooling down are also part of this zone.

Zone 1: Endurance Training

This zone includes both the short daily base runs (around 10-15 kilometers) as well as the long weekly run (25-30 kilometers). The intensity is 70-80% of your FTP. The goal is to stimulate and develop your muscles and aerobic capacity.

Zone 2: Tempo Endurance Training

This zone includes the higher intensity brisk tempo blocs (3-5 kilometers). The intensity is 80-90% of your FTP. The goal is to stimulate and develop the transition zone between the aerobic and anaerobic systems and your pace endurance.

Zone 3: FTP Training

This zone comprises the longer interval sessions (800-1,000-1,200 meters, for example 5*1000 meters). The goal is to stimulate and develop your FTP. The intensity is 90-100% of your FTP.

Zone 4: VO$_2$ max Training

In this zone the shorter interval sessions are done (400-600 meters, for example 10*400 meters). The goal is to stimulate and develop your VO$_2$ max. The intensity is 100-110% of your FTP.

Zone 5: Anaerobic Capacity Training

This zone consists of very short intensive intervals (200 meters, for example 10*200 meters). The goal is to stimulate and develop your anaerobic capacity and speed. The intensity is 110-150% of your FTP.

Zone 6: Neuromuscular Power

This zone includes the high-speed sprint sessions (50-100 meters). They can be done with a flying start. These sessions stress and develop the neuromuscular power. The intensity has to be above 150% of your FTP.

With a running power meter you can easily determine your own FTP. You do not need to perform complicated tests at a physiological lab or with mobile breathing gas analysis equipment (i.e., ergospirometry).

67. WHY SHOULD YOU TRAIN WITH POWER METERS?

Running is the greatest metaphor of life because you get out of it what you put into it. —Oprah Winfrey

In the previous chapters, we have paid attention to the theory and the practice of power meters. We have shown that the Stryd power data are accurate and reliable. Also, we have dealt with some useful applications, such as determining your running economy (RE), your functional threshold power (FTP) and your personal training zones. In this chapter we will provide an overview of the most important reasons why training with this new technology may help you optimize your fitness and performance.

1. **For the first time you can quantify your running economy.**

   We believe this to be a revolutionary breakthrough. We expect a lot from this application. Now you can quantify exactly how much energy you are using to run at a certain speed. And because you get the data daily and in real time on your smartphone or computer, you can start experimenting on how you can reduce the energy cost of running and thus improve your RE. In an earlier chapter we explained that you can easily calculate the specific energy consumption of your run (c, in kJ/km/kg) by dividing your specific power (in watts/kg) by your speed (in m/s). Your c value should be around 0.98 kJ/kg/km, which is equivalent to an RE of 201 ml O_2/kg/km. See how high your c and RE are and try to reduce them by optimizing your running form!

2. **For the first time you can train systematically to improve your running form.**

   Until now we were all a bit in the dark when it came to improving our running form. You could read books and get tips from coaches and other runners, but you could not measure the impact of changes in your running form. Now you can calculate on a daily basis your c and RE values, so you can directly see the impact of changes (e.g., increasing your cadence, knee lift, arm drive and so on). We realize that this will not be easy because various parameters influence each other, nor is it easy to change your running form as this has become habituated during many years of training. Also you should be careful to prevent injuries. But we believe that this application will change and improve the traditional views on running form, as soon many thousands of runners will start experimenting and sharing their results with the running community!

3. **You get a better picture of your workouts, so you can optimize them.**

   In the past, runners based their training on how they felt. Listen to your body. Are you tired, or can you give something more? Since the introduction of the GPS watches many athletes base their training on pace. The additional information you get from an HR meter is also useful as it indicates how your body responds to the training.

   But now you can really measure your running power, which is the best and most accurate reflection of the intensity of your training. Your power data will immediately respond to changes in pace, as opposed to the HR which always lags behind. The following figures of a workout with 400-meter intervals by author Ron illustrate this. The first figure is the output of the Stryd PowerCenter, the second figure shows the same workout in Garmin Connect.

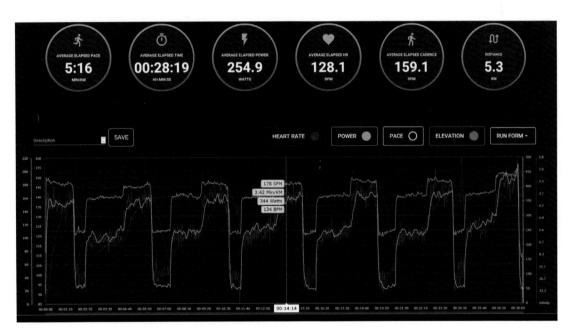

Workout with 400-meter intervals presented in Stryd PowerCenter.

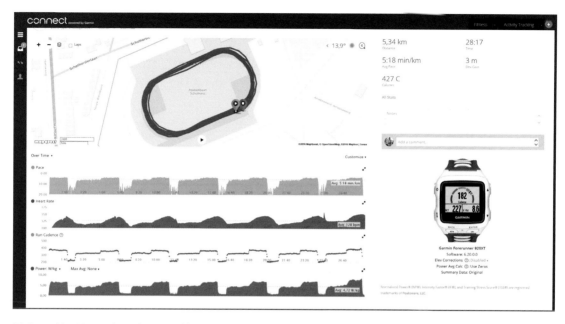

Workout with 400-meter intervals presented in Garmin Connect.

In this book we have shown that many aspects affect your workouts and races. Examples include hills, wind, footing, temperature, accelerations and your fitness (which could be affected by a recent disease or break from training). All of these aspects affect the effectiveness of your workout. Principally, power is the correct parameter representing the intensity of your efforts, so it is better to optimize your workouts based on real-time power data. The figure below illustrates (for the same exercise with 400-meter intervals) that there can be a substantial difference between HR-based training zones and power-based training zones. We note that the Stryd is not perfect yet in this respect, as the impact of wind and footing are reflected only indirectly in the data.

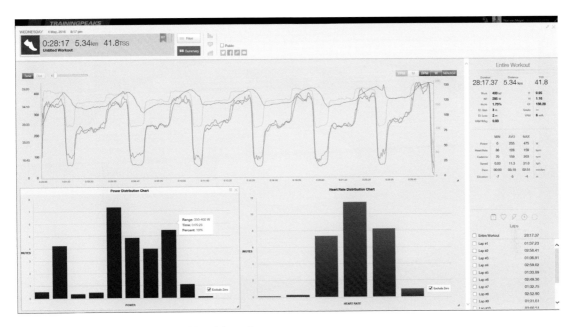

Workout with 400-meter intervals presented in TrainingPeaks.

4. **You get a better picture of your fitness and you can peak at the right time.**

   When you register your power data and RE value on a daily basis, you get a clear and accurate picture of the development of your fitness and performance capability. This also means you can adjust your training program, if necessary, and prevent overtraining. Also you will see the impact of a cold or disease immediately and you can better taper for a race. Various online platforms such as Stryd PowerCenter, Garmin Connect, Strava and TrainingPeaks supply supporting data that you may use for this. In the next chapter we will discuss the details of these apps.

Key data of workout with 400-meter intervals presented in Garmin Connect.

5. **You can share all information with your coach, so you can get better guidance.**

   By sharing all data with your coach, you give him the best insight into your training and the development of your fitness. Your coach can advise you better this way. You can also share your data with apps and online platforms as Stryd PowerCenter, TrainingPeaks, Strava, Garmin Connect and Polar. An example of TrainingPeaks is shown below. This way you build a wonderful database of all your workouts with all the details and can get feedback with trend analysis and correlation of data.

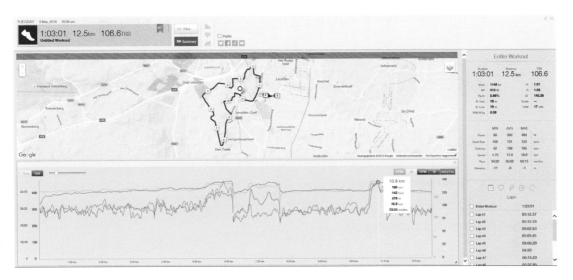

Endurance training with three tempo blocs presented in TrainingPeaks.

68.WHY SHOULD YOU RACE WITH POWER METERS?

Success is measured by racing times, not training mileage.

In the previous chapter we discussed the new opportunities that a power meter provides to optimize your training. In this chapter we will discuss the potential advantages in races. In the next chapter we will give you some tips and tricks for everyday use.

1. ### Maintain perfect pacing throughout the race.

    A famous example of perfect pacing is professional cyclist Chris Froome. On his way up the flanks of Alpe d'Huez we can see that Froome carefully monitors his power meter and pushes exactly the amount of power that he knows he can sustain. He allows competitors like Contador and Nibali to break away and follows at his own pace. The result is usually that Contador and Niabli tire themselves out and are overtaken by Froome after some time.

    As runners, we are used to pacing ourselves based on feel, HR or speed. We try to maintain a constant pace throughout the race, but this is not easy when the conditions change (e.g., hills, wind). Now that we can measure our running power, we finally have access to the most accurate representation of our effort, so we can pace ourselves perfectly.

    An example of these aspects can be seen in the pictures below. Author Ron ran the Rotterdam Marathon on April 10, 2016. Based on previous experiences, Ron had planned to run the race at a constant pace of 4:50/km. He managed to hold on to this strategy for the main part of the race, but fatigue forced him to reduce his pace in the final 12K. All in all, he was quite content with the final result of 3:28:53 (equivalent to an average pace of 4:54/km). However, the Stryd data clearly show that he used too much power at the start (when he got a bit carried away by the pack) and up the Erasmus bridge (twice, after 2K and 27K). The Stryd illustrates this very nicely with the red zones, where Ron spent too much power. We believe that if Ron he had run with constant power (instead of constant pace), the decline in the final 12K would have been less and his race time would have been better.

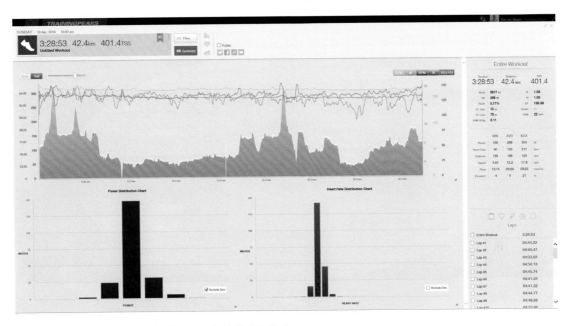

The Rotterdam Marathon by co-author Ron presented in TrainingPeaks.

Power map in Stryd Power Center showing the Rotterdam Marathon of author Ron. The colors indicate differences in power zones.

Another example is given below. Runner JanWillem Nieboer living in Amersfoort, the Netherlands, ran the Berg (mountain) Race by Night and spent too much power (532 Watts) up the Wageningen mountain, tiring himself out and losing a lot of time.

JanWillem Nieboer's Berg Race by Night presented in PowerCenter.

2. Analyze your performance perfectly.

This is similar to what we discussed in the previous chapter on training. Your running power is the best and most accurate measure of your effort. Consequently, it is better to analyze your performance based on power data as compared to feel, HR or pace. An example of such an analysis for the Rotterdam Marathon of author Ron is shown below. The power-to-HR ratio of Ron's marathon was a nice -3.91%, but his pace-to-HR ratio was +5.77% (see next chapter), which confirms that he used too much power at the start and at the Erasmus bridge. He should have run with constant power to obtain an perfect pacing.

In earlier chapters we explained that if heart rate during an all-aerobic workout rises while the intensity (power or pace) stays the same your human engine is not operating efficiently and the aerobic endurance is questionable when the value is worse than 5%. The same is true if heart rate stays the same and power decreases or the pace slows.

Entire Workout

Duration	Distance	TSS
3:28:53	42.4 km	401.4

Work	3617 kJ	IF	1.08
NP	289 W	VI	1.00
Pw:Hr	-3.91%	EF	2.17
El. Gain	75 m	Grade	--
El. Loss	75 m	VAM	22 m/h
VAM W/kg	0.11		

Workout summary of Ron's Rotterdam Marathon presented in TrainingPeaks.

3. **Share your data with your coach and an online platform.**

   This is also similar to what we already covered in the last chapter on training. By sharing all data with your coach, you give him the best understanding of your races and your strong and weak points. The same applies to apps and online platforms such as Stryd PowerCenter, TrainingPeaks, Strava, Garmin Connect and Polar applications. In this way you build a wonderful database of all your workouts with all the details. You will get feedback with trend analysis and correlation of data that you can use to analyze your performance in more detail.

69. TIPS AND TRICKS FOR USING POWER METERS

Fitness is the new wealth! —Erben Wennemars

Experiences in Cycling

For many years physician and co-author of our book *The Secret of Cycling*[2] Guido Vroemen has advised cyclists and triathletes on training with power meters. Some of his tips and tricks are given below.

Pay attention to the options for data analysis. These will increase your understanding of your workout and performance. In this chapter we will help you to understand the options for data analysis and the associated parameters.

The first time you run with a power meter, you'll notice quickly that the power data may vary significantly. This is not surprising, because the power meter responds directly to the accelerations in three dimensions (forward, lateral and vertical). A handy trick is to use the three- or ten-second average power setting of your Garmin. Your watch then shows average values over three or ten seconds so that the variations are limited and the information is better visualized. After finishing your run, you can see all that data on your computer or tablet. Several apps are available for this, including TrainingPeaks. They also have a smoothing feature that allows the data to be averaged and the graphs better visible. TrainingPeaks is one of the most popular apps, so we will use it as an example in this chapter.

Because running power meters such as the Stryd are a recent development, you may experience some interface problems with older running watches. Depending on the brand and even watch model there are differences. Author Hans gets the power data in his Garmin 630 in the running mode on the cadence screen (which reads out no higher than 500 watts because a cadence higher than 500 is unrealistic). Ron uses a Garmin 920XT and he has to switch this to the cycling mode to get his power data. This also means that TrainingPeaks shows the data as cycling results. This can be corrected manually by converting it in the app to running results. The standard cycling mode of the Garmin does not have a screen for pace. As a solution Ron can get the pace on his Garmin in cycling mode by using the special Stryd Pace app which is available through IQ Connect apps for Garmin. By zapping between cycling and running modes in the TrainingPeaks app on your computer or tablet more information can be obtained (e.g., a rate-to-HR ratio instead of a power-to-HR ratio). For Strava this applies accordingly. Try it out! The Stryd can also be used as a stand-alone device on your chest band. Then you have to synchronize the data after your workout and you do not see the real-time power data during your workout or race. A very useful service of TrainingPeaks is that your threshold power value is calculated from your race or workout. If this improves you can be notified by e-mail and you can optimize your zones with the new value. YouTube videos on the TrainingPeaks website explain how to use this app.

Which Parameters Can Be Reported?

Average power (watts, W)

This speaks for itself. This parameter equals all measured values divided by the total number of readings. The average power is calculated including the zeros readings.

Power per kilogram (watts/kg)

For your running performance, your specific power is most relevant. This is the power divided by your body weight. The higher your specific power is, the faster you will run. Previously we have shown that the maximum limit of the human power during one hour (functional treshold power, FTP) is 6.4 watts/kg for men and 5.7 watts/kg for women.

Normalized power (NP, in watts)

There is often a misunderstanding about the difference between average power and normalized power. Some people think that normalized power is equal to the average power but without the zeros. That is not the case. The normalized power represents the power that you would have needed to run at a constant speed. Variations in speed cost more effort—and therefore more power—than maintaining a constant speed.

Variability index (VI)

This is a parameter which is calculated by dividing the normalized power by the average power, so it indicates the variability of your workout. If you've run constantly with few ups and downs than the VI will be 1.0.

Training Stress Score (TSS)

Training Stress Score (TSS) is a parameter which includes both the intensity and duration in order to get a good picture of the total load of the workout or race. The calculation assumes that if you ran one hour at the intensity of FTP, this corresponds to 100 TSS points. If you ran two hours with an intensity of 80% of the FTP you will get $(0.8)2*2*100 = 128$ TSS points.

Intensity Factor (IF)

This parameter says something about how intense a training or race has been compared to your FTP. The IF is calculated by dividing the normalized power by the FTP.

Work or energy consumed in kJ

By using a power meter, it is easy to calculate the energy you have used to run. Since the metabolic efficiency is about 25%, your body will have consumed about four times as much energy. Since one kCal equals 4.18 kJ, the energy consumption of your body in kCal roughly equals the kJ indicated by your power meter.

Peak power

This table shows what your best values were for various time intervals. By collecting all the power data the best values of all time or of the current workout can be assessed.

Efficiency factor (EF)

This parameter is calculated by dividing the normalized power by the average heart rate of the workout or race. By comparing this value with similar sessions, you can see whether you improved your aerobic efficiency. The value in itself is not very important. But an increase or a decrease means something. If the ratio rises then this means that you have more power at the same heart rate, or the same power at a lower heart rate. In short, you got more efficient and better!

Power-to-HR and pace-to-HR ratios

If the heart rate increases during aerobic endurance training while the intensity (power or pace) remains the same, the aerobic base is insufficiently developed. The same applies when the heart rate remains the same but the power output decreases. For assessing this ratio, the endurance training (or race) is divided into two parts. TrainingPeaks compares the ratio of the first half with that of the second half. With a decrease in the second half of +5% or higher, improvement of the aerobic base is necessary and possible.

Velocity ascended in meters (VAM)

This parameter provides in watts/kg and in m/h an indication of the specific power and speed needed to cope with differences in altitude, such as hills.

Some Examples

The figures below give an example of how results of workouts in Garmin Connect and TrainingPeaks are reported. The example is the Rotterdam Marathon that Ron ran on April 10, 2016. Of course Ron immediately calculated his running efficiency. His c value (specific energy consumption in kJ/kg/km) was 1.071. Apparently Ron was less efficient than the 0.98 we always use as default in the model calculations in this book. That value (and even slightly better), he gets only on a track. A variety of the above-mentioned parameters are shown in the figures. Interestingly, various apps calculate parameters such as TSS differently. The underlying algorithms are owned by the app providers and to underline this they even show the copyright symbol (©).

Ron was very pleased with his VI of 1.00. In Garmin Connect the his IF value was 0.965 and in TrainingPeaks 1.08. The explanation is simple. The VI is the normalized power divided by FTP (the power that you can maintain for one hour). So for the marathon, the VI should be lower than 1.0. However, at the time of the marathon, Ron's FTP was not yet properly entered in TrainingPeaks (nor in Garmin Connect). For TSS the examples show values of 323 (Garmin Connect) and 401 (TrainingPeaks).

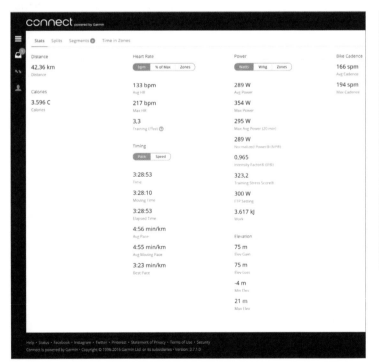

Running parameter summary from Ron's Rotterdam Marathon presented in TrainingPeaks.

Running parameter summary from Ron's Rotterdam Marathon presented in Garmin Connect.

70. LABORATORY TESTING

Running provides relaxation and creativity. —Tim Noakes

The performance lab of a sports medical center offers various tests. In this chapter we elaborate on the testing of the aerobic system of a runner on a treadmill. To test the aerobic system the load is step-by-step increased by increasing the speed of the treadmill. Such a test goes beyond your anaerobic threshold until you (nearly) reach your maximum effort level. This is called the threshold test. This test provides an accurate assessment of your threshold speed, threshold heart rate and even threshold power.

Threshold Test

In this test ergospirometry is used to determine the threshold accurately. In addition to the HR and blood pressure, the composition of the exhaled air is measured breath-by-breath, including the concentrations of oxygen (O_2) and carbon dioxide (CO_2). The software generates various graphs that show how the energy production in the body develops. During this test various parameters are determined which provide information on your physical fitness. With this information, specific individual limitations can be diagnosed, and training schedules and training advice can be optimized.

Protocol Threshold Test

In order to ensure that the body gets the opportunity to reach a new equilibrium at the next step, the duration of a step should be sufficiently long. A three-minute step length is suitable; shorter steps are not advised. The starting speed or pace is determined based on previous performances of the runner. It should be at least 5 km/h slower than the 10K race speed. Each step the speed is increased by one km/h. Once the anaerobic threshold has been reached, the duration of the steps are reduced to one minute until the maximum speed is reached. Take care that the runner does not stumble or fall at the maximum speed. A special harness may improve safety.

Which Parameters Are Measured?

Ventilation

The ventilation is the volume of exhaled air (VE) in one minute. The VE is calculated from the number of breaths per minute, the respiratory rate or frequency (Rf), and the volume per breath, the tidal volume (TV).

VE = Rf*TV

At rest the Rf is about 10-12 times per minute and the TV is about 500-1000 ml. Thus, the VE at rest is about 5-10 l/min. During maximal effort the respiratory rate Rf may increase to 60-70/min and the TV up to 3-4 liters (depending on total lung volume). So during maximum effort the VE can be up to 200 l/min or more.

Circulation

The circulation, also known as cardiac output (CO), is calculated from the heart rate (HR) and the volume of blood circulated per stroke (SV).

CO = HR*SV

At rest, the resting heart rate (RHR) is about 50-60 bpm (well-trained athletes have lower values) and the SV is about 60-80 ml, so the CO at rest is some 4-5 l/min.

During maximum effort HR may increase up to 200 bpm and the SV of well-trained athletes to 150-200 ml. Consequently the CO during maximum effort can increase to 30-40 l/min.

The stroke volume (SV) cannot yet be measured simply during a test. The heart rate (HR) is determined from the electrocardiogram (ECG).

Oxygen concentration

During the test the oxygen content in every breath is determined. By determining the difference with the outside air (20.93% oxygen), the oxygen uptake by the body can be calculated. At maximum effort the maximum oxygen uptake (VO_2 max) can be determined.

Carbon dioxide concentration

The amount of carbon dioxide is determined in the exhaled air and compared with the outside air (0.03% CO_2). Consequently, the CO_2 production by the body can be calculated.

Respiratory quotient (RQ) or respiratory exchange ratio (RER)

This parameter indicates the sources of energy that your body uses. The RQ is the amount of CO_2 produced (in l/min) divided by the amount of O_2 used (in l/min).

$$RQ = VCO_2/VO_2$$

If only fatty acids are used, RQ is 0.7. If glycogen (carbohydrates) are burned exclusively, RQ is 1.0. At an RQ of 0.85, the fuel mix consists of 50% fatty acids and 50% glycogen. This parameter is useful for assessing the fat and glycogen consumption during various efforts.

Equivalents (VE/VO$_2$ and VE/VCO$_2$)

These parameters say something about the amount of air required to ventilate one liter of oxygen, or exhale one liter of carbon dioxide.

Aerobic threshold (first ventilatory threshold)

This is the threshold where the production of lactic acid starts. At this point the lactic acid can still be easily removed and broken down by your body. Consequently, the concentration of lactic acid hardly increases. This threshold is between zone 1 and zone 2. Graphically this point can be recognized as the point where the VE/VO$_2$ starts rising.

Anaerobic threshold (second ventilatory threshold)

From this point on you produce so much lactic acid that it cannot be broken down sufficiently. So lactic acid starts to accumulate. The further you get above this threshold, the shorter you can maintain this intensity. This threshold is between zone 3 and zone 4. Graphically this point can be recognized as the point where both VE/VO$_2$ and VE/VCO$_2$ no longer remain constant and will rise.

The maximum oxygen uptake capacity (VO$_2$ max)

The maximum oxygen uptake is measured in milliliters per minute (ml/min). In order to make the parameter comparable with other runners it is divided by the body weight (in kg) and expressed as ml/kg/min. For more information about VO$_2$ max also see one of the earlier chapters.

The running economy (RE)

This is the amount of oxygen that is used by the runner to run one kilometer at a certain submaximal speed. At every submaximal speed the oxygen uptake is measured in ml/min/kg and the running economy can be calculated in ml/kg/km. As an example we use an oxygen uptake at 12 km/h of 45 ml/min/kg. Consequently, this runner has an RE of 5 x 45 = 225 ml/kg/km; it takes him five minutes to run one kilometer. Running economy is a very important parameter because it tells you how efficient your running style is and how much energy you use to run one kilometer. World-class marathon runners have an RE of 180 ml O$_2$/kg/km. Average runners have an RE of 210-240 ml O$_2$/kg/km.

Author Ron at the treadmill for a combined ergospirometry and running power test.

Running Power Treadmill Test

In an earlier chapter we looked into the impact of the specific energy cost of running (c, in kJ/kg/km). We can also express the specific energy cost of running in terms of the specific oxygen uptake (in ml O_2/kg/km). This can be determined in the laboratory with a treadmill test as explained above. As the energy value of 1 ml of O_2 is equal to 19.5 J and the metabolic efficiency can be set at 25%, the following relationship holds:

c = (19.5*0.25/1000)*RE

This means an RE of 201 ml O_2/kg/km is equivalent to our standard value for c of 0.98 kJ/kg/km. Obviously, the c and the RE are not the same for all runners and in all conditions.

We can also determine the specific energy cost of running (c) at the treadmill test. This can be easily done by wearing a running power meter. Of course authors Hans and Ron did so at the sports performance lab of Guido Vroemen. The c value (in kJ/kg/km) can be easily calculated by dividing the average specific power (watts/kg) by the average speed (in m/s). The results of the combined ergospirometry and running power treadmill test are given in the table below.

As can be seen the c values of Hans and Ron were not entirely constant during the test. Is seems that their c values increased somewhat with speed. One explanation for this phenomenon could be that they ran more economically at higher speed. As we discussed in an earlier chapter, it would be very interesting to see which factors determine the c and RE in practice and how runners can improve their running economy by optimizing their running form.

Combined Ergospirometry and Running Power Treadmill Test						
	Hans (58 kg)			Ron (80 kg)		
Step	Power	VO$_2$	c	Power	VO$_2$	c
(km/h)	(watts/kg)	(ml/kg/min)	(kJ/kg/km)	(watts/kg)	(ml/kg/min)	(kJ/kg/km)
10	2.46	40	1.13			
11	2.79	44	1.10	3.85	43	1.26
12	3.17	47	1.05	3.98	47	1.19
13	3.48	49	1.04	4.03	48	1.12
14	3.81	52	1.02	4.19	50	1.08
15	4.34	54	0.96			

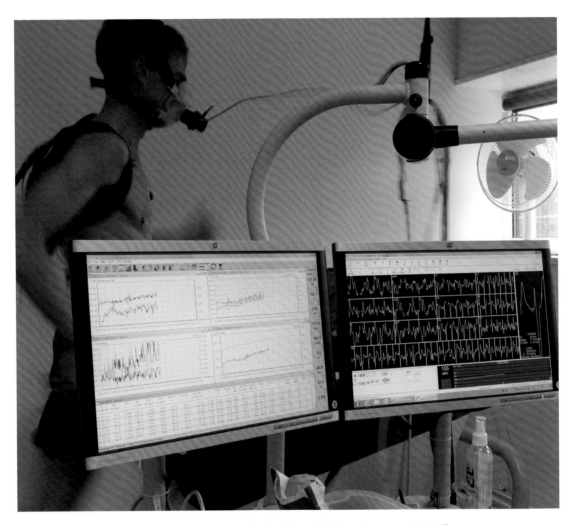

During a ergospirometry test various parameters are determined which provide information on your physical fitness.

PART VI

THE MYTHS OF
RUNNING

71. THE SUB TWO-HOUR MARATHON?

Marathon racers discover the peace inside the pain.

Recently, the media reported on the Sub2hrs Project Team[85]. They have set a goal to break the dream barrier of two hours for the marathon. The project aims to get a budget of $30 million, half of which is earmarked for race organizers and athletes. The team with lead-scientist Yannis Pitsiladis and athlete manager Jos Hermans has identified ten research areas which should contribute to faster times. These areas include nutrition, biomechanics, physiotherapy, race preparation, training, race course analysis, bio-energetics and bio-informatics. This sounds very inspirational, but how realistic is the goal of a sub two-hour marathon? We felt challenged to calculate the possibilities and limitations with our model. The results of our analysis will be discussed in this chapter.

How Strong Is the Current Marathon World Record?

In an earlier chapter, we have already analyzed the current world records in athletics. The table shows the results for the distances from 3,000 meters up to and including the marathon. For all records, we have calculated the required specific power (in watts/kg) with our model and transferred this to the equivalent FTP (also in watts/kg), using Riegel's formula. The table shows clearly that the level of most world records is more or less the same (i.e., equivalent to an FTP of 6.30-6.36 watts/kg). The records at the 15, 25 and 30K are somewhat less strong, which is probably related to the fact that these distances are run less frequently.

World Records: Men			FTP
Distance	Time	Name	(Watts/kg)
3,000 m	7:20.67	Daniel Komen	6.32
5,000 m	12:37.35	Kenenisa Bekele	6.33
10,000 m	26:17.53	Kenenisa Bekele	6.36
15 km	00:41:13	Leonard Komon	6.24
20 km	00:55:21	Zersenay Tadese	6.32
21.1 km	00:58:23	Zersenay Tadese	6.34
25 km	01:11:18	Dennis Kimetto	6.22
30 km	01:27:38	Emmanuel Mutai	6.14
42.2 km	02:02:57	Dennis Kimetto	6.30

From our calculations, we conclude that the marathon world record is already quite strong with an equivalent FTP of 6.30 watts/kg. It will not be easy to improve this by 2.5%, which is required for the sub two-hours goal. For completeness sake, we note that all world records in athletics have already been set in ideal conditions (cool, windless) and in orchestrated races (with pacemakers).

Which FTP Is Required to Run a Sub Two-Hours Marathon?

The media have suggested that Kenenisa Bekele could run a sub two-hours marathon if he would devote himself to the marathon and do all the required hard training work. From the table, we note that Kenenisa did have the highest FTP of all the world record holders with a value of 6.36 watts/kg (equivalent to his 10,000 meter world record). We used our program to calculate the impact of the FTP on the marathon race time. The results are given in the figure below. We see that Bekele's FTP of 6.36 watts/kg is equivalent to a marathon time of 2:01:57. This would be an impressive new world record, but it is still two minutes shy of the sub two-hours goal! To reach this goal, an FTP of 6.48 watts/kg would be required, according to our calculations. This value is extremely high and significantly higher than the current limit of the human power. As we showed in earlier chapters, we believe that the limit of clean human power is 6.40 watts/kg, so we feel that the sub two-hours goal cannot be reached in the near future (in an authorized way).

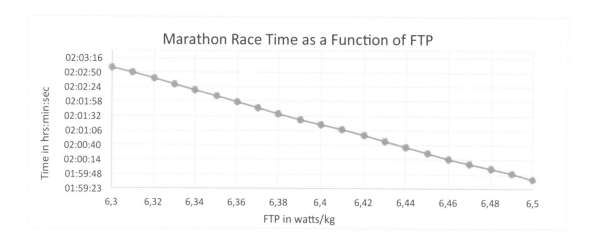

How Much Time Could Be Gained in Ideal Conditions?

So far, we have made the calculations for the standard conditions:

» Windless weather (v_w = 0 km/h)
» Normal air pressure (1,013 mbar)
» Ideal temperature (5-10°C)
» No hills (i = 0%)
» With pacemakers (c_dA = 0.20 m²)

These are the typical conditions of record races. It will not be easy to find better conditions. A higher or lower temperature and the presence of wind or altitude differences will always have a negative impact on the race time. The only options to gain time in an authorized way are:

» The presence of a depression or low air pressure.
» The presence of perfect pacemakers throughout the 42 kilometers.

We have used our model again to calculate the impact of these factors. The results are shown in the table. We see that if a marathon were be run in conditions of low air pressure, a gain of some 22 seconds is possible (due to the lower air resistance). Regarding the impact of pacemakers, we should note that the current world record of Dennis Kimetto was already set with the assistance of pacemakers. As we discussed earlier in this book, we have taken the impact of normal pacemakers into account by reducing the air resistance coefficient (c_dA) from the standard value of 0.24 m² to 0.20 m². As the table shows,

Dennis Kimetto owes already 84 seconds time gain to his pacemakers. We have made an alternative calculation into the impact of ideal pacers, assuming that the c_dA value could be further reduced to 0.18 m^2. This would require perfect shielding throughout the race. In practice this would mean a large group of strong pacers and a small group of elite athletes that will work closely together up to the finish. According to our calculations, this may provide a gain of another 39 seconds.

Impact Conditions on WR Marathon	
Present WR	02:02:57
Without pacers (c_dA = 0.24 m^2)	02:04:21
Ideal pacers (c_dA = 0.18 m^2)	02:02:18
Low pressure (953 mbar)	02:02:35
140-meter altitude gain	02:01:28

How Much Time Could Be Gained Downhill and With a Tailwind?

We read in the media that the sub two-hours team suggested organizing special record races on a course that would give the runners the benefit of a tail wind. Obviously, such a record would not be recognized by the IAAF, as they stipulate that the start and the finish of the marathon be at the same location. The reason for this rule is to avoid incomparable advantages between different courses. This is also why records at the Boston Marathon are not recognized, as the finish in Boston is 140 meters downhill from the start. As the table above shows, this 140-meter gain in altitude provides a gain in race time of 89 seconds!

To illustrate how big the impact of a tailwind is, we have used our model to calculate the race time that Dennis Kimetto could run with his FTP of 6.30 watts/kg, provided he could benefit from a tailwind throughout the race. The results are shown in the figure below.

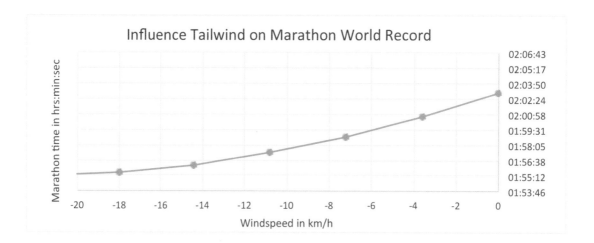

The figure shows that with a tailwind it would be a piece of cake for him to reach the sub two-hours mark! He could already reach this with a light breeze of 5 km/h. Obviously, the reason is that he will be literally supported by the wind throughout the race. This will reduce the air resistance drastically.

As we saw from the example of the Boston Marathon, it may also be easy to reach the sub two-hours goal running downhill. We have calculated that Dennis Kimetto could reach this goal with his FTP of 6.30 watts/kg with a gain in altitude of 280 meter.

In summary, we do not believe that the goal of a sub two-hours marathon can be reached in the near future in a regular fashion as this would require an FTP of 6.48 watts/kg. On the other hand, it will be relatively easy to reach this goal in specially organized races where the runners can benefit from running downhill or with a tailwind. However, we believe that reaching the goal in this way will not be very inspirational, as a matter of fact it seems a bit like cheating...

In 2014 Dennis Kimetto from Kenya won the 41st Berlin Marathon in the world record time of 2:02:57.

72. NUTRITION, SUPPLEMENTS AND BEET JUICE

Running is about finding your inner peace and so is a life well lived. —Dean Karnazes

Regularly, new items or books are published on products or diets that are supposed to make us more healthy or fit. Most of these reports fall in the categories of humbug or scam. The scientific literature on nutrition[6-12,80] concludes that there is no such thing as a miracle product. Moreover, a normal healthy and varied diet suffices to prevent deficiencies, even for the elite athletes. Supplements are required only in exceptional cases or extreme efforts like the Tour de France or Ironman triathlons.

What Constitutes a Healthy Diet?

In an earlier chapter, we learned that first and foremost a healthy diet should be lean and varied. As the general Western diet contains too much fat and calories, the following recommendations can be made:

1. Eat plenty (five to six portions daily) of vegetables and fruit.
2. Eat whole-wheat bread (with lean or fruit filling) and oatmeal porridge as required.
3. Eat one portion of potatoes (no fries), pasta, rice or other grain products daily.
4. Eat one portion of lean meat, fish, poultry or tofu, or another source of protein (like eggs, beans, nuts) daily.
5. Replace butter with olive oil or another liquid oil.
6. Eat or drink lean dairy products, like skin milk, yoghurt or cheese as required (maximum of three portions daily).
7. Drink plenty of water and tea and as little as possible of sodas, beer, wine and sports drinks.
8. Avoid fried products, snacks, refreshments and salted or fried cookies.
9. On occasions you may eat gingerbread, pancakes and low-fat cookies.

This diet will contain the proper amounts and shares of the energy sources (carbohydrates, proteins and fatty acids), but also of the vitamins, trace elements and antioxidants that you require. Be careful to buy fresh products and vary the menu as much as possible. Avoid using ready-made products containing flavoring additives, emulsifiers and salt. Weigh yourself regularly to make sure your weight remains stable and at the desired level.

As was stated above, supplements like sports drinks and energy gels are unnecessary. They should be avoided as they contain a lot of calories, so you will gain body fat!

The only exception to the above rules should be made in the last 2-3 days before running a marathon. Then you should apply the marathon diet (carbo-loading), by increasing the share of carbohydrates in your diet to 70% and reducing the share of proteins and fats to 15% each. This will increase the glycogen stores in your muscles, which will help you to avoid hitting the wall in the final stages of the marathon. On the morning of the marathon, you should take an alimentary breakfast and during the marathon you should drink sports drinks every 5K to supplement the glucose and glycogen used during the marathon. More details on this have been given in an earlier chapter.

Supplements

As stated above, supplements are unnecessary and even unwanted in normal circumstances. We should realize that the human body is capable of synthesizing almost all required compounds from the elements which are present in our nutrition. In our intestines, most of our food is broken down to small and simple compounds. An example is the fact that carbohydrates from potatoes or pasta are broken down to glucose. The glucose is adsorbed by the blood and transported to the cells, where it is used to synthesize glycogen. Finally, the glycogen is used by the cells to produce the energy and power we need for running.

We should also realize that our body has ample stores of many compounds that can be mobilized when needed. As an example, both authors Hans and Ron have experienced that a large amount of their body fat was slowly mobilized and dissolved during the six months in 2012 when they lost weight (in both cases some 10-15 kg). In this period they ate fewer calories, while continuing their training. Consequently, their bodies needed to mobilize their body fat in order to provide the energy and power required for the training. So, contrary to popular belief, you do not have to eat a lot to supply the energy and power needed for running. The human body has ample stores of fat which it can mobilize.

The only exception to this rule applies to some vitamins and trace elements, which our body cannot synthetize itself. These components need to be present in our nutrition. However, also for these components the body usually has some stock available. This means that we just have to make sure that in the long run (months) our nutrition contains sufficient amounts of these components, hence the importance of sufficient variation in our nutrition. Vegetables and fruits contain a lot of vitamins, trace minerals and antioxidants which are very healthy.

After this clarification, the reader will probably understand that there is no such thing as a miracle sports nutrition or supplement. The only proven miracle products are doping substances, like EPO and anabolic steroids. These are mostly injected and influence the hormone system. When consumed orally, EPO is broken down in the intestines and loses its function. Some anabolic substances can be consumed orally, but they are much less effective.

Review of Popular Supplements

Below we will give a review of the impact and the side effects of some popular supplements, based on the scientific literature[6-12,80].

1. *Caffeine*

   Caffeine is not really considered a supplement, as it has become an accepted part of the normal diet. However, it does have a proven ergogenic effect (i.e., a positive impact on the performance in sports). How big the impact is, however, remains uncertain. Different studies have given different results. The small positive impact found in most studies is explained by the fact that caffeine stimulates the conversion of fatty acids. As a result, the glycogen stores are somewhat spared which will help to avoid hitting the wall. Caffeine also is known to have a stimulating effect on the brain and the nervous system. Since 2014 caffeine is no longer on the WADA doping list, but it is recommended that the consumption is limited to 5 mg/kg of body weight. For a runner with a body weight of 60 kg, this means consuming no more than 300 mg or 3-6 cups of coffee or 5-10 cups of tea. In view of the expected small positive impact and because coffee and tea are harmless products, it is recommended to drink some 2-3 cups of strong coffee or tea two hours before the race.

2. *Sodium bicarbonate*

   Sodium bicarbonate increases the pH of the blood and improves the buffering capacity. As a result, the negative impact of lactic acid, which is produced at speeds above the anaerobic threshold, will be neutralized. In literature a positive effect of a few percent has been reported at middle distance races, but there have been mixed results with a dose of 0.3 mg/kg, consumed a few hours before the race. An awkward side effect is that 50% of the test persons got abdominal discomfort. Sodium bicarbonate is not yet on the doping list, but this may change. It could be traced easily on account of the impact on the urine pH. Using it would be pointless for distance runners, but for short and middle distances a small positive effect could be expected, provided of course that the runner does not suffer from diarrhea!

3. *Creatine*
Creatine is present in meat and is produced in the liver. Creatine phosphate is used in the synthesis of ATP in the muscles. Some studies have shown that supplementary intake of creatine (3-5 g/day) improves the recovery process in interval training. Creatine is used in power sports, swimming and cycling. Objections are the possible contamination of the product (e.g. with nandrolone), and the resulting weight increase.

4. *Glycerol*
The consumption of glycerol may lead to a temporary increase of the blood (plasma) volume. Consequently, it has been used to mask the use of EPO since it results in lower levels of hemoglobin and hematocrit. However, proof of a positive impact on the running performance is lacking.

5. *Triglycerides*
Theoretically, the consumption of triglycerides should improve the conversion of fatty acids. However, several studies failed to prove any positive impact in practice.

6. *Branched chain amino acids/L-Tryptophan*
Serotonin is synthesized in the body from the amino acid tryptophan. As a neurotransmitter serotonin has a positive impact on your mood. During exercises, like walking and running, serotonin is produced which makes you feel good. However, during protracted exercise the serotonin level can rise to levels causing fatigue. Theoretically, the level of serotonin could be mitigated by the intake of branched chain amino acids like valine, leucine and isoleucine. In practice mixed results have been found. This also applies to studies that looked into the direct intake of L-tryptophan. Based on current science, the use of these supplements cannot be supported.

7. *Vitamins/antioxidants (A, B1 t/m B15, C, D, E)*
For almost all vitamins it is known that a healthy and varied diet will supply the necessary amounts, so supplementary intake is not necessary. The only exceptions to this rule can be for special sensitive groups, like babies, children, pregnant women, vegetarians, elite athletes and senior citizens. In these cases supplements of vitamin D (discussed in the next chapter) or on occasions vitamin B11 (folic acid), B12 or K may be recommended. In the 1980s there was a lot of interest in vitamin B15, which was thought to boost performances. However, later studies failed to prove any positive effect.

8. *Trace elements (Ca, Cr, B, Fe, Mg, Zn)*

   Also for all trace elements science tells us that a healthy and varies diet will supply all the necessary amounts, so supplementary intake is not necessary. For special groups, including pregnant women, vegetarians and elite athletes, supplementary intake or iron may be recommended to avoid anemia. The recommended daily intake is 10 mg for men and 15 mg for women. Some distance runners have the experience that supplementary intake of magnesium helps to prevent or reduce muscle cramps in the final stages of the marathon. In summary, there is no harm in taking a daily iron pill and occasionally a multi-vitamin pill as a precautionary measure.

9. *Phosphate*

   Phosphate is necessary for the synthesis of ATP, so theoretically supplementary intake could boost recovery. However, in practice no positive impact has been found.

10. *Carnitine*

    Theoretically, carnitine could stimulate the conversion of fatty acids. However, no effect was found in practice.

11. *Spirulina and ginseng*

    No scientific studies have been published that prove a positive effect of these formulations.

Beet Juice

In recent years, the use of beet juice has been more or less a hype in the media[86]. The consumption of beet juice was said to improve the performance in running and cycling. Some studies reported a boost in performance of 3-5%. This would be very significant indeed; no other product besides EPO and anabolic steroids could boast on such an impact!

Theoretically, you could expect some positive impact of the high nitrate (NO_3^-) level of beet juice. The oxygen from the nitrate might play a role in the aerobic processes in the muscles. So, you could hypothesize that it may increase your oxygen uptake capacity and thus improve your performance. However, we should approach this topic critically, as the reported results were obtained with only a limited number of test persons. This means that the results could easily have been influenced by random differences or a placebo effect.

Another reason for a critical attitude follows from the mass balance. In the reported studies the total dose was 1,000 mg NO_3^- (0.5 liter beet juice per day over three days). We have compared this (on a molar base) to the amount of the oxygen used during two hours of running. The result is that the nitrate dose is a factor 1,600 smaller than the oxygen uptake! We believe that it is most unlikely that such a small dose could have such a big impact, particularly as the processes in our body are based primarily on oxygen and not on nitrate.

An argument in favor of beet juice, is the fact that nitrate will be reduced to nitrite and nitrogen monoxide in the stomach. This may lead to some dilation of the blood vessels, which will improve the circulation and reduce the blood pressure.

In view of the above, authors Hans and Ron could not resist the temptation to test it themselves. On the occasion of the 20K at Alphen aan den Rijn in 2013, they served as guinea pigs. During the three days before the race, they took a dose of 1,800 mg of NO_3^-, by drinking beet juice and eating spinach, turnip stalks and beets. Unfortunately, during the race they did not notice any impact at all! Their race times were exactly as could be expected from their training and previous races. Of course, this can hardly be called scientific proof, so we do not want to exclude the possibility that other runners may benefit a little from beet juice. So if you don't mind the taste of beet juice, feel free to try it. We have not repeated the test, as we don't believe we will benefit from it.

Authors Hans and Ron could not resist the temptation to test beet juice themselves.

73. AVOID A VITAMIN D DEFICIENCY!

Nothing will work, unless you do. —Maya Angelou

In winter, the risk of a vitamin D deficit is significant, especially in Northern countries like the Netherlands. Consequently, supplementary intake of vitamin D can be necessary and prudent, particularly for athletes. Authors Hans and Ron (and physician and distance runner Karel Bos, who co-authored this chapter) take a daily vitamin D pill to prevent any negative impact on their performance. What do runners need to know about vitamin D and how may it affect your performance? These questions will be answered in this chapter.

The History of Vitamin D

Historically, vitamin D deficiency[87] has been associated with Rickets, a bone disease which was commonly found in industrial areas in Northern Europe in the 19th century. In the 1920s research showed that it could be treated effectively by:

1. Exposure to UV light and sunlight
2. Intake of codfish oil, butter and milk

After World War II, the Dutch government set up holiday camps to increase the exposure of children to sunlight. Since 1961 vitamin D is also added to margarine in the Netherlands.

Recommended Daily Intake of Vitamin D

The European Food labelling Guideline states a recommended daily intake (RDI) of 5 microgram (μg). However, this does not take into account the risk groups, like senior citizens, pregnant women and breastfeeding women. In the Netherlands a vitamin D deficiency is quite common, in particular amongst groups who remain indoors most of the time, people with dark skin and women wearing burkas or veils.

The Dutch Food Center recommends a daily intake of a supplement of 10 µg for the following groups:

1. Children under the age of 4 years
2. Persons between the ages of 4-50 years with dark skin
3. All pregnant women and breastfeeding women
4. All women over the age of 50 and men over the age of 50
5. All women under the age of 50 wearing veils

They also recommend a daily intake of 20 µg for the following groups:

1. Persons suffering from osteoporosis or living in a nursing home
2. Women over the age of 50 and men over the age of 70 who remain indoors most of the time
3. Women over the age of 50 wearing veils

Sources of Vitamin D

Sunlight

The human body can synthesize vitamin D when exposed to sunlight. People who live in tropical areas produce an estimated 250 µg/day—much more than the RDI. When the skin takes in the sun, the vitamin D production decreases, so the level of vitamin D will never become excessively high. In countries like the Netherlands, only in summer is the UV index of the sun high enough to produce a sufficient amount of vitamin D (some 25 µg after 15 minutes sun exposure of the face, arms and upper body without sun screen). Also, in many Western countries most people stay indoors most of the time or cover their skin, which limits the vitamin D production. Finally, the production of vitamin D reduces with age as a result of skin aging.

Nutrition

Our nutrition generally contains insufficient vitamin D. Only a few products contain vitamin D, in particular codfish oil, fat fish (15-25 µg/portion), some mushrooms and egg yolks. In the Netherlands vitamin D is added to margarine.

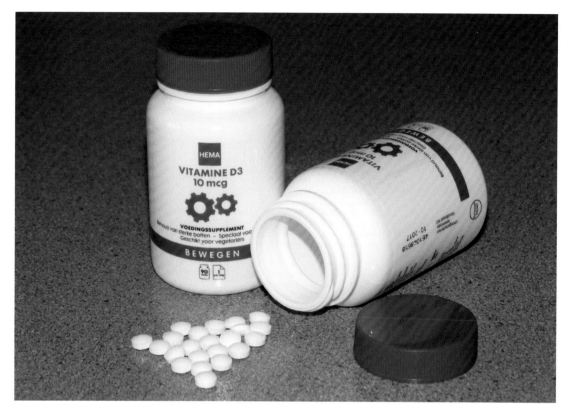

Supplementary intake of vitamin D can be necessary and prudent, particularly for athletes.

Relationship Between Vitamin D and the Performance in Sports

The scientific literature contains many dozens of papers on the relationship between vitamin D and the performance in sports. The following positive effects of vitamin D have been reported[88]:

1. Prevention of injuries, like stress fractures
2. Prevention of diseases, like infections, inflammation and osteoporosis
3. Increased muscle power
4. Improved performance in sports (sprint, swimming, gymnastics, tennis)

In a recent review paper, the following recommendations were made regarding the optimal vitamin D blood level[89]:

1. Prevention of Rickets   25 nmol/L
2. Prevention of stress fractures   100 nmol/L
3. Improved performance in sport   125 nmol/L

Positive proof that vitamin D will improve the running performance is still lacking, This would require a study with a large number of test persons and a professional scientific methodology (e.g., double-blind, randomized).

Experiences of Hans, Ron and Karel

For many years, Hans has been supplementing his diet with 10 µg/day of vitamin D in summer and 15 µg/day in winter. Also, he regularly spends time outdoors, running, gardening and hiking. In May 2014 and in December 2014, he had his blood level checked in the laboratory. The results are given in the table and show that the level of vitamin D in his blood was adequate. The somewhat lower level of December will have been caused by the reduced sunshine in winter.

Vitamin D Data: Hans		
	Blood level (nmol/L)	Intake (µg/day)
May 2014	95.2	10
December 2014	91.8	15

Previously, Ron did not take vitamin D pills. Also, he spends more time indoors as compared to Hans. When he had his blood level checked in June 2014, it was found to be rather low. From then on, he started supplementing his diet too. As a result, his blood levels increased as shown in the table.

Vitamin D Data: Ron		
	Blood level (nmol/L)	Intake (µg/day)
June 2014	55.5	-
July 2014	84.5	50
September 2014	82.7	25
November 2014	71.8	20
January 2015	77.2	30
March 2015	81.8	30
April 2015	61.1	20
July 2015	69.5	20

Based on the data of Ron's table, we drew up a mass balance of vitamin D. We found that around 20 µg/day were broken down or excreted (in summer less, in winter more). So, we concluded that a supplement of 30 µg/day in winter and 20 µg/day in summer would be adequate for Ron.

Co-author Karel has been taking 20 µg/day in winter for many years. He cycles one hour every day and runs three times a week.

Conclusions and Recommendations

1. Vitamin D deficiency is prominent in the Netherlands and may have a negative impact on health and performance in sports.
2. It seems wise to take precautionary measures: take a regular sunbath in summer (a few times per week for 15 minutes; don't overdo it as too much sunshine can cause skin diseases) and supplement the diet with a vitamin D pill.
3. Risk groups and persons with complaints should have their blood level checked, so that informed additional measures can be taken.
4. Runners and other athletes should certainly take the precautionary measures mentioned above to avoid the risk of a negative impact on their performance.
5. The toxic levels of vitamin D are very high (blood level higher than 325 nmol/L), so taking some additional vitamin D does not easily lead to any risk of intoxication.

The human body can synthesize vitamin D when exposed to sunlight.

74. DON'T TAKE TOO MANY PILLS!

The true runner is a very fortunate person. He has found something in him that is just perfect. —George Sheehan

Earlier we learned that the scientific literature on nutrition and supplements tells us that there is no such thing as a miracle product. Even for elite athletes a normal, healthy and varied diet is sufficient and will supply all the necessary elements. Supplements are only required in exceptional cases, such as for specific deficiencies or extreme efforts (Tour de France or Ironman triathlon). Some vitamin formulas can even be dangerous! As an example of such potential problems, we will discuss vitamin B_6 in this chapter.

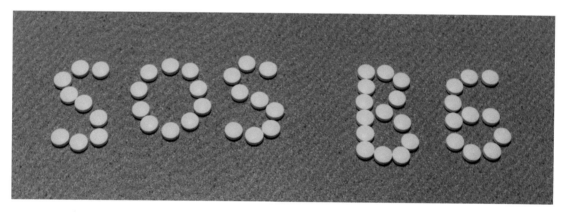

In the Netherlands, vitamin B6 intoxication is diagnosed frequently.

How Vitamin B_6 May Harm Your Health (The Burning Feet Syndrome)

An overdose of vitamin B_6[90] can cause neurological complaints, including tingling and burning feet (burning feet syndrome). In the Netherlands, vitamin B_6 intoxication is diagnosed frequently. One of the reasons is the fact that pills containing a high dose can be bought without prescription. Physician and co-author Karel Bos regularly sees patients with vitamin B_6 intoxication in his medical practice.

The History of Vitamin B$_6$

Vitamin B$_6$ was discovered during research into pellagra, a skin disease which is still prominent in developing countries. In 1934, the Hungarian microbiologist and biochemist Paul Györgi traced a substance that was able to prevent pellagra in rats. One year later, he managed to isolate vitamin B$_6$. The molecular structure was discovered in 1939. Vitamin B$_6$ comprises of three compounds including pyridoxine. This name is also used as the general denomination for vitamin B$_6$.

Vitamin B$_6$ Deficiency Symptoms

Prolonged deficits may lead to anemia, lack of appetite, diarrhea, nervous conditions and a weakened immune system. In the Netherlands deficits are rare, as the normal diet contains sufficient vitamin B$_6$. Deficiencies are only seen in special cases, such as alcoholism and persons with a reduced kidney function.

Recommended Daily Intake

The RDI has been set at 1.5 mg/day by the Dutch Health Council. For special groups, like pregnant women, the RDI is slightly higher, 1.9 mg/day. The maximum acceptable safe intake is considered to be 25 mg/day.

Sources of Vitamin B$_6$

Nutrition

In our food, vitamin B$_6$ is mostly bound to proteins. Very rich sources are chicken and liver. Good sources are meat, fish, eggs, milk and cheese. Vegetable sources are legumes, bananas, nuts, beans, cauliflower, raisins, bread and corn. The normal Dutch diet will easily supply the RDI of 1.5 mg/day.

Vitamin pills

In the Netherlands, vitamin B$_6$ can be bought without a prescription. Pills are sold with a mega dose of 50, 100 or even 250 mg. The bottle instructions recommend a daily intake of 2-4 of these pills! Consequently, it seems likely that in the Netherlands, just like in the USA, many people will use a dose of 1,000 mg. This is equivalent to 40 times the maximum recommended safe intake and even 666 times the RDI! So, it is obvious that people who take these pills regularly run the risk of an overdose and intoxication of vitamin B$_6$!

Risks of an Overdose of Vitamin B$_6$

The scientific literature contains many papers on the risks of an overdose of vitamin B$_6$. It may lead to a degeneration of the peripheral nervous system and parts of the spine (peripheral neuropathy). These effect have been proven clearly at doses of 500 mg/day; patients suffer from tingling and idiosyncrasy of the arms and legs (burning feet syndrome). At lower doses of 50 to 300 mg/day, the symptoms are less obvious.

An Increasing Problem?

Vitamin B$_6$ intoxication is often not recognized, as physicians are not aware of the toxicity of vitamins. For a proper diagnoses it is necessary to analyze the blood level in the laboratory. The normal blood level of vitamin B$_6$ is 35-110 nmol/L. A hospital in the Netherlands issued a warning recently that they were seeing a significant increase in excessive blood values. Some 50% of all samples were higher than the upper limit of 110 nmol/L, with an extreme value of 12,525 nmol/L! They strongly advise not to use any vitamin B$_6$ pills.

Conclusions and Recommendations

1. Vitamin B$_6$ deficiency occurs only rarely in the Netherlands, so it not necessary to take supplementary pills, even for elite athletes.
2. Vitamin B$_6$ intoxication occurs regularly in the Netherlands. It is caused by the intake of pills with a mega dose and can lead to tingling and idiosyncrasy of the arms and legs (burning feet syndrome).
3. Persons having complaints should have their blood level checked in consultation with their physician. If the level is too high, they should stop taking pills immediately. The complaints may continue for as long as a year.
4. To limit the risk of overdosing, it is strongly recommended to reduce the maximum dose of vitamin B$_6$ from 250 to 25 mg/pill. Also the bottle instructions should warn against the risk of overdosing and intoxication.

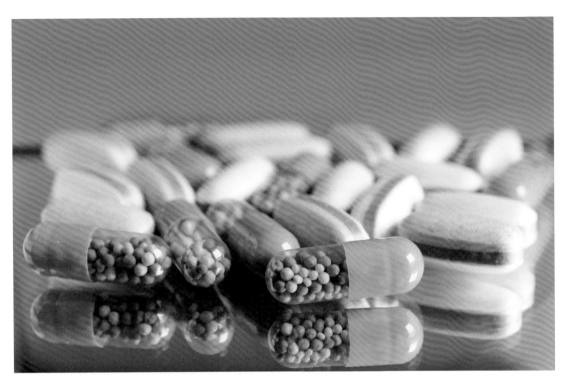

Don't take too many pills!

75. JACK DANIELS' RUNNING FORMULA

If you train your mind for running, everything else will be easy. —Amby Burfoot

In 1979, American coach and physiologist Jack Daniels, together with Jimmy Gilbert, published the groundbreaking book *Oxygen Power*[91], in which he introduced the concept of the VDOT. His VDOT is actually the same as the traditional concept of the VO_2 max, or rather an equivalent value of the VO_2 max. Consequently, the unit is also ml O_2/kg/min. Daniels published elaborate tables, showing which race times you could run at different distances for a certain value of the VDOT. He also made similar tables for the recommended paces in training (distinguished as easy pace, marathon pace, threshold pace, interval pace and speed/repetition pace) as a function of the VDOT. In 1998 Daniels published his second book *Daniel's Running Formula*[8]. This book became a worldwide bestseller with over 140,000 copies sold. It was named the best training book for runners by the magazine *Runner's World*. For decades, Daniels' books have been of great significance to runners and coaches. His tables and formulas are still used worldwide, and in calculators on the internet. In this chapter, we will compare his formulas to ours and mark the differences.

How Fast Can You Run With Your Human Engine?

Daniels expresses the power of the human engine in his concept of VDOT/VO_2 (in ml/kg/min). Empirically, he derived the following formula[92] between the VO_2 and the running speed v (in m/min):

$$VO_2 = -4.80 + 0.182258v + 0.000104v^2$$

In our book, we express the power of the human engine in the specific power (P/m, in watts/kg). Based on the laws of physics and in ideal conditions (flat course and windless weather), we derived the following formula between the specific power and the speed (v, in m/s):

$$P/m = cv + (0.5\rho c_d Av^3)/m$$

Both formulas look more or less similar, which makes sense. On the left side, we see a concept for the specific power (VO_2 and P/m, respectively) and on the right side we see an equation with a number of constants and the speed (v). What are the differences and similarities?

1. First, we should determine the relationship between VO_2 (in ml O_2/kg/min) and P/m (in watts/kg). As the energy value of 1 ml O_2 is equal to 19.5 J and the metabolic efficiency can be set at 0.25, the following relationship holds:

$$P/m = 19.5/60*0.25 = 0.081*VO_2$$

2. Secondly, we see that apparently Daniels has simplified the cubic equation (of v) to a quadratic equation, which will probably be not too far off in normal conditions.

A fundamental disadvantage of Daniels' formula is that it not based on the laws of physics. As a result, he uses the wrong exponent for the air resistance (v^2 instead of v^3). More seriously, he does not take into account the fact that the impact of the air resistance on the specific power (P/m or VO_2, both are related to kg of body weight) should be inversely dependent on the body weight of the runner! Finally, we think it has the drawback that it does not provide the opportunity to calculate the impact of variables, like the air density, the air resistance coefficient (c_dA) and the specific energy cost of running (c, which also reflects the running economy (RE), as we saw earlier).

What happens when we compare the results of both formulas in practice? We have calculated this with our model. The results are given in the figure, for the standard conditions ($Đ$ = 1.205 kg/m³, c_dA = 0.24 m², c = 0.98 kJ/kg/km).

We see that Daniels' formula leads to higher running speeds than our model. One reason to explain this could be that the test runners of Daniels had a higher running economy. In our standard we use the c value of 0.98 kJ/kg/km. Some readers may be more familiar with the concept of running economy (RE, in ml O_2/kg/km). As one ml of O_2 has an energy value of 19.5 kJ and the metabolic efficiency can be set at 0.25, the following relationship holds:

$$c = 19.5/1000*0.25*RE$$

Consequently, a c value of 0.98 kJ/kg/km is equivalent to an RE of 201 mlO_2/kg/km.

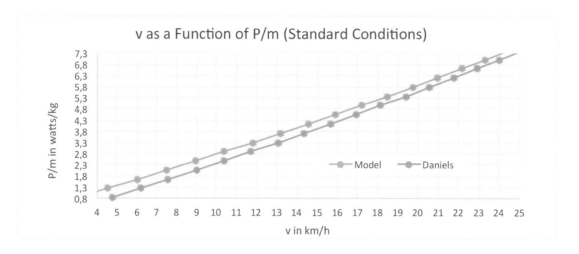

In the figure below we show the results for an alternative calculation (c = 0.93 kJ/kg/km, equivalent to an RE of 191 ml O_2/kg/km).

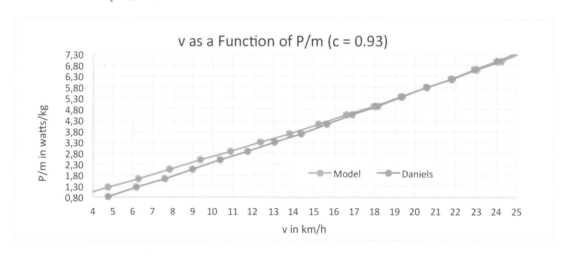

We see that with the improved RE the results match pretty well. As we saw earlier in the chapter on the running economy, an RE of 191 ml O_2/kg/km is rather low, but certainly possible. The RE of the most economical Kenyan runners has been reported to be as low as 180 ml O_2/kg/km. So, we conclude that Daniels probably based his empirical formula on tests with runners with a more than average running economy (which means they had a lower than average RE and c). This seems quite logical as he has been coaching a number of elite runners.

The Power-Time Relationship

Daniels uses the following formula to describe the relationship between power and time:

$\% VO_2 \max = 0.8 + 0.1894393e^{(-0.012778t)} + 0.2989558e^{(-0.1932605t)}$

We use Riegel's formula, which corresponds to the following:

$\% P/m = \% VO_2 \max = (t/10)^{-0.07}$

In both formulas, the time (t) is expressed in minutes. We have calculated the results of both formulas; the results are quite similar and given in the figure below:

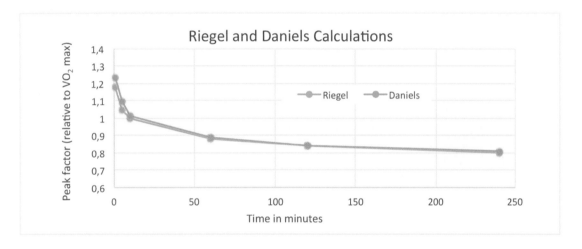

The Impact of the Altitude

In his books, Daniels does not present an explicit formula for the impact of the altitude on the performance of the human engine. Therefore, we have used the data from a table that he gave in his book. We have compared these data with the calculations of our model, based on the formulas of Basset[68] and Cerretelli[69]. The results are presented in the figure.

As the figure shows, Daniels' data seem to underestimate the impact of altitude as compared to Basset's formula. As we discussed in an earlier chapter, Basset's formula seems to give realistic results, so we have used them in our model.

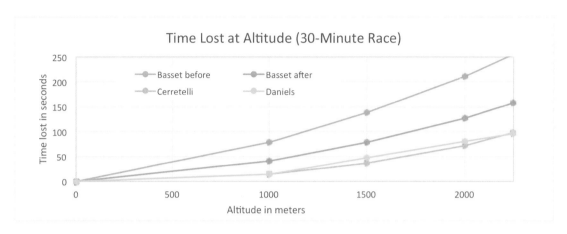

For the impact of altitude, we used Basset's formula.

In summary, we can conclude that for decades Daniels' books and in particular his VDOT tables, have played a major and meaningful role in comparing performances and determining training paces. However, he has based his formulas on empirical relationships, which are not completely accurate according to the laws of physics. Consequently, we prefer our own model, which has both theoretical and practical advantages. As we have shown throughout this book, our model allows us to study the impact of all relevant parameters (such as the body weight, the air density and the factors influencing it, the $c_d A$ value and the specific energy cost of running (c or RE)) separately. We believe that this provides additional insight into the factors influencing the performance and additional opportunities to optimize these factors.

76. PREHISTORIC MAN WAS A DISTANCE RUNNER!

Out on the roads, there is fitness and self-discovery and the persons we are destined to be. —George Sheehan

Nowadays, the marathon is dominated by African runners. In the world-leading marathon times, non-African runners can hardly be found. Although the dominance of African runners is well-known, the debate on the real reasons for this continues. The following aspects are frequently mentioned as contributing factors:

1. They have superior genes/talent/DNA.
2. They live at altitude (2,500 meters).
3. They are small and skinny.
4. They have a simple, non-sedentary life.
5. They train hard and at high intensity.
6. They value a career in running and there is a lot of competition.
7. They are stimulated by the prospect of a more prosperous life.

Most probably, a combination of these factors will be the cause of the phenomenal success of the Kenyans and Ethiopians. A striking aspect is the fact that the large majority of the elite runners originate from a small area, like the Rift valley in Kenya.

Of course, the present dominance of the African runners is not related to the origin of mankind. Still, it was in Africa that around 4 million years ago the first hominids *Australopithecus afarensi* evolved from earlier monkeys, and descended from the trees. The most famous example of these first hominids was Lucy. She was excavated in 1974 and named after "Lucy in the Sky with Diamonds," the Beatles song. Lucy stood and walked erect, but was still very primitive and survived on a diet of carrots and turnips.

Next in the evolution of mankind, was *Homo erectus*, who evolved 1.5 million years ago. The most well-known example is Turkana Boy, who was found in Kenya. He was the prototype of prehistoric man, hunting the plains of Africa as a long-distance runner. His body was clearly adapted to life on the savanna:

1. His body was adapted for running: tall legs, slender pelvis and flexible hips.
2. His body was adapted to daytime hunting: thin body hair allowing it to sweat and lose the heat produced by running.

Turkana Boy hunted in groups and learned to control fire around 1 million years ago.

Later, around 600,000 years ago, *Homo habilis* evolved. It had opposable thumbs and could prepare and use refined tools. Our own species *Homo sapiens* evolved only some 60,000 years ago. Since then, we see a larger brain volume and the development of art, language and technology (including the invention of agriculture).

From archeological research, it is known that from *Homo erectus* onwards, the hominids survived as hunter-gatherers. By working together in groups, they could scavenge bait from large predators. They were also able to catch prey by using their stamina. They chased and exhausted prey as long-distance runners until they could kill them with spears.

The technological progress of the last 100 years has led to the present situation in which most of us live a sedentary life, quite the opposite of the life of prehistoric man. Instead of running and hunting all day to supply a meager menu, we sit behind a desk near the refrigerator and other temptations. No wonder that the physical fitness of most modern day *Homo sapiens* is pretty bad and affluent diseases like heart attacks, diabetes and strokes abound. Our DNA and body posture is still similar to that of prehistoric man, but our lifestyle has changed completely.

Running is an excellent way to reverse this lifestyle change, combat the affluent diseases and improve our health. Research has shown that statistically running adds five years to your lifetime and each hour spent running will add two hours to your life! Moreover, as we run we experience feelings of euphoria and freedom, which may be traced back to the primal feelings of prehistoric man hunting his prey in Africa. Anyway, to authors Hans and Ron, nothing beats a sunrise in the early morning, while running in the great outdoors!

A replica of Lucy is displayed in the Ethiopian National Museum in Addis Ababa. The original bones are archived here too.

77. WHY ARE SPRINTERS ALSO GOOD JUMPERS?

Those seven guys beside you in that lane, they want it as much as you want it. So you want to have it more. This is why you train harder. —Usain Bolt

In this chapter we will apply the laws of physics to some other athletics events. We will look into the long jump and the pole vault. We will show that for both events the sprinting speed is vital for the performance. So, good sprinters also can jump well! Of course, this does not mean that they don't have to train for these events; they will have to master the technique and they will have to develop the specific muscles for the events. Finally, we will apply the laws of physics to race walking.

The Pole Vault

In the pole vault, the speed of the approach is an essential factor in determining the performance. During the sprint approach, the kinetic energy of the athlete increases with his speed in accordance to the following formula[93]:

$$E_{kin} = 0.5mv^2$$

As an example, we use a speed (v) of 10 m/s and a body weight (m) of 70 kg, so the kinetic energy (E_{kin}) becomes $0.5*70*10^2 = 3,500$ joule.

If the athlete has a perfect technique, theoretically he can transform this kinetic energy into the potential energy required for the height of the bar:

$$E_{pot} = mgh$$

Using the same example as above, we can calculate that the athlete may raise his center of gravity to a height (h) = $3,500/(70*9.81) = 5.10$ m. As his center of gravity will be around one meter above the ground, he may jump over a bar height of $5.10+1.00 = 6.10$ meters! We have calculated the relationship between the sprinting speed and the attainable bar height, in accordance with the formulas above. The results are given in the figure and table below.

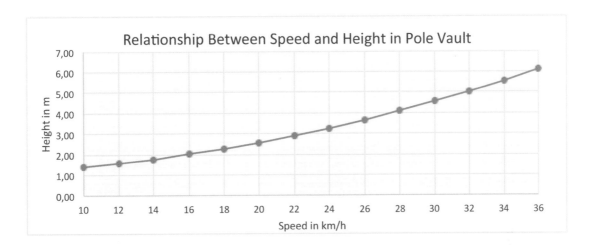

Pole Vault	
v	h$_{tot}$
(km/h)	(m)
10	1.4
12	1.6
14	1.8
16	2.0
18	2.3
20	2.6
22	2.9
24	3.3
26	3.7
28	4.1
30	4.5
32	5.0
34	5.5
36	6.1

We note that the results of the calculations match the results in practice quite well. The current world record by Renauld Lavillenie is 6.16 meters. The current world record of Usain Bolt at the 100 meter (9.58) is equivalent to a speed of 37.6 km/h. According to our theory, Bolt could jump over the mark of 6.55 meter! Our Marathon Man can sprint only 17.4 km/h, so in theory he could jump over the mark of 2.20 meter. As mentioned before, both Usain and our Marathon Man will have to train well to reach this result. Also it is quite possible that they are less talented in jumping than in running.

The pole vault of the Dutchman Peter Braun at the 2015 World Championships in Beijing.

The Long Jump

In the long jump, the speed of the approach is equally important as in the pole vault. At takeoff, the jumper transfers part of his horizontal speed (v_{hor}) to a vertical speed (v_{vert}). As a result, he will move upward and forward in a manner which can be described by the trajectory physics:

$$h = v_{vert}^2/2g$$

$$t = \sqrt{(2*2*h/g)}$$

$$d = (\sqrt{(v_{hor}^2 - 2hg)})*\sqrt{(2h/g)}$$

As an example, we use v_{hor} = 10 m/s and v_{vert} = 4.43 m/s. According to the formulas, the jumper will reach a maximum height (h) of 1.0 m and a distance (d) of 9.0 meters. He will be airborne during t = 1 second. We have calculated the relationship between the approach speed (v) and the distance (d). The results are given in the figure and table below.

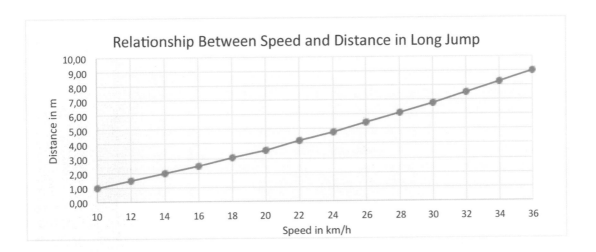

Long Jump	
v	d
(km/h)	(m)
10	0.96
12	1.44
14	1.94
16	2.46
18	3.00
20	3.58
22	4.17
24	4.80
26	5.44
28	6.11
30	6.80
32	7.52
34	8.25
36	9.01

Again, we note that the results in practice match the calculations pretty well. The current world record of Mike Powell is 8.95 meters. Theoretically, Usain Bolt could jump 9.49 meters with his 100-meter speed of 37.6 km/h. Our Marathon Man could jump 2.90 meters with his sprinting speed of 17.4 km/h, provided of course that he has trained sufficiently.

The long jump of the Dutch Nadine Broersen at the 2015 Dutch Championships in Amsterdam.

Race Walking

When walking, your legs make a pendulum motion around the fixed stance point on the ground; your hip moves along the sector of a circle. This means you encounter a centrifugal acceleration equal to v^2/L[94], v being your walking speed in m/s and L the length of your leg in meters. On earth, the centrifugal acceleration can never exceed the gravitational acceleration (g), which is 9.81 m/s². Consequently, the maximum speed before you are released from the ground becomes:

$$v = \sqrt{(gL)}$$

As an example, we use a leg length (L) of 0.9 meter, so the maximum speed in race walking theoretically is only $\sqrt{(9.81*0.9)}$ = 3 m/s or 10.8 km/h. In practice, elite walkers can race faster on account of the wiggling motion of their hips. As a result of this, their center of gravity moves up and down. The current world record in the 10K walk is 37:11, which is equivalent to a speed of 16.1 km/h. Other applications of the above formula include:

1. On account of their shorter legs, children walk much slower than adults, so they have to run to keep up.
2. At the moon, the g value is only 1.6 m/s^2, so the maximum walk speed is only 1.2 m/s or 4.3 km/h!

Conclusions

In summary, we conclude that the laws of physics enable us to calculate the attainable performances in the pole vault, the long jump and in race walking. In an earlier chapter, we showed that Usain Bolt should be able to run the 100 meter in 9.18 seconds at the altitude of Mexico City. This is equivalent to a speed of 10.89 m/s, so theoretically he could attain phenomenal performances in Mexico City: 9.99 meters at the long jump and 7.04 meters at the pole vault!

Germany's Melanie Seeger competes in the Women's 20 km Race Walk final as part of the London 2012 Olympic Games.

78. THE AMAZING ED WHITLOCK

I'll be happy if running and I can grow old together.
—Haruki Murakami

Who Is Ed Whitlock (March 6, 1931)?

Ed Whitlock is a Canadian distance runner, who picked up running in his forties.

In 2003, he was the first (and so far still the only) person over 70 years old to run a marathon in less than 3 hours. At age 73, he ran an amazing 2:54:48! He lives in Milton, Ontario and trains every day for three hours around a cemetery...

Author Hans will never forget the Rotterdam Marathon of 2011. This was the day when he got beaten by an 80-year-old granddad! While preparing for the marathon, Hans had read an item in the media on Ed Whitlock[95], the famous Canadian long distance runner, who planned to attack the world record for the M80 category (masters 80 years and older). At the start, Hans was still confident that he would finish a long way ahead of the amazing 80-year-old runner. However, around the 35K mark, Hans hit the wall and he was passed by a tiny old-timer with number 80 on his shirt. Contrary to Hans, his stride was still powerful and in spite of his embarrassment, Hans could not keep up! That year Ed set the world record at 3:15:53!

Meanwhile, Hans has studied this granddad, so he knows Ed Whitlock is definitely the best master in the history of running. Currently, Ed holds the marathon world records in the year classes of 68, 69, 70, 72, 73, 74, 75, 76, 80, 81, 82 and 85!

In the half marathon, Ed Whitlock owns 10 single-age records ranging from his 1:20:33 at age 68 to 1:50:47 at age 85 years.

He also holds an impressive string of world records at the track, both indoor and outdoor and at distances from 1,500 meters to 10,000 meters. On the road he also holds a string of records on the distances from 10K to the marathon.

The table below lists the official IAAF-recognized world records. For some recent world records ratification is still in progress.

Ed Whitlock's Amazing Streak

His string of records at the marathon is known as Ed Whitlock's Amazing Streak. The figure below clearly illustrates how extraordinary his records are. His records are substantially stronger than could be expected by the regression line. We see that for many years Ed managed to limit the decline in performance to the minimum.

As an example, we can illustrate how amazing his world record of 2:54:48 at the age of 73 is. This is equivalent to an FTP of around 4.50 watts/kg. Already a pretty good number and much better than the 3.75 watts/kg of our Marathon Man. But Ed did this at the age of 73! When we use an age grading of 0.8% per year, this is equivalent to an FTP at the age of 30 of $4.50/(0.992)^{43} = 6.35$ watts/kg! This is even higher than the 6.30 watts/kg of current world record holder Dennis Kimetto!

World Records: Ed Whitlock		
	Age class	Time
Track		
1500 meter	80-84	5:48.93
1500 meter	85-89	6:38.87
Mile	75-79	5:41.80
Mile	85-89	7:18.55
3000 meter	75-79	11:10.43
3000 meter	80-84	12:13.56
5000 meter	75-79	19:07.02
5000 meter	80-84	20:58.12
5000 meter	85-89	24:03.12
10,000 meter	70-74	38:04.13
10,000 meter	75-79	39:25.16
10,000 meter	80-84	42:39.95
10,000 meter	85-89	51:07.53
Indoor		
1500 meter	75-79	5:20.04
1500 meter	80-84	5:48.47
1500 meter	85-89	5:48.47
3000 meter	65-69	10:11.60
3000 meter	70-74	10:52.40
3000 meter	75-79	11:17.21
3000 meter	80-84	12:00.88
3000 meter	85-89	13:41.96
Road		
Marathon	70-74	2:54:48
Marathon	75-79	3:04:54
Marathon	80-84	3:15:54
Marathon	85-89	3:56:33

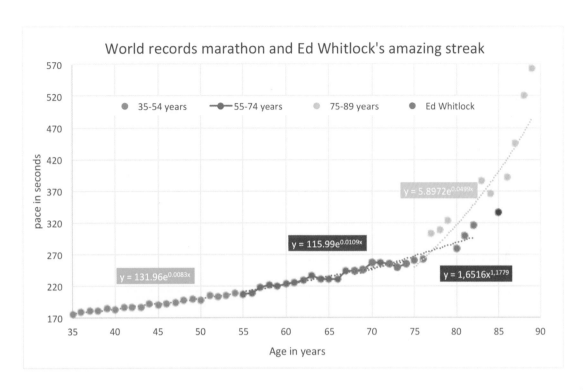

World records marathon and Ed Whitlock's amazing streak

● 35-54 years   ●─●─● 55-74 years   ● 75-89 years   ● Ed Whitlock

pace in seconds

$y = 5.8972e^{0.0499x}$

$y = 115.99e^{0.0109x}$

$y = 131.96e^{0.0083x}$

$y = 1,6516x^{1.1779}$

Age in years

The amazing Ed Whitlock trains daily in a nearby cemetery.

Of course, these are only theoretical calculations, but it clearly shows how unparalleled the performances of Ed really are. It also makes you wonder what he could have run if he had started at a younger age.

Unfortunately, Ed has suffered from injuries since 2012, so he missed the marathon world records at 83 and 84 years. However, at the Canadian Masters Indoor Nationals in March 2016, he smashed the M85 world records at 1,500 and 3,000 meters to 6:38 and 13:41. Wearing 15-year-old running shoes, Ed Whitlock raced through wind and rain at the October 2016 Toronto Marathon to break the men's 85–89 age group world record by 38 minutes. His 3:56:33 shattered the previous mark of 4:34:55, set in 2004.

79. HAILE GEBRSELASSIE: THE GREATEST RUNNER IN HISTORY

Schooling is so important. —Haile Gebrselassie

The Wikipedia page of Haile Gebrselassie mentions that he is widely considered the greatest runner in history[96]. His string of successes include two Olympic titles, nine world titles and 27 new world records at distances ranging from the 2,000 meter to the marathon.

Born in a Tent

Haile was born on April 18, 1973 in a traditional tent in a field near the village Assela, situated about 175 kilometers south of the capital of Ethiopia, Addis Ababa. His parents had no fewer than ten children. Every day Haile ran ten kilometers to school at an altitude of 2,500 meters! His father did not like it at all that Haile did not want to become a farmer like him.

Dutch Connection

In 1992 former Dutch athlete and athlete manager Jos Hermens became the manager for the then 19-year-old Haile. As a result Haile ran many races in the Netherlands, including the 15K Zevenheuvelenloop, which he won frequently (best time 41:38). His last participation was in 2013 as a 40 year old. He won in 42:42. Afterwards he said: "The first five kilometers were too slow, I would rather have finished under 42 minutes."

Haile has also run a world record in the 10EM at Tilburg in 2005 (44:24). He received the nickname Mister Hengelo because of his many world records at the FBK Games held in Hengelo, the Netherlands, including the 5,000 meter (12:56.96 in 1994) and 10,000 meter (26:43.53 in 1995 and 26:22.75 in 1998).

Social Career

Despite being promoted from athletics to the boardroom, Haile still trains every day early in the morning. At nine he is in his office nowadays. Haile invested his prize money initially in real estate. Today Haile is in coffee and car imports, and he owns several resorts. "Do not put all your eggs in one basket" is his corporate philosophy. This multi-sidedness in business approach is quite different from the focus he had as an athlete.

Coffee is the main export product of Ethiopia, and Haile has built a business empire with 1,500 employees. He supports numerous social projects in the area of education and health care (AIDS). Nevertheless Haile remains the nice, smiling and accessible man he always was. Haile says he still experiences daily that sport is important to get rid of stress.

Haile and the Great Ethiopian Run

It's no surprise that Haile is also the president of the organization of the Great Ethiopian Run.

Haile himself won the Great Ethiopian Run in 2001. With 30:04, his time for this 10K road race was not so fast. In spite of the altitude the winner usually finishes below 30 minutes, and often even below 29 minutes. Among the 40,000 participants there are always a lot of fast guys at the start.

How can we assess the performance of Haile in The Great Ethiopian Run?

We know that Haile ran a world record at the 10,000 meter in 26:22.75 in 1998 in Hengelo. In 2002 Haile set a world record 10K road race time of 27:02 at sea level in Doha, the capital of Qatar. With a body weight of 56 kg, Haile's time in Hengelo corresponds to an FTP of 6.37 watts/kg.

Altitude strongly affects the running performance. The air pressure and thus the air density decrease with height, and with this the amount of available oxygen decreases in proportion. In Addis Ababa (2,350 meters) the air pressure is 25% less than at sea level. Therefore you perform considerably less than in a race at sea level. Of course Haile is acclimatized to altitude. As we saw earlier, Basset's formula can be used to assess the impact of the altitude[68]:

%FTP = 99.921-1.8991*h-1.1219*h^2

We can calculate that Haile had only 89.3% of his FTP available. In other words, Haile had an FTP of approximately 6.37*89.3% = 5.67 watts/kg in the 2001 Great Ethiopian Run. With such a FTP a time of 29:24 at the 10K could be expected. In reality Haile ran 30:04 that year. We can explain this by way of the 115 altitude meters which have to be overcome in the Great Ethiopian Run. This road race is certainly not comparable to the flat track in Hengelo.

Interview With Haile

Co-author Ron met Haile at his office located at the seventh floor of an office building named after his wife, the Alem building. In his office is a large family photo. Haile is a real family man. This is also reflected in the name of his company: Haile & Alem International.

Haile is a relation-oriented man in all respects. For example in the car on the way to his office we were alerted by a text message that unfortunately he had to shift the appointment by half an hour. Haile had to do a live interview on the radio first.

Haile and Ron talking about running secrets in Haile's office.

The Orange Lion Guesthouse where Ron was staying in Addis Ababa lies close to the home of Haile and opposite a forest. Haile trains every morning in this forest before he goes to the office. In the afternoon he trains in a gym. Haile says he is in good shape but experiences that it is difficult to combine top athletics with a working life. Haile told Ron that he is 3 kg too heavy. The race weight of the 1.65 m long Haile is 56 kg. With the 15th Great Ethiopian Run in 2015 Haile ended his professional running career.

The PBs of Haile

Gradually we came to talk about Haile's personal bests. He ran his PBs in the first half of his career on the track and in the second half of his career Haile gradually shifted to road races and the marathon.

We know that an FTP of 6.35 watts/kg may be considered to be the maximum value for the human power. On all distances Haile came close to this value. His strongest distances were the 5,000 and 10,000 meter track. His performance at these distances corresponds with FTPs of 6.36 and 6.37 watts/kg, respectively. However, Haile has run phenomenal times in all distances ranging from 1,500 meters to the marathon. His times in the 1,500 meter and the marathon were equivalent to a FTP respectively 6.30 and 6.28 watts/kg!

When we present Haile's PBs in a graph, we see that the exponent in Pete Riegel's famous formula is below -0.07. This means that he is not only an exceptional all-round middle and long-distance runner, but he also has a phenomenal fatigue resistance!

Haile ran his PBs in the first half of his career on the track. At the 10,000 meter of the Sydney 2000 Olympic Games Haile won a blistering sprint finish before Kenyan Paul Tergat.

Haile says he looks back with pleasure at the many races and many records he has run in the Netherlands. The Dutch take a special place in his heart.

PBs of Haile Gebrselassie				
Distance	Venue	Date	Time	FTP
				(watts/kg)
1,500 m	Stuttgart	6-06-99	03:33.7	6.30
1 mile	Gateshead	27-06-99	03:52.4	6.23
2,000 m	Brussel	22-08-97	04:56.1	6.15
3,000 m	Brussel	28-08-98	07:25.1	6.30
2 mile	Hengelo	31-05-97	08:01.1	6.28
5,000 m	Helsinki	13-06-98	12:39.4	6.36
10,000 m	Hengelo	1-06-98	26:22.7	6.37
10 km	Doha (Qatar)	11-12-02	00:27:02	6.21
15 km	Nijmegen	4-09-05	00:41:38	6.21
10 mile	Tilburg	4-09-05	00:44:24	6.27
20,000 m	Hengelo	27-06-98	56:26.7	6.22
20 km	Phoenix (Arizona)	15-01-06	00:55:48	6.30
21.1 km	Phoenix (Arizona)	15-01-06	00:58:55	6.32
25 km	Alphen aan den Rijn	12-03-06	01:11:37	6.22
30 km	Dubai	18-01-08	01:28:01	6.14
42.2 km	Berlin	28-09-08	02:03:59	6.28

Haile as Master Athlete

Haile set his world record at the 10,000 meter at age 25 and his second (and last) world record at the marathon at age 35. At the age of 42 years the running legend put an end to his professional career. But what race times could we expect if Haile continued training and racing?

The figures below show the results of our calculations based on the statistical formulas of Elmer Sterken, as discussed in an earlier chapter. The conclusion is clear. Haile could improve the world records in every five-year age group of the masters.

Haile's eyes began to glisten when he saw our graphs. Older Ethiopians seldom exercise athletics. It is more for younger people. For Haile this is different. "Age is just a number for me," Haile said.

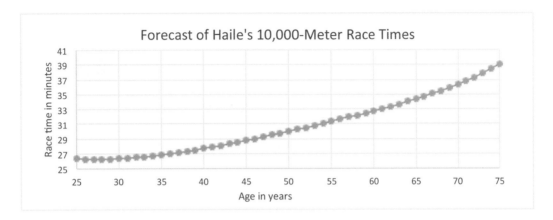

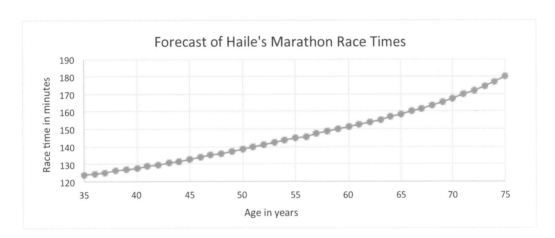

What Can Haile Gebrselassie Perform as a Master Athlete?			
	10,000 m track		
Age class	Forecast Haile	World record	Current world record holder
senior	26:22.7	26:17.5	Kenenisa Bekele (ETH)
M35	26:51.9	26:51.2	Haile Gebrselassie (ETH)
M40	27:42.8	28:30.9	Martti Vainio (FIN)
M45	28:46.5	30:02.6	Antonio Villanueva (MEX)
M50	30:01.4	30:55.2	Peter De Vocht (BEL)
M55	31:20.8	31:51.9	Keith Bateman (AUS)
M60	32:45.1	33:57.6	Michael Hager (GBR)
M65	34:20.1	34:42.2	Derek Turnbull (NZL)
M70	36:16.6	38:04.1	Ed Whitlock (CAN)
M75	39:04.7	39:25.2	Ed Whitlock (CAN)

Marathon		
Forecast Haile	World record	Current world record holder
2:04:26	2:02:57	Dennis Kimetto (KEN)
2:03:59	2:03:59	Haile Gebrselassie (ETH)
2:07:54	2:08:42	Kenneth Mungara (KEN)
2:12:48	2:14:16	Jackson Kipngok (KEN)
2:18:34	2:19:29	Titus Mamabolo (RSA)
2:24:40	2:25:56	Piet van Alphen (NED)
2:31:09	2:36:30	Yoshihisa Hosaka (JPN)
2:38:28	2:41:57	Derek Turnbull (NZL)
2:47:25	2:54:48	Ed Whitlock (CAN)
3:00:21	3:04:54	Ed Whitlock (CAN)

Haile Gebrselassie's unparalleled performance of 2:03:59 in the 2008 Berlin marathon is still a world record of the M35.

469

REFERENCES

1. Hans van Dijk en Ron van Megen, Het Geheim van Hardlopen, April 2014 (2nd edition), NedRun, Leusden, ISBN 978-90-821069-1-6

2. Hans van Dijk, Ron van Megen en Guido Vroemen, Het Geheim van Wielrennen, June 2015, NedRun, Leusden, ISBN 978-90-821069-4-7

3. Hans van Dijk en Ron van Megen, Hardlopen met Power!, April 2012, NedRun, Leusden, ISBN 978-90-821069-7-8

4. www.stryd.com

5. I.Min-Lee et al., Effect of physical inactivity on major non-communicable diseases worldwide: an analysis of burden of disease and life expectancy, The Lancet, 380 (9838), 219-229, July 2012

6. T.Noakes, Lore of Running, 2002, Cape Town, Human Kinetics, ISBN 0-87322-959-2

7. M. L. Foss, S.J. Keteyian, Fox's physiological basis for exercise and sport, McGraw-Hill, 1998, ISBN 0-697-25904-8

8. Jack Daniels, Daniels' Running Formula, Human Kinetics, Champaign, USA, 2012, ISBN 1-4504-3183-6

9. Owen Anderson, Running Science, Human Kinetics, Champaign, USA, 2013, ISBN 0-7360-7418-X

10. Brad Hudson and Matt Fitzgerald, Run Faster, from the 5K to the Marathon, Broadway Books, New York, 2008, ISBN 978-0-7679-2822-9

11. A.E. Jeukendrup, Carbohydrate intake during excercise and perfomance, Nutrition 2004: 20, 669-677

12. M.Fitzgerald, Racing weight; how to get lean for peak performance, 2009, Boulder, Velo Press, ISBN 978-1-934030-51-6

13. Kris Verburgh, De voedselzandloper, Bert Bakker Uitgeverij, Amsterdam, 2012, ISBN 978-90-351-3758-5

14. www.esbnyc.com/event/2015-empire-state-building-run-up-info

15. www.fiets.nl/2015/06/08/wiggins-werelduurrecord-geanalyseerd

16. www.fiets.nl/2015/07/25/hoe-snel-gaat-froome-alpe-dhuez-op

17. ACSM Metablic Equations for Gross VO_2 in Metric Units, certification.acsm.org/metabolic-calcs

18. N. Sherman, Development of a generalized model to estimate the energy cost of walking and running for healthy adults, Journal of Strength hand Conditioning Research, 1998, 12(1), pp 33-36

19. J. Slawinski et al., Changes in spring-mass model parameters and energy cost during track running to exhaustion, Journal of Strength and Conditioning Research, 2008, 22(3), pp 930-936

20. P. Zamparo et al., Eur J Appl Physiol Occup Physiol, 1991, 65(2), pp 183-187

21. A. Sassi et al., The cost of running on natural grass and artificial turf surfaces, Journal of Strength and Conditioning Research, 2011, 25(3), pp 606-611

22. G. Vroemen, personal communication on the test of Wilson Kipsang

23. L. Léger and D. Mercier, Gross energy cost of horizontal treadmill and track running, Sports Medicine 1 (1984), pp 270-277

24. P. Riegel, Time predicting, Runner's World, August 1977

25. P. Riegel, Athletic records and human endurance, American Scientist, 69, May-June 1981

26. L.G.C.E. Pugh, Oxygen intake in track and treadmill running with observations on the effect of air resistance, J. Physiol. (1970), 207, pp 823-835

27. L.G.C.E. Pugh, The influence of wind resistance in running and walking and the mechanical efficiency of work against horizontal and vertical forces, J. Physiol. (1971), 213, pp 255-276

28. C.T.M. Davies, Effects of wind assistance and resistance on the forward motion of a runner, J Appl Physiol, 1980, pp 702-709

29. Alberto E. Minetti et al., Energy cost of walking and running at extreme uphill and downhill slopes, J Appl Physiol, 2002, 93, pp 1039-1046

30. B.I. Rapoport, Metabolic factors limiting performance in marathon runners, PLoS Comput Biol 6 (10): e1000960, doi:10.1371/journal.pcbi.100960

31. hyperphysics.phy-astr.gsu.edu/hbase/biology/atp.html

32. books.google.nl/books?id=v9HL5VyRmZcC&pg=PA292&lpg=PA292&dq=gibbs+energy+from+atp&source=bl&ots=DPSLVfLzSe&sig=z8dV3U1ppOH1S6Pbso4KtT5

33. www.rpi.edu/dept/bcbp/molbiochem/MBWeb/mb1/part2/bioener.htm

34. www.chembio.uoguelph.ca/educmat/chm452/lecture1.htm

35. en.wikipedia.org/wiki/VO$_2$_max

36. www.runningforfitness.org/faq/vo$_2$-max

37. en.wikipedia.org/wiki/List_of_world_records_in_athletics

38. www.world-masters-athletics.org/laws-a-rules/appendixes-and-tables

39. E. Sterken, From the cradle to the grave: how fast can we run?, Journal of Sports Sciences, 2003, 21, 479-491

40. www.world-masters-athletics.org/records

41. en.wikipedia.org/wiki/Lean_body_mass

42. Bob Glover and Shelly-lynn Florence Glover, The competitive runner's handbook, Penguin Books, 1999, New York, isbn 978-0-14-046990-5

43. en.wikipedia.org/wiki/Heart_rate

44. www.firstbeat.com/userData/firstbeat/download/white_paper_vo$_2$_estimation.pdf

45. www.firstbeat.com/userData/firstbeat/download/white_paper_epoc.pdf

46. www.firstbeat.com/userData/firstbeat/download/white_paper_training_effect.pdf

47. www.firstbeat.com/userData/firstbeat/download/white_paper_recovery.pdf

48. www.firstbeat.com/userData/firstbeat/download/white_paper_energy_expenditure_estimation.pdf

49. Rocco Di Michele, relationships between running economy and mechanics in middle-distance runners, PhD-thesis, University of Bologna, 2008

50. Jack Daniels and Nancy Daniels, Running economy of elite male and elite female runners, Medicine and Science in Sports and Exercise, 24, 1992, 4, pp 483-489

51. Philo U. Saunders et al., Factors affecting running economy in trained distance runners, Sports Medicine, 2004 (34) 7, pp 465-485

52. Kyle R Barnes and Andrew E. Kilding, Running economy: measurement, norms and determining factors, Sports Medicine Open, 2015, DOI 10.1186/s40798-015-0007-y

53. S. Magness, Factors affecting distance running performance, www.scienceofrunning.com

54. T. Novacheck, The biomechanics of running, Gait and Posture 7, 1998, 77-95

55. M.N. Scholtz, M.F. Bobbert, A.J. van Soest, J.R. Clark and J. van Heerden, Running biomechanics,: shorter heels, better biomechanics, The Journal of Experimental Biology 211, 3266-3271, 2008

56. Andrew M. Jones, The physiology of the world record holder for the women's marathon, International Journal of Sports Science and Coaching, 2006, (1) 2,pp 101-115

57. H.C. Pinnington, B, Dawson, Energy cost of running on grass compared to soft dry sand, Journal Sci. Med Sport, 2001 Dec 4(4), 416-430

58. S.A. Stefanescu et al., The cost of running on natural grass and artificial turf surfaces, J. Strength Cond Res, 2011 Mar 25(3), 606-611

59. T.M. Lejeune et al., Mechanics and energetics of human locomotion on sand, Journal Experimental Biology, 201, 2071-2080(1998)

60. runsmartproject.com/coaching/2012/02/06/how-much-does-shoe-weight-affect-performance/

61. E.C. Frederick, Physiological and ergonomics factors in running shoe design, Applied Ergonomics, 1984, 15.4, pp 281-287

62. E.C. Frederick et al. Lower Oxygen Demands of running in soft-soled shoes, Research quarterly for exercise and sport, 1986 (57.?), pp 174-177

63. Philip E. Martin, Mechanical and physiological responses to lower extremity loading during running, Medicine and Science in Sports and Exercise, 17, 1985, pp 427-433

64. N.J. Hanson, K. Berg, J.R. Meendering, C. Ryan, Oxygen Cost of running barefoot vs running shod, Int. J. Sports Med., 2011; 32, 401-406

65. Joel Fuller et al., The effect of footwear on running performance and running economy in distance runners, Sports Medicine, 45 (3), November 2014

66. Herman Pontzer, A new model predicting locomotor cost from limb length via force production, The Journal of Experimental Biology 208, 2005, pp 1513-1524

67. nl.wikipedia.org/wiki/Schaal_van_Beaufort

68. www.ncbi.nlm.nih.gov/pubmed/10589872

69. P. Cerritelli, Limiting factors to oxygen transport on Mount Everest, J. Appl. Physiol. 40: 1976, pp 558-667

70. A. Baker and W.G. Hopkins, Altitude training for sea-level competition, www.sportsci.org

71. www.alpedhuez21.fr

72. Will Le Page, Optimum Temperature for Elite Running Performance, University of Tulsa, USA, April 2011

73. El Helou N, Tafflet M, Berthelot G, Tolaini J, Marc A, et al. (2012) Impact of Environmental Parameters on Marathon Running Performance. PLoS ONE 7(5):e37407. doi:10.1371/journal.pone.0037407)

74. Matthew R. Ely et al., Impact of weather on marathon performance, Medicine and Science in Sports and Exercise, 2007, (39), 3, pp 487-493

75. en.wikipedia.org/wiki/Wet-bulb_temperature

76. R. Still, Wet-bulb temperature from relative humidity and air temperature, Journal of Applied Meteorology and Climatology, 2011 (50), pp 2267-2269

77. John R. Brotherhood, Heat stress and strain in exercise and sport, Journal of Science and Medicine in Sport, 2008 (11), pp 6-19

78. Alan St Clair Gibson, Jos J. De Koning, Kevin G. Thompson, William O. Roberts, Dominic Micklewright, John Ragli, Carl Foster, Crawling to the Finish Line: Why do Endurance Runners Collapse? Implications for Understanding of Mechanisms Underlying Pacing and Fatigue Sports Med (2013) 43:413–424DOI 10.1007/s40279-013-0044-y

79. en.wikipedia.org/wiki/Wind_chill

80. A.E. Jeukendrup, Carbohydrate intake during excercise and perfomance, Nutrition 2004: 20, 669-677

81. www.stryd.com

82. www.youtube.com/watch?v=pqACzgjVxqs

83. www.dcrainmaker.com/2015/01/stryd-first-running.html

84. Jim Vance, Run with power, 2016, Velo Press, Boulder, CO, ISBN 978-1-937715-43-4

85. www.sub2hrs.com

86. fellrnr.com/wiki/Beetroot_and_Running_Performance

87. en.wikipedia.org/wiki/Vitamin_D

88. www.vitamindwiki.com/tiki-index.php?page=Sports&redirectpage=

89. www.vitamindwiki.com/Sports+benefits+from+up+to+50+ng+of+Vitamin+%25E2%2580%2593+meta-analysis+-+Nov+2012

90. en.wikipedia.org/wiki/Vitamin_B_6

91. J. Daniels and J. Gilbert, Oxygen Power, 1979

92. J. Daniels, R. Fitts and G. Sheehan: Relationship between VO_2 and running velocity, in Conditioning for Distance Running- the Scientific Aspects, John Wiley and Sons, New York, 1978

93. Cliff Frohlich, Effect of wind and altitude on record performance in foot races, pole vault and long jump, Am. J. Phys. 53 (8), August 1985, pp726-730

94. R. McNeill Alexander, Walking and running, The mathematical gazette, 1996 (80), pp 262-266

95. en.wikipedia.org/wiki/Ed_Whitlock

96. en.wikipedia.org/wiki/Haile_Gebrselassie

CREDITS

Photo

Thanks to the following agencies and individuals for their kind permission to use their photographs as reference:

- » Mukhlid Alotaibi p. 67
- » Marco Barabino p. 159
- » Atty and Hans van Dijk p. 14, 175, 254
- » dpa Picture-Alliance GmbH p. 91, 141, 169, 183, 189, 235, 253, 263, 269, 277, 315, 337, 347, 357, 365, 385, 395, 427, 439, 443, 457, 465
- » Jeroen Eck p. 24, 75
- » Geert Hakze p. 294
- » Marleen van Hoorn p. 214
- » iStockphoto p. 10, 21, 41, 59, 68, 87, 182, 287, 301, 303, 335, 433, 448
- » Henk Knapen p. 333
- » Erik van Leeuwen p. 29, 55, 79, 85, 105, 125, 167, 206, 211, 247, 249, 275, 281, 295, 339, 352, 378 (the runner only), 454, 456
- » Ron van Megen: All other photos
- » Pioneer p. 31
- » Coen Schilderman p. 179
- » Desirée Schippers: Author photos
- » Jo Schoonbroodt p. 239
- » Wim Slangewal p. 35
- » Huub Snoep p. 63
- » Jaap Stijlaart p. 215
- » Harry van 't Veld p. 388
- » Cor Vos Fotopersburo p. 299
- » Guido Vroemen p. 399
- » Ed Whitlock p. 458, 462
- » Wikimedia Commons, license CC BY-SA 3.0 p. 327

Graphics

Hans van Dijk, Ron van Megen

Design

Cover design, inside layout, typesetting: Sannah Inderelst

Editing

Editing: Anne Rumery, Kristina Oltrogge

BECOME A BETTER RUNNER WITH MEYER & MEYER SPORT!

Jeff Galloway

NUTRITION FOR RUNNERS

Using material from renowned nutritionist Nancy Clark, Jeff Galloway gives the reader tips on what to eat, when to eat, how much to eat, and how to combine all that with your training schedule while still retaining the chance to enjoy other aspects of life.

232 p., in color,

55 photos, 8 illus.,

paperback, 6 1/2" x 9 1/4"

ISBN: 9781782550273

$ 15.95 US

Jeff Galloway

THE RUN WALK RUN® METHOD

Jeff's innovative ideas have opened up the possibility of running and completing a marathon to almost everyone. Philosophically, Jeff believes that we were all designed to run and walk, and he keeps finding ways to bring more people into the positive world of exercise.

2nd revised edition

192 p., in color,

38 photos, 13 charts,

paperback, 6 1/2" x 9 1/4"

ISBN: 9781782550822

$ 19.95 US

MEYER & MEYER Sport
Von-Coels-Str. 390
52080 Aachen
Germany

Phone   +49 02 41 - 9 58 10 - 13
Fax   +49 02 41 - 9 58 10 - 10
E-Mail   sales@m-m-sports.com
Website   www.m-m-sports.com

All books available as E-books.

MEYER
& MEYER
VERLAG